WHEN STATES GO BROKE

When States Go Broke collects insights and analyses from leading academics and practitioners who discuss the ongoing fiscal crisis among the American states. No one disagrees with the idea that the states face enormous political and fiscal challenges. There is, however, little consensus on how to fix the perennial problems associated with these challenges. This volume fills an important gap in the dialogue by offering an academic analysis of the many issues broached by these debates. Leading scholars in bankruptcy, constitutional law, labor law, history, political science, and economics have individually contributed their assessments of the origins, context, and potential solutions for the states in crisis. It presents readers – academics, policymakers, and concerned citizens alike – with the resources to begin and continue that important, solution-oriented conversation.

Peter Conti-Brown is an Academic Fellow at the Rock Center for Corporate Governance at Stanford Law School and the Stanford Graduate School of Business. His research focuses on banking regulation and financial and fiscal crises, and includes articles published in the *Stanford Law Review*, *UCLA Law Review*, and the *Washington University Law Review*, among other law journals.

David A. Skeel, Jr., is the S. Samuel Arsht Professor of Corporate Law at the University of Pennsylvania Law School. He is the author of *The New Financial Deal: Understanding the Dodd-Frank Act and Its (Unintended) Consequences* (2011), *Icarus in the Boardroom* (2005), and *Debt's Dominion: A History of Bankruptcy Law in America* (2001), as well as coeditor with Michael Klarman and Carol Steiker of *The Political Heart of Criminal Procedure* (2011), a collection of tribute essays to William J. Stuntz.

When States Go Broke

THE ORIGINS, CONTEXT, AND SOLUTIONS FOR THE AMERICAN STATES IN FISCAL CRISIS

Edited by

Peter Conti-Brown

Rock Center for Corporate Governance
Stanford University

David A. Skeel, Jr.

University of Pennsylvania School of Law

CAMBRIDGE UNIVERSITY PRESS
Cambridge, New York, Melbourne, Madrid, Cape Town,
Singapore, São Paulo, Delhi, Mexico City

Cambridge University Press
32 Avenue of the Americas, New York, NY 10013-2473, USA

www.cambridge.org
Information on this title: www.cambridge.org/9781107023178

© Cambridge University Press 2012

This publication is in copyright. Subject to statutory exception
and to the provisions of relevant collective licensing agreements,
no reproduction of any part may take place without the written
permission of Cambridge University Press.

First published 2012

Printed in the United States of America

A catalog record for this publication is available from the British Library.

Library of Congress Cataloging in Publication data
When states go broke : the origins, context, and solutions for the American states in fiscal crisis / [edited by] Peter Conti-Brown, David Skeel.
  p. cm.
Includes bibliographical references and index.
ISBN 978-1-107-02317-8 (hardback)
  1. State government bankruptcy – United States. 2. Finance, Public – United States – States. I. Conti-Brown, Peter, 1981– II. Skeel, David A., 1961–
KF1535.S73W54 2012
336'.01373–dc23   2012006886

ISBN 978-1-107-02317-8 Hardback

Cambridge University Press has no responsibility for the persistence or accuracy of URLs for external or third-party Internet Web sites referred to in this publication and does not guarantee that any content on such Web sites is, or will remain, accurate or appropriate.

Contents

List of figures	page vii
List of tables	ix
List of contributors	xi
Acknowledgments	xiii

Introduction: The Perennial Crisis for the American States
PETER CONTI-BROWN 1

PART I. THE ORIGINS OF THE STATES IN FISCAL CRISIS

1 Fiscal Institutions and Fiscal Crises
ISABEL RODRIGUEZ-TEJEDO AND JOHN JOSEPH WALLIS 9

2 Obligations Without the Power to Fund Them
DAMON A. SILVERS 40

3 Public Pension Pressures in the United States
OLIVIA S. MITCHELL 57

4 Structural Challenges in State Budgeting
JOSH BARRO 77

PART II. THE LEGAL AND POLITICAL CONTEXT OF PUBLIC DEBT

5 What States Can Learn From Municipal Insolvency
CLAYTON P. GILLETTE 99

6 Market Discipline and U.S. Federalism
  JONATHAN RODDEN   123

7 American States and Sovereign Debt Restructuring
  ADAM FEIBELMAN   146

PART III. EVALUATING SOLUTIONS

8 State Bankruptcy from the Ground Up
  DAVID A. SKEEL, JR.   191

9 Fiscal Federalism and the Limits of Bankruptcy
  ADAM J. LEVITIN   214

10 Extending Bankruptcy Law to States
   MICHAEL W. MCCONNELL   229

11 Bankruptcy For the States and By the States
   GEORGE TRIANTIS   237

12 Labor and the States' Fiscal Problems
   CATHERINE FISK AND BRIAN OLNEY   253

Epilogue – David A. Skeel, Jr.   315
Index   317

Figures

1.1	Adoption of first constitutional debt restrictions, by decade	*page* 25
1.2	Number of states that have a constitutional debt restriction, by decade	25
1.3	Adoption of first constitutional BBR, by decade	28
1.4	Number of states that have a constitutional BBR, by decade	29
1.5	Number of adoptions of RDFs, by decade	30
1.6	Number of state rainy day funds, by decade and type	30
1.7	Limits on traditional TELs and property tax limitations, by decade of first adoption	31
1.8	Number of states that have traditional TELs and property tax limits, by decade	32
1.9	Adoption of constitutional fiscal institutions	32
1.10	Number of states that had adopted each type of constitutional fiscal institution, by decade	33
3.1	Anticipated year of exhaustion for state pension fund assets	68
4.1	Pie chart of state and local tax sources in 2008	79
4.2	Graph of pupil-teacher ratios and education spending as a share of GDP over time	88
6.1	The growth of federal grants relative to state and local current expenditures	134
6.2	Credit default swaps for selected U.S. states	137
6.3	Credit default swaps for selected U.S. states and member states of the European Monetary Union	138

6.4 Debt-to-GDP ratios for European countries and U.S. states   139
12.1 Unadjusted Hourly Compensation – Public and Private Sector Compared: 2011   265
12.2 Adjusted Hourly Compensation – Public and Private Sector Compared: 2011   266
12.3 Public Pension Plan Funding Ratios by Extent of Collective Bargaining Rights: Fiscal Year 2009   277
12.4 Median Budget Gap by Extent of Collective Bargaining Rights: Fiscal Year 2012   280
12.5 Median Budget Gaps by Extent of Collective Bargaining Rights, Fiscal Years 2009–2011   280
12.6 Median State Workforce as a Percentage of Total Workforce by Extent of Collective Bargaining Rights: 2009   281
12.7 Median State Labor Expense as a Percentage of State Budget by Extent of Collective Bargaining Rights: Fiscal Year 2009   282

Tables

1.1	Government revenues as a share of GDP	*page* 13
1.2	Government debt as a percentage of GDP	14
1.3	Hypothetical Budgets	16
3.1	Present value of aggregate state defined benefit plan liabilities, alternative scenarios	63
3.2	Year of public plan exhaustion for alternative asset returns, under ongoing and termination scenarios	67

Contributors

Josh Barro is the Walter B. Wriston Fellow at the Manhattan Institute for Policy Research, where he specializes in state and local fiscal policy. He received his AB from Harvard College.

Peter Conti-Brown is an Academic Fellow at the Rock Center for Corporate Governance at Stanford Law School and the Stanford Graduate School of Business. He writes in the areas of banking, bankruptcy, corporate, and administrative law, with a particular focus on the law, economics, and history of financial and fiscal crises, public and private debt regulation, and central banking. He is a graduate of Stanford Law School and Harvard College.

Adam Feibelman is the Sumter Davis Marks Professor of Business and Corporate Law at Tulane Law School where he researches and writes on banking, bankruptcy, and sovereign debt.

Catherine Fisk is the Chancellor's Professor of Law at the University of California, Irvine. She is the author of three books and dozens of articles on labor law. She received a JD from the University of California, Berkeley, and an AB from Princeton University.

Clayton P. Gillette is the Max E. Greenberg Professor of Contract Law at NYU School of Law, where he teaches in the areas of state and local government law and commercial law.

Adam J. Levitin is a Professor of Law at Georgetown University Law Center where he specializes in bankruptcy, commercial law, and financial regulation. He received his JD from Harvard Law School.

Michael W. McConnell is the Richard & Frances Mallery Professor of Law and Director of the Constitutional Law Center at Stanford Law School and Senior Fellow at the Hoover Institution. He was previously a Circuit Judge on the United States Court of Appeals for the Tenth Circuit.

Olivia S. Mitchell is the International Foundation of Employee Benefit Plans Professor at the Wharton School of Business at the University of Pennsylvania and a Research Associate at the National Bureau of Economic Research. Her research focuses on the economics and public policy of private and public pensions. She received an MA and PhD in Economics from the University of Wisconsin-Madison, and an AB in Economics from Harvard University.

Brian Olney is a JD candidate at the University of California, Irvine, and received a BA from Wesleyan University. From 2001 to 2010 he worked for the Service Employees International Union, focusing on health care.

Jonathan Rodden is Professor of Political Science and W. Glenn Campbell and Rita Ricardo-Campbell National Fellow at the Hoover Institution, Stanford University. He is the author of *Hamilton's Paradox: The Promise and Peril of Fiscal Federalism*.

Isabel Rodriguez-Tejedo is a professor in the Department of Economics at the University of Navarra (Spain). She received her PhD in Economics from the University of Maryland.

Damon A. Silvers is the Director of Policy and Special Counsel for the AFL-CIO and has served in various local, state, and federal government capacities, including as the Deputy Chair of the Congressional Oversight Panel for TARP from 2008 to 2011. He received a JD, MBA, and AB, all with honors, from Harvard University.

David A. Skeel, Jr., is the S. Samuel Arsht Professor of Corporate Law at the University of Pennsylvania Law School. He is the author of *The New Financial Deal: Understanding the Dodd-Frank Act and Its (Unintended) Consequences* (2011), *Icarus in the Boardroom* (2005), and *Debt's Dominion: A History of Bankruptcy Law in America* (2001), as well as coeditor with Michael Klarman and Carol Steiker of *The Political Heart of Criminal Procedure* (2011), a collection of tribute essays to William J. Stuntz.

George Triantis is Professor of Law at Stanford Law School. Prior to joining the Stanford Law School faculty in 2011 he was the Eli Goldston Professor of Law at Harvard Law School. He specializes in bankruptcy, contracts, and corporate law.

John Joseph Wallis is Professor of Economics at the University of Maryland and Research Associate at the National Bureau of Economic Research.

Acknowledgments

This book began as a conference at Stanford University, in May 2011. We thank Dan Siciliano and Rock Center for Corporate Governance at Stanford University, Michael McConnell at the Constitutional Law Center at Stanford Law School, and Dean Larry Kramer for generous support for the conference, and we thank also the many participants for those helpful discussions. Our thanks also to Trish Gertridge and her staff for making the conference come to pass.

We also thank Blair Hodges for his work on the index and John Berger and his staff at Cambridge University Press for excellent editing.

Introduction: The Perennial Crisis for the American States

PETER CONTI-BROWN

In the summer of 2011, people throughout the world watched with rapt attention as Republican leaders in the U.S. Congress and President Barack Obama squared off against each other in a high-stakes, down-to-the-wire negotiation over the fate of the country's ability to issue new debt to fund its many financial obligations. The so-called debt ceiling debate illustrated the toxicity and potency of political-fiscal brinkmanship. Eventually, the crisis was averted – or at least forestalled – as a compromise was reached, new debt issued, and the tarnished credit of the United States relatively unbroken.[1]

In light of the attention paid to the political theater that preceded raising the debt ceiling, many citizens would be forgiven in thinking that the United States exists as a sole economic entity for the purposes of fiscal policy. This, of course, is erroneous. The several states of America independently participate as debtors to a vast array of creditors, from their own employees to the anonymous masses of the bond markets; from targeted lenders to the recipients of the states' safety nets. And while Congress and the President engaged in a time-consuming game of political chicken during the summer of 2011, a phenomenon as central to the American system as federalism itself continues to fly under the radar: The American states, in their individual governmental capacities, are in extraordinary debt.

Although the states' debt problems are not, at present, reported above the fold in leading national newspapers, they persist with a relentlessness that academics, policymakers, and citizens should heed. The unique history, context, and structure of the American states in debt require hard and careful thinking, planning, and action.

---

[1] Although Standard & Poor's did downgrade the U.S. credit for the first time in the credit rating agency's history, markets have continued to treat U.S. debt as among the safest available.

This volume gathers some of the leading scholars and commentators on issues relating to state debt crises to provide that level of thoughtful engagement not otherwise available in a single volume. These academics and practitioners from a variety of disciplines and backgrounds address this basic quandary: How do we understand and navigate the reality that state governments, by all accounts, appear unable to meet their obligations to their many claimants, from employees in the form of wages, pensions, and health care; citizens, in the form of welfare spending, infrastructure, education, and nearly every other government service; investors, in the form of general and specific debt; and indeed, any other individual or institution who interacts with state governments? At stake in this crisis is the very essence of state government, with the difficult and highly contested questions of what state governments ought to be, what state governments presently are, and how any difference between the two can be bridged in a contentious political climate.

Although frequently riding backseat to the more pressing concerns of sovereign – especially the United States – fiscal woes, nearly everything about the question of states' fiscal crises is fraught with urgency and controversy. In 2011 alone, tens of thousands of protesters filled the streets in Madison, Wisconsin, to challenge or support that state's efforts to redefine its relationship to its public employees' unions; legislators in Indiana absconded out of state with hopes to avoid votes on controversial issues on similar matters; the state of California began for a time paying its creditors with IOUs because the state was simply unfunded; Mayor Bloomberg of New York City proposed to lay off thousands of teachers in an already stretched school district to bridge the gap left by state cuts in Albany. And in a recent report, it was determined that the country of Iraq enjoys a higher credit rating than the state of Illinois.

What, then, might be done about these crises? Are federal bailouts of the states political nonstarters or predetermined by the nature of our union? Is serious tax reform a frank and inevitable necessity or so politically toxic as to be dismissed out of hand? Are unions' collective bargaining rights driving the states over a precipice, or are unions nothing but tangential figures in this story, paraded out as easy scapegoats by politicians eager to avoid the harder issues at stake? Would a mechanism for states to restructure their debts, similar to bankruptcy, resolve the problem or make it worse? Is such a mechanism even possible as a matter of law, or, for that matter, politics? What can we learn from the experiences of other public entities who have engaged in debt restructuring, whether foreign sovereigns or municipalities?

The authors who have contributed to this volume address these and related questions. The authors, taken together, agree on very little. Some consider the rhetoric of the conversation in general and even the title of the book overblown. Others think the problems are far graver than this Introduction has described. All authors, however, contribute to some aspect of this conversation and inform readers, challenge conventional thinking, and encourage those who seek to understand these problems to dig deeper than they have already done to understand what, exactly, is the problem in the American states today, and, as importantly, how it can be resolved.

The book is organized, as its subtitle suggests, into three subsections: origins, context, and solutions. In the first section, five scholars provide essentially a historical context for the states' problems, each highlighting different elements of the issues faced. Economic historians John Wallis and Isabel Rodriguez-Tejedo discuss, in illuminating detail, the ways in which states over the last two centuries have responded to fiscal crises and evaluate the current state of the states against that historical backdrop. Olivia Mitchell, the leading economist studying private and public pensions, provides a thorough introduction to the nature of state pensions and the ways in which funding commitments can create ballooning liabilities when the assumptions undergirding those commitments change. The Manhattan Institute's Josh Barro contributes a chapter on the basic mechanics of state budgetary processes. And Damon Silvers, former Deputy Chair of the Congressional Oversight Panel and present Director of Policy for the AFL-CIO, takes a fundamentally different tack, laying the problems facing the states at the feet of the political and economic changes that states have experienced over the last thirty years. Silvers highlights in particular two phenomena. First, the changing nature of recessions, from those that were steep, deep, relatively short-lived, and related to the business cycle, to those that are long, shallow, and the consequence of financial crises. Second, Silvers analyzes the ways in which New Federalism, championed by President Ronald Reagan and his supporters and extended during subsequent Administrations, takes from the federal government the responsibility of massive welfare provision and gives that responsibility to the states – a responsibility they are not always best situated to bear.

In the second section, we learn more about how insolvency regimes have functioned elsewhere in the world and elsewhere in the United States. In his contribution to the volume, Clayton Gillette, a leading scholar of both local and state government law and commercial law, leads readers through the context of municipal bankruptcy, comparing and contrasting the relatively well-established system of municipal bankruptcy with the problem of state insolvency. In the process, he discusses how the fundamentally different relationship between states and the nation on the one hand versus states and their subentities on the other complicates, perhaps irretrievably, the ways in which the solutions for municipal bankruptcy can be made applicable to the problems of state debt.

Of course, cities and states are not the only political entities that face debt crises, as the events in the United States and especially Europe throughout 2011 can amply attest. In this sense, Adam Feibelman, a scholar of bankruptcy and sovereign debt, ably introduces the history and implications of the regimes currently in place to allow sovereigns to restructure their debts in times of crisis. Feibelman's detailed case studies of sovereign default will be of interest to those readers interested in how, specifically, resolving sovereign debt crises can – and cannot – compare to the debt crises facing the states.

Political scientist Jonathan Rodden performs a similar analysis but focuses instead on the theoretical structure of fiscal federalism, a topic he has reinvigorated over the last decade. Rodden views the basic problem of fiscal federalism through the familiar lens of moral hazard in that subnational entities may attempt to displace their debts to the national sovereign, thus avoiding the costs of their debts, both economic and political. Rodden also helpfully compares the structure of the U.S. states to other fiscal federations, most relevantly the European Union, itself in a more acute fiscal-federalist crisis than the United States has yet faced.

In the final section of the book, the authors explore, in some detail, a proposal to allow states to restructure their debts in a process akin to bankruptcy. David Skeel, the volume's co-editor and the leading academic proponent of the proposal, lays out – with specificity not presented in his other writing on this topic – the strong case for bankruptcy and responds to many criticisms that have been lodged against the proposal. The three authors that follow Skeel do not make much of the bankruptcy proposal. Adam Levitin argues, for example, that the problem facing states is not financial, but political, and as a consequence, state bankruptcy proposals are solutions looking for a specific problem. Michael McConnell, former federal appellate judge and leading constitutional law scholar, is, for the purposes of the volume, expressly agnostic as to the policy benefits of state bankruptcy. He does, however, explain the very real constitutional problems that these proposals face, problems not addressed by making state bankruptcy a voluntary procedure.

George Triantis, another leading bankruptcy and commercial law scholar, presents a middle ground. He argues that the concept of a single state bankruptcy regime belies the political, institutional, and financial variation that exists among states. He argues instead that states should pass, themselves restructuring regimes that are more tailored to their own economic and political realities, and that such proposals should be evaluated on their own bases, with reference to the states that pass them.

Finally, stepping out of the context of state bankruptcy, labor law scholars Catherine Fisk and Brian Olney present the case that public unions have been a scapegoat in this process and present a sensible alternative to the widely adopted argument that states need only throw the unions out in order to resolve their crises. Fisk and Olney discuss how labor law – as opposed to bankruptcy law – can help resolve the state debt crises. David Skeel concludes the volume with an epilogue on the state of the states, and the relevance of this project extends beyond the political zeitgeist of any single moment.

This book expends significant energy on assessing the strengths and weaknesses of state bankruptcy proposals. But the book is not about state bankruptcy per se, but something far broader, and more important. The American states face a perennial fiscal crisis, made painfully obvious each time recession devastates the economy. To quote one of Warren Buffett's perhaps overused nuggets of axiomatic wisdom, "You only find out who is swimming naked when the tide goes out." Because of a combination of political, fiscal, and economic factors, the states are chronically swimming naked. This book represents an effort to understand the basic structure of this perennial problem, and, hopefully, point toward mechanisms that would mitigate the problems when they arise.

PART I

The Origins of the States in Fiscal Crisis

1

Fiscal Institutions and Fiscal Crises

ISABEL RODRIGUEZ-TEJEDO AND JOHN JOSEPH WALLIS

1. TAXING, SPENDING, AND BORROWING

American states came into existence as self-constituting legal entities in 1776. Since then they have continued to face the persistent problem of what and how much to tax, on what and how much to spend, and whether some expenditures should be financed through borrowing. These problems are not new nor will they ever go away as long as there are states. The current state fiscal crisis (2009 to 2011) is one in a series of crises that will be repeated in the future. Fiscal crises arise when revenues unexpectedly fall, expenditures unexpectedly rise, or some combination of the two produces a situation in which taxes must rise, spending must decrease, and/or borrowing must increase. Hope springs eternal in America, however, and for close to 200 years, state governments and their citizens have regularly tried to prevent the next crisis from occurring by changing the constitutional rules that constrain state government taxing, spending, and borrowing. The term "fiscal constitutions" includes constitutional provisions regarding taxing, spending, and borrowing. How and why the rules of fiscal constitutions have changed and the interaction of the rules with fiscal crisis over time is our concern.[1]

At three points in the past – the 1840s, the 1870s to 1880s, and the 1930s – one or more states reached a point at which they were forced to default on interest payments on their bonded debt. In several instances states actually went so far as to repudiate their obligations. Although the sound and fury over the predicament of states in the recession that began in late 2007 can make it seem as though the current crisis is unprecedented, it is not. Some states are in a tight spot, but no tighter than they have

---

[1] This chapter builds on the ideas and information presented in Rodriguez-Tejedo and Wallis (2010).

been on a couple of occasions since the 1930s, and states in general are in much better shape now than they were in the 1840s or the 1930s, or the southern states were after the Civil War. Over the last 200 years, succeeding generations of Americans have had to learn and relearn the lesson that a popular democracy does not automatically guarantee a government capable of sustainable fiscal policies. Americans have been less amendable to learning the lesson that changing the rules to solve the last fiscal crisis may make the next fiscal crisis worse, or at least different. There is a pronounced pattern of crisis and response in the historical record, a pattern that we call "recursive" institutional change, in which new constitutional changes respond to a crisis exacerbated by a previous constitutional change. Rather than admitting that the fundamental underlying problem is that no government can ensure fiscal sanity through constitutional rules alone, Americans keep searching for the magic set of rules. Fiscal sustainability results from mature and realistic politics. Understanding why politics in America is sometimes neither mature nor realistic goes beyond the scope of this chapter, but an important conclusion is that the fiscal crisis facing states in 2011 is a political problem more than a constitutional or economic problem.[2]

In a global context, American state and local governments manage extremely sophisticated systems of public finance. In the first decade of the twenty-first century, state and local governments combined borrow roughly $300 billion a year to finance capital and infrastructure investments. Subnational governments in the countries that are clients of the World Bank, with about 60 percent of the world's population, borrow only about $5 billion a year. American state and local governments rarely default (in the sense of missing interest payments). In a comparative perspective, the American system works very well.

From an economic standpoint, a very desirable feature of American constitutional provisions is that they coordinate who benefits from specific decisions to tax, spend, and borrow with the people who pay the taxes or bear the costs. From the 1840s on, changes in constitutions have often been directed toward ensuring that those who pay taxes to finance debts have a say in whether the debt is incurred (a bond referendum, for example). Where government activity takes place – a state, a county, a city, a school

---

[2] For an excellent discussion of how political forces have generated the current fiscal crisis in California, see Cain and Noll (2010). On May 17, 2011, the *Economist* magazine recently published a series of articles on constitutional change and politics in California, based in part on Cain and Noll's analysis.

district, or a special district – often results from the political advantages of financing infrastructure investment through borrowing in jurisdictions where a majority of the citizens and voters benefit from the investment. This chapter describes how and why these institutional arrangements developed over time. At the conclusion, we provide a few suggestions about which parts of current fiscal constitutions are working well and which are causing problems.

After reviewing state finances in a historical perspective, we examine more carefully what a state budget is to see where decisions are made in the political process about taxing, spending, and borrowing that might be affected by constitutional rules. In section V, we show how states have enacted a series of reforms to their fiscal constitutions. We close with a synthesis of the history that points out why fiscal constitutions have changed over time and a simple proscription for how we might think about changing constitutions in the future.

II. THE STATE GOVERNMENT FISC IN AMERICAN HISTORY

It seems best to determine clearly right from the beginning what a fiscal crisis is and is not. A fiscal crisis is caused when revenues and expenditures change relative to one another in a way that strains the capacity of the government to finance its activities, usually to the extent that a state must deliberately change its taxing, spending, or borrowing policies. Two aspects of the definition are important. One is that a fiscal crisis is largely self-defined by the actions and attitudes of the state in which the crisis occurs – that is, fiscal crises are always political as well as economic events. Second, the definition of a fiscal crisis has nothing to do with the size of the government or with the amount that a government borrows. Big state governments are no more or less likely to find themselves in a fiscal crisis than small governments; what matters is the relative amount of revenues and expenditures. We should be careful not to infer that a state whose taxes and expenditures (TEL) comprise 10 percent of the income of state residents is no more likely to have a fiscal crisis than a state whose (TEL) account for 5 percent of state income. What matters most is the relative size of revenues and expenditures. Likewise, states may borrow lots of money without causing a fiscal crisis. State governments in the United States regularly borrow more than $150 billion a year to finance things like highways, schools, public buildings, and other capital investments without causing fiscal crises. In 2007, the year of the last Census of Governments, total state debt outstanding was $936 billion, and debt issued in that fiscal year by states totaled $161 billion ($92 billion in debt was repaid)[3]; 2007 was not a crisis year. Yet, Indiana defaulted on its debts in 1841, when the total debt was only $12 million! Today, the average state has $20 billion in debt.

To meaningfully compare Indiana's $12 million debt in 1841 with its $19 billion state debt in 2007 requires that we appropriately adjust debt figures by population, income, and inflation. Tables 1.1 and 1.2 give basic information on the size of state governments and the size of state debts over time from the 1840s to 2007, where size is kept in perspective by measuring total government revenues and government debt as a percentage of gross domestic product (GDP) in each year. Local and national government revenues and debts are included for comparison. There are many interesting numbers and trends in Tables 1.1 and 1.2. In 1841, on the eve of the default crisis during which Pennsylvania, Maryland, Indiana, Illinois, Michigan, Mississippi, Louisiana, Arkansas, and the territory of Florida defaulted on their bonded debts, state government debt outstanding was 12 percent of GDP, whereas state revenues were only 1 percent of GDP. After the default crisis in 1841 and 1842, state debts as a share of GDP trended down steadily until 1913, whereas state revenues remained around 1 percent of GDP. State governments grew steadily smaller in relation to both local and national governments over the second half of the nineteenth century. In 1913, local government debt was more than double national and state government debt combined, and local government revenues were only slightly smaller than national government revenues. Local governments undertook the lion's share of borrowing for infrastructure investment (roads, schools, and public utilities) in the late nineteenth and early twentieth centuries. The national debt in 1913 was a carryover from financing the Civil War and the Spanish-American War.

In the twentieth century, these patterns changed again. State governments began growing as states assumed responsibility for constructing highways after the invention of the automobile. States took over a much larger share of the responsibility for public welfare services in the 1930s and beyond. State revenues grew from roughly 1 percent of GDP at the beginning of the twentieth century to 9 percent at the end of the century. State debts also grew, from about 1 percent to 6 percent of GDP. State borrowing grew more slowly than state revenue collection (and spending) over the course of the twentieth century (Wallis 2000, 2001).

---

[3] Census of Governments, *State and Local Government Finances by Level of Government and by State: 2006–07.*

TABLE 1.1. *Government revenues as a share of GDP*

	National	State	Local	Total
1840	1.7%	1.0%	1.4%	4.0%
1850	1.9%	1.0%	1.2%	4.2%
1860	2.5%	1.3%	1.6%	5.4%
1870	4.7%	1.1%	2.6%	8.4%
1880	2.8%	0.7%	2.2%	5.7%
1890	2.7%	0.9%	2.8%	6.4%
1900	2.6%	1.0%	3.6%	7.2%
1902	3.0%	0.8%	4.0%	7.8%
1913	2.4%	0.9%	4.2%	7.5%
1922	5.8%	1.7%	5.2%	12.6%
1927	4.7%	2.1%	6.0%	12.8%
1934	6.0%	3.8%	7.6%	17.4%
1940	7.0%	5.0%	5.8%	17.9%
1946	22.3%	3.7%	3.6%	29.5%
1952	20.4%	4.1%	4.0%	28.5%
1957	19.3%	4.6%	4.7%	28.6%
1962	18.5%	5.2%	5.5%	29.2%
1967	19.7%	5.7%	5.4%	30.8%
1972	18.4%	6.9%	6.2%	31.5%
1977	19.2%	7.6%	6.0%	32.8%
1982	21.6%	8.2%	6.2%	36.1%
1987	21.0%	9.1%	6.9%	37.0%
1992	20.8%	9.3%	7.3%	37.5%
1997	19.3%	9.7%	6.7%	35.7%
2002	17.9%	7.2%	6.4%	31.5%
2007	18.5%	11.2%	7.4%	37.0%

After the initial burst of state borrowing in the 1830s, followed by the default crisis of 1841 and 1842, state governments did not grow relative to the economy over the rest of the nineteenth century, and state debts declined relative to GDP. Southern states defaulted and renegotiated their debts after the Civil War and Reconstruction. Arkansas defaulted on its debts at the beginning of the Great Depression. Other than those incidents, states have managed to pay interest and principal on their debts on time. State governments grew steadily in the twentieth century, both with respect to national and

TABLE 1.2. *Government debt as a percentage of GDP*

	State	Local	National	Total
1841	12.3%	1.6%	0.3%	14.3%
1870	4.2%	6.1%	29.0%	39.3%
1880	2.6%	7.1%	18.0%	27.7%
1890	1.7%	6.7%	8.3%	16.8%
1902	1.2%	10.1%	6.3%	17.7%
1913	1.0%	10.3%	3.0%	14.3%
1922	1.5%	12.2%	31.3%	45.0%
1932	4.8%	27.9%	33.2%	65.9%
1942	2.0%	9.9%	41.8%	53.8%
1952	1.9%	6.5%	59.9%	68.3%
1962	3.8%	10.0%	42.3%	56.1%
1972	4.8%	10.4%	26.0%	41.3%
1982	4.5%	7.9%	28.3%	40.7%
1992	5.9%	9.5%	47.3%	62.7%
1997	5.5%	9.2%	45.3%	59.9%
2002	6.0%	9.8%	33.3%	49.1%
2007	6.7%	10.5%	35.8%	53.0%

local government, as well as relative to GDP. The size of the state fisc grew more rapidly than the size of state debt. The situation in 2007, on the brink of the current recession, was not particularly precarious in historical terms. State borrowing was not out of control or exploding. State governments continued to slowly grow relative to the economy, as they had for most of the twentieth century. There were reasons that states became more susceptible to economic downturns over the twentieth century, largely having to do with the structure of their revenues and expenditures. In 1900, roughly three-quarters of state revenues came from property taxes. Sales and income taxes became more important sources of revenue as the century progressed. In 2007, sales taxes and personal income taxes accounted for more than half of all state revenues. Both sales and income taxes are more variable with respect to economic conditions over time than the property tax. In addition, during the 1930s, states assumed a much larger role in the provision of welfare services of a variety of types. Just as income tax revenues decline in economic recessions, expenditures for welfare services rise, putting the states in a bind from both the taxing and spending side.

III. BUDGETS AND DEBTS

How revenues, expenditures, and debts are measured plays a critical role in how we think about fiscal institutions and fiscal crises. It seems straightforward to say that states should balance their budgets by ensuring that the amount of money that comes into the treasury equals or exceeds the money that goes out. In principle, that is what a fiscal constitution is designed to do. A very simple statement of the principle was included in the Nevada constitution of 1864, Article 9, section 2:

> The Legislature shall provide by law for an annual tax, sufficient to defray the estimated expenses of the State for each fiscal year; and whenever the expenses of any year shall exceed the income, the Legislature shall provide for levying a tax sufficient, with other sources of income, to pay the deficiency, as well as the estimated expenses of such ensuing year or two years.

Nevada articulated the idea that the state government should raise enough money to cover expenditures, and if it does not, it should raise taxes in a sufficient amount to make up the deficit over the next two years. In Nevada in 1864, any deficit was supposed to be remedied automatically by raising taxes. This is not the prevailing sentiment in 2011.

A budget that simply counts money in and money out, however, runs into several problems, including borrowed funds and principal repayment, separation of funds for different purposes, and how questions about timing are accounted for. Table 1.3 sketches out a set of budget models, each more complicated than the next moving down the table. Individual lines in the table represent items in the budget. An equal sign (=) is included to indicate what items in the budget are "balanced" against each other. Budget A is money in equals money out. Budget B recognizes that, at the beginning of the fiscal year, the state possesses cash (or other assets), and over the course of the fiscal year those assets can be drawn down or added to. Whether the cash at the beginning of the year should be included in money in or not varies from state to state. Nevada was explicit about expenses exceeding income; presumably in Nevada, cash balances were not included in either income or expenses. In the 1830s, Maryland received money from the national government from the surplus revenue disbursement. Maryland recorded the disbursement as revenue, put the money in a bank account, and later when the money was withdrawn from the bank, counted it as a revenue again! You can see why cash balances (and other assets) are something that a budget or budget rules may want to deal with explicitly and segregate from the money in/money out calculation. The development of

TABLE 1.3. *Hypothetical Budgets*

A.	Money in	=	Money out
B.	Cash at beginning		Cash at end
	Money in	=	Money out
C.	Cash at beginning		Cash at end
	Loans		Principal repaid
	Net money in	=	Net money out
D.	Cash at beginning		Cash at end
	Loans		Principal repaid
	Money into general fund	=	Money out of general fund
	+ Money into fund X	=	+ Money out for purpose X
E.	Cash at beginning		Cash at end
	Loans		Principal repaid
	+ Money into general fund	=	+ Money out of general fund
	+ Money into fund X	=	+ Money out for purpose X
Capital Budget			
	+ Loans		+ Principal repaid
	+ Money in for capital funds	=	+ Money out for capital projects
Sinking Fund			
	+ Money in for sinking fund	=	Principal repaid + Bonds purchased

"rainy day" funds (RDF) in the twentieth century was an attempt by states to deal deliberately with cash balances and the accounting rules for taking money in and out of cash and other assets.[4]

Part of the problem with cash balances is timing: Revenues and expenditures do not occur at the same time over the course of the year, and so the balance in the treasury at any point in time may be large or small in a way that does not reflect the true condition of state finances. States often keep several sets of accounts: one is essentially "checks written" and the other is "checks cleared."[5] In many states, a set of checks written accounts is

---

[4] Inman (2010) recommends that Congress begin thinking about ways to encourage states to maintain larger cash balances in their budgets through RDFs.

[5] In the nineteenth century, these accounts were often recorded in terms of warrants issued. Warrants were claims that the state treasurer was obliged to redeem.

kept by the treasurer and included in published state reports, and another account of checks cleared is kept by the auditor (or comptroller) and also published in state reports. The two accounts differ intrinsically by time, and sometimes they disagree in amounts, which usually leads to an investigation of the treasurer. In the nineteenth century, it was common for the state to keep a set of accounts with the treasurer. The money in the treasurer's accounts was literally the treasurer's money.[6] At the end of the treasurer's term, there would be a settling up. Occasionally, the treasurer's books did not balance. As the nineteenth century progressed, states gradually integrated their financial accounts, and the treasurer became an officer of the state government rather than an independent actor.

When money is borrowed and repaid, a problem with double counting arises. A state that borrows $10 million to build a bridge, builds the bridge, then repays the principal over time with money raised in taxes, will have received more than $20 million in revenues (the $10 million loan plus the taxes necessary to repay the principal and any interest accrued) and more than $20 million in expenditures ($10 million to build the bridge, $10 million in principal repayment, and any interest paid). Revenues and expenditures will be more than twice what they should be. To avoid this type of double counting, loans are typically excluded from revenues and principal repayment is excluded from expenditures when accounts are drawn up. You can see how this complicates a simple "money in equals money out" idea of balance. It is possible to have a balanced "money in equals money out" budget, with borrowing, if loans are counted as revenues! This is another reason that simple constitutional provisions like Nevada's can be problematic. A budget that accounts for double counting is shown in Budget C in Table 1.3. Loan revenues and principal repayment expenditures are segregated in the budget from money in and money out (loans and principal repaid do not equal one another in any given budget year, but do over time.) In this table, loans and principal repayment are shown on different lines than net money in (money in net of loan revenues) and net money out (money out net of principal repayments).

Another problem arises when citizens wish to dedicate a particular revenue source to a particular purpose. For example, many states allocate a fixed portion of revenues from state lotteries to fund education. That produces a budget that includes segregated funds, with their own

---

[6] This led in some states to the confusing way in which revenues and expenditures are reported. State revenues are "debits" to the treasurer's account, and expenditures are "credits" to the treasurer's account, even though revenues are credits to the state, and expenditures are debits.

accounts, as in Budget D. Budget D poses a very important problem. Is a budget balanced if the sum of the general fund and the special fund are in balance, or should each fund be considered separately? Further, how should transfers between the general fund and the special fund be treated?[7] The distinction of special funds dedicated to particular purposes began to play a larger role in constitutional regulation of borrowing in the late nineteenth century.

Currently, the term "general" is used in two related, but different, ways with respect to revenues and funds to reflect both accounting standards and concepts in public finance. Most states distinguish between a general fund and special funds in their own budgets, as a way of segregating revenues for specific purposes. Some states have extensive arrays of special funds, whereas other states have fairly unified budgets. The second meaning of "general" is in the standard accounting procedures used by the Census of Governments, in which "general revenues" are revenues from the general operation of government, and special or "non-general" revenues are money received for special purposes like insurance trust funds (unemployment insurance and social security, for example), revenues from public enterprises like utilities (a water company or transit authority, for example), or from state liquor stores.[8]

Budget E represents a budget in which special funds for a number of purposes have been created. One is a capital budget, which records money borrowed and expended on long-term capital infrastructure like highways, public buildings, and utilities. Revenues in the capital budget may be transfers from the general fund, or they may be dedicated revenues from particular revenue sources. Although the capital budget must be balanced, capital budgets explicitly allow for borrowing and principal repayment to be counted as money in and money out. Likewise, many states have a sinking fund (possibly more than one if several debts are segregated) in which money from the general fund or specific revenue sources is regularly deposited and then is available to repay the principal on debt when the debt matures. Sinking funds are sometimes authorized

---

[7] This is a central problem in accounting for revenues, expenditures, and debt with respect to the Social Security Trust fund in the national budget. Currently, the Congressional Budget Office keeps a consolidated budget, a budget with items that are "on budget," and a budget with items that are "off budget."

[8] The standard census public finance categories are described in various publications of the Census of Governments. When looking at individual states, it is important to keep in mind that each state defines its general fund in a specific and idiosyncratic ways, and that the state definitions vary from the Census definition.

to purchase debt on the open market when interest rates rise and the market price of bonds falls.[9]

Today, most state budgets are at least as complicated as Budget E. In the eighteenth century, they were more like Budget A, and since then budgets have transformed through stages. There is no ideal form of a state budget, although there are accepted accounting standards for budget rules and professional associations of state budget officers. What is certain is that the shape that budgets take is a result of political expediency as much as accounting transparency. Nowhere is this more true than in the concept of a balanced budget and the procedures regulating and accounting for government borrowing.

IV. FISCAL CONSTITUTIONS

Over the last two centuries, states developed four main types of constitutional provisions governing fiscal processes. The first and most widespread type regulates government borrowing through procedural requirements on debt issue or actual limits on amounts of debt. The second type, also widespread, includes provisions that require a balanced budget and sometimes stipulate that the budget be passed following certain procedures. The third type is RDFs that require or allow a state to save funds in good years to be available to meet deficits in lean years. The fourth type includes tax and expenditure limits that cap the level of taxes, expenditures, or both in absolute or relative terms. Tax and expenditure limits may also include procedures that affect legislative rules about taxes or expenditures – for example, a two-thirds supermajority in the legislature to raise taxes. The details of these provisions vary widely. Our purpose is to outline the main features of fiscal constitutions rather than to analyze the differences in state constitutions across states and over time.

The first fiscal provisions inserted into state constitutions in the 1840s dealt with government debt. The concepts of debt restrictions and debt limitations are often confused, because states as well as scholars sometimes use the two terms interchangeably. To be clear, a debt "limitation" is a limit on the total amount of debt a state (or local) government can issue. The limit can be an absolute limit (say, $300,000) or a relative limit (say, 1 percent of assessed property valuation). A debt restriction, sometimes

---

[9] For an interesting case in which the allocation of a sinking fund became a political issue, see Miller's discussion of the sinking fund in New York established to build up funds to repay the bonds issued to build the Erie Canal.

called a procedural debt restriction, allows a state (or local) government to create new debt as long as a particular procedure is followed. For clarity, for the remainder of this chapter we will call procedural debt restrictions debt "procedures." Be aware, however, that these terms are unique to this chapter and are not widely used. Unfortunately, the widely used terms are used indiscriminately, so a reader usually cannot be sure whether it is a debt limit or debt procedure at issue.

The most common kind of debt procedure requires the state legislature to follow three steps. First, the legislature identifies the purpose for which the debt will be issued and calculates the annual cost to service the debt. Second, the legislature must raise taxes by that amount. Third, voters must approve the debt and the new taxes in a special bond referendum. Other debt procedures may require a legislative supermajority approval – two-thirds or three-quarters of both houses of the state legislature – or approval in two consecutive sessions of the legislature.

The difference between debt procedures and debt limitations cannot be over emphasized. State constitutions typically are concerned with procedural restrictions that shape the incentives of political actors, both officeholders and voters. The point of debt procedures is not to make it impossible for states to borrow, but to put procedural hurdles in the way of borrowing so that legislatures and voters are more conscious of the decisions they make. Many states combine a debt limitation with a debt procedure. The 1849 California constitution, for example, allowed the legislature to borrow up to $300,000 without voter approval (a limitation), but allowed the state to borrow unlimited amounts with voter approval (a procedure). This type of debt limitation is a "casual" limit because it only limits the amount of debt the legislature is allowed to incur without invoking the debt procedure. The California constitution still has the 1849 limit of $300,000 on casual debt and a procedural restriction on the issue of other debt.

In terms of the budgets presented in Table 1.3, a debt procedure attempts to sustain fiscal balance through restrictions on the political process by which borrowing is authorized. Debt procedures attempt to affect the amount of loans taken out by the state. Whether loans are counted as revenues or not does not really matter because loans have to be repaid and principal repayments will ultimately balance out loan revenues, although with double counting. In the early nineteenth century, some states counted loans as revenues in their accounts. The key point to remember is that the first attempts to regulate borrowing did not do so in the framework of a balanced budget but by tweaking the political process through which borrowing was authorized. States began adopting debt procedures in the 1840s, long before balanced budget restrictions (BBR) became commonplace.

It is important to keep in mind as well that even a state with a strict debt limit in its constitution can still amend the constitution to allow debt to be issued for a specific purpose, or in a specific amount. Constitutional amendments that allow debt for a specific purpose, what we have called "itemized debt," are also quite common. Amending the constitution is always a debt procedure available to politicians, governments, and citizens.

Debt procedures do not limit the amount of debt that can be issued, and as advocates of less government borrowing learned that debt procedures would not eliminate borrowing, they began pressing for more explicit balanced budget provisions. Balanced budget provisions require state governments to adopt budgets that raise enough revenue to cover expenditures. Balanced budget provisions are quite variable. The simple statement in the 1864 constitution of Nevada articulated the principle that legislatures should raise revenues sufficient to cover expenditures. Whether the Nevada provision would prohibit or limit state borrowing, however, would depend on how revenues and expenditures were measured and, thus, whether loans and principal repayment were included or excluded from the amount to be balanced.

In the beginning of the twentieth century, more complicated balanced budget provisions started to be included in state constitutions and in state legislation. These provisions were more forward looking and apply more formal guidelines. In 1938, New York adopted a constitutional provision that required the governor to submit a balanced budget to the state legislature every year. Article 7, section 2:

> Annually, on or before the first day of February, the governor shall submit to the legislature a budget containing a complete plan of expenditures proposed to be made before the close of the ensuing fiscal year and all moneys and revenues estimated to be available therefor, together with an explanation of the basis of such estimates and recommendations as to proposed legislation, if any, which he may deem necessary to provide moneys and revenues sufficient to meet such proposed expenditures. It shall also contain such other recommendations and information as he may deem proper and such additional information as may be required by law.

Section 2 was followed by fourteen more sections that specified legislative procedures for implementing a balanced budget and then a complicated set of debt limitations and restrictions. In the 1930s and later, the (BBR) in many states became increasingly strict, limiting the ability of the state to run casual deficits that they could eventually make up.

The more strict BBR had two elements. First, they made explicit what parts of the budget needed to be in balance. They often referred explicitly to balance in the general fund of the state and implicitly or explicitly excluded special funds, capital budgets, and sinking funds from the balance requirement. Second, formal balanced budget procedures were aimed at the budgeting process as much as balancing the budget. Budgets had to be in balance ex ante not ex post, and as a result, the ability of state legislatures to make informal adjustments without resort to long-term borrowing was significantly reduced. BBR were aimed at defining what was included in the money in/money out category and then attempting to force governors and legislatures to balance those amounts ex ante. Even states with sound fiscal practices occasionally would find themselves in a situation in which their forward-looking budgets were out of balance. Legislatures were then required either to raise taxes, to lower spending, or to ask voters for borrowing approval. When budgets prove to be out of balance expost, states would either have to borrow, following their debt procedures, or figure out ways to raise revenues and/or cut spending. Most states allow a certain amount of what we call "casual" debt, like the $300,000 in the California constitution, which allows legislatures and executives to borrow to smooth out small fiscal bumps without invoking the debt procedure.

BBR created more pressure on legislatures to pass balanced budgets, and a move to ease the constraints of balanced budget provisions first appeared in the 1940s and became widespread in the 1980s: the RDF fund. A RDF fund explicitly addressed the presence of cash assets at the beginning and end of the fiscal year. A typical RDF required legislatures to put away money in good years that would be available to supplement tax revenues in lean years. This meant that states would carry forward cash balances that would grow in normal years.[10] The RDFs take advantage of the cash balance part of the budget identified in budget B in Table 1.3 to achieve balance with more flexibility over time.

There was a technical effect as well. Money put into the RDF was counted as an expenditure in the year the contribution was made, but

---

[10] In fiscal year 2008, states held cash and security holdings of $3.8 trillion. Of this, $2.7 trillion were held by insurance and pension trust funds, $500 billion in sinking funds and bond funds of various types, and the remaining $600 billion in other funds.

withdrawals from the funds and the expenditures based on those withdrawals were not counted as expenditures in the later year.[11] RDF could be drawn on when conditions warranted. This gave states more flexibility in managing finances over time and allowed states to meet the letter of the balanced budget rules in years when the state was running down its assets.[12] Rather than borrowing to meet temporary shortfalls, the state could draw down its RDF. The RDFs were adopted on a widespread basis in the 1980s and 1990s. Again, the terms of the RDF provisions varied widely from state to state.

Like debt procedures, BBR did not stop the growth of state governments in the mid-twentieth century. The most recent type of fiscal constitutional provision is a direct limitation on TEL. Famously in California, Proposition 13 limits the property tax rate to 1 percent of the assessed value of the property (it has other provisions as well). Tax and expenditure limits are attempts to fix the size of government budgets, sometimes in absolute terms but more often as a percentage of a relevant economic measure like per capita income or assessed property value or as a percentage of the previous year's budget (limiting budget growth). In the next section, we draw a distinction between property tax limitations (PTL), which have been around since the late nineteenth century, and TELs, which are more comprehensive attempts to limit revenues and expenditures and only became common after 1980.

TELs are attempts to define the budget structure in a particular way and the limit parts of the budget (or budget growth over time). TELs have not proven particularly effective at actually limiting the size of state government budgets because of the inherent ability of state governments to move or divide budget categories. The procedural parts of TELs, like Proposition 13's two-thirds requirement to raise tax rates, have certainly had an effect on the politics of public finance, one that we return to later.

[11] The California constitution authorized RDFs in 1979 (along with an expenditure limitation). The language of Article 13.B, section 5, reads: "Each entity of government may establish such contingency, emergency, unemployment, reserve, retirement, sinking fund, trust, or similar funds as it shall deem reasonable and proper. Contributions to any such fund, to the extent that such contributions are derived from the proceeds of taxes, shall for purposes of this Article constitute appropriations subject to limitation in the year of contribution. Neither withdrawals from any such fund, nor expenditures of (or authorizations to expend) such withdrawals, nor transfers between or among such funds, shall for purposes of this Article constitute appropriations subject to limitation."

[12] By a strict interpretation of a constitutional provision like the 1864 Nevada balanced-budget provision, using a RDF would be "unconstitutional," because money in would be less than money out.

V. THE PATTERN OF FISCAL CONSTITUTIONS OVER TIME

It is easy to see that states adopted constitutional provisions sequentially by looking at the timing of constitutional changes across states. This section describes the recursive process of institutional change as a response not only to the original economic conditions but also to the unexpected consequences of previous modifications in fiscal constitutions. From a static perspective, debt restrictions, balanced budget rules, TELs, and RDFs may seem independent instruments that states use to address everyday economic problems. In this section, we look at the timing of their adoption and put it in its historical context, and a clear pattern of crisis and response emerges.

Debt Procedures and Limitations

Figure 1.1 shows the number of states that adopted their first debt procedure or limitation in each decade between the 1830s and the 1950s and after. Figure 1.2 shows the cumulative total number of states that have a debt procedure or limitation in place over the same period. States began implementing debt restrictions in the 1840s, when ten states changed their constitutions (Wallis 2005). States were responding to the default crisis of 1841 and 1842. Whereas Indiana banned debt outright, and a few other states put strict limits on the amount of debt – Ohio for example – most states adopted debt procedures rather than debt limits. Several southern states defaulted on their debts after the Civil War. By 1900, most states had a debt procedure or debt limit of some type, the only regional exception was New England.

Although the new debt procedures did have an effect on the amount of debt incurred by states, they had the unexpected effect of shifting government borrowing to the local level. As Tables 1.1 and 1.2 show, local governments grew in size relative to state governments over the end of the nineteenth century and into the beginning of the twentieth century. In the 1870s, a number of local governments, primarily those who had borrowed money to invest in railroad construction, defaulted on their debts. In response, states began extending debt procedures and debt limits to local governments as well (Wallis and Weingast 2008).

Just as the unexpected effect of debt procedures at the state level was the growth of local government borrowing, so the extension of debt procedures to local governments had the unexpected effect of increasing the number of local governments called "special districts" or "special purpose

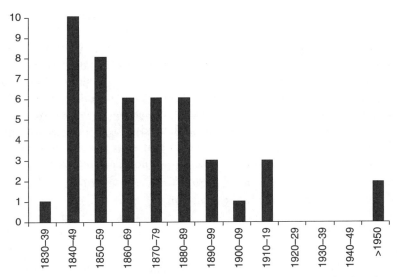

FIGURE 1.1. Adoption of first constitutional debt restrictions, by decade.

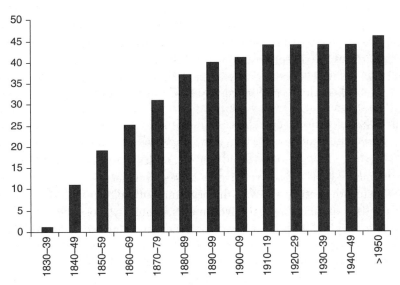

FIGURE 1.2. Number of states that have a constitutional debt restriction, by decade.

governments." Governments that faced a bond referendum requirement before they could issue debt were confronted with the difficulty of mobilizing political support among a majority of voters. Many socially useful projects do not benefit a majority of a state's voters. The direct benefits of a project like the Erie Canal or an intrastate highway accrue primarily to people who live in close proximity to the transportation route (or citizens of other states that enjoy lower transportation costs). Because most voters do not benefit directly from the project, they vote against the bond referendum for good reason.

Moving borrowing from the state to the local level enabled governments to more closely match the geography of those who benefited from an infrastructure project with the geography of those who paid for the project. When local governments were required to authorize new bond issues through a majority rule referendum, both state and local governments responded by creating new government forms that either had boundaries that specifically matched beneficiaries and taxpayers, like a water or sewage district, or began to more carefully craft matches between revenue sources and repayment obligations.

The creation of special governments with tailored geographic boundaries had a long history in the provision of education by school districts. In 1940, when the first comprehensive count of governments in the United States was taken, there were 155,166 governments: 1 national; 48 state; 3,050 counties; 16,220 municipal governments (cities); 18,919 towns and townships; 108,579 school districts; and 8,299 special governments. In 2007, the number of governments had fallen to 89,476, and the number of school districts had shrunk to 13,051, but the number of special districts had risen to 37,281.[13]

The second change was to tailor specific revenue sources to repay specific debt obligations. The "special fund doctrine" held that constitutional debt procedures only applied to debts payable from the general revenues of the state (or local) government, what is usually called "general obligation" (or GO) debt. If bonds were issued that were payable only from specific, special revenue sources, and the bondholders only had recourse to those revenue sources for repayment, then perhaps the debt procedure did not hold for those obligations. Courts in some states agreed with the logic of the special fund doctrine, and in those states, special funds proliferated. Many states began issuing "revenue bonds," bonds payable out of

---

[13] All numbers taken from the Census of Governments. The smallest number of governments in the United States was in 1972, at 78,269. The number of special districts grew from 23,885 in 1972 to 37,281 in 2007.

a specific revenue stream and not the general obligation of the taxpayers. Special purpose governments and revenue bonds backed by specific (special) revenue sources spread rapidly between the 1880s and the 1930s.

One can view these two developments as attempts by politicians to evade constitutional debt procedures and debt limits, as in Briffault's excellent summary of state fiscal constitutions at the end of the twentieth century: *Balancing Acts* (1996). However, neither special districts nor revenue bonds produced a wave of irresponsible borrowing and subsequent defaults. It is important to understand why. As we discussed briefly in the Introduction, the key political problem with government borrowing is whether the people who benefit from the investments of the borrowed funds are the same people who pay the taxes that repay the debt. The idea that the identity of those who benefited should be explicitly matched to those who paid was embodied in the first debt procedures adopted in the 1840s through the bond referendum requirement. The identity of beneficiaries and taxpayers was extended by special districts and revenue bonds, which matched the geographic and functional distribution of beneficiaries and taxpayers, respectively. Highway trust fund revenues that come from gasoline taxes are a good example of a functional matching. Those who gained paid, whether through a geographic manipulation of government boundaries or by tying the repayment of bonds to specific revenue sources that benefited specific groups in the economy. Debt procedures and limits, therefore, did little to limit the growth of state (and local) governments. They did enable American governments to dramatically expand the amount of infrastructure investment publicly financed and, to a significant extent, made state and local governments larger rather than smaller. As we saw earlier, the growth in state government began in earnest in the early twentieth century, following the invention of the automobile and widespread public investment in highways (Wallis 2001).

Balanced Budget Restrictions

The desire to restrain the size of government that was part of the motivation for debt restrictions and limits led some states to impose limits on the state's ability to raise revenues. Between 1860 and 1930, fourteen states incorporated limits to property taxation in their constitutions. These PTLs differ from what is normally understood by tax limits in that they do not restrict either the amount the state may raise through taxes nor the overall maximum tax rate. They simply restricted the maximum property tax rate that could be applied. At the time, however, a limit to property taxes would

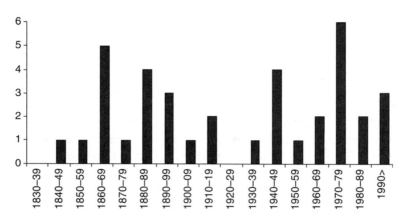

FIGURE 1.3. Adoption of first constitutional BBR, by decade.

be an important restriction on state finances because in 1900 about three-quarters of state revenues came from this source.

Viewed in terms of the size of governments, the changes did not work. Debt procedures and limits, even when paired with PTLs, did very little to limit the growth of state (and local) governments. BBR followed, written to bring some sort of equilibrium between revenues and expenditures. Figure 1.3 shows the number of BBRs adopted in each decade from the 1840s to the 1990s. We can see how BBRs were also adopted in the nineteenth century, although less widely than debt restrictions. Unlike debt restrictions, BBRs were not adopted in a "cascade," with a surge of adoptions followed by a constant (but diminishing) stream of followers. Instead, the adoption of BBRs was concentrated in two distinctive periods. The first wave of BBR adoptions occurred in the 1860s and 1880s, with less technical rules aimed at providing some sense that total revenues should be at least as great as total expenditures (like Nevada). During the Great Depression, state governments came under substantial fiscal strain, both during the downturn of 1929 to 1933 and as they began assuming more responsibility for social welfare programs under the New Deal (Wallis 1984). The second wave of BBR adoptions took place in the twentieth century. These later restrictions were more likely to require that the governor submit a balanced budget to the legislature and that the legislature pass a balanced budget. Figure 1.4 shows the cumulative total of states with BBRs and gives a sense of the staggered nature of the adoption of BBRs, in contrast to the concentrated adoptions of debt restrictions. Although both the first debt restrictions and BBRs were put in place in the

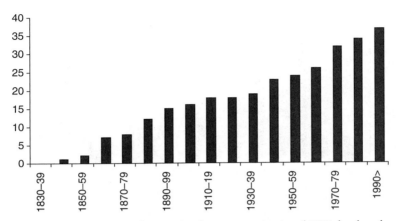

FIGURE 1.4. Number of states that have a constitutional BBR, by decade.

1840s, debt restrictions were adopted much more rapidly than BBRs. In fact, of the forty states with both measures, the average debt restriction was adopted forty-seven years before the adoption of a BBR. The average date of adopting a state's first debt restriction was 1872, whereas the average date of adopting a state's BBR was 1919.[14] In total, forty-six states have some form of debt restriction and forty-two, some form of BBR. Only one state, West Virginia, adopted a BBR (1863) before they adopted a debt restriction (1872). In every other state debt restrictions either preceded the adoption of a BBR, or the two were adopted simultaneously.[15]

RDFs and TELs

The combination of debt restrictions and BBRs (especially those drafted in the second wave) made it more difficult for states to respond to adverse economic shocks. The need to actually pass balanced budgets without access to fast and easy borrowing required new taxes or the reduction of expenditures during economic contractions. The formal adoption of RDFs (also known as "budget stabilization funds") can be considered in part as a response to the limited ability of state finances to respond to economic changes. By putting money away in good years, states could hope to meet

[14] This is the average date that the first debt restriction or BBR was adopted, excluding the states that never adopted a measure.
[15] States that entered the Union in the 1840s, beginning with Wisconsin in 1848, were very likely to adopt both measures in their first constitution.

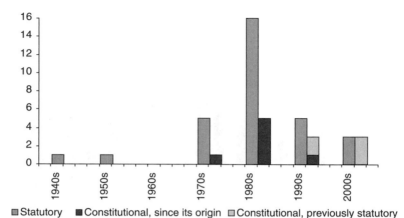

FIGURE 1.5. Number of adoptions of RDFs, by decade.

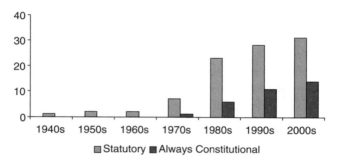

FIGURE 1.6. Number of state rainy day funds, by decade and type.

their BBR without having to resort to tax increases or expenditure cuts and without needing to call in the debt procedure. The widespread adoption of RDFs is often considered a response to the crisis of the 1980s, but it cannot be easily understood without the set of restrictions imposed by debt restrictions and BBRs. Figure 1.5 gives the number of states that put RDFs in place in each decade from the 1940s to the 2000s, and Figure 1.6 gives the cumulative number of states with rainy-day funds by decade. Because RDFs were often adopted by statute rather than constitutional amendment, the graphs distinguish statutory RDFs from constitutional funds. As we can see in the graphs, by 1979, thirty-two states had adopted a BBR, whereas only six states had RDFs. In the 1980s, however, twenty-one states adopted RDFs: sixteen by statute and five by constitutional amendment.

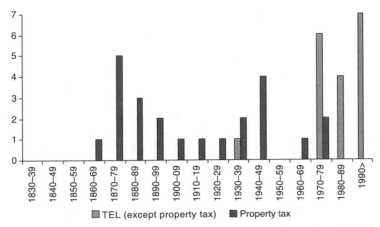

FIGURE 1.7. Limits on traditional TELs and property tax limitations, by decade of first adoption.

Limits to TEL came at roughly the same time as RDFs. As we discussed, the first of these limits were not TELs in the comprehensive sense because they regulated only one particular aspect of taxation: property taxes. Figure 1.7 shows the number of states that adopted their first TELs or PTLs in each decade between the 1830s and the 1990s and after. Figure 1.8 shows the cumulative total number of states that have each type of limitation in place over the same period. The first TELs are implemented as the wave of strong BBRs comes to an end, followed closely by the widespread adoption of RDFs. More states have adopted RDFs, forty-five, than have adopted any sort of TEL, thirty-five.

VI. HISTORICAL PATTERNS AND RECURSIVE INSTITUTIONAL CHANGE

The historical record reveals two broad common patterns in the timing of the adoption of fiscal measures. Figures 1.9 and 1.10 give an overview of these patterns. Figure 1.9 shows the distribution of adoptions over time, and Figure 1.10 presents the total number of states that have adopted each type of institution by decade. First, there is a crisis and response pattern. Debt restrictions were first adopted in the mid-nineteenth century after the default crisis in 1841 and 1842, although it took the remainder of the century for debt procedures to spread to all states. Debt procedures for local governments were adopted after the wave of local government defaults in

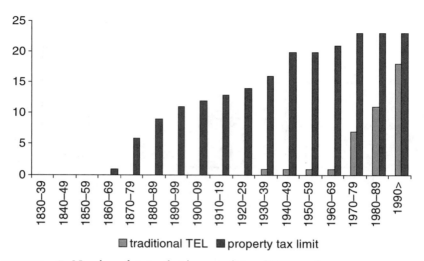

FIGURE 1.8. Number of states that have traditional TELs and property tax limits, by decade.

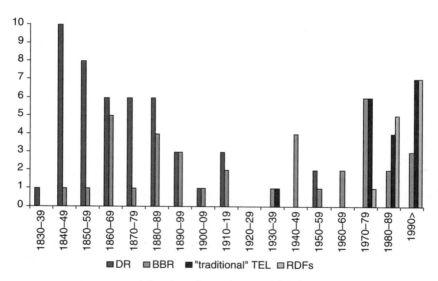

FIGURE 1.9. Adoption of constitutional fiscal institutions.

the 1870s. Weak BBRs were adopted in the late nineteenth century, and stronger BBRs were adopted in the 1930s and thereafter, again in response to a period of fiscal stress and increasing state fiscal responsibilities. RDFs

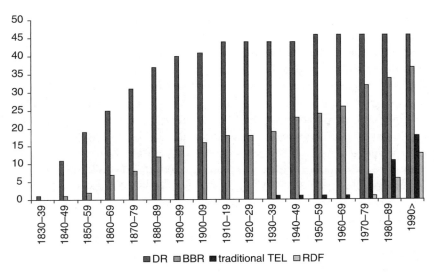

FIGURE 1.10. Number of states that had adopted each type of constitutional fiscal institution, by decade.

and TELs were adopted in the 1980s after another round of fiscal strain in the recessions of 1975 and of 1981.

The second pattern is recursive institutional change. Each new wave of constitutional reforms tends to address a problem created by the last wave of constitutional reforms. State adoption of debt procedures in the 1840s shifted more borrowing to local governments. Local defaults resulted in debt procedures for local governments in the 1880s and later. BBR were a response to the growing size of state governments. The first debt restrictions preceded the first BBRs by roughly forty years, and only one state adopted a BBR before they adopted a debt restriction. A similar pattern appears when we compare BBRs and the adoption of RDFs and TELs.

State fiscal constitutions can seem a bit odd if we think of them as an integrated set of rules and constraints. States regulate and limit debt issuance in their constitutions, however, those same states regularly borrow large quantities. BBRs exist in forty states, however, those states still run deficits and fiscal imbalances. The wording of debt procedures and BBRs are often intertwined and seem to imply that the government should not borrow at the same time that the constitution provides a procedure for borrowing. Tax and expenditure limits that call for refunds to taxpayers when the economy is doing well seem at odds with RDFs that require money to be set aside in a special fund under the same circumstances.

Part of the explanation is that state constitutions are historical documents. They are not created and designed in a cohesive way. Waves of constitutional change have washed through the American states. Each wave was designed to address a specific historical problem; however, each wave brought unanticipated consequences that played out in unexpected ways. Later waves of changes were often needed to address problems created by earlier changes. As a result, later changes may appear as ways of circumventing the intent of existing provisions by irresponsible policy makers and inconsistent voters.[16] There is another interpretation, however. Successive rounds of constitutional changes have not, by in large, led to defaults and excessive debt. In general, fiscal constitutions have provided state governments with the ability to navigate economic cycles while providing the infrastructure and services citizens desired. American fiscal constitutions actually work pretty well, but how they work is often misperceived.

The pattern of recursive institutional change stands out in the historical record. The first debt restrictions increased the cost of borrowing at state level, which resulted in an increase of local debt. After the restrictions on debt were extended to the local level in the 1870s, new ways of issuing debt made their way into the system. The creation of special districts and public authorities made it possible to create a majority consensus to finance projects that would not have met the procedural requirements of the general provisions, and revenue-generating projects were granted exemptions from the usual procedures via revenue bonds. BBRs were introduced in two distinct waves: The earlier simply required some sense of balance, whereas the latter one focused on more detailed, technical procedures. When BBRs were combined with debt procedures, however, states found themselves strongly tied to the economic cycle. When borrowing became politically more costly under the BBR, tax increases and expenditure cuts became necessary to pass balanced budgets, adding to the economic hardship of already contracted economies. RDFs provided a state with a tool to retain some countercyclical fiscal capabilities while still complying with the existing restrictions on their budgets.

The second part of the explanation for the apparent inconsistencies in fiscal constitutions must acknowledge the confusion over the meaning of the term "limit." There is the semantic difference stressed throughout

---

[16] Briffault makes this argument explicitly, and similar arguments are often used to frame these questions in the legal and political science literature.

the chapter that most fiscal constitutions have debt procedures as well as debt limits, and BBRs and RDFs are about procedures rather than strict limits. (TELs are an exception, to which we will return.) People often talk about debt limits when they are really talking about debt procedures and confusion results. There is a further, substantive confusion about the nature of a constitutional limit. Even a state with a strict constitutional limit on revenues, expenditures, or debt issues can still amend its constitution. A state that prohibits state debt entirely can amend its constitution to allow itemized debts for specific purposes. This procedural possibility is often overlooked. Every state has a procedure for changing the constitution, and any constitutional limit can be regarded as binding only in the context of that power to amend the limit. Ultimately, every possible constitutional limit can be overridden by a constitutional procedure.

Part of the patchwork quality of fiscal constitutions, therefore, results from the power of constitutional procedures over constitutional limits. This is not an aspect of constitutional design that we want to change; it is an extremely valuable feature of American constitutions that enables us to pull off a neat trick: stable constitutions that are nonetheless flexible. It can produce frustration on the part of people who believe that the constitution says that debt is prohibited and then find that their state still borrows.

The third part of the explanation for apparent inconsistencies in fiscal constitutions lies in the deeper meaning of state budgets. Think about the complicated budget shown in the final panel of Table 1.3, Budget E. The different waves of fiscal constitutional provisions have been directed at regulating different parts of the budget. The first wave of procedural restrictions aimed to regulate the amount of loans a state incurred. The second wave of BBRs addressed the structure of the budget, what was in the general fund, and what was not, and then attempted to specify that money in must equal money out in the general fund part of the budget. The third wave of RDFs was explicitly addressed to the problem of how beginning and ending cash balances (or asset positions) were to be determined over the course of time and how accumulations and drawdowns of cash balances would be treated under the terms of the BBR. Tax and expenditure limitations, although sometimes perceived as an overall restriction on the size of the budget, have turned out in practice to be attempts to regulate the money in (taxes) or money out (expenditures) line in the general fund budget. TELs have not been particularly effective at limiting the size of government, largely because of the ability to shift revenues and expenditures in or out of the general fund.

We have not explicitly considered the structure of budget funds in this chapter because segregated funds are present in state budgets and in state constitutions from very early on. Budget funds do not, therefore, come in the kind of reform waves that we are identifying. Nonetheless, segregating funds, particularly matching specific revenue sources to specific expenditures and specific debts, is an important part of fiscal constitutions. Voters are often willing to approve higher taxes, spending, and debts when a specific purpose is identified and accounts are kept segregated to ensure that the separation of the special fund from the general fund is maintained.[17]

Stepping back from a single moment in time and taking a longer view of how fiscal constitutions developed over the last two centuries does not resolve all of the apparent inconsistencies in the constitutions; however, it does provide us with a better perspective to evaluate what has happened. State governments began with a set of constitutional changes that focused first on the procedures for incurring loans and creating state debts. These reforms were extended to local governments and played a role in stimulating more special governments. State, local, and special governments probed the extent to which they could avoid the requirements of voter approval by creating special funds that did not obligate taxpayers in general. BBRs were both an attempt to limit the overall size of government (an attempt that failed) and to specify what the budget was and the procedures required to bring a budget into being. The balanced budget procedures produced unexpected fiscal crises in times of economic downturns and resulted in the adoption of RDFs. This makes sense in historical terms, even if specific provisions seem in conflict with each other. What can we learn from this history?

VII. LESSONS

Several lessons can be drawn from this history to inform the ongoing debate over taxes, expenditures, deficits, and debts. State governments have been in financial crises before, and undoubtedly they will experience them again in the future. Fiscal crises have not led to widespread default for over a century, and in light of the large amount of infrastructure investment that states undertake, American states have a good fiscal record. One part of the lessons to be learned, then, is why fiscal constitutions in America have worked relatively well.

---

[17] We have not explicitly examined the constitutional dimensions of special funds, which is clearly a productive area for future research.

After the first state default crisis in the 1840s, states moved toward systems that required taxpayers to approve new debt issues and the taxes necessary to service the debts. Adoption of state-level debt procedures resulted in some borrowing moving to the local level and a round of local government defaults in the 1870s that led to the provision of local debt procedures. This, in turn, led to an increase in special districts, created by both state and local governments. These changes all helped align those who benefit with those who pay. Rather than limiting the level of government borrowing, these provisions have made state and local governments relatively good credit risks, particularly in the case of special districts and revenue bonds for specific purposes in which debt repayment is tied to specific revenue sources. Private credit markets are able to evaluate the riskiness of individual bond issues, rather than relying on the general fiscal health of the general fund of a state. Indeed, as we have seen, provisions of fiscal constitutions often create incentives for state governments to move fiscal budgeting out of the general state fund and into specific categories.

The other historical lesson to learn is why states have continued to change their constitutions in ways that appear to be less effective. Absolute or relative limit amounts of state debt, taxes, and expenditures have not fared as well as debt procedures. State governments grew over most of the twentieth century, despite the proliferation of balanced budget amendments, RDFs, and tax and expenditure limitations. We see these waves of constitutional reform as a response to earlier constitutional changes. Whether BBRs have worked depends on what you think their purpose actually is. If the purpose was to prevent state government borrowing, they have not worked in general. If it was to limit the growth of state budgets, they have not worked, again in general. If it was to ensure that states are fiscally responsible, they have worked, however, it is not clear whether their marginal contribution has been positive or negative. That is, states are not markedly more responsible in the latter half of the twentieth century than they were before. BBRs complicate the dimension of timing between revenues and expenditures. Although BBRs may seem desirable to the extent that they encourage fiscal responsibility in the short run, we have seen that the rule is tricky to establish in practice. States often respond over time by reshaping their budgets.

A strict short-term application of a BBR can aggravate a fiscal crisis and make state budgets more pro-cyclical. There have certainly been times, like the current crisis, when BBR have caused fiscal crises for political reasons because the mandate for governors and legislators to pass budgets that are balanced ex ante gives pivotal political groups political leverage when revenues unexpectedly fall. One reaction to BBRs has been the adoption of RDFs on a wider scale, which is probably a good thing. RDFs can allow states to work around the cycle while maintaining fiscally responsible policies.

Limits on taxes, expenditures, and debt have not worked very well either. These limits are transparent attempts to limit the size of state governments and must be evaluated as ineffective in light of the continued gradual growth of state government. In part, this is simply because constitutions can always be amended. Even a strict prohibition on state borrowing can be changed by a constitutional amendment. Voters who approve of the idea that government be limited in general may also approve increases in the size of government for particular purposes. There is nothing wrong with such an outcome. When unforeseen circumstances present themselves, policy makers may need to work around the limits or amend the constitution. Furthermore, limits expressed in absolute terms are likely to become obsolete quickly.

More serious is the tendency for tax and expenditure limits to include provisions that skew the political costs of taxation and expenditure, often in ways that work directly against the intent of the limit. For example, some states have implemented provisions that require a supermajority rule for raising taxes in the legislature, however, they have left the voting rules for authorizing expenditures and debt at the majority level. Raising the political cost of raising taxes while leaving the cost of spending and borrowing unchanged has probably resulted in more borrowing. In the long run, this will cause problems.

The idea that making taxes more difficult to raise procedurally will either limit the size of government or the amount of government debt ignores the lessons that states learned in the nineteenth century. When increases in expenditure or debt are linked to tax increases, voters respond to the higher taxes. Rather than making it harder to raise taxes, proponents of smaller governments might want to consider making it easier to raise taxes and more closely tying tax increases to increases in expenditure or debt (precisely what debt procedures do). Voters would then be much more directly aware of the trade-off between costs and benefits than they are in the current environment, where taxes are not raised when expenditures and debts increase. This is easiest to see at the national level, but it applies at all levels of government. The question to raise taxes ought to be presented with that of borrowing so that a clear connection may be made between the two. Tax restrictions that limit the ability to increase revenue jeopardize this critical connection. BBRs, at least the ones we have seen so far in history, do not manage to make a clear link between expenditures and taxation, for reasons we have discussed.

Unintended consequences result no matter what aspects of fiscal constitutions are being considered. In subsequent rounds of financial difficulties, fiscal provisions may play out differently than expected or cause new problems. If we want to stick with what has worked in the past, we should abandon attempts to limit the size of state governments but insist that taxes increase whenever debts go up.

REFERENCES

Briffault, Richard. *Balancing Acts: The Reality behind State Balanced Budget Requirements*. New York: The Twentieth Century Fund Press, 1996.

Cain, Bruce and Noll, Roger. "Institutional Causes of California's Budget Problem." *California Journal of Politics and Policy*, 2 (3), pp. 1–37, 2010.

Inman, Robert. "States in Fiscal Distress." NBER Working paper 16086, June 2010.

Kiewiet, D. Roderick and Szakaly, Kristin. "Constitutional Limitations on Borrowing: An Analysis of State Bonded Indebtedness." *Journal of Law, Economics, and Organization*, 12 (1), pp. 62–97, 1996.

Kousser, Thad, McCubbins, Mathew D., and Moule, Ellen. "For Whom the TEL Tolls: Can State Tax Expenditure Limits Effectively Reduce Spending?" *State Politics and Policy Quarterly*, 8 (4), pp. 331–361, 2008.

Miller, Nathan. 37. Cornell University Press, 1962.

National Association of State Budget Officers. *Fiscal Survey of the States*. Washington, DC: National Association of State Budget Officers, 2010.

Rodriguez-Tejedo, Isabel and Wallis, John Joseph. "Lessons for California from the History of Fiscal Constitutions." *California Journal of Politics and Policy*, 2 (3), pp. 1–19, 2010.

Wallis, John Joseph. "The Birth of the Old Federalism: Financing the New Deal." *Journal of Economic History*, 44, pp. 139–159, 1984.

Wallis, John Joseph. "American Government Finance in the Long Run: 1790 to 1990," *Journal of Economic Perspectives*, 14(1), pp. 61–82, 2000.

Wallis, John Joseph. "A History of the Property Tax in America." In Wallace E. Oates, ed., *Property Taxation and Local Government Finance*. Cambridge, MA: Lincoln Institute of Land Policy, 2001.

Wallis, John Joseph. "Constitutions, Corporations, and Corruption: American States and Constitutional Change, 1842 to 1852." *Journal of Economic History*, 65 (1), pp. 211–256, 2005.

Wallis, John Joseph and Weingast, Barry R. "Dysfunctional or Optimal Institutions: State Debt Limitations, the Structure of State and Local Governments, and the Finance of American Infrastructure." In Garrett, Grady, and Jackson, eds., *Fiscal Challenges: An Interdisciplinary Approach to Budget Policy*. New York: Cambridge University Press, 2008.

2

Obligations Without the Power to Fund Them

DAMON A. SILVERS

The roots of the fiscal crisis of the states lie in the intersection of a series of explicit and implicit understandings reached in the nineteenth century, with the economic realities of modern government. States have not generally had the authority to borrow to fund operating expenses since the Civil War. However, since the Great Depression, states have had partial responsibility for large-scale countercyclical spending through the unemployment insurance system and the Medicaid system. This tension has become deeply problematic as a result of two changes over the last thirty years. First, the nature of recessions since the early 1980s has changed so that recessions that were brief and steep and driven by the business cycle have been replaced by ones that are long, shallow, and driven by the bursting of financial bubbles. Second, our politics since the 1970s have been increasingly an expression of the belief that the United States should have modern government without the tax policies necessary to pay for it – most dramatically embodied recently by Tea Party signs saying "Keep Your Government's Hands Off My Medicare." Tax revenues in good times are not enough to fund long-term public investment or to set aside the reserves necessary under this system to fund countercyclical expenditures in bad times. The result is that, looked at as a whole, our federal system has difficulty engaging in needed levels of countercyclical spending in economic crises, and the resulting public sector layoffs worsen the nation's economic problems just when public spending should be a counteracting weakness in the private economy.

The United States is fortunate compared to Europe in that we have a set of fundamental understandings in our federal system that can work through good economic times and bad economic times. However, the current set

---

This chapter reflects the author's views alone and not those of the AFL-CIO

of fiscal policies being pursued both by states and by the federal government is putting those understandings under a great deal of strain. This is dangerous for the health of the country. In response, some in academic life have suggested the often-tempting route of looking for extra-political solutions to political problems, such as creating a bankruptcy proceeding for states. Setting aside the enormous legal difficulties involved in such an undertaking, state bankruptcy is not a substantive solution so much as it is an expression of despair at the possibility of political processes coming up with substantive solutions. Real solutions to the fiscal crisis of the states need to begin with an understanding of the real causes of the problem and then proceed to possible substantive solutions.

The real problem lies in asking states to undertake countercyclical responsibilities without providing them with a fiscal structure for doing so – a problem compounded by inadequate revenue at either the state or federal level necessary to support a modern government in the execution of its economic responsibilities. The real threat represented by this problem is not the fiscal collapse of the states. States can and will cut their spending; however, that "solution" is in fact the problem – the collapse of countercyclical spending structures in a prolonged economic crisis feeding a more prolonged and painful crisis and the inability of states to perform vital functions like the provision of education and investment in infrastructure during recessions. The solution does not lie in measures to accelerate procyclical steps but in measures that allow states to perform the role we have asked them to play in economic downturns.[1]

In undertaking this analysis, this chapter distinguishes between two types of public-sector fiscal problems. On the one hand, there are situations in which a government can meet its obligations but refuses to do so – refuses to raise taxes or cut spending so that its finances are stable over time. A government that does this is dysfunctional; however, it is not insolvent. An insolvent government, like an insolvent business, is one that cannot in any manner repay its debts as they come due no matter what decision politicians make. The entity in question is so economically weak or has such large debts that attempts to raise taxes or to cut spending lead to economic shrinkage at a level that renders fiscal measures self-defeating. Greece is in this position currently. At least one U.S. state found itself in this position in the Great Depression; however, no U.S. state is anywhere near this situation today.

---

[1] This chapter owes much to Alice Rivlin's work on the subject, particularly *Another State Fiscal Crisis: Is There a Better Way?* BROOKINGS INSTITUTION CCF BRIEF NO. 23 (December 2002).

I. SOME CAVEATS ABOUT DATA

There are multiple, inconsistent sets of aggregate data on state and local government finances. The Census Bureau, the General Accounting Office, and the Treasury Department all maintain distinct data sets. In addition, there are problems within the states themselves. It is difficult on an aggregate basis within the confines of an exercise of this sort to distinguish between proceeds of asset sales and other unsustainable sources of cash and sustainable tax and fee revenues. Finally, among the most difficult areas to get consistent data are the flows of funds between federal, state, and local governments. In a way, the difficulty in looking at state government data in isolation from federal and local government data proves the larger point of this chapter, which is the integration of states into a larger, national system of government finance. Consequently, the data in this chapter must be understood as illustrative and not definitive.

II. A BRIEF PRIMER ON THE FISCAL IMPLICATIONS OF THE FEDERAL SYSTEM

In our Constitution, states are not mere instrumentalities of the national government. They have an independent political and economic existence. In this way, they are fundamentally different from localities – cities and counties – which are instrumentalities of states. In the early years of the Republic, states asserted at various times notions of broader sovereignty, which included on some occasions borrowing money and printing money. The most profound assertion of state sovereignty was the claim, made at various times for various reasons during the early years of the Republic, that states were really independent of the federal government and could choose to leave the federal government if they wished. This assertion turned out not to be true, though it was settled not by the courts but at Appomattox.

However, before the Civil War, in response to the prolonged economic crisis of the 1840s, some states sought to engage in what would later be called Keynesian stimulus – they borrowed money to maintain government expenditures where tax revenues were insufficient to do so. When states were unable to repay their borrowings, they went through painful periods of fiscal adjustment that led to the adoption in most states of rules forbidding states to run operating deficits and limiting borrowing to funding discrete capital investments.

The result was a federal system in which the federal government did not control or guarantee state finances. However, states were neither monetary policy actors nor really fiscal policy actors. Consider by contrast the European Union (EU) in which member governments have relinquished authority over monetary policy but have full fiscal policy authority.

This system, however, left an important question unanswered. What would happen if a state could not pay its debts – either because it was in a Greek-like situation in which its economy simply could not support its debts or because of political paralysis of the kind that threatened the United States during the debt ceiling debate of the summer of 2011? Even though states had made this problem more theoretical than practical in most cases by limiting their borrowing, it was still an issue in times of deep economic distress when states found they could not repay funds borrowed to make capital investments.

There have always been three possible answers: first, the Federal government would rescue states that got into trouble; second, states could be forced by the courts to honor their commitments by increasing taxes; and third, states could effectively default – that is, fail to honor their commitments. During the period from the Civil War until the Great Depression, no state reached a fiscal crisis deep enough to place these options into focus. This was largely a result of the limited nature of government countercyclical spending in the pre-New Deal era and the relatively short length of pre-Depression economic crises.

However, the length and severity of the Depression produced unmanageable fiscal strains on some states, particularly those affected not just by the Depression but also by the natural disasters of the prolonged drought of the 1930s and the ensuing Dust Bowl. As a result, Arkansas attempted to default on state obligations. Arkansas's creditors sued, asserting that there was no bankruptcy proceeding covering states, and as a result, creditors had a right to sue to force payment from an insolvent state – a remedy that could encompass judicially ordered tax increases to fund any such payments. Arkansas's creditors prevailed, establishing the one clear modern precedent in this area as to what the federal court system would do if a state refused to pay its creditors. The implication was that, although it might be costly for creditors to enforce their right to payment from states, that right was absolute and could not be restructured in a bankruptcy or quasi-bankruptcy process.[2]

---

[2] See *Hubbell v. Leonard*, 6 F. Supp. 145 (1934).

Similar issues were presented in New York in the aftermath of the New York City fiscal crisis of the 1970s. In *Flushing National Bank v. Municipal Assistance Corporation of New York*, the New York Court of Appeals found that the phrase "faith and credit" in the New York State Constitution barred the New York Legislature from changing the terms of local government debt. The case suggested the court could well follow a similar approach should the State of New York seek to unilaterally alter the terms of its own debt by legislative action.[3]

Since the Great Depression, the states' countercyclical spending role in economic downturns increased through the creation of, first, unemployment insurance, and then Medicaid. Both these programs were administered at the state level and involved substantial state obligations. A demand for these programs naturally rose in recessions. Nonetheless, the issue of state insolvency did not arise for decades following the Great Depression because economic downturns were relatively shallow and brief. By the time states felt their full effect, their revenues were already on the way to recovery.

The federal fiscal system that resulted was one in which states were only able to do limited borrowing and, as a practical matter, were supported by the federal government in times of economic distress. However, their debts were not guaranteed by the federal government and generally traded at a small premium after accounting for tax subsidies in terms of yield to the yield of federal government obligations of similar duration.

The combination of ad hoc federal support for states during economic downturns and the willingness of courts on the few occasions the matter was tested to order repayment effectively transformed what had originally been a genuinely federal system into a system that was federal in name only – a system in which the finances of states was sufficiently intertwined with that of the federal government to constitute one fiscal system.

In this system, states have a peculiar status – they cannot borrow to fund operating expenditures, but at the same time, they have an absolute duty to pay their debts, a duty enforced by federal courts and made real by the states' taxing authority, with a hazy implicit federal guarantee lying about someplace in the background. States appear almost to have been designed never to go broke – with obligations that are small in relation to tax revenues, the power to raise taxes, and ultimately an enforceable legal duty to do so to meet a state's contractual obligations.

---

[3] 358 N.E. 2d 848 (1976).

The fundamental reason companies seek bankruptcy protection – an inability to meet their obligations and a danger that a liquidation will destroy value – has no meaning for a state. The only sense in which a state could go broke would be if, despite the general prohibition on borrowing for operating purposes, a state incurred obligations that could not be paid back without taxation so punitive as to set off an economic downward spiral, and the federal government stood aside and let it happen – essentially the situation now faced by Greece and Ireland and the EU.

States have found ways to enter into long-term obligations despite the general ban on doing so; however, no U.S. state faces obligations beyond the power of its taxing authority to meet, and the states as a whole are not remotely near such a circumstance. The truth is the states' fiscal crises are political, not financial, in nature.

III. HALFWAY TO KENYESIANISM– THE RISE OF COUNTERCYCLICAL EXPENDITURES AT THE STATE LEVEL

Prior to the New Deal, what passed for countercyclical spending in the United States was done at the state or local level. Relief programs were state level, but the spending was modest, and states, by virtue of their fiscal structure, were limited in what they could do to stimulate their economies in an economic downturn. There was also relatively little federal spending on roads and other infrastructure before the New Deal.

The Great Depression began in different parts of the country at different times. Agricultural regions of the United States faced Depression conditions as a result of falling commodity prices during much of the 1920s. States in the hardest hit regions of the South and Midwest made efforts at countercyclical spending in the late 1920s, largely focused on road building, only to be hit by a combination of the national Depression and a series of partially man-made natural disasters with serious economic consequences, culminating in the Dust Bowl.[4]

The combination of state level efforts to combat unemployment – largely through infrastructure spending that could be funded by project borrowing – led to state and local spending and state and local debt increasing significantly as the economy shrank. State and local spending in 1932 was 14.5 percent of GDP – today, state and local expenditures only

---

[4] *See, e.g.*, ARTHUR M. SCHLESINGER, JR., THE AGE OF ROOSEVELT: THE CRISIS OF THE OLD ORDER, 1919–1933 (Boston, Houghton Mifflin Co. 1957).

reach around 11 percent.⁵ State and local government debt almost doubled from 1922 to 1932, reaching an astounding 32.8 percent of GDP in 1932.⁶ Partly, this was a result of the increase in government spending to counteract the effects of the Depression, but far more important in driving these percentages was the decrease in GDP – which fell almost in half from 1929 to 1932 – and the consequent decrease in tax revenue.⁷ Meanwhile, the federal government under the Hoover administration was running up surpluses until 1931, and federal spending remained essentially flat until 1932.⁸ In 1933, state and local government debt was $19 billion, and federal government debt was only $22 billion, almost all of which was the result of military spending during World War I. By comparison, today state and local debt is less than a third of federal debt.⁹

By 1932, the poorest states in the United States were in the situation faced currently by Greece – they could not raise taxes to pay off their debts as their economies shrank, not in the sense that they could not reach political agreement to do so but in the sense that you cannot get blood from a stone. The state in the worst condition was Arkansas, which stopped making payments on its interest and principal in 1933. Ultimately, the state's

---

5   U.S. Census Bureau, *Series Y 671–681. State and Local Government Expenditures by Character and Object, and State and Local Government Debt: 1902 to 1970*, HISTORICAL STATISTICS OF THE UNITED STATES: COLONIAL TIMES TO 1970, Part 2, at 1127; BUREAU OF ECONOMIC ANALYSIS, CURRENT DOLLAR AND "REAL" GROSS DOMESTIC PRODUCT; Office of Management and Budget, *Historical Tables*, Table 15.3 – TOTAL GOVERNMENT EXPENDITURES AS PERCENTAGES OF GDP: 1948–2010.

6   State and local government debt was $10,109,000,000 in 1922 and $19,205,000,000 in 1932. U.S. Census Bureau, *Series P 188–201. – State and Local Government – General Revenue and Expenditure, and Gross Debt: 1890–1945*, HISTORICAL STATISTICS OF THE UNITED STATES: 1789–1945, at 314; BUREAU OF ECONOMIC ANALYSIS, CURRENT DOLLAR AND "REAL" GROSS DOMESTIC PRODUCT.

7   GDP in 1932 was $58.7 billion in current dollars. BUREAU OF ECONOMIC ANALYSIS, CURRENT DOLLAR AND "REAL" GROSS DOMESTIC PRODUCT. U.S. Census Bureau, *Series Y 671–681. State and Local Government Expenditures by Character and Object, and State and Local Government Debt: 1902 to 1970*, HISTORICAL STATISTICS OF THE UNITED STATES: COLONIAL TIMES TO 1970, Part 2, at 1127.

8   U.S. Census Bureau, *Series P 89–98 Federal Government Finances – Treasury Receipts, and Surplus or Deficit: 1789 to 1945*, HISTORICAL STATISTICS OF THE UNITED STATES: 1789 TO 1945, at 297–298.

9   U.S. Census Bureau, *Series Y 671–681. State and Local Government Expenditures by Character and Object, and State and Local Government Debt: 1902 to 1970*, HISTORICAL STATISTICS OF THE UNITED STATES: COLONIAL TIMES TO 1970, Part 2, at 1127; U.S. Census Bureau, *Series P 132–143. – Federal Government Finances – Public Debt: 1791–1945*, HISTORICAL STATISTICS OF THE UNITED STATES: 1789–1945, at 305; U.S. Census Bureau, *Table 468, Federal Budget Debt: 1960 to 2010*, STATISTICAL ABSTRACT OF THE UNITED STATES; U.S. Census Bureau, *Table 441, State and Local Governments – Expenditures and Debt by State: 2007*, STATISTICAL ABSTRACT OF THE UNITED STATES.

bondholders recognized there was nothing to be done but to negotiate a restructuring. However, it was during this period that some creditors sued Arkansas seeking payment, resulting in a judicial opinion that states could not go bankrupt, and that if necessary, courts could order states to raise taxes to meet their obligations. Fortunately for all concerned, Arkansas's major creditors understood that such a course of action would be futile in a context in which Arkansas's economy had essentially collapsed.

Arkansas's fiscal crisis is an all but forgotten footnote in American history rather than a beginning of a major calamity, because starting in the same year in which Arkansas defaulted – 1933 – the federal government began to assume the dominant role as the agent both of countercyclical spending and of major infrastructure investment. Although the Depression continued for another seven years, and GDP did not return to 1929 levels until 1940, overall state and local borrowing rose only from $19.2 billion in 1932 to $20.2 billion in 1940.[10] In its place, federal spending expanded dramatically – increasing from $4.6 billion in 1932 and 1933 to $8.2 billion in 1936.[11]

If the Civil War settled the question of whether states were independent in the sense that they could potentially have their own fiscal and monetary policies, the Great Depression resolved the question of whether the states, so constrained, could manage the effects of a profound economic downturn on their own. In the Great Depression, the poorer states – our equivalents of Greece – could not maintain a modern government without federal help. That help came largely in the form not of transfer payments to states but of direct federal spending that allowed states to pull back, and that sparked renewed economic growth, restoring states' revenues.

Although the New Deal involved a dramatic increase in federal spending, much of it in temporary programs, the New Deal's lasting impact on American government was its creation of permanent systems of social insurance and countercyclical spending. The most important form of explicitly countercyclical spending created by the New Deal was national unemployment insurance. However, the way that program was created was through setting standards and subsidies for states to create their own unemployment insurance programs. Although these programs were

---

[10] BUREAU OF ECONOMIC ANALYSIS, GROSS DOMESTIC PRODUCT PERCENT CHANGE FROM PREVIOUS PERIOD; U.S. Census Bureau, *Series Y 671–681. State and Local Government Expenditures by Character and Object, and State and Local Government Debt: 1902 to 1970*, HISTORICAL STATISTICS OF THE UNITED STATES: COLONIAL TIMES TO 1970, Part 2, at 1127.

[11] U.S. Census Bureau, *Series Y 605–637. Federal Government Expenditure, by Function: 1902–1970*, HISTORICAL STATISTICS OF THE UNITED STATES: COLONIAL TIMES TO 1970, Part 2, at 1124.

funded by premiums paid by employers, those premium structures were inevitably set to fund layoffs at rates at which they occur in normal times. Even well-designed programs – with excess premiums designed to fund in advance the benefits that will be needed during downturns – will face cash flow issues when a very deep recession occurs. In such circumstances, states that lack a capacity to borrow for operations will inevitably need assistance from the federal government.

For example, between 1990 and 1992, state unemployment benefits paid out increased 90 percent.[12] In the 2001 recession, unemployment benefits paid out per year increased 160 percent over 2000 levels and stayed at that level for two years.[13] In the economic crisis that began in 2008, state payments (the majority of which were made possible by federal subsidies) went from $32.7 billion in 2007 to $43.5 billion in 2008 to $120 billion in 2009 and to $156 billion in 2010 as Congress extended unemployment benefits in light of the unprecedented extent and length of the crisis.[14] Even with unprecedented federal aid, state borrowing from the federal government to fund unemployment benefits is projected to reach $63 billion by the end of 2012 according to the U.S. Department of Labor.[15]

The New Deal unemployment insurance system was a kind of half Keynesianism. It created a national unemployment benefits system but left the financing of it ad hoc as states continued to have no capacity to borrow from private markets for operations and had to rely on the willingness of the federal government in times of economic crisis to assist the states either through grants or loans.

IV. MEDICAID – THE EXPANSION OF THE UNEMPLOYMENT INSURANCE MODEL OF COUNTERCYCLICAL SPENDING

Between the adoption of the unemployment insurance system as part of the Social Security Act in 1936 and the creation of Medicaid in the 1960s, there

---

[12] U.S. Census Bureau, *No. 585. Social Welfare Expenditures, by Source of Funds and Public Program: 1980 to 1992*, STATISTICAL ABSTRACT OF THE UNITED STATES 1995, at 375.

[13] U.S. Census Bureau, *Table 548. State Unemployment Insurance – Summary: 1990 to 2004*, STATISTICAL ABSTRACT OF THE UNITED STATES 2005, at 369.

[14] U.S. Census Bureau, *Table 538. Government Transfer Payments to Individuals by Type: 1990 to 2008*, STATISTICAL ABSTRACT OF THE UNITED STATES: 2011, at 351; FY 2010 CONGRESSIONAL BUDGET JUSTIFICATION, EMPLOYMENT AND TRAINING ADMINISTRATION, STATE UNEMPLOYMENT INSURANCE AND EMPLOYMENT SERVICE OPERATIONS (2009), at 29 (projected figure includes state and federal unemployment benefits, including extended benefits and Trade Adjustment Assistance benefits).

[15] PRESIDENT'S BUDGET PROJECTION FOR FY 2012.

were no serious economic downturns on the scale of the Great Depression. At the same time, rising federal infrastructure expenditures and economic growth led to state highway expenditures falling as a percentage of GDP even as the United States was in the middle of the largest infrastructure investment effort in human history – state and local highway expenditures were 2.9 percent of GDP in 1932 and 1.7 percent of GDP in 1960.[16] As a result of these developments in tandem with unprecedented economic growth, states and local government debt fell from 33 percent of GDP to 13 percent of GDP.[17]

Against this backdrop, Congress and President Johnson enacted the Medicaid program in 1965.[18] Medicaid provided health care to poor families for the first time on a national basis. Medicaid, unlike Medicare and Social Security, is highly dependent on overall economic conditions: The worse the economy, the more people are eligible for Medicaid. Like unemployment insurance and food stamps, Medicaid is a countercyclical program; however, unlike food stamps and like unemployment insurance, Medicaid is significantly funded by the states.

Medicaid enrollment has grown with increasing inequality and the decline of employer paid health insurance. Rising enrollments and medical inflation have led to Medicaid costs rising 104 times in nominal terms from 1967 to 2007.[19] As a percentage of GDP, Medicaid costs rose from 0.8 percent of GDP to 2.3 percent of GDP, with states' shares increasing to 1 percent of GDP.[20]

Since the program's foundation, state contributions to Medicaid have averaged 42 percent of total Medicaid spending.[21] Because of increases in

---

[16] U.S. Census Bureau, *Series Y 682–709. State and Local Government Expenditure, by Function: 1902 to 1970*, HISTORICAL STATISTICS OF THE UNITED STATES: COLONIAL TIMES TO 1970, Part 2, at 1127–1128; BUREAU OF ECONOMIC ANALYSIS, CURRENT DOLLAR AND "REAL" GROSS DOMESTIC PRODUCT.

[17] U.S. Census Bureau, *Series Y 671–681. State and Local Government Expenditures by Character and Object, and State and Local Government Debt: 1902 to 1970*, HISTORICAL STATISTICS OF THE UNITED STATES: COLONIAL TIMES TO 1970, Part 2, at 1127; BUREAU OF ECONOMIC ANALYSIS, CURRENT DOLLAR AND "REAL" GROSS DOMESTIC PRODUCT.

[18] Title XIX, Social Security Amendments of 1965, Pub. L. 89–97 (codified as amended in scattered sections of 42 U.S.C.).

[19] U.S. DEPARTMENT OF HEALTH AND HUMAN SERVICES, CENTERS FOR MEDICARE AND MEDICAID SERVICES, NATIONAL HEALTH EXPENDITURES BY TYPE OF SERVICE AND SOURCE OF FUNDS: CALENDAR YEARS 1960 TO 2009.

[20] U.S. DEPARTMENT OF HEALTH AND HUMAN SERVICES, CENTERS FOR MEDICARE AND MEDICAID SERVICES, NATIONAL HEALTH EXPENDITURES BY TYPE OF SERVICE AND SOURCE OF FUNDS: CALENDAR YEARS 1960 TO 2009; BUREAU OF ECONOMIC ANALYSIS, CURRENT DOLLAR AND "REAL" GROSS DOMESTIC PRODUCT.

[21] U.S. DEPARTMENT OF HEALTH AND HUMAN SERVICES, CENTERS FOR MEDICARE AND MEDICAID SERVICES, NATIONAL HEALTH EXPENDITURES BY TYPE OF SERVICE AND SOURCE OF FUNDS: CALENDAR YEARS 1960 TO 2009.

federal medical assistance percentages (FMAP) during recessions, this percentage has typically fallen as Medicaid expenditures have risen. The most dramatic FMAP intervention by far since the enactment of the program occurred in 2009, when, as a result of the economic crisis, total Medicaid spending grew at a rate of 9 percent, driven by a 7.5 percent increase in enrollment; however, because of the American Recovery and Reinvestment Act (ARRA), state Medicaid expenditures fell 9.8 percent.[22]

This FMAP change was a critical contributor to the ability of states to close their budget gaps in 2009 and 2010, and the projected absence of such support in 2012 is a significant reason for the projection of very large budget gaps in the states going forward.

However, the underlying nature of what happens to Medicaid in a severe economic downturn is shown by the enrollment numbers. Medicaid enrollment from 2007 to 2011 will likely increase 28 percent, according to the Kaiser Family Foundation survey of state Medicaid administrators.[23]

This is the most serious example to date of the consequences of creating programs with countercyclical features but leaving the question of federal support for state obligations under those programs to the short-term federal budget process. Of course, as long as federal elected officials are willing to use the federal government's borrowing power to fund these countercyclical programs, the structures work in recessionary times; however, if they are unwilling to do so, states are left with the choice of either paring back on countercyclical programs, with profoundly negative social and economic consequences, or paring back on other state responsibilities, such as infrastructure investment, education funding, and law enforcement.

V. TAXES – STRUCTURAL INADEQUACY AND PRO-CYCLICALITY

State and local governments are funded by a wide variety of taxes – including income taxes, sales taxes, property taxes, and a range of fees for

---

[22] U.S. DEPARTMENT OF HEALTH AND HUMAN SERVICES, CENTERS FOR MEDICARE AND MEDICAID SERVICES, NATIONAL HEALTH EXPENDITURES BY TYPE OF SERVICE AND SOURCE OF FUNDS: CALENDAR YEARS 1960 TO 2009; U.S. DEPARTMENT FOR HEALTH AND HUMAN SERVICES, CENTERS FOR MEDICARE AND MEDICAID SERVICES, MEDICARE ENROLLMENT: NATIONAL TRENDS 1966 – 2009, MEDICARE AGED AND DISABLED ENROLLEES BY TYPE OF COVERAGE ALL AREAS, AS OF JULY 1, 1966–2009. The ARRA temporarily increased the federal share of Medicare payments by $87 billion.

[23] THE KAISER COMMISSION ON MEDICAID AND THE UNINSURED, HOPING FOR ECONOMIC RECOVERY, PREPARING FOR HEALTH REFORM: A LOOK AT MEDICAID SPENDING, COVERAGE AND POLICY TRENDS RESULTS FROM A 50-STATE MEDICAID BUDGET SURVEY FOR STATE FISCAL YEARS 2010 AND 2011, 31 (2010).

services. According to the Organization for Economic Co-operation and Development (OECD), U.S. total taxes, including federal state and local taxes, were 24 percent of GDP in 2009.[24] The Office of Management and Budget estimates that federal tax revenues were 14.9 percent of GDP in 2009, whereas state and local taxes were 10 percent of GDP.[25] Federal tax collections in 2009 were the lowest as a percentage of GDP since a brief period in the late 1940s and early 1950s when the United States was demobilizing from World War II and had not yet begun the cold war military buildup.[26] The OECD has found that the United States is at the bottom of the OECD countries in terms of taxes as a percentage of GDP, behind all but Mexico and Chile.[27]

State tax revenue raising capacity has suffered from economic change and political attack, starting with the tax revolts of the 1970s. With the transition to a more service-based economy and the rise of Internet-based transactions, less economic activity is now subject to sales taxes. States have competed with each other to attract economic activity by offering tax incentives to employers. Complex national and international businesses have become expert at avoiding state taxes and defeating collection efforts. Finally, states and localities were uniquely vulnerable to a real estate bubble and bust, as they derived a large portion of their revenue from the combination of property taxes and fees from real estate transactions.

As a result, tax revenues, which averaged 0.6 percent of GDP less than expenses for state and local governments in the 1970s, averaged 0.8 percent of GDP less than expenses in the 1980s and 1990s and 1.1 percent less in the 2000s.[28]

State and local government revenues have also become more vulnerable to economic cycles. In the 1989 recession, state and local government revenues rose as a percentage of GDP from 9.7 percent of GDP in 1987 to 9.9

---

[24] OECD, Table A. Total tax revenue as percentage of GDP (2010).
[25] Office of Management and Budget, *Historical Tables, Table 15.1 – Total Government Receipts in Absolute Amounts and as Percentages of GDP: 1948–2010*, BUDGET FOR FISCAL YEAR 2012, 340–341.
[26] Office of Management and Budget, *Historical Tables, Table 15.1 – Total Government Receipts in Absolute Amounts and as Percentages of GDP: 1948–2010*, BUDGET FOR FISCAL YEAR 2012, 340–341.
[27] OECD, op. cit.
[28] Office of Management and Budget, *Historical Tables, Table 15.1 – Total Government Receipts in Absolute Amounts and as Percentages of GDP: 1948–2010*, BUDGET FOR FISCAL YEAR 2012, 340–341; Office of Management and Budget, *Historical Tables, Table 15.3, Total Government Expenditures as Percentages of GDP: 1948–2010*, BUDGET FOR FISCAL YEAR 2012, 344–345.

percent of GDP in 1991. In the 2001 recession, state and local government revenues fell from 10.0 percent of GDP in 2001 to 9.8 percent in 2002 and 2003; however, in both these recessions revenues rose in nominal dollar terms. By contrast, in the current economic crisis, state and local revenues fell by $60 billion in nominal dollars between 2008 and 2009. The decline in state tax revenues as of the first quarter of 2011 compared to precrisis levels was 9 percent.[29]

Of course, it is the nature of governments to face falling revenues in times of economic crises. National governments have the option of borrowing; however, states do not. In the postwar era, this was less of a problem because of the short duration of recessions. The characteristics that made states more resilient in business cycle-driven downturns now make them more vulnerable, and more dependent on federal aid, in longer economic crises driven by financial collapse and asset deflation.

VI. THE CHANGING NATURE OF ECONOMIC CYCLES

The degree to which countercyclical spending strains state finances is a function of the length of periods of high unemployment. Following the Great Depression, the United States went through a prolonged period of business cycle-driven recessions, characterized by steep but brief drops in employment. Then, starting with the recession of the late 1980s, the U.S. economy appears to have shifted to a pattern of economic cycles driven by financial bubbles, with periods of high unemployment that last much longer than was true in the postwar era.

The economic crisis that began in 2007 has many features in common with the long, shallow recessions of 1990 and 2001. Unfortunately, it also shares the depth of earlier business cycle recessions. This is not surprising because the current crisis was preceded by an unprecedented bubble in housing, which affected the balance sheets of the majority of U.S. households and provoked a financial crisis on a different scale from earlier finance-driven recessions. However, it means that for states, the combination of rising Medicaid and unemployment expenses and falling revenues seems likely to be with us for some time – well beyond the ability of states to absorb the lost revenues and increased expenses.

---

[29] Office of Management and Budget, *Historical Tables, Table 15.1 – Total Government Receipts in Absolute Amounts and as Percentages of GDP: 1948–2010*, BUDGET FOR FISCAL YEAR 2012, 340–341.

VII. CONSEQUENCES – PART I – THE SOURCES AND MAGNITUDE OF STATE SHORTFALLS

As of July 2011, the Center on Budget and Policy Priorities estimates total state budget shortfalls of $130 billion in 2011, $103 billion in 2012, and $46 billion in 2013. Federal aid under ARRA, commonly known as the "stimulus act," was $59 billion for the fiscal year 2011 and is projected to be $6 billion for 2012 – meaning the likely levels of shortfalls that actually have to be addressed are $71 billion in 2011 and $97 billion in 2012.[30]

By comparison, if tax revenues had kept pace with expenditures at the level of the 1980s and 1990s, states and localities would have 0.3 percent of GDP, or $42 billion in additional revenue annually. Or, to look at just one of the sources of pro-cyclical obligations, using 2009 expenditures as a reference point, 2012 Medicaid expenditures reverted as of July 1, 2011, to pre-ARRA formulas. Unless Congress takes further action, state obligations under Medicaid will rise $41 billion – accounting for 40 percent of the majority of projected shortfalls for 2012. The actual impact of Medicaid on the 2012 shortfalls will be significantly higher as a result of increases in medical costs and in Medicaid enrollment between 2009 and 2012.

By comparison, state and local government debt over the last thirty years has varied from 12 to 18 percent of GDP and is currently at 16 percent, with interest payments on the debt at 4 percent of all state and local spending – the same level as it was in 1980.[31] State and local debt totaled $2.6 trillion in 2008, with unfunded pension liabilities of $660 billion, for a total of major obligations of almost $3.3 trillion.[32] These obligations are approximately one-quarter the size of the U.S. national debt, whereas state and local government revenues are two-thirds of federal government revenues.

State and local government debt today is approximately $10,000 per capita, or approximately 25 percent of per capita income. By comparison, the total debt of state and local government in Arkansas in 1932 was $255 million, or $142 per capita, whereas personal income per capita was $151,

---

[30] Elizabeth McNichol, Phil Oliff, and Nicholas Johnson, Center on Budget and Policy Priorities, States Continue to Feel Recession's Impact (2011).
[31] Office of Management and Budget, *Table 15.6 – Total Government Surpluses or Deficits in Absolute Amounts and as Percentages of GDP: 1948–2010*, Budget for Fiscal Year 2012, 350–351,.
[32] Office of Management and Budget, *Table 15.6 – Total Government Surpluses or Deficits in Absolute Amounts and as Percentages of GDP: 1948–2010*, Budget for Fiscal Year

having fallen from $303 in 1929. That represents per capita state and local debt of 94 percent of per capita income.[33]

VIII. CONSEQUENCES – PART II – HOW THE RESPONSE TO STATE SHORTFALLS IS HURTING THE U.S. ECONOMY

States that must make countercyclical expenditures with no way to finance them make up their budget gaps by cutting public services, laying off public employees, and reducing investment in public goods. The consequences are that the layoffs add to mass unemployment and slow down economic recovery. The cuts in public services, particularly education, do long-term damage to the nation's workforce, and the reductions in public investment both cut back on jobs and impair our country's long-term competitiveness.

State and local governments eliminated 550,000 jobs from September 2008 through August 2011.[34] In May and June 2011, large public sector job cuts all but overwhelmed increasingly weak private sector job creation, leaving total job growth in June 2011 at only 18,000 jobs.[35] In August 2011, public sector job losses did overwhelm weak private sector job creation, leaving net job creation in the U.S. economy at an improbable level of 0. Since 2008, twenty-one states have proposed identifiable and deep cuts in education from prekindergarten through twelfth grade. At least twenty states have proposed major, identifiable cuts in higher education.

IX. SOLUTIONS – REFEDERALIZATION OF COUNTERCYCLICAL SPENDING OR STRUCTURED FEDERAL SUPPORT FOR STATES

During the 1980s, President Ronald Reagan proclaimed a public policy doctrine he called the New Federalism. The idea of the New Federalism was that a variety of governmental functions that had been undertaken by

---

2012, 350–351; The Pew Center on the States, The Widening Gap: The Great Recession's Impact on State Pension and Retiree Health Care Costs, 1 (2011).

[33] It is not possible to obtain the equivalent of GDP for Arkansas in the Depression. The only data available for this type of comparative analysis is income-based data. U.S. Census Bureau, *Table 215 – State Finances: Revenues and Expenditures by States, 1932*, STATISTICAL ABSTRACT OF THE UNITED STATES 1939, at 224; *Table 226, – Net Debt of State and Local Governments: 1902–1937*.

[34] U.S. BUREAU OF LABOR STATISTICS, EMPLOYMENT, SITUATION SUMMARY (NATIONAL) (SEPTEMBER 2, 2011).

[35] U.S. BUREAU OF LABOR STATISTICS, THE EMPLOYMENT SITUATION – JUNE 2011.

the federal government in a standardized, national fashion were actually better done by the states in a decentralized fashion.

Reagan's New Federalism from a fiscal perspective was more a slogan than a reality. The balance between state and federal spending was not altered much during the Reagan years; however, divided responsibility for countercyclical spending has been a feature of the United States' governmental structure since the New Deal. More recently, in an age of conservative dominance of the federal government, liberal Democrats saw opportunities to expand the role of government at the state level that did not exist at the federal level. Conservatives often favored decentralization for its own sake and, in particular, felt more comfortable that, in diverting resources and power to states, state governments were more likely to use those resources and power in accordance with conservative values. Neither party recognized that in doing so it was setting the stage for inevitable fiscal instability given the nature of state governments.[36]

As long as recessions were brief, these issues were uncomfortable but manageable for state governments and had relatively little impact on the larger economy. With the rise of recessions driven by financial bubbles, the impact of states' inability to fund countercyclical spending has become much more serious, both for states and for the nation's economy and long-term competitiveness.

The solution to the problem of funding countercyclical expenditures could be either funding such expenditures exclusively at the federal level, as food stamps are, or by putting in place statutory mechanisms to provide expanded federal aid to the states when unemployment rises over certain levels.

The key for policy makers is not to be fooled into thinking that states or municipalities, with a few exceptions at the municipal level, are insolvent. They are almost all meeting their obligations and show every sign of being able to continue to do so. The crisis is not one of bankruptcy but of the costs to our country's economy and our long-term competitiveness from the way in which states manage through recessions.

The policy challenge posed by the fiscal crisis of the states is at one level parallel to the broader, long-term challenge facing the United States of how to fund the operations of a modern state on a sustainable basis and, in particular, how to fund desperately needed increases in the level of public investment. The irony of the U.S. problem is that, as Standard &

---

[36] See Richard P. Nathan and Fred C. Doolittle, *The Untold Story of Reagan's "New Federalism,"* THE PUBLIC INTEREST, 77 (Fall 1984), pp. 96–105.

Poor's recently pointed out in a credit rating report, it is a political problem, not an economic problem.[37] Simply put, the United States has ample wealth and income to fund a public sector and a level of public investment comparable to those of other developed societies. Our nation's problem is that the wealthy are powerful enough to block taxes but not powerful enough to dismantle the modern state. Large majorities want government to undertake basic functions like public education, maintenance of public parks, provision of a social safety net, and construction and maintenance of physical infrastructure. No one wants the unemployed to starve or to go without health care. Large majorities favor a more progressive tax system to pay for these services and investments. While we continue to more or less have a modern government, we seem unable to enact the revenue measures necessary to fund it or the intergovernmental mechanisms necessary in a federal system to manage economic cycles.

Even in an economic crisis as severe as the one we are currently experiencing, the federal-state transfers necessary to keep states economically healthy are relatively small amounts compared to the aid given to the financial system or the tax breaks offered or renewed at a federal level since 2007. It is not an issue of money; it is an issue of political honesty and political will – the honesty to admit that states are not really fiscally independent of the federal government and the will to act responsibly in accordance with that reality.

---

[37] Standard & Poor's, *United States of America Long-Term Rating Lowered to 'AA+'Due to Political Risks, Rising Debt Burden; Outlook Negative* (August 5, 2011) (pointing to "the difficulties in bridging the gulf between the political parties over fiscal policy" as a major cause of S&P's pessimism about the nation's long-term financial stability).

3

Public Pension Pressures in the United States

OLIVIA S. MITCHELL

Of late, public employee pension plans have received a great deal of scrutiny and media attention.[1] One reason is that some in the private sector are experiencing "pension envy" on learning that public pension benefits are often more generous than those paid to private sector employees. For instance, benefits on average replace 56 percent of pay for employees with thirty years of work in the public sector (66 percent if they are not covered by Social Security) versus 46 percent for private-defined benefit-covered workers (Clark 2011). Another reason is that financial markets – investors, rating agencies, and insurers – are devoting much more attention than ever before to the financing demands of public sector pension plans when considering whether a state may be able to sustain, and surely to increase, efforts to borrow as a means of smoothing the deleterious impact of the financial crisis (Fitch 2011; Moody's 2011; Standard and Poor's 2011). This chapter discusses why public pensions have warranted so much interest of late, devoting particular attention to their financing, funding status, recent developments, and reform options.

We show that many state pension plans will be able to pay promised benefits for some time, but there is enormous cross-state heterogeneity. Several states will surely require substantial new revenue soon, or they will need to institute benefit cuts if they are to return their plans to long-term solvency.[2] What remains to be seen is how the burden of returning

---

The author acknowledges research support from the Pension Research Council/Boettner Center at the Wharton School of the University of Pennsylvania and helpful comments from Robert Clark and Peter Conti-Brown. Opinions and conclusions expressed herein are solely those of the author and do not represent the opinions or policy of any institution with which she is affiliated. © 2011 Mitchell. All rights reserved.

[1] A Google search provided 65 million results in September 2011.
[2] For lack of space we do not take up solvency issues facing federal employee pensions nor the national Social Security system; neither can we focus on municipal pension financing

the plans to financial health will be borne, and how key stakeholders will implement reforms in these systems if they are to once again become viable before time runs out.

I. A BRIEF BACKGROUND ON STATE PENSION PLANS

Public sector pensions in the United States cover approximately 20 million public sector (nonfederal) employees and around 7 million retirees (Staman 2011). The vast majority of U.S. public pension plans are of the defined benefit (DB) variety in which retiree payments are specified as a stream of periodic payments for life with the amounts based on retirees' salary and years of service. In contrast, most private-sector employees with pensions have defined contribution (DC) plans; in these, contributions are specified as a percent of pay, but no particular benefit payout is specified.[3]

Labor market analysts are in agreement that pensions are one of many forms of deferred compensation offered to enhance employers' ability to recruit, incentivize, and eventually retire employees.[4] The United States has had a rich tradition of offering pensions to public employees, beginning with disability pensions for the militia during the colonial period (Clark, Craig, and Wilson 2003; Clark, Craig, and Ahmad 2009; Clark 2011). Thereafter, the U.S. Continental Congress established disability programs for members of the armed services during the Revolutionary era, which were later converted to old-age pension programs for veterans. In the mid-nineteenth century, many U.S. cities provided benefits for their superannuated teachers, firefighters, police officers, and other public personnel as part of a broad effort to reform civil service jobs and to move them into a merit-based system rather than one based on patronage (Clark et al. 2003). Most federal employees were covered by retirement pensions by 1930, although the federal approach to retirement provision has also evolved over time (Hustead and Hustead 2001).

The first U.S. state credited with establishing a statewide retirement plan is Massachusetts, which in 1922 began to cover general public employees

---

or public employee retiree health insurance obligations. For analysis of these, see Clark and Morrill (2010, 2011), McElhaney (2009), Mitchell and Anderson (2009), and Mitchell and Hustead (2000).

[3] For useful overviews of U.S. public pension plans, see Mitchell (2000); Mitchell and Anderson (2009); Mitchell et al. (2000); and Mitchell and Hustead (2000); more recent studies include Pew Center on the States (2010a, 2010b, 2011).

[4] Pensions are also a useful way for employees to save for retirement in a tax-qualified vehicle (McGill et al. 2010).

(Craig 2003). Thereafter, several states moved to implement pensions (mostly DB plans) in response to the passage of the national Social Security Act in 1935, which explicitly excluded public sector employees. In 1950, an amendment to that act permitted governmental units to enter Social Security; currently, public employees in seven states are still not included in the U.S. Social Security system.[5]

II. THE STRUCTURE OF PUBLIC SECTOR-DEFINED BENEFIT PLANS

Workers covered by DB pension promises receive compensation in the form of labor earnings as well as claims to future streams of pension payments in retirement. Accordingly, an employee accrues a future promise of benefits each year on the job, an accrual that constitutes a liability of the pension plan. Generally, retirement benefits are determined by a formula (often collectively bargained) in which payments rise with the worker's salary level, age and/or time on the job (tenure), retirement age, and perhaps other factors (Mitchell et al. 2000).

In the early 1900s, few state pension plans were funded – few had accumulated assets sufficient to back the benefits accrued by active workers (Craig 2003). Indeed, most early plans were run on a pay-as-you-go model in which annual benefit payments were covered by annual employee and employer contributions, as well as dedicated taxes (e.g., property tax levies or one-time asset sales; c.f. Civic Federation 2007). Over time, however, states began to link pension contribution levels to actuarial calculations, which meant that each participant's expected future pension payments would be calculated and – at least in principle – money would be set aside each year to finance those future benefits. To the extent that contributions were also invested, the pension fund's accumulated investment earnings were also used to pay benefits. From this perspective, then, the notion of a fully funded DB plan evolved: It is a fund that has, at any given date, sufficient money to pay all accrued vested benefits.[6]

---

[5] States still not participating in Social Security include Alaska, Colorado, Louisiana, Maine, Massachusetts, Nevada, and Ohio. Additionally, some local government workers do not participate, including groups in California, Connecticut, Illinois, Kentucky, Missouri, and Texas (Clark 2011). In 1983, the right to withdraw from Social Security was revoked.

[6] This refers to vested benefits; vesting occurs when the worker has earned a legal right to the future benefit stream. In the corporate sector, this funding concept is called the "termination" or "shutdown liability," referring to the ability of a plan to pay all promised benefits

The first states to thus structure their plans – sometimes referred to as "scientific" pension plans in the 1920s – were New Jersey, Ohio, and Vermont (Craig 2003). A key rationale for using these actuarial calculations was to ensure that sufficient funds would be set aside to pay workers' accrued benefits. In practice of course, full funding is inherently a moving target: Future benefit projections rely on assumptions about wage increases, labor turnover, mortality patterns, inflation, and other factors, and asset returns also are not reliably forecasted. Accordingly, DB plans must periodically adjust contributions and/or benefits to rectify funding shortages.[7]

III. RECENT CONCERNS ABOUT STATE PENSION PLANS

A major debate has recently exploded regarding public sector pension problems, driven in part by the ongoing economic recession, which drastically cut state tax collections by 30 percent in 2009 (and revenue streams have not recovered quickly; c.f. Cooper 2011). Consequently, many states face substantial budget challenges on many fronts due to extraordinary unemployment insurance bills, rising Medicaid expenditures due to aging populations, and the need to pay for major infrastructure improvements. In addition, most state governments must balance their operating budgets, making it difficult to come up with the needed cash to remedy pension shortfalls at the same time that other pressing fiscal needs have emerged.[8]

---

even if the plan sponsor were to shut down (Pension Benefit Guaranty Corporation n.d.). The public sector has often used different accounting and financial reporting standards (GASB 2006).

[7] Pension cost concepts to this end are described by Winklevoss (1993) among others. It must be noted that not everyone favors 100% funding of public pensions. From a practical viewpoint, the Government Accountability Office (GAO) (2008: 19) notes that funding at an 80-percent level might be sensible because "…it is unlikely that public entities will go out of business or cease operations as can happen with private sector employers, and state and local governments can spread the costs of unfunded liabilities over a period of up to 30 years under current GASB standards. In addition…it can be politically unwise for a plan to be overfunded; that is, to have a funded ratio over 100 percent. The contributions made to funds with 'excess' assets can become a target for lawmakers with other priorities or for those wishing to increase retiree benefits." Bohn (2011), among others, offers theoretical arguments pro and con.

[8] An active discussion is underway regarding the potential for state bankruptcy in the wake of the crisis; c.f. Skeel (2011). Barclays (2011) noted that pension underfunding plays a role in this process because Standard & Poor's downgraded New Jersey's GO rating to AA- from AA, citing its concern about the state's pension system underfunding. They

These exigencies are now competing with the need to hike contributions to meet public pension funding requirements. Such shortfalls were partly the result of the approximately $1 trillion in losses sustained by plan assets during the financial market implosion (Munnell et al. 2011b). In addition, public sector employees have been retiring in record numbers, increasing the drain on pension assets sooner than expected.[9] Public plans have also gotten into financial trouble for longer-standing reasons, including the fact that states have historically cut pension contributions and raised benefit promises in good economic times rather than taking advantage of robust periods to build up a financial cushion to protect against downturns (Schieber 2011). Public plan contributions have also fallen short of what they should have been. For instance, according to Greenhouse (2011), the fifty states together owed $117 billion to their pension plans in 2009 but, in fact, only contributed $73 billion. Contribution shortfalls of this nature have persisted because state DB plans follow rules set by their legislatures rather than by a centralized accounting authority; this permits politicians to adjust payment targets in times of fiscal stringency.[10]

Public pensions have also been roundly critiqued of late regarding how they measure their assets and liabilities. On the asset side, rather than reporting the market value or the amount for which the assets could be sold in the capital market, public DB pensions are permitted to "smooth" the time period over which the valuation is conducted (most public plans smooth assets over five or more years; Barclays 2011). Although such smoothing does reduce reported plan funding volatility, it also means that, after a substantial market crash such as the one that began in 2008, reported asset values and returns do not portray a plan's economic funding status as of any given moment. For instance, at year-end 2009, the fifty-state total of

---

also indicated that Moody's expressed concern regarding Illinois state bonds because of pension funding shortfalls.

[9] For instance, retirement rates for Ohio public school teachers rose between 2009 and 2010 by 20% and 50% for highway patrol officers, as workers responded to uncertainty about the state's pension underfunding (Rowl 2011).

[10] The Government Accounting Standards Board (GASB) requires public sector employers to report annual required contribution (ARC) amounts, but as Barclays (2011: 44) notes, this "is not a government funding requirement. ... While the ARC prescribes what an employer should contribute to cover current (normal) costs incurred and pay down the UAAL [*unfunded liabilities*], actual contributions do not always equal the ARC because governments are free to determine their own funding schedules. In addition, during times of fiscal stress, states may choose to defer or cut their pension contributions" (italicized phrase added).

assets computed using actuarial values exceeded the assets' market value by over 20 percent (Barclays 2011).

Another thorny issue has to do with how the public pension plan liabilities are measured. This is difficult because DB plan liabilities are of very long duration – they include the sum of benefits that must be paid this year, next year, the year afterward, and so forth, until the last surviving pension plan participant dies. If we define B_t as the retirement benefits a DB plan is obligated to pay to all retirees in any given year (t); r, the discount rate used to convert current future benefits into today's dollars; and assuming that the last possible year the final plan survivor (including spouses) will die is 90 years from now, then the expected present value (EPV) of the benefit stream may be expressed as follows:[11]

$$\text{EPV Benefits} = B_0 + B_1/(1+r) + B_2/(1+r)^2 \ldots + B_{90}/(1+r)^{90}$$

Naturally, many assumptions are required to forecast future DB plan obligations, including wage growth and inflation, turnover and retirement patterns, mortality improvements, and so forth.[12] However, an underappreciated and very powerful factor driving the liability measure is r, the discount rate. For corporate pensions, the U.S. government requires private DB plans to use discount rates consistent with the cost of corporate borrowing (the corporate yield curve). By contrast, public pension accounting permits DB plans to discount future benefit promises at the projected rate of return expected on plan assets, rather than what it would cost the state to borrow. What this means is that public DB plan sponsors today regularly use discount rates higher than 8 percent, despite the fact that they will probably not earn long-term asset returns of this magnitude anytime soon.[13]

As is evident from the formula above, when a DB plan sponsor selects a high discount rate for computing funding levels, this mechanically lowers plan-measured liabilities. What might be less obvious is that seemingly small changes in r have profound implications for pension funding and contribution requirements. For instance, Winklevoss (1993) noted that a single percentage point increase in the discount rate shrinks measured plan

---

[11] We refer the interested reader to McGill et al. (2010) for a more detailed discussion of plan cost methods.

[12] Another issue worth mentioning here is that public plan liabilities often are broader than corporate pension liabilities in that the former include future or projected benefits as well as accrued vested benefits earned as a function of salary and service to date.

[13] Wilshire Consulting (2011) expects the median state pension fund to earn 6.5% per year on its investments, assuming asset allocations of 64% equity (31% U.S., 18% non-U.S., 6% real estate, and 9% private equity) and 36% fixed income (27% U.S., 9% other).

TABLE 3.1. *Present value of aggregate state defined benefit plan liabilities, alternative scenarios*

		Assumed discount rate		
		State-chosen[a]	Taxable muni[b]	Treasury[c]
(1)	Total Plan Liabilities*	$2.80 trillion	$3.21 trillion	$5.20 trillion
(2)	Total Plan Assets **	$1.94 trillion	$1.94 trillion	$1.94 trillion
Difference (1–2)		$0.86 trillion	$1.27 trillion	$3.26 trillion

Notes:
* Plan liabilities measured using the accumulated benefit obligation (ABO) accrual methodology; see Rauh (2010).
** Assets estimated as of December 2008.
[a] Benefits discounted at the state-chosen discount rate, usually 8%.
[b] Benefits discounted at municipal bond rates based on zero-coupon municipal yield curve as of January 30, 1999.
[c] Benefits discounted at the zero-coupon Treasury yield curve as an approximation for a default-free rate.
Source: Derived from Rauh (2010) Table 1.

actuarial liabilities by 15 to 20 percent; Munnell et al. (2011a, 2011b) show that raising the discount rate by two percentage points, from 8 to 10 percent, staves off the date at which a public plan will exhaust its assets – and hence be unable to pay benefits – by a dozen years. In other words, selecting a high discount rate will mean substantially lower pension liabilities – implying, in turn, lower contributions required to finance retiree promises.[14]

To illustrate the stakes in this highly charged debate, Table 3.1 reports how state DB plan funding projections respond to different discount rate assumptions. In the leftmost column, liabilities are $2.8 trillion when discount rates chosen by the states (usually 8 percent) are used. The middle column uses the taxable municipal bond yield curve, and here liabilities are larger, at 115 percent of commonly reported levels. The final column – where a Treasury bond yield curve is used – pegs state pension liabilities at 185 percent of the first column (Rauh 2010). Clearly, the choice of discount rate makes an enormous difference in measuring the size of benefits promised to retired workers. After subtracting out plan-reported asset levels, the net underfunding also varies rather dramatically: In the first column, underfunding using state discount rates amounts to $0.86 trillion;

---

[14] For instance, when New York State raised its assumed interest rate in 1991 from 8% to 8.75%, this lowered the government's annual required contribution by $325 million (Hsin and Mitchell 1994).

in the second column, the estimate is half again as large with the municipal bond rate; and using Treasury rates boosts public pension underfunding to $3.26 trillion.[15] In other words, using the state-selected discount rates, the ratio of state pension assets to liabilities (A/L) comes to 69 percent indicating an estimated shortfall of almost one-third overall; however, the A/L ratio is only 37 percent using the least risky rate, implying that assets fall short of promised benefits by almost two-thirds.

The economic rationale for using a less-risky discount rate is that public pension benefits are often deemed to be very secure promises. In fact, they are frequently guaranteed by state constitutions and backed by the full faith and credit of the state tax base (Staman 2011; National Education Association 2004).[16] For this reason, financial economists argue that the discount rate for valuing future public pension benefits should be close to a risk-free Treasury rate (Brown and Wilcox 2009; Novy-Marx and Rauh 2011a). Furthermore, conformity with private pension accounting would suggest that a state's borrowing rate is a better assumption than the (usually much higher) expected return on assets. Additionally, from the perspective of transparency, Wilcox (2008: 1) contends that:

> some have argued that because state and local governments do not exist to generate a profit, or because public plan sponsors cannot go out of business or be acquired by a competitor, market-based estimates are irrelevant for them. Others have argued that policy makers need other information aside from market-based estimates in order to make sound decisions on behalf of their constituents... [But] in order to be useful, an estimate of plan liabilities must provide an analytically sound answer to a coherent, well-specified question. Market-based estimates of plan liabilities meet that test.

On the other hand, some actuaries and plan administrators continue to argue strongly in favor of the conventional approach. One reason is that it is believed to generate more stable contribution rates than the alternative (Segal Associates 2011).[17] Another reason, according to Miller (2008: 2) is that:

---

[15] This pattern is similar to those reported by the U.S. Congressional Budget Office (Russek 2011) and Munnell et al. (2011b).

[16] The Little Hoover Commission noted that (2011: i) "[p]ension benefits promised to retirees are irrevocable, as are the promised benefits that current workers have accrued since their employment began. It also remains difficult to alter the theoretical, yet-to-be earned benefits for current workers. This situation, reinforced by decades of legal precedent, leaves little room for state and local governments to control mounting retirement costs, particularly when the only venue for change is the bargaining table."

[17] See also Angelo et al. (2010), Lav and McNichol (2011), and Society of Actuaries (SOA) (2006).

by retaining the traditional practice of using reasonably probable investment returns as the basis for discounting future obligations... actuaries and accountants faithfully support the primary purpose of a public pension plan – which is to establish a funding plan that has the best possible chance of equitably balancing the interests of today's taxpayers and tomorrow's retirees. Many ... would agree with me that using risk-free rates of return to value public plans (which enjoy a long-term horizon and capacity to prudently assume equity risks) will almost assuredly over-burden today's taxpayers. Such an MVL regime would perversely shift the entire normal market risk premium to the benefit of future generations at the expense of their forebears.

Yet change is in the wind. Several states are currently litigating cases that would allow legislatures to alter and amend pension benefit and contribution formulas; these may render public pension promises less immutable than anticipated in the past.[18] New rules are also being developed by the Government Accounting Standards Board (GASB 2010), which will use a bond discount rate for underfunded pension liabilities (though expected asset returns will still be used to value funded plan liabilities; Segal Associates 2011). Meanwhile, although two of the major rating agencies, Standard & Poor's and Moody's, are still using reported funding ratios using state-determined discount rates, Fitch is moving toward more conservative rates to make plan funding rates comparable across states (Barclays 2011; Fitch 2011; Moody's 2011). It is also evident that public pension discount rate choices have been selected opportunistically: For instance, states experiencing fiscal problems reduce required contribution flows by selecting higher pension discount rates (Hsin and Mitchell 1994), and less well-funded plans are more than 2.5 times more likely to use a discount rate greater than 8 percent, compared to better funded plans (Park 2009). Although the great discount rate debate is far from over, it seems probable that the economic perspective will eventually prevail.

IV. HOW IMPORTANT IS THIS?

The debate over exactly which public pension underfunding measure to use ultimately boils down to what these shortfalls mean to stakeholders

---

[18] For a discussion of litigation underway on public plan benefit changes, see Barclays (2011) and Snell (2011). Walsh (2011) reports that judges in Colorado and Minnesota have refused to hear complaints about reductions in the cost-of-living adjustments for public pension recipients. For a discussion of other reforms, see Brown, Clark, and Rauh (2011).

and which stakeholders will be most affected when pension promises made to teachers, police, firefighters, and other state employees cannot be met. In the past, state pension contributions averaged 4 percent of annual state budgets, a level low enough that some argue there is little need for concern (Munnell, Aubry, and Quinby 2010). Nevertheless, this logic is flawed because the historical experience does not reflect the large, new financing shortfalls resulting from the financial crisis, recession, and other longer-term problems. For example, Novy-Marx and Rauh (2011a) estimate that contributions to public pensions will need to rise more than three-fold, to 14 percent of public sector revenue, to achieve full funding over the next 30 years. Average contributions would have to rise to 41 percent of payroll, and on average this could amount to a per-household average tax increase of $1,400 per year.

Of course, attempting to raise taxes this much could have potentially very serious consequences. Some public sector entities are already finding it difficult to borrow in the capital market as a result of the economic and financial crisis, and rating agencies are now paying much closer attention to whether pension shortfalls are exacerbating this problem. Explicit state debt totaled $2.4 trillion in 2010 (Maguire 2011: 5), and many states face limited capacity to borrow further. It is also worth noting that the pension-financing burden is not spread evenly. For instance, more than 20 percent of all general state transfers and revenues received by the State of Illinois are currently required to pay for pensions (Barclays 2011: 1).[19] To amortize their shortfalls over the next thirty years, New Jersey and New York households would face immediate and continuing tax hikes of more than $2,200 per household. California and Illinois residents would confront a yearly tax increase of over $1,900; although at the low end, Indiana residents would need to pay only $329 more per year to fund state pensions over the next three decades (Novy-Marx and Rauh 2011c: 40). Many municipalities and even some states are also aware that raising taxes may shrink the tax base.[20]

If needed revenues are not raised, however, a large number of public plans are likely to run quite short on cash within the decade (see Table 3.2). Munnell et al. (2011b) estimate the exhaustion date for public plans under two scenarios, an "ongoing" framework assuming that plan sponsors pay the full costs required in future years versus a "termination" framework

---

[19] This figure includes pension benefits and debt service on pension obligation bonds.
[20] For instance, Epple and Schipper (1981) report that a large component of public pension shortfalls is capitalized in property prices.

TABLE 3.2. *Year of public plan exhaustion for alternative asset returns, under ongoing and termination scenarios*

Assumed return on assets	Ongoing	Termination
6%	2025	2022
8%	2029	2025
10%	2035	2029

Notes: See text for definitions.
Source: Derived from Munnell et al. (2011a) Table 4.

assuming that benefit payments must rely solely on existing assets. If a relatively high 6-percent discount rate is assumed (yet one below what most plans currently use), they predict that public plans will exhaust their assets in 2022 on average if they terminated immediately and paid only already-accrued benefits. The exhaustion year is pushed back – but only slightly – to 2025, assuming that new contributions continue to flow in and benefit accruals continue to rise. Either way, these dates are alarming, particularly for baby boomers expecting a pension cash flow for two to three decades in retirement. It is also striking that the exhaustion date forecasts are quite unresponsive to higher discount rates.

There is also substantial variation around the averages, as illustrated in Figure 3.1. Here, the projected dates of exhaustion for public pensions in Illinois, Indiana, Connecticut, and New Jersey will take place by 2020, along with Hawaii, Louisiana, and Oklahoma. A dozen more states face cash strictures by 2025, with about the same number by 2030. States projected to be in better shape include Alaska, Florida, Nevada, New York, and North Carolina. It should be noted that these projections assume that investments return 8 percent per year; moreover, the analysis does not take into account reforms already made as well as potential future changes (Angelo et al. 2010). However, as we shall see, the reforms currently underway may not do much to remedy the problems, at least for those facing the most serious shortfalls.

V. REFORMS UNDERWAY

In response to the fiscal pressures identified above, several public plan sponsors have proposed and implemented reforms that they hope will alleviate these pension pressures. As noted by the Government Accountability Office (GAO) (2010), one rather worrisome approach has been to tilt

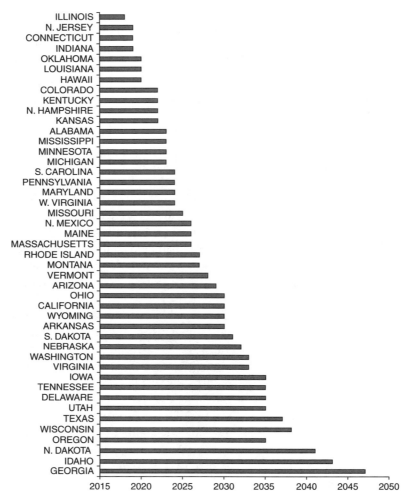

FIGURE 3.1. Anticipated year of exhaustion for state pension fund assets.
Note: Projections assume the funds earn 8% on assets, and all future contributions are used to pay for new benefits in full.
Source: Derived from Rauh (2010: table 1).

pension portfolios into riskier investments in the hope of making higher expected returns. For instance, New Jersey's public pension council recently approved a one-third increase in the maximum permitted allocation to alternative investments including hedge funds and private equity (Tangel 2011); Illinois's and Pennsylvania's funds have been writing credit default swaps and international interest rate swaps (Harris 2011). Some states have also issued special pension obligation bonds (POB) to generate cash that is then deposited in the pension system; nevertheless, this has proven an expensive way for some states to raise money.[21] Even when these are admissible assets for pension plans, they also involve substantially more risk, and given extant underfunding, it is unclear if such investments are consistent with a well-thought-out approach to pension risk management.[22]

An increasingly prevalent way to raise plan revenue involves asking employees to pay more for their own pensions. In 2010, a dozen states boosted employee pension contributions; to date in 2011, fourteen states including Wisconsin and Florida have also legislated contribution increases (Greenhouse 2011).[23] The governor of New York in 2011 has requested a doubling of employee contribution rates from 3 to 6 percent of pay; in Oregon, the proposed hike is from 0 to 6 percent.

Besides boosting investment returns and raising contributions, the only other way to reduce pension underfunding is to curtail expenditures. Of late, many such efforts have been set in motion (National Association of State Retirement Administrators n.d.). Changing the rules for retirees is usually seen as most difficult, although changes in cost-of-living adjustments clearly reduce the purchasing power of retiree benefits.[24] Altering prospective benefits for existing workers is also difficult because many state statutes and constitutions protect not only accrued but also prospective benefits for current employees. In addition, current employees are usually covered by collective bargaining contracts, which require joint union/management agreement to bring about any change. For these reasons, it has been somewhat less difficult (and less controversial) to adjust benefit formulas for future employees – those not yet hired. For instance,

---

[21] Barclays (2011) reports that, if states were to issue $700 billion in 30-year debt at an interest rate of 6% to 7.5% to finance their public plans, annual debt service would amount to about 7% to 8% of state tax revenues.

[22] In fact, some financial economists and actuaries have recommended otherwise (c.f. Black 1989, Gold and Latter 2009, Lucas and Zeldes 2009, and Peskin 2001, among others). Maurer, Mitchell, and Rogalla (2008) develop an explicit model to examine what asset allocation would minimize worst-case pension costs using a Monte Carlo framework and a stochastic present value approach, combined with a conditional value at risk measure. They show that funding public pension obligations requires being explicit about the level of risk that the plan fiduciary is willing to take on, which in turn requires explicit attention to risk bearing by present and future generations.

[23] For a detailed list of changes in 2011 to date, see Snell (2011).

[24] As noted above, Colorado, Minnesota, and South Dakota have recently sought to restrict cost-of-living adjustments (COLA); a full list of 2011 COLA changes appears in Snell (2011) and NASRA (n.d.).

numerous states have raised the number of years required to vest in (gain a legal entitlement to) eventual benefits; in addition, the retirement age has been raised in several cases, along with the number of years required for unreduced benefits (Snell 2011).

Some have proposed switching from a DB to a DC plan to reduce future benefit costs. To date, two states, Alaska and Michigan, have mandated DC plans for new hires; ten additional states offer as options either defined contribution or hybrid plans (mixed DB and DC). It is worth noting, however, that reducing costs for the not-yet-hired would not be expected to affect the already accrued benefits – also known as the "legacy benefits" – and their underfunding inherited from the past.[25]

At the end of the day, the size of the public pension shortfall remains dauntingly large and discouragingly expensive to fix. And few of the changes explored to date will help fill the gap very much, including changes in the cost-of-living escalators (COLA) often applied to benefits postretirement. According to Novy-Marx and Rauh (2011a: ii):

> a one percentage point reduction in COLAs would reduce total liabilities by 9–11%, implementing actuarially fair early retirement could reduce them by 2–5%, and raising the retirement age by one year would reduce them by 2–4%. Even relatively dramatic policy changes, such as the elimination of COLAs or the implementation of Social Security retirement age parameters, would leave liabilities around $1.5 trillion more than plan assets under Treasury discounting. This suggests that taxpayers will bear the lion's share of the costs associated with the legacy liabilities of state DB pension plans.

CONCLUSIONS

This brief overview has argued that the recent financial and economic crises have exacerbated the breadth and depth of pension financing challenges by undermining state revenue collections, wounding pension investment performance, and spiking pension liabilities. Fewer active workers remain to support retirees than ever before, and even if equity returns did rise strongly and persistently, it is unlikely that this will happen soon enough to cure the most seriously challenged plans. And it is worth remembering that many state pension problems arose for deeper reasons, including the lack

---

[25] Bergen and Garcia (2011) indicate that the Securities and Exchange Commission (SEC) has been exploring how the state of Illinois has been able to argue that benefit reductions applying only to new hires can be described in a state bond offering as reducing pension contributions immediately and through 2045.

of public pension transparency, the overreliance on risky asset returns to measure pension liabilities, and the inability to meet contribution requirements on a regular basis. As a result, too many U.S. state pension systems have become underfunded, and several face enormous challenges in the not-too-distant future if they are to return to solvency.

As a result of the recent "perfect storm," what was once seen as a safe defined benefit promise has now been transformed into a much riskier retirement offering. Given that U.S. state pensions are not guaranteed by federal backing, it is possible that a public plan might even be unable to continue paying promised benefits. Although modern U.S. history offers no examples of state bankruptcies, some municipalities have had to renegotiate their obligations in recent decades.[26] This in turn raises questions about how public pensions are governed and whether the existing structures are capable of ensuring managerial oversight of operations and accountability. Pension trustees are the designated "holders of the pension purse strings," faced with the difficult challenge of balancing the often-conflicting interests of public sector active and retired workers, taxpayers, and consumers.[27] Those seeking to remake and strengthen public pensions will need to return the plans to affordability, while making them more resilient to financial, economic, demographic, and political pressures.

REFERENCES

Angelo, Paul, Keith Brainard, Mitra Drazilov, and Paul Zorn. (2010). "Analysis of Joshua Rauh's Paper, Are State Public Pensions Sustainable?" National Association of State Retirement Administrators. http://nasra.org/resources/RauhResponse.pdf

Bader, Lawrence N. and Jeremy Gold. (2007). "The Case Against Stock in Public Pension Funds." *Financial Analysts Journal.* 63(1): 55–62.

Barclays. (2011). *States' Pensions: A Manageable Longer-Term Challenge.* Barclays Capital Municipal Credit Research Special Report. May 2011.

Bergen, Kathy and Monique Garcia. (2011). "SEC Probes Illinois Pension Savings Projections: Securities and Exchange Commission Inquiry Won't Affect Bond Sale Plans, Quinn Says." *Chicago Tribune,* January 25.

Black, Fischer. (1989). "Should You Use Stocks to Hedge Your Pension Liability?" *Financial Analysts Journal.* 45(1): 10–12.

Bohn, Henning. (2011). "Should Public Retirement Plans be Fully Funded?" *Journal of Pension Economics and Finance.* 10: 195–219.

---

[26] These include Cleveland, Ohio; Bridgeport, Connecticut; and Vallejo, California (c.f. Barclays 2011).

[27] For further discussion of public plan governance, see Useem and Mitchell (2000) and Yang and Mitchell (2008).

Brown, Jeffrey R., Robert Clark, and Joshua Rauh. (2011). "The Economics of State and Local Public Pensions." *Journal of Pension Economics and Finance.* 10(2): 161–172.

Brown, Jeffrey R. and David W. Wilcox. (2009). "Discounting State and Local Pension Liabilities." *American Economic Review.* 99(2): 538–542.

Civic Federation. (2007). *Dedicated Revenue Sources for State Pension Funds: A Civic Federation Brief.* Chicago: The Civic Federation. http://civicfed.org/sites/default/files/civicfed_240.pdf

Clark, Robert. (2011). "State and Local Pension Plans in the United States." Presented at the International Workshop on Civil Service and Military Pension Arrangements in Selected Countries of the Asia-Pacific. PIE Hitotsubashi University, Tokyo, January 20–21.

Clark, Robert L., Lee A. Craig, and Neveen Ahmed (2009). "The Evolution of Public Sector Pension Plans in the United States." In *The Future of Public Employee Retirement Systems.* Olivia S. Mitchell and Gary Anderson, eds. Oxford: Oxford University Press: 241–266.

Clark, Robert L., Lee A. Craig, and John Sabelhaus. (2011). *State and Local Retirement Plans in the United States.* Northampton, MA: Edward Elgar Publishing.

Clark, Robert L., Lee A. Craig, and Jack W. Wilson. (2003). *A History of Public Sector Pensions in the United States.* Philadelphia: University of Pennsylvania Press.

Clark, Robert and Melinda S. Morrill. (2010). *Retiree Health Plans in the Public Sector: Is There a Funding Crisis?* Northampton, MA: Edward Elgar.

Clark, Robert L. and Melinda S. Morrill. (2011). "The Funding Status of Retiree Health Plans in the Public Sector." *Journal of Pension Economics and Finance.* 10(2): 291–314.

Cooper, Michael. (2011). "Pension Fund Losses Hit States Hard, Data Show." *New York Times*, January 5.

Craig, Lee A. (2003). "Public Sector Pensions in the United States." EH.Net Encyclopedia. Edited by Robert Whaples, March 16. http://eh.net/encyclopedia/article/craig.pensions.public.us

Epple, Dennis and Katherine Schipper. (1981). "Municipal Pension Funding: A Theory and Some Evidence." *Public Choice.* 37(1): 141–178.

Fitch Ratings. (2011). *Enhancing the Analysis of U.S. State and Local Government Pension Obligations.* Special Report. February 17. http://www.fitchratings.com

Gold, Jeremy and Gordon Latter. (2009). "The Case for Marking Public Plan Liabilities to Market." In *The Future of Public Employee Retirement Systems.* Olivia S. Mitchell and Gary Anderson, eds. Oxford: Oxford University Press: 29–57.

Government Accountability Office (GAO, 2008). "State and Local Government Pension Plans: Current Structure and Funded Status." Statement of Barbara D. Bovbjerg, Director of Education, Workforce, and Income Security, before the Joint Economic Committee of the US Congress. Washington, DC: July 10.

Government Accountability Office (GAO, 2010). "State and Local Government Pension Plans: Governance Practices and Long-term Investment Strategies Have Evolved Gradually as Plans Take on Increased Investment Risk." Report to the Ranking Member, Committee on Finance, U.S. Senate.

Government Accounting Standards Board (GASB, 2006). "Preliminary Views of the Government Accounting Standards Board on Major Issues Related to Pension Accounting and Financial Reporting by Employers." http://www.gasb.org/cs/ContentServer?c=Document_C&pagename=GASB/Document_C/GASBDocumentPage&cid=1176156938122

Government Accounting Standards Board (GASB, 2006). "Why Governmental Accounting and Financial Reporting Is and Should Be Different." http://www.gasb.org/cs/ContentServer?c=Page&pagename=GASB%2FPage%2FGASBSectionPage&cid=1176156741271

Greenhouse, Steven. (2011). "States Lean on Public Workers for Bigger Pension Contributions." *New York Times*, June 15. http://www.nytimes.com/2011/06/16/business/16pension.html

Harris, Alexandra. (2011). "Illinois Pension Fund uses OTC Derivatives to Recoup Returns, Jeopardizes Pensions." *Medill Report*, June 10. http://news.medill.northwestern.edu/chicago/news.aspx?id=166746&print=1

Hsin, Ping-Lung and Olivia S. Mitchell. (1994). "The Political Economy of Public Pensions: Pension Funding, Governance, and Fiscal Stress." *Revista de Analisis Economico*. Special Issue on Pension Systems & Reform. P. Arrau & K. Schmidt-Hebbel, eds., 9(1): 151–168.

Hustead, Edwin C. and Toni Hustead. (2001). "Federal Civilian and Military Retirement Systems." In *Pensions in the Public Sector*. Olivia S. Mitchell and Edwin C. Hustead, eds. Philadelphia: University of Pennsylvania Press: 66–104.

Jones, Norman L., Brian B. Murphy, and Paul Zorn. (2009). *Actuarial Methods and Public Pension Funding Objectives: An Empirical Examination*. Presentation at the Society of Actuaries Public Pension Finance Symposium, May.

Lav, I. and E. McNichol. (2011). "Misunderstandings Regarding State Debt, Pensions, and Retiree Health Costs Create Unnecessary Alarm." Center on Budget and Policy Priorities Report, January 20. http://www.cbpp.org/cms/index.cfm?fa=view&id=3372

Little Hoover Commission. (2011). *Public Pensions for Retirement Security*. Milton Marks Commission on California State Government Organization and Economy Report. Sacramento, February.

Lucas, Deborah J. and Stephen P. Zeldes. (2009). "How Should Public Pension Plans Invest?" *American Economic Review Papers and Proceedings*. 99(2): 527–532.

Maguire, Steven. (2011). *State and Local Government Debt: An Analysis*. Washington, DC: Congressional Research Service.

Maurer, Raimond, Olivia S. Mitchell and Ralph Rogalla. (2008). "The Victory of Hope over Angst? Funding, Asset Allocation, and Risk-Taking in German Public Sector Pension Reform." In *Frontiers in Pensions Finance*. Dirk Broeders, Sylvester Eijffinger, and Aerdt Houben, eds. Cheltenham: Edward Elgar: 51–81.

McElhaney, Stephen T. (2009). "Estimating State and Local Government Pension and Retiree Health Care Liabilities." In *The Future of Public Employee Retirement Systems*. Olivia S. Mitchell and Gary Anderson, eds. Oxford: Oxford University Press: 19–28.

McGill, Dan M., Kyle N. Brown, John J. Haley, Sylvester J. Schieber, and Mark Warshawsky. (2010). *Fundamentals of Private Pensions* 9th ed. Oxford: Oxford University Press.

Miller, Gerard. (2008). "Presentation by Girard Miller: Comments before the Public Interest Committee of the American Academy of Actuaries." Washington, DC: Academy of Actuaries, September 4. http://www.actuary.org/events/2008/forum_statements_septo8/oral/miller.pdf

Mitchell, Olivia S. (2000). "Developments in Pensions." In *Handbook of Insurance*. G. Dionne, ed. Boston: Kluwer Academic Publishers: 873–899.

Mitchell, Olivia S. and Gary Anderson, eds. (2009). *The Future of Public Employee Retirement Systems*. Oxford: Oxford University Press.

Mitchell, Olivia S. and Ping-Lung Hsin. (1997). "Public Sector Pension Governance and Performance." In *The Economics of Pensions: Principles, Policies, and International Experience*. S. Valdes-Prieto, ed. Cambridge: Cambridge University Press: 92–126.

Mitchell, Olivia S. and Edwin Hustead, eds. (2000). *Pensions for the Public Sector*. Philadelphia, PA: University of Pennsylvania Press.

Mitchell, Olivia S., David McCarthy, Stanley C. Wisniewski, and Paul Zorn. (2000). "Developments in State and Local Pension Plans." In *Pensions for the Public Sector*. Olivia S. Mitchell and Edwin Hustead, eds. Philadelphia, PA: Univ. of Pennsylvania Press: 11–40.

Moody's. (2011). *Combining Debt and Pension Liabilities of U.S. States Enhances Comparability*. New York: Moody's Investor Services, January 26.

Munnell, Alicia H., Jean-Pierre Aubry, Josh Hurwitz, Madeline Medenica, and Laura Quinby. (2011a). "Funding of State and Local Pensions in 2010." Boston: Center for Retirement Research 17.

Munnell, Alicia H., Jean-Pierre Aubry, and Laura Quinby. (2010). "The Impact of Public Pensions on State and Local Budgets." CRR Brief 13, October.

Munnell, Alicia H., Jean-Pierre Aubry, and Laura Quinby. (2011b) "Public Pension Funding in Practice." *Journal of Pension Economics and Finance*. 10(2): 247–268.

Munnell, Alicia H., Kelly Haverstick, and Jean-Pierre Aubry (2008). "Why Does Funding Status Vary Among State and Local Plans?" Boston College Center for Retirement Research Brief.

National Association of State Retirement Administrators (NASRA, n.d.). *Public Fund Scorecard*. http://www.publicfundsurvey.org/publicfundsurvey/scorecard.asp

National Council on Public Employee Retirement Systems (NCPERS) and Cobalt Community Research. (2011). *The 2011 NCPERS Public Fund Study: Preliminary Results*. NCPERS.

National Education Association. (2004) *NEA Issue Brief on Pension Protections in State Constitutions*. NEA Collective Bargaining & Member Advocacy.

Novy-Marx, Robert and Joshua D. Rauh. (2009). "The Liabilities and Risks of State-Sponsored Pension Plans." *Journal of Economic Perspectives*. 23(4): 191–210.

Novy-Marx, Robert and Joshua D. Rauh. (2011a). "Policy Options for State Pension Systems and Their Impact on Plan Liabilities." *Journal of Pension Economics and Finance*. 10(2): 173–194.

Novy-Marx, Robert and Joshua D. Rauh. (2011b). "Public Pension Promises: How Big Are They and What Are They Worth? *Journal of Finance*. 66(4): 1207–1245.
Novy-Marx, Robert and Joshua D. Rauh. (2011c). "The Revenue Demands of Public Employee Pension Promises." Kellogg School of Management Working Paper, June.
Park, Youngkyun. (2009). "Public Pension Plan Asset Allocations." *EBRI Notes*. 30(4).: 1–12.
Pension Benefit Guaranty Corporation (n.d.). "Plan Termination Fact Sheet." Washington, DC: PBGC. http://www.pbgc.gov/res/factsheets/page/termination.html
Peskin, Michael. (2001). "Asset/Liability Management in the Public Sector." In *Pensions in the Public Sector*. Olivia S. Mitchell and Edwin Hustead, eds. Philadelphia: University of Pennsylvania Press: 195–217.
Pew Center on the States. (2010a). *Roads to Reform: Changes to Public Sector Retirement Benefits Across States*. Washington, DC: Pew Center, November.
Pew Center on the States. (2010b). *The Trillion Dollar Gap*. Washington, DC: Pew Center, November.
Pew Center on the States. (2011). *The Widening Gap: The Great Recession's Impact on State Pension and Retiree Healthcare Costs*. Washington, DC: Pew Center, April.
Rauh, Joshua D. (2010). "Are State Public Pensions Sustainable? Why the Federal Government Should Worry About State Pension Liabilities." *National Tax Journal (Forum)* 63(10): 585–601.
Rowl, Daryl. (2011). "Follow the Exit Signs." *The Columbus Dispatch*, June 26. http://www.dispatch.com/live/content/local_news/stories/2011/06/26/follow-the-exit-signs.html?sid=101
Russek, Frank. (2011). *The Underfunding of State and Local Pension Plans*. Economic and Budget Issue Brief. Congressional Budget Office, May.
Schieber, Sylvester J. (2011). "Political Economy of Public Sector Retirement Plans." *Journal of Pension Economics and Finance*. 10(2): 269–290.
Segal Associates. (2011). *Actual Cost vs Market Price: Does Market Valuation of Pension Liabilities Fit the Public Sector?* Washington, DC: Segal Report, June.
Skeel, David. (2011). "A Bankruptcy Law – Not Bailouts – For the States." *Wall Street Journal*, January 18.
Snell, Ronald K. (2011). *Pensions and Retirement Plan Enactments in 2011 State Legislatures*. National Council on State Legislatures.
Society of Actuaries (SOA) and American Academy of Actuaries. (2006). *Pension Actuary's Guide to Financial Economics*. Society of Actuaries and American Academy of Actuaries. http://www.actuary.org/pdf/pension/finguide.pdf
Staman, Jennifer. (2011). *State and Local Pension Plans and Fiscal Distress: A Legal Overview*. Washington, DC: Congressional Research Service.
Standard and Poor's (2011). *U.S. States' Pension Funded Ratios Drift Downward*. New York: Global Credit Portal Ratings Direct Report.
Tangel, Andrew. (2011). "NJ Taking Risks to Boost Pension Pool, May Double Up on Alternative Investments." *NorthJersey.com*, May 17.

U.S. Census Bureau. (2010). "State and Local Public Employee Retirement System Assets Drop Nearly $180 B in 2008 Census Bureau Reports." U.S. Department of Commerce Press Release, March 25. http://www2.census.gov/govs/retire/fyo8pressrelease.pdf

Useem, Michael and Olivia S. Mitchell. (2000). "Holders of the Purse Strings: Governance and Performance of Public Retirement Systems." *Social Science Quarterly*. 81(2): 489–506.

Walsh, Mary Williams. (2011). "Two Rulings Find Cuts in Public Pensions Permissible." *New York Times*, June 30.

Wilcox, David. (2008). "The Disclosure of Market Value of Assets and Liabilities by Public-Sector Defined-Benefit Pension Plans." Comments before the Public Interest Committee of the American Academy of Actuaries. Washington, DC, September 4. http://www.actuary.org/events/2008/forum_statements_septo8/oral/wilcox.pdf

Wilshire Consulting. (2011). *2011 Wilshire Report on State Retirement Systems Funding levels and Asset Allocation.* Santa Monica: Wilshire Consulting.

Winklevoss, Howard E. (1993). *Pension Mathematics with Numerical Illustrations.* Philadelphia: University of Pennsylvania Press.

Yang, Tongxuan (Stella) and Olivia S. Mitchell. (2008). "Public Pension Governance, Funding, and Performance: A Longitudinal Appraisal." In *Pension Fund Governance: A Global Perspective on Financial Regulation.* John Evans and John Piggott, eds. Cheltenham: Edward Elgar: 179–199.

4

Structural Challenges in State Budgeting

JOSH BARRO

In managing their budgets, states face several structural challenges that are quite different from the challenges of federal budgeting. Every state except Vermont has a balanced budget requirement; although these requirements vary in strength, they do significantly limit the ability of states to engage in deficit spending. Therefore, unlike the federal government, states face significant cyclical budgeting challenges, as they seek to balance their budgets even during recessions.

Like the federal government, states also face secular – that is, noncyclical – budgeting challenges created by expenses that grow faster than the economy and tax sources whose bases are eroding. However, whereas the federal government can paper over those secular challenges for a long time by running structural deficits, states are compelled to take action so that expenditures do not grow significantly faster than revenues. In other words, state lawmakers must respond with much greater vigilance to budget pressures than their federal counterparts.

Because the budgets of states and localities are closely intertwined, it makes little sense to discuss the budgeting challenges of states in isolation. In nearly every state, local governments depend to a significant extent on grants-in-aid paid for by state level taxes.[1] Budget pressures affecting localities often bubble up to the state level and vice versa – for example, as local governments have faced increasing legal and political barriers to levying property tax, there has been increased pressure for states to raise sales and income taxes to make aid payments to local governments. In addition, the division of budgetary responsibilities among states and their subsidiary

---

[1] As of 2008, intergovernmental revenue from states accounted for 29 percent of local government expenditure nationally, and for at least 20 percent in forty-eight of fifty states. Census of State and Local Governments, U.S. Census Bureau, via Tax Policy Center State and Local Finance Data Query System (SLFDQS). http://slfdqs.taxpolicycenter.org/

entities varies widely from state to state. In 2008, direct expenditures by municipalities ranged from 67 percent of all state and local expenditure in Nevada to just 21 percent in Hawaii.[2]

Given these interconnections, this chapter will deal jointly with the budgeting challenges of state and local governments. As New Jersey Governor Chris Christie made clear in his 2010 budget address, it is impossible to bring fiscal reform to a state facing structural budget gaps without considering state and local expenditures together.[3] Together, states and localities must restructure so that tax receipts remain predictable and sufficient and expenditures do not grow faster than the economy.

The broad prescription for how states and localities should make and keep their budgets sustainable is simple: They should set spending priorities that are affordable and enact a tax code that will raise sufficient and reliable revenue to pay for those priorities while doing minimal damage to the economy. States should avoid policies that exacerbate either cyclical or structural gaps between expenditures and revenues. However, governments have often fallen into traps, with program costs that grow on autopilot at a rate faster than the economy and taxes in which receipts swing wildly and do not keep pace with the economy.

The budgetary traps that states and localities fall into come in a few broad areas. On the revenue side, these are taxes that are highly volatile or have problems with insufficiency – that is, receipts that grow too slowly. On the expenditure side, these are programs in which costs tend to grow faster than the economy or are too difficult for policy makers to control.

I. REVENUE CHALLENGES

States and localities face three primary challenges on the revenue side, with one problem roughly relating to each of the three major taxes most states and localities rely on. These three big taxes – taxes on personal income, general sales, and property – each account for between 23 and 31 percent of state and local tax receipts (See Figure 4.1). Income taxes are a growing share of the state and local revenue mix, and at the same time, those taxes are growing more volatile, making it more challenging for state lawmakers

---

[2] SLFDQS

[3] "We cannot and should not make state government shrink only to let local government expand." Budget address of New Jersey Governor Chris Christie, March 16, 2010. http://abclocal.go.com/wabc/feature?section=news/local&id=7333237

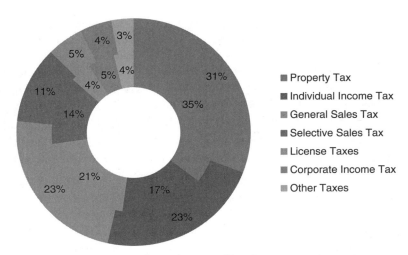

FIGURE 4.1. Pie chart of state and local tax sources in 2008.

to plan their budgets. Political resistance has decreased local governments' ability to rely on property tax, historically a very stable source of revenue. Additionally economic changes are undermining the sufficiency of the sales tax, which is leading states to raise tax rates.

II. VOLATILITY

One of the most remarkable features of state and local tax collections over the last several decades is their stability. From 1985 to 2008, state and local tax receipts varied within a narrow band from 10.0 percent of national personal income to 10.9 percent.[4] (Over the same period, federal receipts have ranged much more widely, from 16.1 to 20.6 percent.)[5]

However, in recent years, the trend has been toward greater revenue volatility. Because spending needs of governments are not very volatile, sharp changes in revenues either require significant changes in the tax code or significant changes to government spending. As such, the increase in revenue volatility is a worrying trend.

As Don Boyd of the Rockefeller Institute noted in March 2011, states had particular difficulty foreseeing the sharp drops in revenue that resulted from recessions in 2001 and 2009. He writes:

---

[4] SLFDQS
[5] Historical Tables, Office of Management and Budget.

> [N]egative surprises... have become larger and more troubling over time. During the three main years of the 1990–92 fiscal crisis for states, revenue was at least 5 percent below forecast in 25 percent of states. During the comparable years of the downturn that began in 2001, 45 percent of forecasts were off by at least that amount. And in 2009 – admittedly the most-difficult-to-forecast year of the current crisis – fully 70 percent of all projections missed the mark by similar proportions, while half of the states had truly big problems with collections coming in more than 10 percent below forecast levels...
>
> [I]f revenue forecasts are prone to more and larger errors than was the case in an earlier era, something must have changed. Indeed, that's the case: The relationship between state tax systems and the economic activities to which they apply has evolved significantly over the past few decades.
>
> In 1978, the personal income tax represented just over one-quarter of total state tax revenue. In 2008, it was above 35 percent. During that time, the nature of the income that is typically subject to state tax has evolved. Decades ago, taxable income was overwhelmingly dominated by salaries and wages. These may decline during recessions, but usually by relatively modest amounts. Although such regular income is still the largest share of the taxable base, capital gains and bonuses play a much more important role now.[6]

This effect can also be seen when considering state and local governments together. From 1977 to 2008, personal income tax rose from 17 percent of state and local tax collections to 23 percent. At the same time, the most stable source of state and local tax revenue, property tax, declined from 35 percent of state and local taxes to 31 percent.[7] This shift, coupled with the increasingly volatile nature of personal income itself, has made revenue volatility a larger problem for states.

Some states have exacerbated the volatility problems associated with personal income tax by placing an above-normal reliance on income tax or by having greater income tax progressivity. For example, California falls into both of these categories. Personal income tax forms a somewhat above-normal share of California state and local tax receipts (30 percent),[8] but the state also has one of the country's most progressive income taxes, with the top 1 percent of taxpayers paying 7.1 percent of their incomes in personal income tax. (Each of the bottom four quartiles pays less than 2

---

[6] http://www.rockinst.org/observations/boydd/2011-03-rising_volatility_state_tax_systems.aspx
[7] SLFDQS.
[8] SLFDQS.

percent).[9] As a result, the top 10 percent of tax filers were paying about 71 percent of California personal income taxes as of 2008.[10]

High-income taxpayers tend to have especially volatile incomes, in part because a relatively large share of their income consists of capital gains. Capital gain income, as Boyd notes, tends to be extremely volatile. In the case of California, taxable capital income rose from $33 billion in 1996 to $118 billion in 2000, only to fall back to $33 billion by 2002.[11]

Corporate income tax is even more volatile than personal income tax; however, this tax accounts for less than 5 percent of state and local tax receipts. Corporate tax volatility is a significant problem for the handful of states that rely heavily on corporate taxes (such as Alaska and New Hampshire) but is secondary nationally to personal income tax volatility.

Although volatility is most problematic in income taxation, it is also a concern for states relying heavily on sales tax. Historically, sales tax receipts have been more stable than income tax receipts because household consumption does not change as much as household income in recessions. However, the recent downturn has featured marked weakness in state sales taxes. For example, state sales tax receipts in the third quarter of 2009 were off 9 percent from a year earlier, with personal income tax receipts off 12 percent.[12] That was the worst year-over-year drop in state sales tax receipts in fifty years. By contrast, in the 2001 downturn, sales tax receipts were generally flat even as income tax receipts were plunging.[13]

States can mitigate tax volatility by relying more on property tax and less on sales and income taxes. However, states can also make choices about the structure of sales and income taxes to mitigate or increase volatility. Sales tax bases tend to be heavily weighted toward durable goods, with services and nondurables often receiving tax preferences. In recessions, durable goods purchases tend to be weaker than consumption overall, which undermines the stability of sales tax receipts. A broader sales tax base would result in lower volatility.

[9] ITEP, "Who Pays" report, 2009 data. http://www.itepnet.org/whopays.htm
[10] California Franchise Tax Board Annual Report, Appendix Table B-3: http://www.ftb.ca.gov/aboutFTB/Tax_Statistics/2009.shtml
[11] California Franchise Tax Board Annual Report 2004. http://www.ftb.ca.gov/aboutftb/annrpt/archive_index.shtml
[12] Lucy Dadayan, Rockefeller Institute, "Final Quarter of 2009 Brought Still More Declines in State Tax Revenue," February 2010. www.rockinst.org/pdf/.../finance/.../2010-02--23-State_Revenue_Flash.pdf
[13] Donald Boyd and Lucy Dadayan, Rockefeller Institute, "Sales Tax Decline in Late 2008 Was the Worst in 50 Years," April 2009. http://www.rockinst.org/pdf/government_finance/state_revenue_report/2009-04-14-(75)-state_revenue_report_sales_tax_decline.pdf

One strategy states have used to cope with volatility in income tax receipts is the imposition of temporary income taxes following downturns. California imposed such a tax in 1991 and again in 2009. Four other states (New York, New Jersey, Maryland, and Hawaii) also imposed temporary income tax increases in the recent recession, generally focused on high-income tax filers. With the exception of Hawaii's temporary tax, which is set to expire in 2015, and a portion of New York's tax, these taxes have all been allowed to sunset in the nascent economic recovery.[14]

Some states also mitigate the volatility of the income tax by offering a tax preference for capital income. This reduces the state's reliance on volatile capital gains and dividends and shifts more reliance to a more stable wage income. Eight states currently offer a tax preference for capital income.[15]

III. SALES TAX INSUFFICIENCY

In general, sales tax bases tend to focus on taxation of sales of tangible personal property. While a handful of small states (Hawaii, New Mexico, and South Dakota) apply sales tax broadly to most services, a majority of states with sales taxes apply tax to fewer than one-third of the services identified as potentially taxable by the Federation of Tax Administrators.[16] Many states also exempt certain "necessity" goods from sales taxation; while forty-five states levy a sales tax, only fourteen apply that tax to grocery food (many at a reduced rate).[17] Most exempt prescription drugs[18] and gasoline[19], whereas a handful even exempt over-the-counter medication[20] and clothing.

This choice to include only some kinds of consumption in the sales tax base is problematic for a few reasons. First, it is distortionary: Consumers

---

[14] Josh Barro, "Temporary Tax Increases Actually Proving Temporary," National Review Online, June 13, 2011. http://www.nationalreview.com/agenda/269499/temporary-tax-increases-actually-proving-temporary-josh-barro

[15] Institute on Taxation and Economic Policy. http://www.itepnet.org/pdf/capitalidea0111.pdf

[16] Timothy Hurley, "Curing the Structural Defect in State Tax Systems: Expanding the Tax Base to Include Services," 61 Mercer L. Rev. 491 (2010).

[17] Federation of Tax Administrators, "State Sales Tax Rates and Food & Drug Exemptions (As of January 1, 2012)." http://www.taxadmin.org/fta/rate/sales.pdf

[18] "State Sales Tax Rates and Food & Drug Exemptions (As of January 1, 2012)."

[19] Tax Foundation, "State Gasoline Tax Rates as of January 1, 2011." http://www.taxfoundation.org/taxdata/show/26079.html

[20] "State Sales Tax Rates and Food & Drug Exemptions (As of January 1, 2012)."

are induced to consume more of the untaxed items and fewer of the taxed items than they otherwise would. The choice to focus the tax base specifically on durable goods, by exempting food and in some cases clothing, also exacerbates revenue volatility, as discussed.

The focus on goods over services is also problematic because services are growing as a share of the economy, and therefore, the sales tax base is shrinking. In 1979, sales tax bases represented 58.9 percent of personal income nationally; by 1996, that figure had fallen to 41.9 percent as a result of changes in consumption patterns.[21] This means that, without a change in tax rates, sales tax receipts will tend to decline as a share of the economy over time. If government spending needs grow roughly in line with the economy, this will leave states searching for new sources of revenue.

A secondary, but growing, problem that is undermining sales tax bases is the increasing prevalence of online sales. In general, a retailer is only obligated to collect sales tax on sales made to states where the retailer has a physical presence.[22] Although a number of states have enacted so-called Amazon Tax laws that broadly construe the idea of "physical presence" – counting online retailers' local affiliate marketers as an in-state presence – in practice, states are having little success in getting Amazon and other online-only retailers to collect and remit sales tax. This problem is likely to worsen over time as online retailing continues to grow.

Despite an eroding tax base, sales tax receipts have actually been growing slightly as a share of state and local tax collections over the last several decades, rising from 21 percent in 1977 to 23 percent in 2008.[23] This is because governments have responded to the shrinking sales tax base by raising rates: The mean state sales tax rate rose from 3.5 percent in 1970 to 5.2 percent in 2003.[24]

[21] William Fox, "Can the Sales Tax Survive a Future Like Its Past,", in *The Future of State Taxation*, ed. David Burnori, Urban Institute Press, Washington, DC, 1998. http://books.google.com/books?id=WZzTK_5nIOEC&pg=PA33&lpg=PA33&dq=%22Can+the+State+Sales+Tax+Survive+a+Future+Like+Its+Past?%22&source=bl&ots=JDFI4fHJjs&sig=L95JOfNylLZ8jYA2ILh7dEww1rQ&hl=en&ei=_x8hTp6bLqa3oAGHgp3JAw&sa=X&oi=book_result&ct=result&resnum=3&ved=0CCkQ6AEwAg#v=onepage&q=%22Can%20the%20State%20Sales%20Tax%20Survive%20a%20Future%20Like%20Its%20Past%3F%22&f=false

[22] If tax is not collected on a taxable sale, the purchaser is legally obligated to pay a compensating "use tax," generally reported on a state income tax form; however, compliance is low.

[23] SLFDQS.

[24] Iris Lav, Elizabeth McNichol, and Robert Zahradnick, "Faulty Foundations: State Structural Budget Problems and How to Fix Them," Center on Budget and Policy Priorities, 2005.

This is not a shift to which we should be indifferent; states are much better off raising revenue with a sales tax that has a broad base and a low rate than a narrow base and a high rate. Higher sales tax rates increase the distortion of the sales tax by exacerbating the difference in treatment of taxed goods and untaxed services. In addition, because the deadweight loss of a tax is a function of the tax rate squared, a sales tax with a higher rate will do more damage to the economy than a lower-rate sales tax even if it does not raise more total revenue.

It would be better for states to respond to the problem of sales tax revenue insufficiency by broadening their sales tax bases so that tax receipts will rise in line with the economy. Such a move would allow states to cut sales tax rates now and avoid the need to raise them in the future. However, efforts to broaden sales tax bases have generally proved unpopular.

Most famously, Florida officials enacted and then swiftly repealed[25] a wildly unpopular[26] tax on services in 1987. The tax was widely credited with severely damaging the career of Governor Bob Martinez and serves as a cautionary tale for politicians who seek to expand the sales tax base. In the last two years, efforts to expand sales tax bases have been defeated or significantly watered down in Connecticut, Georgia, Illinois, Maine, Maryland, Massachusetts, and Rhode Island. In Maine's case, a revenue neutral tax reform that cut income tax rates by expanding the sales tax base was overturned by a people's veto with 61 percent of the vote in 2010.[27]

IV. PROPERTY TAX LIMITATIONS

Whereas income taxes have been on the rise for decades, with sales tax rates rising just enough to offset erosion of the tax base, one major source of state and local tax receipts has been in decline: property tax. Although still the largest tax source for state and local governments, property tax receipts have declined from 35 percent of state-local tax receipts in 1977 to 31 percent in 2008. Most of the rise in income taxes can be thought of as offsetting the property tax decline.

This trend can be traced to the property tax revolts that began in the late 1970s, most famously California's Proposition 13, which sharply limits

---

[25] http://articles.latimes.com/1987-12-12/news/mn-6754_1_service-tax
[26] http://articles.orlandosentinel.com/1987-12-06/news/0160370279_1_services-tax-central-florida-general-sales-tax
[27] http://hosted.ap.org/dynamic/files/elections/2010/by_state/ME_Question_0608.html?SITE=MEPOPELN&SECTION=POLITICS

local governments' ability to levy property tax. Faced with more restricted local revenue streams, states began offering bigger local aid payments and needed bigger state tax sources to finance them.

In New Jersey, the trade-off is supposed to be explicit: Income tax receipts go not to the general fund but to the Property Tax Relief Fund, all of which is earmarked for local aid. (Some sales tax revenue also goes to this fund.) However, local aid has not been effective at relieving the property tax burden; although the income tax was established in 1976 for the purpose of relieving property taxes, the state still has the country's highest property taxes.[28] (The income tax has also been raised several times. The top rate at enactment was 2.5 percent and is 8.97 percent today; for 2009, there was a temporary top rate of 10.5 percent.)

In some other states, property tax relief measures have had the effect of holding down property taxes while leading other taxes to grow faster. Massachusetts, which enacted a property tax cap in 1980, has seen slow growth in property taxes through 2008: just a 22 percent inflation-adjusted rise in property tax per capita, versus 62 percent nationally. However, the gap in growth of overall state-local tax collections was much smaller: 58 percent in Massachusetts and 70 percent nationally.[29] This reflects the fact that limitations on property tax encourage greater dependence on other tax sources.

In some states, particularly those in the Northeast with especially high property tax burdens, restrictions on property tax make sense, even if the result is a shift toward income and sales taxation. In general, the shift away from property tax toward income tax is a negative trend because property taxes appear to be less economically damaging than sales or income taxes per dollar of revenue raised.[30]

In addition, because real property is immovable, it is one of the easiest taxes to administer at the local level. Although local sales and income taxes exist, their usefulness is limited by the ease with which transactions can flee across municipal borders. Therefore, limits on property tax often mean a choice to move fiscal decision making from city halls to state capitals. This creates new budgetary challenges for both city and state officials. City officials must balance their books with fewer revenue tools available. State

[28] Tax Foundation, "Property Taxes on Owner-Occupied Housing by State, 2009." http://taxfoundation.org/taxdata/show/1913.html
[29] Josh Barro, "Do Property Tax Caps Work: Lessons for New Jersey from Massachusetts," Manhattan Institute, June 2010. http://www.manhattan-institute.org/html/cr_62.htm
[30] Jens Arnold, "Do Tax Structures Affect Aggregate Economic Growth? Empirical Evidence from a Panel of OECD Countries," OECD, 2008.

officials come under greater pressure to appropriate large and growing amounts for local aid instead of telling the city officials to fix their own budget problems.

California provides the starkest example of the effects of property tax limitations. In 1977, property tax accounted for 42 percent of all state and local tax collections in California. Proposition 13, enacted in 1978 and effective for 1979, sharply reduced property taxes and then restrained their growth. Property tax reached a trough of 22 percent of California state and local tax collections by 2000, before rising to 28 percent in 2008 on the strength of the property bubble.

Although Proposition 13 has sharply constrained property tax, it has also led to a major increase in California's reliance on income tax. In 1977, California collected just 1.9 percent of state personal income in personal income tax; by 2008, that figure had nearly doubled to 3.5 percent. (Nationally, average personal income tax collections rose much more modestly, from 1.8 to 2.5 percent.)[31] This shift has meant increased volatility and decreased efficiency in California's tax code. It has also meant the increased centralization of California's fiscal apparatus: With few means to levy additional revenue of their own, localities are increasingly dependent on Sacramento.

The increasing demand for sales and income tax revenue that results also pushes marginal rates upward, damaging the economy. Of course, lower property taxes provide some offsetting economic benefits. But property tax limits are often structured so that the relief they provide does not come at the margin – rebates and homestead exemptions place more money in the hands of homeowners, but they do not incentivize economic activity. The rent-control-like provisions of Proposition 13, which provide greater value to homeowners the longer they stay in the same house, not only fail to encourage productivity but distort economic behavior.

V. EXPENDITURE CHALLENGES

Two of the largest areas of state and local government expenditure – health care and education – are experiencing long-term cost growth at rates significantly in excess of economic growth. This means that state governments must either grow their spending as a share of the economy or cut back on services provided. States and localities also face challenges related to two aspects of employee benefits – health insurance and pensions – that

[31] SLFDQS.

have in recent years seen cost growth that has significantly outpaced economic growth.

VI. SECTORAL CHALLENGES

About half of state and local spending goes toward education and health care. As of 2008, education accounted for 29 percent of state and local government spending. Total expenditures on health care are less easy to quantify because the spending is fragmented among several Census reporting categories. However, a reasonable estimate is that at least 22 percent of state and local budgets are spent on health care. This includes spending reported to the Census Bureau in the health and hospitals category (7 percent of budgets), public welfare payments to private vendors for medical care (principally Medicaid and CHIP – 10 percent), and public employee health benefits (5 percent).[32] Some other components of health spending, such as disproportionate share payments made to private hospitals for uncompensated care, are excluded from this figure.

Over the last few decades, both health care and educational costs have grown at paces significantly faster than general inflation, but for different reasons. The drivers of health care inflation are largely beyond the control of state and local officials, meaning that healthcare inflation is a problem for them to cope with rather than resolve. The primary driver of rising education costs has been a conscious choice to hire more staff and significantly reduce student-teacher ratios.

VII. THE TEACHER EXPLOSION

In 1970, America had nearly 46 million students in public primary and secondary schools and nearly 2.1 million public school teachers. By 2009, enrollment had grown 7 percent to 49.3 million. Over the same period, the number of teachers employed in public schools grew an astonishing 54 percent, to 3.2 million.[33] Over this period, the national pupil-teacher ratio in public schools declined from 22.3 to 15.6 (see Figure 4.2).

---

[32] Data from SLFDQS, except health benefits estimate is based on data from SLFDQS and Bureau of Labor Statistics (BLS) Employer Cost for Employee Compensation data, and vendor payments data is directly from 2008 Census of State and Local Governments. There is some overlap between the education and health spending figures, as both figures include the cost of health benefits for educational employees.

[33] Digest of Educational Statistics 2010, National Center for Education Statistics, calculations based on Tables 3 and 4. http://nces.ed.gov/programs/digest/d10/

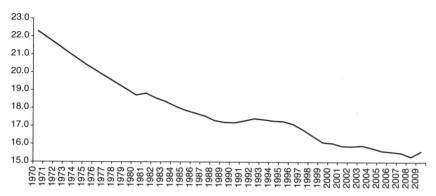

FIGURE 4.2. Graph of pupil-teacher ratios and education spending as a share of GDP over time.

Despite this increase in staffing ratios, the share of GDP that goes toward state and local expenditure on education has only increased modestly since 1977 (the earliest year for which data are available). State and local expenditure on education declined from 6.3 percent of GDP in 1977 to a trough of 5.4 percent in 1984 and has since gradually risen to 6.8 percent as of 2008.[34]

However, the modest growth in educational expenditure as a share of the economy was possible only because public school students have become a smaller share of the population. Indeed, public school enrollments declined from 1971 through 1984, when the last of the baby boomers graduated from high school. As a result, public school students made up 20 percent of the U.S. population in 1977, but just 16 percent in 2008[35]; however, the share of GDP devoted to public education expenditure increased.

The U.S. Department of Education projects that public school enrollments will continue to grow over the next ten years, but more slowly than the overall population. However, pupil-teacher ratios are projected to continue declining by another full point to 14.6 students per teacher. If state and local governments hope to continue achieving declines in student-teacher ratios, they will have to continue devoting a larger share of personal income to government educational expenditures – and find revenue sources that allow them to do so.

[34] SLFDQS.
[35] Digest of Educational Statistics 2010, and U.S. Census Bureau Population Estimates.

VIII. RISING MEDICAL COSTS

For decades, medical services have been increasing in cost at a rate greater than general inflation. Over the same period, state governments have significantly increased their commitment to spend on medical services. By far the largest of these increases has been in the Medicaid program, which pays for acute care for indigent adults and children and nursing care for people of all ages.

From 1975 to 2002, federal and state Medicaid expenditures grew by an average of 7.1 percent per year in excess of the general inflation rate. Approximately 62 percent of that increase was a result of the fact that, on average, costs per recipient rose at a rate of 3.9 percentage points higher than inflation. The remainder of the increase was a result of greater enrollment, with annual growth in recipients just over 3 percent a year (significantly faster than general population growth).[36] Since 2002, Medicaid enrollment and costs per enrollee have continued to outpace population growth and general inflation, respectively.[37]

On average, the federal government pays for 57 percent of state Medicaid expenses, with the size of the federal share varying based on a state's per capita income.[38] States with higher per capita incomes must pay for more of their own Medicaid expenses, though no state is responsible for more than 50 percent of its Medicaid costs.[39]

For 2009 and 2010, the FMAP formula used to determine state Medicaid shares was adjusted as an economic stimulus measure, with each state seeing its share of Medicaid cost responsibilities reduced by 6.2 percentage points. A smaller adjustment was also in effect for the first six months of 2011.[40] Aside from this extraordinary measure, the state share of Medicaid expenditure has generally been flat over time, meaning that as Medicaid costs have expanded, states have needed to find revenues to cover a proportionate share of those rising costs.

---

[36] http://www.cbo.gov/ftpdocs/73xx/doc7387/07-13-Medicaid.pdf

[37] http://www.kff.org/medicaid/upload/8152.pdf

[38] In general, the non-federal share of Medicaid expense is borne by state governments. However, two states (New York and North Carolina) require county governments to pay for a significant percentage of Medicaid. See http://www.empirecenter.org/pdfs/HM-01.pdf

[39] "FMAP: The Federal Share of Medicaid Costs," National Health Policy Forum, Georgetown University, 2009. http://ccf.georgetown.edu/index/cms-filesystem-action?file=research%2Fabout+medicaid%2Fbasics+fmap.pdf

[40] "Update – Extra Federal Support for Medicaid," Health Affairs Health Policy Brief, August 2010. http://www.healthaffairs.org/healthpolicybriefs/brief.php?brief_id=22

The Congressional Budget Office anticipates that Medicaid spending per beneficiary will continue to grow at a rate above GDP per capita for the foreseeable future: As of 2007, they were expecting an annual gap of 2.2 percentage points.[41] This means that both the federal and state governments will have to find additional sources of revenue to accommodate continued growth of Medicaid spending relative to the economy.

That is in addition to any growth in costs as a result of expanded enrollment. Historically, enrollment increases have been driven by expansions of eligibility. Although the 2010 health care law includes a major expansion of Medicaid eligibility for low-income adults, this will be financed almost entirely by the federal government. Upon implementation of the law in 2014, the federal government will pay 100 percent of the cost of expanded coverage, gradually declining to a permanent rate of 93 percent in 2019. As a result, states are expected only to shoulder $21 billion of the $464 billion cost of Medicaid expansion through 2019.[42] Accordingly, the main structural challenge for state budgets from Medicaid is tied to rising costs per enrollee, not new enrollment.

IX. EMPLOYEE BENEFITS

Although Medicaid costs receive a great deal of attention in Washington and in state capitals, it is worth noting that states and municipalities spend about half as much on health benefits for their own employees as they do on Medicaid – approximately 5 percent of all state and local spending. These costs, too, are rapidly expanding, with the average premium for public employee single-coverage health insurance rising nearly 160 percent from 1996 to 2009. This pace of growth has outpaced the growth of premiums in the private sector by about 20 percent.[43] State and local governments have been less effective in coping with health inflation than private employers, and therefore, their benefit loads are more affected by health care inflation.

Pension benefits also pose a significant challenge for state and local governments. A large majority of public employees receive retirement benefits through "defined benefit" pension systems in which governments

---

[41] http://www.cbo.gov/ftpdocs/89xx/doc8948/01-31-HealthTestimony.pdf
[42] Kaiser Family Foundation. http://www.kff.org/healthreform/upload/Medicaid-Coverage-and-Spending-in-Health-Reform-National-and-State-By-State-Results-for-Adults-at-or-Below-133-FPL.pdf
[43] Josh Barro, "Cadillac Coverage: The High Cost of Public Employee Health Benefits," Manhattan Institute, July 2011. http://www.manhattan-institute.org/html/cr_65.htm

make a promised, fixed payment during retirement. Governments set aside invested funds to support the promises of future pension benefits, but the risk associated with those investments is borne by taxpayers, as governments make the promised pension payments regardless of the performance of the supporting assets.

In total, pension contributions made up 3.8 percent of state and local direct expenditure as of 2008. However, a key word there is "contributions" – states and localities have no obligation under federal law to make actuarially sufficient contributions to their pension funds, and many fail to do so. It is not possible to underfund forever – a failure to make contributions today creates unfunded liabilities that must be satisfied in later years. If states and localities were complying with the recommendations of their actuaries, pension contributions would rise to 5 percent of budgets.[44]

However, that 5-percent figure represents a floor of what governments should be paying, not a ceiling. In recent years, government pension accounting standards have come under significant criticism from financial economists for allowing governments to understate their liabilities.[45] This understatement of liabilities allows governments to contribute less to their pension funds than would be required under the more conservative standards used in the private sector. If state and local governments adopted private sector-style standards, required contributions would be closer to 9 percent of budgets.[46]

It is unlikely that municipalities will adopt these accounting standards or markedly increase their contributions to pension funds. However, this does not mean that governments will not experience a growth in pension costs that outpaces revenue growth or economic growth. Inherent in the accounting standards used by governments today is an assumption that the equity-heavy portfolios in which pension fund assets are invested will continue to perform in line with their historical average. An extended period of underperformance will create growing gaps in pension funding, which will need to be closed with greater taxpayer contributions to pension funds.

---

[44] Alicia Munnell, Jean-Pierre Aubry and Laura Quinby, "The Impact of Pensions on State and Local Budgets," Center for Retirement Research at Boston College, October 2010. http://crr.bc.edu/images/stories/Briefs/slp_13.pdf

[45] Josh Barro, "Dodging the Pension Disaster," National Affairs Issue 7 (Spring 2011), pages 3–20. http://www.nationalaffairs.com/publications/detail/dodging-the-pension-disaster

[46] Munnell, Aubry, and Quinby, "The Impact of Pensions on State and Local Budgets."

In other words, pension costs are a pro-cyclical force in state and local budgets – during downturns, when the economy is weak and tax receipts anemic, pension contributions will claim a growing share of tax receipts. Conversely, when the stock market soars, required pension contributions will decline, and state and local governments will get fiscal windfalls when they are least needed. Therefore, pension systems exacerbate the fiscal risks that economic downturns pose to state and local governments.

X. ADDRESSING STRUCTURAL CHALLENGES

State and local governments face an array of structural budgetary challenges. Each of their three major tax sources is troubled: Property taxes are hemmed in by political resistance; sales taxes have insufficient bases and are increasingly volatile; and income taxes are volatile and also increasingly necessary because of the decline of property tax. Meanwhile, two of the largest state and local expenditure areas – education and health care – are experiencing cost growth faster than the economy, and public pension and health care benefits are also seeing fast rises in cost.

For the last several decades, states have sought to paper over these problems. For example, they have responded to the shrinking sales tax base by raising rates and to income tax volatility by imposing temporary taxes. Many have resorted to borrowing in order to run structural budget deficits, often by failing to make required payments into pension funds. However, the recent economic stagnation, and the havoc it has wrought on state revenues, has made these strategies untenable. In these difficult times, states and their localities need structural reforms to keep expenditures and revenues in line.

On the revenue side, state and local governments must take steps to make their tax systems more sufficient and less volatile. On the expenditure side, they should review priorities in an effort to stem cost growth in the fastest growing areas. Additionally, they should reform employee benefits to reduce both cost growth and exposure to risk from the equity markets.

XI. TAX REFORM FOR STATES

States have a number of objectives in designing their tax codes, but five principles should be key among them.

- Efficiency: Taxes should be designed to minimize distortion of economic activity. In general, this means applying low tax rates to broad tax bases.

- Equity: Taxes should be designed to treat similar taxpayers similarly ("horizontal equity") and to apply higher tax rates to taxpayers with greater ability to pay ("vertical equity").
- Sufficiency: Taxes should be designed so that, over the long term, tax receipts grow in line with the economy.
- Stability: Taxes should be designed so that tax receipts grow at a consistent rate over time, with minimal declines in recessions and spikes during economic booms.
- Simplicity: Taxes should be easy to understand and comply with.

No tax system will perform perfectly along any of these dimensions, and indeed, some are in tension with each other: An increase in tax progressivity will tend to increase equity but decrease efficiency. However, some tax systems perform better across the five dimensions than others.

The most worrying trend over the last forty years, from the perspective of ideal state and local taxation, is the decline of property tax in favor of income tax and, to a lesser extent, sales tax. Sales tax faces major challenges on all of the first four of these dimensions, especially equity and sufficiency. Income taxes face severe stability problems and, especially in states with high income tax rates, are poor performers on efficiency.

Property taxes are highly stable, more efficient than sales or income taxes,[47] and only slightly regressive.[48] Property taxes do suffer from some problems with horizontal equity – particularly, many jurisdictions tax owner-occupied homes at rates more favorable than those for rental, commercial, and industrial properties, which creates economic distortions in favor of homes and away from other kinds of real estate. The main sufficiency challenges with property taxes are political – restrictions on property tax are politically popular, leading many states to artificially restrict localities' ability to levy property tax.

The typical state would do well to buck the national aversion to property tax and to use higher property taxes to reduce the income and sales tax burdens. States should also broaden their income and especially sales tax bases. For example, states that use the federal income tax base should switch to taxing federal adjusted gross income. States and localities should add more consumer services to their sales tax bases. These base broadenings can be used to further reduce tax rates and would improve both the stability and the efficiency of sales and income taxes.

---

[47] Arnold, "Do Tax Structures Affect Aggregate Economic Growth?"
[48] ITEP, "Who Pays."

This set of tax reforms is not much different from rolling back the clock a few decades to a time when property tax rates were higher, income and sales tax rates were lower, and sales tax bases made up a larger share of the economy. In the case of state and local taxation, the way we used to do it really was better.

XII. CONTROLLING HEALTH CARE AND EDUCATION COSTS

Tax reforms that increase the stability and sufficiency of state and local revenues can make it easier for states to meet their spending needs; however, if state expenditures grow faster than the economy, such reforms will not be enough. It is important for states to manage areas of excess cost growth so they can live within their means.

In the education area, this means critically evaluating the explosion in per-pupil spending, driven by massive increases in staffing relative to student populations. Are schools really getting benefits from lower student-teacher ratios that justify the extreme costs of staffing up? States should also continue to pursue education reforms like charter schools and vouchers that allow for students to be educated by lower-cost providers than traditional public schools.

Health care cost explosions are a tougher challenge for state and local governments. Policies that impact health care inflation are largely under the purview of the federal government. However, there are two key areas where state and local lawmakers have the option to control costs.

The first includes several options to increase the supply of medical services and, therefore, drive down prices. States can give their residents access to lower-cost health care options by legalizing retail health clinics and increasing the scope of practice for nurse practitioners. These measures lower the cost of health care overall, including health care that is paid for by the government.

Additionally, states should reevaluate their choices about which health expenditures are the government's responsibility. In some states, including New York, coverage for long-term care under Medicaid has become unaffordably generous. These states should consider moves such as reducing the number of home health aide hours made available to beneficiaries and reducing reimbursement rates to nursing homes.

States and localities should also reevaluate the health benefits they offer to their own employees. As of 2009, the value of health benefits offered to state and local workers exceeded the private sector average by $800 for single coverage and $1,300 for family coverage.[49] Realigning these benefits with those offered in the private sector would save taxpayers tens of billions of dollars a year and somewhat reduce the burden of health care inflation on state budgets.

Finally, states should enact reforms that give them more control over the costs of employing workers and give municipalities similar control. Because 43 percent of state and local budgets go toward compensation,[50] an ability to manage compensation costs is essential to making ends meet. Particularly, states should remove decisions about health and pension benefits from collective bargaining, or impose restrictions on what may be bargained in these areas. Several states, including Massachusetts, New Jersey, Ohio, and Wisconsin, have enacted good reforms in this area in 2011.

The structural budgetary challenges facing states are substantial, as we have seen with the economic troubles following the 2008 real estate crash. State lawmakers will look to the federal government for help and, in some areas (particularly health care costs), an increased federal role may be the best way to overcome state-level budgeting challenges. In general, however, states have the ability to reform their tax and expenditure systems to alleviate budget gaps, if only they can summon the political will to do so.

---

[49] Barro, "Cadillac Coverage."
[50] Josh Barro, "Tools for Better Budgets: Options for State and Local Governments to Manage Employee Costs," Manhattan Institute, March 2011. http://www.manhattan-institute.org/html/ib_09.htm

PART II

The Legal and Political Context of Public Debt

5

What States Can Learn From Municipal Insolvency

CLAYTON P. GILLETTE

Any discussion of a statutory regime for restructuring state debts inevitably invites comparison to the existing scheme for managing municipal insolvency under Chapter 9 of the Bankruptcy Code.[1] This is not to say that a state bankruptcy regime would have to follow the procedures established for municipalities. One could imagine a state bankruptcy regime far different from the current form of Chapter 9, such as a minimalist regime that limited judicial intrusion or creditor intervention but gave the state substantial flexibility to impose an orderly mechanism for restructuring its debts, or a regime that covered only a subset of obligations that states incur.[2]

Nevertheless, examination of Chapter 9 should lead drafters of potential legislation governing states to avoid procedures that have proven inefficient in the municipal context and might even suggest that the entire enterprise of providing a federal scheme for state debt adjustment is misguided. That is not to say that a state bankruptcy procedure should simply reflect a "cleaned-up" version of Chapter 9. Many of the features of Chapter 9 reflect a constitutional relationship between states and their political subdivisions that is quite different from the relationship between the federal government and the states, and the relative autonomy of fiscally distressed states provides them with alternatives to bankruptcy that are less available to municipalities. This chapter explores the successes and failures of Chapter 9 and relates them to the options that states have for addressing their own insolvency.

Many thanks to the participants at the Conference on "When States Go Broke" for comments on a prior version of this paper and to Vanessa Mueller for valuable research assistance.

[1] 11 U.S.C. §§ 901ff.
[2] See e.g., Steven L. Schwarcz, "A Minimalist Approach to State 'Bankruptcy,'" 59 UCLA L. Rev. 322 (2011).

1. THE LIMITED UTILITY OF MUNICIPAL BANKRUPTCY

Unfortunately, our ability to extrapolate from municipal bankruptcy to the state setting is dramatically reduced by the infrequency with which Chapter 9 has been invoked. Omer Kimhi's exhaustive analysis indicates that between 1976 and the beginning of 2009, only about forty general-purpose municipalities filed under Chapter 9, and only about thirty filings were approved.[3] Chapter 9 is used primarily by single-purpose districts – governmental entities such as water districts or park districts that provide only one of the many services offered by general purpose municipalities. About 180 districts successfully filed for bankruptcy during the period that Kimhi studied.[4]

Additional characteristics of those municipalities that file under Chapter 9 reduce the ability to extrapolate meaningfully to the state context. The median population of those general-purpose municipalities that did file is about 1,000 residents. The precipitating cause of bankruptcy has tended not to be long-term financial difficulties that require reformation of structural fiscal arrangements but one-off events such as tort damage awards that have constituted a substantial percentage of the insolvent municipality's budget.[5] Even filings by relatively large cities such as Vallejo, California (population 120,000), do not begin to approximate state populations. Thus, the Chapter 9 experience provides little basis for estimating the efficacy of using similar procedures to resolve fiscal distress caused by endemic financial burdens in large jurisdictions that provide a broad spectrum of public goods. If the low utilization of Chapter 9 is probative of anything, its lack of use reveals the limited utility of a state bankruptcy regime insofar as it suggests that large, general-purpose jurisdictions find the process inhospitable.

Of course, the paucity of Chapter 9 cases may be attributable to other factors. First, its use may have been less necessary because municipalities have not suffered widespread fiscal distress since the enactment of Chapter 9 at the end of the Depression, although several major cities courted financial disaster during the 1970s and in the recession of the 1990s.

Second, bankruptcy, even if desirable, may be underutilized because it is unavailable to a substantial number of municipalities. The Bankruptcy

---

[3] Omer Kimhi, "Chapter 9 of the Bankruptcy Code: A Solution in Search of a Problem," 27 Yale J. Reg. 351, 359 (2010).
[4] Id.
[5] Id., at 360–361.

Code permits a municipality to take advantage of Chapter 9 only if the state of which it is a political subdivision has "specifically authorized" it to file the requisite petition for relief.[6] The standard explanation for this requirement is that it is constitutionally required to avoid federal interference with the state prerogative.[7] Only about half the states have provided the relevant authorization.[8] Many of those states that do permit their subdivisions to seek bankruptcy protection place substantial restrictions on its use. For instance, Connecticut requires a municipality to obtain the permission of the governor,[9] Michigan requires authorization from a state-appointed emergency financial manager,[10] and Louisiana requires state officials to approve both the petition for entering bankruptcy and the plan proposed for emerging from it.[11] New York grants its municipalities greater discretion over the filing decision but is clearly in the minority in doing so.[12] One state, Georgia, has expressly prohibited its municipalities from filing.[13] The reluctance of states to embrace the bankruptcy option for their political subdivisions may be related to the state's desire to retain substantial control over the fiscal affairs of its political subdivisions or may reflect an evaluation that local default will not necessarily create adverse statewide effects that offset the moral hazard associated with bankruptcy. In short, the state may consider its political subdivisions to be small enough to fail. However, failure to authorize Chapter 9 may also indicate something about states' willingness to accept a similar procedure for themselves. State refusal to allow its municipalities to take advantage of Chapter 9, that is, may indicate an institutional commitment to minimize federal intervention into nonfederal fiscal affairs, and that rationale would apply equally to state insolvency.

Alternatively, the state's refusal to authorize municipal filings, or at least to allow filing unconditionally, may reflect the view that the state itself is

---

[6] 11 U.S.C. § 109(c)(2).
[7] See e.g., In re City of Vallejo, 403 B.R. 72, 76 (Bankr. E.D. Cal. 2009).
[8] For a survey of jurisdictions, see H. Slayton Dabney, Jr. et al., *Municipalities in Peril: The ABI Guide to Chapter 9* 95–111 American Bankruptcy Institute: Alexandria (2010). Many states provide limited authorization, allowing some, but not all, political subdivisions to file.
[9] Conn. Gen. Stat. Ann. § 7–566.
[10] M.C.L.A. § 141.1523.
[11] La. Rev. Stat. Ann § 13:4741.
[12] N.Y. Local Fin. Law § 85.80 permits a municipality or its emergency financial control board to file a petition under a federal bankruptcy law without further authorization but may not do so if certain bonds of the municipality are outstanding.
[13] Ga. Code Ann. § 36–80–5.

in a better position to resolve municipal fiscal distress than a bankruptcy court. As a basic tenet of state and local government law, states have the authority to create, destroy, or alter the powers of their political subdivisions. When municipalities have suffered fiscal distress, states have used their plenary authority to provide assistance, although the form of that assistance has varied widely. I will discuss later in this chapter the implications of state assistance for creation of a counterpart for providing federal assistance to distressed states.

Third, states may reject Chapter 9 for their municipalities (or eligible municipalities may reject the bankruptcy option) on the view that the time and expense that the process requires is a game not worth the candle. That is not an implausible view. The recent bankruptcy proceedings involving Vallejo, California, required the city to spend in excess of $10.6 million in lawyers' fees alone.[14] Again, this characteristic portends limited utility for a state bankruptcy regime. Given that a state is likely to face more creditor groups than any of its local governments, states may eschew even streamlined procedures that require substantial negotiations with creditors, court appearances, and the working out of debt adjustment plans that could entail substantial expenses or impose more difficulties than they solve. At the very least, the issue of cost may constrain the scope of a statutory scheme that states may be willing to employ.

States, however, might prefer a bankruptcy alternative for themselves, even if they deny the option to their political subdivisions. I have elsewhere analyzed how municipal threats to file for bankruptcy can be used strategically to procure more favorable terms for a state bailout than would otherwise be available.[15] Local officials have a credible threat that they prefer bankruptcy because current law prohibits bankruptcy courts from interfering with the political apparatus of a bankrupt municipality, including any alteration of the locality's spending or taxing power. State bailout schemes, on the other hand, are likely to extract substantial budgetary and maybe structural authority from assisted municipalities, thus depleting the power of local officials. Local officials can use the bankruptcy threat to reduce the concessions demanded by the state for a bailout. A state may want to deny municipalities the ability to engage in such opportunistic behavior. But, as I suggest later in this chapter, a fiscally distressed state

[14] See Alison Vekshin, "Vallejo Bankruptcy Morass Spurs States to Prevent Other Filings," Bloomberg, April 27, 2011, available at http://www.bloomberg.com/news/2011-04-27/vallejo-municipal-bankruptcy-morass-prompts-u-s-states-to-prevent-filings.html.
[15] See Clayton P. Gillette, "Political Will and the Strategic Use of Municipal Bankruptcy," U. Chi. L. Rev., forthcoming, 2012.

may nevertheless desire to retain the strategic option for its own dealings with the federal government and, thus, want to preserve for itself the same bankruptcy option that it denies to its political subdivisions.

II. CRITERIA FOR ENTERING BANKRUPTCY

Evaluating the utility of state bankruptcy in light of Chapter 9 requires analysis of that statutory scheme and consideration of how analogous provisions might affect states. For those municipalities that are entitled to employ Chapter 9, the variations from the more commonly known tenets of corporate bankruptcy are substantial. Under the convenient legal fiction that a municipality holds its governmental property in trust for its constituents, creditors cannot seize the governmental assets of a municipality. They may not levy on the fire engines or the school buildings because a locality is in default. It is plausible that a municipality could be subject to a mandamus action to increase taxes or reduce services to pay creditors. For instance, during the 1970s New York City fiscal crisis, the New York Court of Appeals insisted that a legislatively enacted moratorium on payment of city debt was invalid because the state constitution mandated that municipal debts be paid, even if tax limits had to be exceeded.[16] That ruling implied that the city was obligated to increase taxes if necessary and that judicial orders to that effect could be forthcoming. However, nineteenth century and Depression experience with mandamus actions or garnishment of taxes gave little solace to creditors, as local officials tended to resign rather than comply with court orders, and courts exercised discretion to deny equitable remedies to creditors in order to preserve municipal services.[17] It remains unclear whether courts in other jurisdictions would similarly demand municipal tax increases, especially in the absence of analogous constitutional mandates given concerns for the adverse effects on municipal residents, or whether any such orders would produce net tax revenues given that mobile taxpaying firms might exit rather than pay rates that compensated creditors rather than provided services to residents. Indeed, even the New York court did not order immediate payment to creditors. Rather, the court declined to mandate immediate payment out of trepidation for subsequent "market and governmental

---

[16] See Flushing National Bank v. Municipal Assistance Corp. for the City of New York, 358 N.E.2d 848 (N.Y. 1976).
[17] Robert S. Amdursky & Clayton P. Gillette, *Municipal Debt Finance Law* 241–245 Little Brown: Boston. (1992).

disruptions." Instead, the court essentially ordered the legislature to find a means of providing payment to creditors in short order.[18] Although practical implications may insulate municipalities from mandated tax increases, states enjoy even greater immunity from creditors' efforts at redress, as the Eleventh Amendment insulates them from federal lawsuits brought by individuals to recover money.[19] Indeed, much of the early history of the Eleventh Amendment was written over the bodies of creditors who unsuccessfully sought to recover on defaulted state bonds.[20]

Most of the law dealing with municipal insolvency, therefore, concerns the adjustment of existing obligations rather than their enforcement. Chapter 9 does not provide for liquidation of the municipality or readjustment of its boundaries, regardless of how those tasks might ultimately redound to the fiscal health of residents.[21] Essentially, bankruptcy means that there is a system for the reduction of municipal debts, the rejection of onerous contracts, and the issuance of new debt to provide capital that might facilitate financial recovery. The distressed municipality itself controls a great deal of that process. The decision to deploy Chapter 9 must be voluntarily undertaken by the municipality.[22] Creditors cannot, as in the corporate setting, force a municipality into the process. The filing of such a petition stays any creditor actions against the municipality[23] and thus allows debtors to avoid the costs and disruptions that attend claims made outside of Chapter 9 or state efforts to direct municipal financial affairs. Creditors are also prohibited from proposing a plan for adjustment that might lead to emergence from bankruptcy.[24] That feature, too, lies within the exclusive domain of the municipality.

The ability to exploit these entitlements under Chapter 9 depends on qualification as a "municipality." The Bankruptcy Act defines a municipality as a "political subdivision or public agency or instrumentality of a State."[25] Not every public entity within the state will qualify. Recent

---

[18] 358 N.E.2d at 855.
[19] U.S. Const. 11th Amendment.
[20] See e.g., Principality of Monaco v. Mississippi, 292 U.S. 313 (1934); Hans v. Louisiana, 134 U.S. 1 (1890); In re Ayres, 123 U.S. 443 (1887); Louisiana v. Jumel, 107 U.S. 711 (1883).
[21] For an argument to expand the scope of municipal bankruptcy to consider these possibilities, see Michael W. McConnell and Randal C. Picker, "When Cities Go Broke: A Conceptual Introduction to Municipal Bankruptcy," 60 U. Chi. L. Rev. 425 (1993).
[22] 11 U.S.C. §§301, 303, 901(a).
[23] 11 U.S.C. §§ 362, 922. See In re Jefferson County, 2012 WL 32921 (Bkrtcy.N.D.Ala.).
[24] 11 U.S.C. § 941.
[25] 11 U.S.C. § 101(40).

decisions include pronouncements that the New York City Off-Track Betting Commission satisfied the criteria,[26] but the Las Vegas Monorail Company[27] and the Orange County Investment Pool[28] did not, although the former was a nonprofit corporation exempt from federal taxation and had issued tax-exempt bonds sponsored by the Nevada Department of Business and Industry, and the latter was a product of state statutes and an instrumentality of the county that handled investments for governmental entities. Relevant factors in qualifying as a municipality include the existence of a right to tax or exercise eminent domain, a grant of sovereign immunity by the state, the purposes of the entity, its susceptibility to state control, and the extent to which it exercises powers typically associated with governments.

Similar definitional problems are likely to affect state bankruptcy proceedings. States have created multiple public entities to implement state policies, ranging from housing authorities that provide home buyers below-market financing, to building authorities that assist states in the construction of office buildings by providing access to credit markets without implicating state constitutional debt limitations, to port and transportation authorities that provide public goods but receive funding from user fees rather than general taxes. Whether these entities would be entitled to take advantage of any debt adjustment process available to the state generally or whether their debts will be implicated by a state bankruptcy is a difficult and complicating issue that requires consideration in the formulation and use of any such statutory scheme.

Additionally, to enter bankruptcy, a municipality must be insolvent. For Chapter 9 purposes, insolvency requires that a municipality be unable currently or prospectively to pay its bills as they become due. Unfortunately, this test – which is not a prerequisite to bankruptcy filings outside of Chapter 9 – raises a variety of questions that are not easily answered. The first test, involving current nonpayment of debts, seems relatively straightforward; however, the second test looks to future capacity to pay. That necessarily raises issues of how prospective is "prospective" and what steps a municipality must take to avoid nonpayment before it can be considered insolvent. For instance, one might contend that a locality must tax to the top of its revenue hill – the point at which increases in tax rates generate

---

[26] In re New York City Off-Track Betting Corp., 427 B.R. 256, 265 (Bankr. S.D.N.Y. 2010); In re County of Orange, 183 B.R. 594 (Bankr. C.D. Cal. 1995).
[27] In re Las Vegas Monorail, 429 B.R. 770 (Bankr. Nev. 2010).
[28] In re County of Orange, 183 B.R. 594 (Bankr. C.D. Cal. 1995).

reductions in tax collections because taxpayers exit the jurisdiction – before it can be considered insolvent.[29] However, one might also contend that prospective incapacity falls short of that point if tax increases and service cuts would reduce local services to a level that an arbiter finds unacceptable, even if fiscally plausible. Ultimately, the insolvency requirement imposes on courts the obligation to make difficult determinations about a locality's prospects for meeting payments in the future as well as in the present. Wholly apart from the institutional issues related to judicial second-guessing of municipal budgets, the speculative nature of future fiscal capacity suggests that the test has limited relationship to the need for debt adjustment. To the extent that the requirement is intended to serve as a gatekeeper against frivolous filings, both market discipline and the other prerequisites to using Chapter 9 may serve as more accurate constraints. Certainly, that is likely to be the case with states, which are sufficiently dependent on access to credit markets that they would be highly unwilling to compromise outstanding indebtedness other than in the most dire of circumstances. As a consequence, the insolvency requirement is likely to be either superfluous or counterproductive in the state setting.

Judicial involvement in defining "insolvency," however, is only one manifestation of a broader issue that affects federal bankruptcy proceedings for sub-federal entities. As a doctrinal matter, Chapter 9 provides courts with very limited explicit authority in municipal bankruptcy. Section 904 expressly bars the court, without the consent of the debtor, from interfering with the political or governmental powers of the debtor municipality, any of its property or revenues, or its use or enjoyment of any income-producing properties.[30] Many commentators and courts consider this nonintervention principle to be constitutionally required.[31]

Nevertheless, there are serious practical limits to the nonintervention principle. Courts retain substantial discretion to determine whether the locality has cleared a variety of vague obstacles necessary to obtain relief under Chapter 9. As I noted, the formal doctrinal requirement that a municipality be insolvent to file a Chapter 9 petition depends significantly on judicial determinations of prospective inability to pay, which may entail implicit mandates to increase taxes or reduce services. The judicial

---

[29] See e.g., In re City of Bridgeport, 129 B.R. 332, 337 (Bankr. D. Ct. 1991); Andrew Haughwout et al., "Local Revenue Hills: Evidence from Four U.S. Cities," 86 Rev. Econ. & Stat. 570 (2006).
[30] 11 U.S.C. § 904.
[31] In re New York City Off-Track Betting Corp., 427 B.R. 256, 264 (Bankr. S.D.N.Y. 2010) (citing sources).

determination that Bridgeport failed that test meant that the city did not qualify for debt adjustment under Chapter 9.[32]

Similarly, the court must confirm the plan that the municipality proposes to exit bankruptcy, and that confirmation is contingent on satisfying a "best interest of the creditors" standard.[33] A court obviously retains substantial discretion to condition that confirmation on the inclusion of tax increases or service reductions.[34] The result is that, notwithstanding formal limitations on judicial authority, courts have the capacity in bankruptcy to do indirectly what they could not do directly. One potential failing of the municipal bankruptcy system has been the inability to wrestle directly with the implications of the indirect authority of judges, that is, whether to allow judicial intervention to be explicitly asserted or constrained. It would be difficult to fathom a state bankruptcy procedure that did not provide similar discretion to judges, unless the process entailed simply a formal mechanism by which a state was entitled to propose a plan that had to be accepted by both creditors and the courts. As a consequence, any proposed state bankruptcy systems might be assisted by a more candid and explicit understanding of the appropriate judicial role.

Finally, municipal bankruptcy law allows municipal debtors to reject executory contracts.[35] A major issue under current law involves whether such powers include the rejection of existing collective bargaining agreements, which may include the pension and benefit obligations that have proven so burdensome to both municipalities and states.[36] Although Congress enacted a provision of the Bankruptcy Code that limited the general ability of debtors to reject collective bargaining agreements, Congress did not include that provision within those sections of the Bankruptcy Code that are incorporated into Chapter 9. Congress did, however, include in Chapter 9 the relatively expansive capacity to reject contracts, which the Supreme Court had previously interpreted to include collective bargaining agreements.[37] A couple of lower courts – including a recent decision arising out of the Vallejo, California, bankruptcy – have interpreted the

---

[32] In re City of Bridgeport, 129 B.R. 332 (Bankr. D. Ct. 1991).
[33] 11 U.S.C. § 943(b)(7).
[34] See e.g., David L. Dubrow, "Chapter 9 of the Bankruptcy Code: A Viable Option for Municipalities in Fiscal Crisis?," 24 Urb. Law. 539, 582 (1992); Fano v. Newport Heights Irrigation Dist., 114 F.2d 563 (9th Cir. 1940).
[35] 11 U.S.C. §§ 365(a), 901.
[36] See Pew Center on the States, The Widening Gap: The Great Recession's Impact on State Pension and Retiree Health Costs (April 2011), available at http://www.pewcenteronthestates.org/initiatives_detail.aspx?initiativeID=85899358839.
[37] NLRB v. Bildisco & Bildisco, 465 U.S. 513 (1984).

Bankruptcy Act as permitting rejection of collective bargaining agreements in at least some circumstances,[38] but those decisions remain controversial in the absence of an authoritative statement by Congress or the Supreme Court. Any new statutory scheme that permitted state bankruptcy filings would benefit by providing an explicit answer to the issue of rejecting executory labor agreements, given the dominance of those contractual obligations in explaining current state fiscal distress.

III. ALTERNATIVES TO STATE BANKRUPTCY

State Default

Of course, the relevant question in deciding whether states can benefit from some form of federal procedure for debt restructuring is, "As compared to what?" The costs of state bankruptcy proceedings might be substantial, but they are excessive only if there exists a less burdensome alternative for resolving state fiscal distress. Some historical perspective is useful here, insofar as it reveals how states have addressed fiscal difficulties both for themselves and for their political subdivisions in the absence of a bankruptcy regime. As I will develop, the immunities that states enjoy essentially allow them to structure debt adjustment outside of bankruptcy, though often at a cost that suggests a formal bankruptcy alternative may be preferable.

The historical perspective also makes clear that the availability of a bankruptcy regime does not necessarily mean that a state will take advantage of it (assuming that, as in the case of municipalities under Chapter 9, states would have sole discretion over the decision to take advantage of the federal scheme). States have, in the past, demonstrated a capacity to exploit various strategies to shift the risk of imprudently incurred debt from residents of a besieged locality to its creditors. During nineteenth-century financial crises, municipalities frequently sought to avoid debt obligations, either by seeking judicial declarations that bonds were invalid or by enlisting the state's assistance in more circuitous avenues for repudiation. Declarations of invalidity were frequently employed to reject claims against municipalities for payment of railroad aid bonds that had been issued to provide financing for promoters who promised that commercial benefits generated by railroad development would render payment of

---

[38] See In re City of Vallejo, 432 B.R. 262, 270 (E.D. Cal. 2010); In re County of Orange, 179 B.R. 177 (Bankr. C.D. Cal. 1995).

the debts painless.[39] Eric Monkkonen's history of debt during the period leads him to the conclusion that "state and local governments frequently colluded against the debt holders' interests."[40] State officials did not refuse bailouts to impose fiscal discipline on their cities; they did so because they were able to impose losses on bondholders with relative impunity, compared to what they might suffer at the hands of the electorate if they used state funds to rescue profligate local officials.

Perhaps the high point of state intervention to shift risks ex post occurred in the late 1870s. In 1859, the city of Mobile, Alabama, had issued bonds secured by a special tax to be imposed on the good residents of that city. Just after the bonds became due, the Alabama Legislature, in its infinite wisdom, enacted two pieces of legislation. First, it dissolved the City of Mobile, the nominal issuer of the debt. Second, it created a new municipality with the oddly similar name of Port of Mobile. The latter contained about 95 percent of the taxable property of the now defunct City of Mobile and about 14/15s of its residents. When holders of the bonds issued by the City of Mobile sought to require Port of Mobile officials to impose the special tax that secured the obligations, they were informed that the Port of Mobile owed no such debt and the nominal debtor, the city of Mobile, no longer existed. Maybe it was the unfortunate resemblance of the relevant localities' names, but the U.S. Supreme Court saw right through their scheme. In *Port of Mobile v. Watson*,[41] the Court declared the Port of Mobile to be the legal successor to the City of Mobile and to be liable for its debts.

Other joint efforts between cities and their states proved more successful, leading Monkkonen to conclude, for instance, that "the city of Duluth and the Minnesota state legislature used legal maneuvers to cheat the city's bondholders of the early 1870s out of any hope of full debt recovery."[42] Even where states have not explicitly assisted local debt avoidance, they have frequently stood by while municipalities sought to shift losses to creditors. When the Washington Public Power Supply System, or WPPSS, triggered what was then the largest-ever default on municipal bonds in the 1980s, the states that were involved did not discourage the ultimately successful effort to have the contractual obligations that served as security for

[39] Amdursky & Gillette, supra note 17, at 90–96.
[40] Eric Monkkonen, *The Local State: Public Money and American Cities* 110 Stanford University Press: Stanford. (1995). See Alberta M. Sbragia, *Debt Wish* 50–61 University of Pittsburgh Press: Pittsburgh (1996).
[41] 116 U.S. 289 (1886).
[42] Monkkonen, supra note 27, at 24.

the bonds invalidated on the grounds that they were outside the authority of the municipalities that had entered into them.[43]

States in the nineteenth century engaged in equally blatant acts of interference with creditors' bargains on their own behalf. States either fully repudiated debts or, more frequently, passed legislation altering the terms or limiting the sources of payment for outstanding debts. Louisiana reduced interest rates on outstanding bonds, notwithstanding that it had explicitly agreed when the bonds were issued that a specific tax was dedicated to their payment, that a contract with bondholders was intended, and that it would be a felony for a state officer to use the designated tax proceeds for any purpose other than paying principal and interest on the bonds.[44] Bondholders became sufficiently exasperated that they were able to induce legislatures in New Hampshire and New York to enact legislation allowing their citizens to assign claims on repudiated bonds to those states and, thus, authorize them to bring a lawsuit against the defaulting jurisdiction in federal court. Ultimately, the Supreme Court determined that these acts constituted ineffective schemes to circumvent the debtor state's Eleventh Amendment immunity.[45]

Some instances of repudiation involved largely a political agenda, such as arguments in southern states that post-Civil War debts had been imposed by the "conquering" government.[46] However, repudiation was also used in the face of general fiscal distress, such as in Michigan, where the failure of a bank involved in a sale of state bonds prior to the payment of bond proceeds into the state treasury caused a fiscal crisis that precluded full payment of principal and interest on the debt,[47] and Minnesota, where the constitution was amended to prohibit the legislature from levying a tax to pay previously issued railroad aid bonds – an act invalidated some 21 years later.[48] States gave various justifications for their rejection of creditors' claims: The issuance of the debt was unauthorized (the railroad aid bond cases); the law providing authorization was unconstitutional;

---

[43] See e.g., Chemical Bank v. Washington Pub. Power Supply Sys., 666 P.2d 329 (1983). Of course, the municipalities in those cases had strong positions on the underlying law. Perhaps one should interpret the state's nonintervention as respectful of the cities' legal position.

[44] Louisiana v. Jumel, 107 U.S. 711 (1883).

[45] New Hampshire v. Louisiana, 108 U.S. 76 (1883).

[46] B. U. Ratchford, *American State Debts*, 204 Duke University Press: Durham (1941, 1966).

[47] William A. Scott, *The Repudiation of State Debts*, 161–164 Thomas Y. Crowell: New York. (1893).

[48] Id. at 152–161; Ratchford, supra note 45, at 230–232.

officials had failed to comply with the laws authorizing issuance of the bonds.[49] Where authority existed, however, these revisions of bond terms and statutory prohibitions on payment constituted clear violations of the Contracts Clause of the federal Constitution. The states' immunity under the Eleventh Amendment, however, made declarations of unconstitutionality superfluous, as creditors had little recourse for recovery from a recalcitrant state treasury.

More recent developments suggest a mixed reaction to states that intervene to avoid their own debts or those of their political subdivisions. States that seek some accommodation with creditors may find both solace and frustration in the Depression-era cases in which states, perhaps less blatantly contemptuous of the claims of creditors than in the nineteenth century, sought to compromise outstanding obligations in the face of genuine fiscal incapacity. In a case involving New Jersey's effort to adjust the debt of the City of Asbury Park, the Supreme Court validated an extension of maturity and amendment of payment terms over the objection of minority creditors, who asserted that the moratorium violated the Contracts Clause.[50] This time the Court applied a pragmatic construction to that clause. In a bit of judicial legerdemain, Justice Frankfurter concluded that the positive opportunity for repayment under the new terms could not be said to impair an obligation that was, as a practical matter, worthless as a result of judicial reluctance to grant writs of mandamus requiring the collection of taxes necessary to pay debts and the practice of tax collectors of resigning rather than complying with such orders.[51] Perhaps the Court's optimism was well founded, as the Court noted that the market value of the bonds in question had actually increased after the composition plan had been enacted. The result is that states may retain some flexibility to impair obligations, even outside a formal bankruptcy procedure, without running afoul of constitutional prohibitions. Thus, under the ruling in *Faitoute*, states might be able to impose on creditors the type of debt adjustment that they could procure within a bankruptcy process. Although one might fear that a state would be overly restrictive in mandating adjustments, the constraint of a need to return to bond markets could serve to counter tendencies to limit bondholder recoveries.

Congress, however, has subsequently overridden the direct result of *Faitoute* by providing in the Bankruptcy Act that a state may not prescribe

---

[49] Amdursky & Gillette, supra note 17, at 90–96; Scott, supra note 47, at 201–210.
[50] Faitoute Iron & Steel Co. v. Asbury Park, 316 U.S. 502 (1942).
[51] See Amdursky & Gillette, supra note 17, at 273–274.

a method of composition of municipal indebtedness that binds nonconsenting creditors.[52] That restriction may itself be suspect as a direct regulation of the states.[53] However, the reasoning of *Faitoute* in allowing states in dire circumstances to compromise debts may have some staying power in the event that Congress removed the statutory prohibition, even if it did not enact a complete formal state bankruptcy regime.[54] Indeed, the repeal of that prohibition may be sufficient to induce states and creditors to reach accommodations without the costs that attend a Chapter 9-like process.

Even without the legal authority to compromise debts, states might simply create what amounts to a functional equivalent by committing a partial or full default and, thus, unilaterally adjust debts without the intervention of a formal bankruptcy process. The state's capacity to impose adjustments by selectively paying only some creditors emanates primarily from the difficulty aggrieved creditors would have in securing recovery. The Eleventh Amendment denies creditors the ability to recover money from the state in federal court, regardless of whether the action is brought against the state or individual officers of the state, as long as the state is the real party in interest.[55] That proposition holds true even if the state's failure to pay is based on an allegedly unconstitutional state statute, such as one that allegedly violates the Contracts Clause.

Some Depression-era cases suggest possible inroads on Eleventh Amendment immunity. After Arkansas enacted a statute diverting designated revenues that had been pledged to the payment of certain bonds, a federal district court enjoined the state treasurer of Arkansas from disbursing the proceeds of those fees and taxes other than in accordance with the bond contract.[56] A statute requiring an alternative disposition of the proceeds was void as an unconstitutional impairment of the obligation of contract.[57] Whether such a holding would survive more contemporary readings of the Eleventh Amendment that cast a broad net of immunity

---

[52] 11 U.S.C. § 903(1).
[53] See McConnell & Picker, supra note 21, at 454 n. 127.
[54] Id. at 479–481.
[55] See Barry v. Fordice, 814 F. Supp. 511, 513–14 (S.D. Miss. 1992), aff'd, 8 F.3d 1 (5th Cir. 1993) (collecting cases).
[56] Hubbell v. Leonard, 6 F. Supp. 145 (E.D. Ark. 1934). Indeed, it is questionable whether the decision was correct at the time, given potential conflict with prior Supreme Court constructions of state immunity in which the state had enacted an allegedly unconstitutional statute, such as in Louisiana v. Jumel, 107 U.S. 711 (1883).
[57] 6 F. Supp. at 151.

against actions, including those seeking equitable relief, that implicate the state treasury remains to be seen.[58]

Post-default, bondholder recourse in state courts is a more complicated issue, contingent on the vagaries of state law. The Mississippi Supreme Court has concluded that the state's mere act of entering into a contract, such as by the issuance of bonds, constitutes a waiver of immunity from suit in state court for a breach of that contract, although it does not appear that the waiver applies equally to Eleventh Amendment immunity.[59] Many other state courts have reached the same conclusion[60]; however, other states appear to be less generous. The Arkansas constitution, for instance, preserves the state's immunity in the state courts, although the legislature has created a claims commission to pay legal debts of the state.[61] Other states, such as Connecticut, appear ambivalent on the issue, making waivers of immunity dependent on the language of individual statutes authorizing the underlying contracts.[62]

Even where the state has subjected itself to suit in its own courts, creditors' capacity to enforce a judgment remains precarious. Again, federal courts are likely to be unhelpful. Mandamus to require a state official to pay funds out of the state treasury is no more justiciable in federal court than is an action against the state to establish a breach.[63] Sale of pledged state assets that secured bonds might not constitute an action against the state if the pledgee has possession of the property so that no action against the state/pledger is necessary to foreclose on the pledge[64]; however, states tend not to deliver possession of their property as collateral.

Again, the cases arising out of municipal defaults are instructive about the possible consequences of efforts to enforce obligations after a state default. Those cases suggest that enforcement is again contingent on particular statutes and judicial willingness to disadvantage residents for the

---

[58] See e.g., Pennhurst State School & Hospital v. Halderman, 465 U.S. 89, 100–101 (1984); Cory v. White, 457 U.S. 85, 90–91 (1982); Edelman v. Jordan, 415 U.S. 651, 661–669 (1974); Parden v. Terminal Ry., 377 U.S. 184, 187 (1963).
[59] Grant v. Mississippi, 686 So.2d 1078, 1091–92 (Miss. 1996).
[60] See e.g., George & Lynch, Inc. v. State, 57 Del. 158, 197 A.2d 734 (1964); Pan-Am Tobacco Corp. v. Dep't of Corr., 471 So. 2d 4, 5 (Fla. 1984); Grant Const. Co. v. Burns, 92 Idaho 408, 443 P.2d 1005 (1968).
[61] Ark. Consti. Art. 5, § 20; Ark.Code Ann. § 19-10-201; Drake v. Smith, 390 A.2d 541, 546 (Me. 1978).
[62] See Conn. Gen. Stat. § 3–20a(c); 184 Windsor Ave., LLC v. State, 274 Conn. 302, 875 A.2d 498 (2005); Withers v. Univ. of Kentucky, 939 S.W.2d 340 (Ky. 1997).
[63] Louisiana v. Jumel, 107 U.S. 711 (1883).
[64] Christian v. Atlantic and North Carolina R.R. Co., 133 U.S. 233, 241–242 (1890).

benefit of creditors in a time of fiscal distress. Courts have been unwilling to mandate payments on municipal debt that would interfere with the "essential functions" of the issuer.[65] Alternatively, courts have structured the terms of the writ to protect the issuer's financial viability.[66] Payment of judgments may be subject to legislative appropriation, although some state constitutions include special protections for holders of state bonds. Georgia's constitution, for instance, requires taxation and appropriation of amounts necessary to pay outstanding general obligation bonds and requires the state fiscal officer to cure any deficiency in the sinking fund for such bonds by setting aside the first revenues thereafter received in the state's general fund.[67] Maryland requires that any debt be accompanied by a tax sufficient to pay principal and interest and prohibits the repeal of such tax or the diversion of its proceeds to other purposes until the debt has been discharged.[68] Minnesota requires the state auditor to levy an annual tax sufficient to pay principal and interest on faith and credit bonds of the state that come due in the "ensuing year and to and including July 1 of the second ensuing year."[69] However, the protections that mandate collection of funds sufficient to pay debt service are not self-executing. There remains a question of whether a state court exercising equitable powers during a time of extreme fiscal need would mandate the payment of the funds to bondholders.

I do not mean by that statement to assume that courts will necessarily be reluctant to enforce the creditors' bargain. As I indicated, the New York Court of Appeals famously invalidated the New York legislature's efforts to assist New York City by adjusting the terms of certain New York City debt in 1975.[70] Even as it carefully elided any federal constitutional issue, the court ultimately invalidated the effort to transform the city's short-term obligations – those that fell due within a year of issuance – into three-year obligations. The court determined that the legislation violated state constitutional requirements that required payment of the city's general obligations, even if tax limits had to be exceeded. The city's pledge of its faith and credit to the notes was not, in the court's view, a "best efforts" clause to be overridden by claims of fiscal distress. Rather, it was, in the court's

---

[65] See e.g., Defoe v. Town of Rutherfordton, 122 F.2d 342, 344 (4th Cir. 1941).
[66] See e.g., East St. Louis v. United States ex rel. Amy, 120 U.S. 600 (1887); Borough of Fort Lee v. United States ex rel. Barker, 104 F.2d 275 (3d Cir. 1939).
[67] See Ga. Consti. Art. VII, § 4, par. 3.
[68] Md. Consti. Art. III, § 34.
[69] Minn. Consti. Art. XI, § 7.
[70] Flushing National Bank v. Municipal Assistance Corp., 358 N.E.2d 848 (N.Y. 1977).

words, "both a commitment to pay and a commitment of the city's revenue generating powers to produce the funds to pay." New York's constitution does not contain an identical mandate with respect to state bonds; however, it does require the state comptroller to pay principal and interest on bonds from revenues applicable to the general fund of the state without a specific appropriation should the legislature fail to appropriate funds for debt service,[71] and one would imagine that courts following the *Flushing National Bank* rationale would find a similar mandate to pay debts in such a provision, notwithstanding state fiscal distress.

All this suggests that, bankruptcy aside, states are likely to employ the default option in a manner that balances the interests of both residents and creditors. A state's willingness to use default to sacrifice the interests of creditors is constrained by its need to return to bond markets as well as by legal principles. Unlike nineteenth-century state interventions such as the Port of Mobile situation, the New York legislature was not attempting to save the city from suffering any harm by shifting losses to creditors. To the contrary, the Moratorium Act followed the imposition of serious constraints on New York City's political and budgetary processes and was arguably enacted largely to demonstrate to Washington that any federal bailout would not displace the penalties that the city would suffer in the debt markets subsequent to a default. At the same time, even courts sympathetic to the need to satisfy obligations will not necessarily uphold the creditors' bargain at all costs. Although the Court of Appeals in *Flushing* purported to demand that the city pay its debts, the court carefully constructed its remedy to avoid dire consequences. It concluded,

> in order to minimize market and governmental disruptions which might ensue it would be injudicious at this time to allow the extraordinary remedies in the nature of injunction and peremptory mandamus sought by plaintiff. Plaintiff and other noteholders of the city are entitled to some judicial relief free of throttling by the moratorium statute, but they are not entitled immediately to extraordinary or any particular judicial measures unnecessarily disruptive of the city's delicate financial and economic balance.[72]

In effect, the court was imposing less on the city than on the legislature to work out an accommodation that would satisfy creditors who now held a transferable entitlement (to receive payment) that had been assumed previously by the state and the city (to avoid payment). Thus, the court was

---

[71] N.Y. Consti. Art. 7, § 16.
[72] 358 N.E.2d at 855.

essentially authorizing, under state law, a state debt adjustment plan with the caveat that it required more consent of creditors than might be necessary under the cramdown provisions of a bankruptcy regime.

The current legal regime, therefore, indicates that, although states may be able to fashion the equivalent of a bankruptcy regime outside of a formal process, doing so is likely to engender substantial costs. The negative consequences for repudiating states do not necessarily entail being completely shut out of the bond markets. Indeed, the nineteenth-century bonds on which Louisiana's post-issuance alteration of terms led to the Supreme Court decision upholding the state's immunity had themselves been issued to exchange an earlier issue at a compromised rate.[73] The latter series of bonds had nevertheless been accepted by bondholders (who may have come to regret their decision after the state's default). Accounts of more recent acts of state repudiation suggest that the primary financial effects involve substantial litigation and negotiations between the state and its creditors to work out mutually acceptable arrangements in the face of competing fiscal and political demands rather than an absolute inability to reenter the bond markets. One might expect that prolonged litigation on defaulted bonds, and its attendant costs, would predominate even more in an age in which vulture funds specialize in purchasing defaulted sovereign debt at substantial discounts and seeking recovery in multiple forums.[74] Indeed, the saga of nineteenth-century state repudiation has continued through litigation in which holders of bonds on which Mississippi defaulted in the 1840s and 1850s have sought redress in both federal and state court as late as the 1990s.[75]

These costs suggest that states might prefer a formal bankruptcy process that permits debt adjustment without the attendant litigation and negotiation costs that are inevitable outside that process. Again, it is not clear that a state version of Chapter 9 would provide that process, as municipal bankruptcy entails its own unwieldy costs, evident in Vallejo's experience. However, a state bankruptcy need not mimic those provisions. Instead, state bankruptcy might provide a more orderly process of bringing all creditors to the table simultaneously and thus authorizing a more systematic, structured adjustment of debts and rejection of burdensome contracts than is attainable through the process of selective default by the state and

---

[73] Louisiana v. Jumel, 107 U.S. 711 (1883).
[74] See e.g., NML Capital v. Republic of Argentina, 2009 WL 721736 (S.D.N.Y.).
[75] Barry v. Fordice, 814 F. Supp. 511 (S.D. Miss. 1992), aff'd, 8 F.3d 1 (5th Cir. 1993); Grant v. Mississippi, 686 So.2d 1078 (Miss. 1996).

uncertain enforcement by courts with substantial discretion. A process that limited the administrative costs of orderly disposition of claims, therefore, might allow the state to provide both stability for bondholders and opportunities for recovery from fiscal distress through a means that can now only be approximated through indirection.

Federal Bailout

Federal bailouts that would enable a fiscally distressed state to meet its obligations constitute the opposite pole from default or state-controlled "bankruptcy." Although bailouts may take a variety of forms – from grants to loans to advances of future intergovernmental transfers – and may involve stringent or lenient conditions, I will treat them as monolithic. Here, too, the experience of municipalities provides some guidance. Historically, municipalities in financial difficulty have been able to obtain aid from the state, at least where the consequences of local distress threaten to spill over to other municipalities or to the state itself. The difficulty attached to bailouts lies in the moral hazard that they entail. Ideally, the rescuing jurisdiction will seek, ex ante, to minimize the risk that its political subdivisions will need to avail themselves of financial assistance and, ex post, to inflict sufficient pain on profligate jurisdictions and their officials to discourage requests for aid in all but the most extreme circumstances.[76]

The constitutional relationship between states and their political subdivisions makes the ability to satisfy those conditions much easier than is the case when those same states require federal assistance. The constitutional structure of states generally allows them to exercise plenary power over their municipalities, subject to state constitutional restraints on municipal authority.[77] State constitutions, at least as a formal matter, tend to reduce the risk of municipal fiscal distress by restricting the borrowing and spending capacities of their municipalities. Debt limitations have been largely honored in the breach[78] and arguably fail to reflect a realistic relationship between debt capacity and capital needs. Nevertheless,

---

[76] See e.g., Robert P. Inman, "Transfers and Bailouts: Enforcing Local Fiscal Discipline with Lessons from U.S. Federalism," in Jonathan Rodden et al., *Fiscal Decentralization and the Challenge of Hard Budget Constraints* 35, 59–60 MIT Press: Cambridge. (2003).

[77] See Lynn A. Baker and Clayton P. Gillette, *Local Government Law* 237–250 Thomson Reuters/Foundation Press: New York. (4th ed. 2010).

[78] See e.g., Richard Briffault, "The Disfavored Constitution: State Fiscal Limits and State Constitutional Law," 34 Rutgers L.J. 907 (2003); Amdursky & Gillette, supra note 17, at 159–221; Robert H. Bowmar, "The Anachronism Called Debt Limitation," 52 Iowa L. Rev. 863 (1967).

they provide at least some check on municipal fiscal recklessness. Municipalities may also be subject to balanced-budget requirements and spending limitations that purport to impose a degree of fiscal discipline, notwithstanding the capacity of municipal officials to circumvent constitutional or statutory requirements with off-budget expenditures or other forms of fiscal illusion.[79]

Perhaps most importantly, once a locality approaches the precipice of fiscal distress, the state is entitled to take over its governance and displace its elected officials. The plenary authority of states allows them to create, abolish, or alter the governance structure of their political subdivisions. This scope of control permits the state to extract a significant price from its localities that require a bailout. When political subdivisions enter fiscal distress, states can essentially place them into receivership, eliminate democratically elected governments, and replace them with appointed oversight or financial control boards that have substantial authority over budgeting, expenditure, and revenue raising. During the past forty years, since the fiscal crisis that led to the imposition of financial control boards in New York and Cleveland, state-imposed financial control boards have displaced substantial functions of elected local governments in Erie County, New York; Nassau County, New York; Benton Harbor, Michigan; Chelsea, Massachusetts; the Chicago School Board; Philadelphia; and Washington, D.C. The authority that these boards exercise ranges from approval of local budgets to actual involvement in drafting the budget. Many states allow the board to issue debt secured by dedicated revenues of the rescued jurisdiction that has priority over other debt of the municipality secured by general revenues. Some allow the board to reject existing contracts, including collective bargaining agreements.[80] Perhaps most importantly, boards can restructure outstanding debt through a combination of negotiation and issuance of new debt with longer duration.[81] States may also have the capacity to recoup any funds provided in a bailout in relatively short order, thus further reducing the incentives of municipal officials to exploit state largesse without necessity. For instance, Virginia allows the state to provide funds in the event of a

---

[79] See e.g., M. David Gelfand, "Seeking Local Government Integrity Through Debt Ceilings, Tax Limitations, and Expenditure Limits: The New York City Fiscal Crisis, the Taxpayers' Revolt, and Beyond," 63 Minn. L. Rev. 545 (1978).
[80] See e.g., M.C.L.A. § 141.1519(1)(k).
[81] See Actions Taken by Five Cities to Restore Their Financial Health, Hearing Before the Subcommittee on the District of Columbia of the Committee on Government Reform and Oversight, House of Representatives, 104th Cong., 1st Sess. (1995).

threatened municipal default but requires that local aid be withheld from the locality until the state has been repaid.[82]

The federal government's capacity to enlist either ex ante or ex post measures or incentives to deal with moral hazard in a proposed bailout of states is much more restricted. Although state constitutional limitations on state debt and expenditures are as notoriously porous as those placed on municipalities, they impose at least some self-imposed fiscal discipline. However, the federal government retains no control over state fiscal policies that might increase the potential for federal intervention. Indeed, to the extent that the federal government reduces interest rates for state borrowing by exempting the interest on sub-federal governmental bonds from taxation, the federal government arguably increases the risk of bailout by inducing more borrowing than would otherwise occur.

That raises the issue of whether the federal government ought, as the price of a bailout, to be entitled to exercise authority over state fiscal affairs analogous to the authority that states exercise over their distressed municipalities. Even ex post, federalism concerns would complicate any effort by the federal government to regulate state fiscal conduct. It is, for instance, difficult to conceive of the federal government appointing a financial control board that exercised authority over California tax and expenditure policies or had the capacity to reject or approve public contracts, much as we might like to see one.

Nevertheless, extracting from the states some relinquishment of fiscal control as a price of federal bailouts may not be so far-fetched, or at least so unconnected from federal interests that such a strategy should trigger fatal federalism concerns or designate federal control an unconstitutional condition of providing aid. Presumably, the federal government would provide a bailout only at the request of the state and only because the consequences of a threatened state default included a substantial risk of contagion to other states or to the federal government. In an ideal world, credit markets would distinguish perfectly between distressed and non-distressed jurisdictions. In reality, however, markets may treat one state's fiscal distress as indicative of difficulties in at least some other jurisdictions. In addition, the default of a state could adversely affect financial institutions that were substantial creditors of that state and, thus, create instability in financial markets far beyond the state and municipal market. In short, any federal intervention is likely to be predicated on an understanding that fiscal federalism can generate perils by allowing decentralized entities to impose

[82] Va. Code Ann. § 15.2-2659.

negative effects on other jurisdictions and on the federal government, in addition to generating the benefits of inspiring inter-jurisdictional competition, inducing officials to deliver services more efficiently to minimize exit of net tax payers, and allowing preference satisfaction.[83] If these more negative effects warranted federal intervention, then it is difficult to contend that the invocation of federalism should be sufficient to prevent the demand of substantial federal control over the state policies that generated the need for federal intervention in the first instance.

One might conclude that the concurrent availability of bankruptcy and bailout provides states with an optimal choice for resolving fiscal distress and would induce states to select whichever regime optimally advanced social interests. States that believed they are best positioned to adjust debts in a manner that minimally impinged on the provision of state services and access to credit markets could select the bankruptcy/default route, whereas states that feared more dire consequences from default could bargain instead with the federal government on the terms of a bailout.

What is optimal from the state's perspective, however, is not necessarily ideal from the broader social perspective, and the choice between bailouts and bankruptcy could affect the terms of each to federal detriment. If bailouts with teeth were desirable to address the moral hazard issue, then the concurrent availability of state bankruptcy could be problematic. States would presumably prefer bailouts with weak conditions to bailout with strong conditions. In the presence of a federally authorized formal state bankruptcy regime, however, the very decision of the federal government to provide a bailout would necessarily reflect the decision that, from the federal perspective, bailout was preferable to bankruptcy. That is, the federal government could plausibly determine that default and adjustment in bankruptcy could impose spillovers that exceeded the costs associated with a federal bailout. If the state has control over the decision to take advantage of the bankruptcy option, it has a strategic advantage over the federal government in that it can threaten to exercise the less preferable (from the federal perspective) bankruptcy rather than accept the strong conditions of a federal bailout. This would induce the federal government

---

[83] See Jonathan A. Rodden, *Hamilton's Paradox* Cambridge University Press: Cambridge. (2006); Erik Wibbels, *Federalism and the Market* Cambridge University Press: Cambridge (2005); Daniel Treisman, *The Architecture of Government: Rethinking Political Decentralization* Cambridge University Press: Cambridge. (2007); Erik Wibbels, "Federalism and the Politics of Macroeconomic Policy and Performance," 44 Am. J. Pol. Sci. 687 (2000).

to reduce the conditions to induce the state to eschew bankruptcy and instead impose only weak bailout conditions.[84]

The possibility that states would use the threat of an undesirable bankruptcy to reduce the conditions of a bailout suggests reason to be dubious of making these potential means of addressing state fiscal distress available simultaneously. The federal government cannot and probably should not attempt to pre-commit against ever providing a bailout of a distressed state. Thus, the risk of strategic uses of bankruptcy should be considered in deciding the propriety or at least the conditions for allowing states to employ a statutory process for debt adjustment. Of course, in the absence of a formal bankruptcy regime, states might exploit the same strategic advantage against harsh bailout conditions simply by threatening to default. However, the same costs of default outside of bankruptcy that allegedly warrant creation of a formal debt adjustment process may also reduce the credibility of strategic threats to default. In that event, the very cost-reducing strength of formal state bankruptcy becomes a weakness insofar as it facilitates state avoidance of the kinds of conditions that might make bailout palatable.

CONCLUSION

The current fiscal distress of states bears at least some family resemblance to the distress that cities have suffered in both recent and distant history. The solutions that have been offered for cities provide some evidence about the utility of various bankruptcy and bailout regimes for the states, notwithstanding the different legal status that states enjoy relative to their political subdivisions. The history of municipal distress, however, does not necessarily provide a road map for states and, in some sense, may provide a negative road map, that is, an indication of what should not be done. That, of course, does not mean that the strategies employed to assist fiscally distressed municipalities do not translate at all to the state context. Rather, it means that ways in which those strategies have been utilized should be analyzed carefully, both to consider whether they have helped to resolve existing fiscal distress and to inhibit its recurrence. Strategies for aiding insolvent states may provide a structured and relatively costless mechanism for adjusting debts. However, they may also be used to insulate the state from ameliBoratives that appear harsher but also provide a

---

[84] For further development of the strategic use of bankruptcy by municipalities against the state and the federal government, see Gillette, supra note 15.

superior means of discouraging excessive debt and the imposition of costs on less profligate jurisdictions. The lesson to be learned from the history of municipal fiscal distress is that proposed solutions are often affected by political demands, legal entitlements, market constraints, and judicial discretion. Any proposal that purports to resolve the problems that distressed states face must consider those implications rather than assume that the imposition of a statutory regime will provide a panacea.

6

Market Discipline and U.S. Federalism

JONATHAN RODDEN

INTRODUCTION

Like each of the last fiscal contractions, the Great Recession has brought some underlying structural deficiencies of American federalism to the surface. As the U.S. states struggle with unprecedented debt burdens and unfunded liabilities, the policy community seems to have entered another of its periodic reflections aimed at "rethinking" or "reinventing" American fiscal federalism.

Today's juncture for American federalism seems especially crucial for several reasons. First, the depth of the unfunded pension problem is becoming clearer to elites and the general public. Second, the unsustainable fiscal paths of large and important states like California and Illinois have generated a perception that a wave of public sector defaults is on the horizon. Third, recent events in the European Union (EU), combined with rescues of large American financial and automobile firms, have raised the specter of another round of costly public sector bailouts that would permanently change the basic structure of American federalism.

Deep concern about the future of U.S. federalism is warranted. However, as scholars begin thinking about reform options, it is important to get a clear diagnosis of the problem. It is also important to understand what works relatively well in the United States in broad comparative perspective.

After all, the challenge of managing fiscal policy in a multilayered federation is not unique to the United States in the early twenty-first century. In fact, it was the subject of debate among the framers of the U.S. Constitution, and it has presented serious challenges in contexts as diverse as the nineteenth-century United States, late twentieth-century Latin America, and of course, the European Monetary Union (EMU) in the twenty-first century.

This chapter focuses on the problem of fiscal discipline and provides a broad overview of the options for the future of U.S. fiscal federalism. It draws a contrast between market-based and hierarchical solutions and argues for a reform agenda that bolsters the former.

Underlying all federal fiscal systems is a basic moral hazard problem. When the central and lower-level governments both have authority to tax and spend, individual lower-level governments can harbor the belief that unsustainable fiscal burdens will ultimately be borne by other members of the federation through bailouts. Like a child with a credit card, lower-level governments can borrow unsustainably based on the implicit guarantee of the higher-level parent.

In both families and federations, there are two very different ways to solve this problem. The most obvious is to take away the credit card or to put a strict credit limit into place. Limit the access of lower-level governments to all forms of borrowing, federalize some of the unsustainable obligations, and use the deeper pockets of the central government to help arrange credit for infrastructure and to help manage the business cycle. Demonstrating a prescient understanding of the moral hazard problem, Alexander Hamilton favored this centralized, hierarchical solution.

In fact, Hamilton's assumption of Revolutionary War Debt was the first of many attempts to use a debt controversy as an opportunity to centralize fiscal authority. Debt assumptions and conditional bailouts in the wake of debt crises have been crucial centralizing moments in the history of the Argentine, Brazilian, Mexican, and German federations, among others. The most ardent European centralizers view the current crisis as a unique opportunity to create an integrated European fiscal system. In the United States as well, the current fiscal crisis might be viewed as an opportunity to finally complete a project of centralization that started in the 1930s.

However, there is another way to solve the moral hazard problem. In families, a child can transition to adulthood and borrow based on his own income as the parents send a clear message that they will not assume debts in the future. In federations, if the central government can commit not to intervene in the fiscal affairs of lower-level governments, the latter can approach credit markets as miniature sovereigns. Ideally, creditors would assess their creditworthiness without assuming an implicit central guarantee, and local fiscal decisions would be governed by market discipline rather than hierarchical administrative controls.

This solution to the moral hazard problem, however, is only as good as the central government's commitment not to bail out the lower-level governments. Looking across the Atlantic at the European crisis, or closer to home at General Motors and Bear Stearns, the "no bailout" commitment of the federal government would appear to be completely lacking in credibility. The idea of market discipline in federations has fallen on hard times.

Nevertheless, this chapter will go against the grain of current policy discourse and argue that in contrast to many other federations, market discipline has worked well in the United States for more than a century, and although it is currently being challenged as never before, it can be maintained. As we consider short- and long-term policy reforms, including something like the introduction of state-level bankruptcy procedures, we should do so with the goal of shoring up rather than dismantling the nineteenth-century edifice of market discipline.

I will argue that a hierarchical system of top-down regulation is unlikely to work well in the United States, and in spite of first-glance appearances, the state governments and their creditors and voters are not currently behaving as if they expect large-scale federal interventions in the future. On the contrary, leaders in many states have made more progress than the federal government in making hard choices to achieve long-term fiscal sustainability. In short, there is ample evidence that market discipline is still working.

The second section will expand on the basic problem of fiscal discipline in federations. The third section will discuss hierarchical and market-based solutions, and the fourth will explain the disastrous intermediate category that fosters indiscipline. Section 5 will briefly review the origins and functioning of market discipline in the United States. Section 6 will examine threats to market discipline that have arisen in recent decades. The penultimate section will consider and reject the proposition that market discipline can no longer function. The final section opens the door to an agenda for reform aimed at bolstering market discipline.

I. THE PROBLEM OF FISCAL DISCIPLINE IN FEDERATIONS

All federations must face up to a basic problem that can be conceptualized in the language of game theory as a dynamic game of incomplete information (see Rodden 2006). When lower-level governments face a serious, long-term, negative revenue shock requiring fiscal adjustment, they are tempted to avoid the political pain of expenditure cuts or tax increases. This temptation is driven by the belief that the higher-level government can eventually be compelled to assume its debts. Thus, even if lower-level governments know that their fiscal decisions are not sustainable in the long run, they can avoid adjustment because of an implicit higher-level guarantee.

The lower-level government generally does not have full information about this implicit guarantee. The higher-level government often makes some sort of formal no-bailout pledge, and its leaders publically state that bailouts are impossible. However, lower-level governments can often see that these promises are not credible. They look to the final stage of the game, the eve of default for the lower-level government, and attempt to project whether the higher-level government will prefer bailouts to default.

Lower-level officials are not the only ones attempting to make these assessments. Market actors like fund managers, banks, and credit rating agencies also attempt to look down the game tree and evaluate the higher-level government's likely reaction at the moment of default.

They look for a variety of clues to the central government's likely behavior. They evaluate the process through which a bailout would be decided and the political incentives of the actors. If the legislature must vote for a bailout, what is the probability that the requisite majority would favor a bailout? This is driven in part by the number of insolvent provinces and the nature of their legislative representation. If the executive has wide-ranging authority to provide a bailout unilaterally, how might the chief executive contrast the political pain associated with bailouts with that associated with default? This trade-off is shaped by the nature of the chief executive's regional support base.

Some of the most crucial questions are about the creditors. Who are they, and how powerful are they in the political process? If they are a diffuse group of foreign individual investors, perhaps the domestic political costs of default will be sufficiently low to make it a relatively attractive option. On the other hand, if the debt of the lower-level governments is an important part of the portfolio of the largest domestic banks, default might be extremely unattractive.

Lower-level officials and market actors will also derive clues from the basic architecture of the system of fiscal federalism. When the lower-level governments provide some of the most politically sensitive public services, like health care and unemployment insurance, and these services are funded almost entirely by taxes that are levied and collected by higher-level governments, voters are likely to blame the higher-level governments for service disruptions. When the political blame for local service disruptions is quickly directed at the central government, the credibility of its no-bailout pledge is undermined, and market actors are more likely to perceive an implicit guarantee.

Perceptions about the credibility of the central government's no-bailout commitment are crucial for local fiscal decision making. If everyone believes with perfect certainty that the central government cannot commit, lower-level governments will have no incentives to adjust to negative shocks, and market actors have weak incentives to punish them or to distinguish between the creditworthiness of the various lower-level governments.

If lower-level governments and market actors perceive the central government's commitment as perfectly credible, lower-level governments will have strong incentives to adjust, and market actors will face strong incentives to monitor their creditworthiness because default is a very real possibility. Of course democratically elected governments will often avoid adjustment as long as possible, but eventually, the costs of doing so become prohibitive.

Although these perfect information benchmark scenarios are instructive, a crucial point is that local officials and market actors often operate under substantial uncertainty. Decisions must be made based on bets about the credibility of the higher level government's no-bailout commitment, using all observable information to inform their evolving beliefs.

As such, central government policies vis-à-vis lower-level governments are important not only because of the direct incentives and restrictions they place on lower-level governments but also because they send valuable signals to players who are always updating their beliefs in a repeated game. Government policies can bolster or undermine the no-bailout commitment, thus altering incentives of lower-level governments, creditors, and even voters.

II. TWO PATHS TO FISCAL DISCIPLINE: HIERARCHY AND MARKETS

If the higher-level government is unable to commit to not provide bailouts, it faces an obvious and severe moral hazard problem. Consider a typical unitary country in Europe, or a highly centralized developing country that has recently made a transition from dictatorship to democracy. Taxation is highly centralized and the central government has taken on primary responsibility for most public services. Lower-level governments are mere conduits for delivering services that are funded through intergovernmental transfers. In Europe, the central government often makes a formal commitment to achieve roughly equal levels of service provision throughout the country.

In such settings, it is common knowledge that any attempt by the higher-level government to forswear bailouts would lack credibility. It would be politically and, in some cases, constitutionally impossible to allow a local government to default.

In such situations, it would be disastrous to allow lower-level governments to approach credit markets and borrow without limits. Thus, central governments in fiscally-centralized countries typically attempt to regulate the access of lower-level governments to all forms of borrowing (Von Hagen and Eichengreen 1996). Bond issues and bank loans are strictly monitored and limited by the central government. In some cases, the central government undertakes all borrowing on behalf of local governments and then allocates infrastructure finance according to its own assessments of needs. To the extent that public employee compensation and pension programs provide windows for borrowing, these are regulated as well. Any attempts to smooth local government expenditures over the business cycle are clearly in the domain of the central government.

This type of hierarchical system has been in place in the relatively homogeneous unitary countries of Europe for much of the twentieth century, where there is no pretense of viewing local governments as sovereign borrowers.

However, the story is quite different in some federations, where even after the centralization associated with two world wars and the Great Depression, states and provinces held on to significant authority well into the postwar era. When the powers of the central government are limited and the constituent units of the federation possess significant autonomous taxing authority, the central government might be able to credibly commit to allow them to default.

In this scenario, lower-level governments can approach credit markets as sovereign borrowers, and creditors face incentives to collect information about the sustainability of their finances. The desire to borrow at attractive rates would provide incentives for governments to make sustainable choices. Moreover, competition with other states or provinces over mobile citizens and firms would provide additional incentives for prudence and a sustainable debt burden.

This vision of decentralized, competitive federalism has been attractive to fiscal conservatives from Friedrich von Hayek to James Buchanan and has been portrayed by Barry Weingast as an engine of growth and prosperity. In fact, an enthusiasm for this style of federalism lurks behind much of the optimism about fiscal decentralization in the development community in the early 1990s.

III. WHEN FEDERATIONS FAIL

The problem with this rosy scenario, however, is that it rarely comes to fruition. Through a series of painful crises, we have learned that it can be very difficult for the central government to fully commit.

In some decentralized federations, a combination of constitutional and informal political constraints retarded the process of fiscal and administrative centralization that characterized the first half of the twentieth century in much of the world. These restraints are a double-edged sword. On the one hand, by limiting the capacity and incentives of the center to intervene in the fiscal affairs of lower-level governments, robust federalism can bolster the central government's no-bailout commitment and sow the seeds of market discipline. On the other hand, it can also prevent the central government from monitoring and regulating the borrowing of lower-level governments.

In such federations, as a result of the wide-ranging powers of the lower-level governments to tax, spend, and borrow, the stakes are very high if the center's commitment is in any way compromised. In the late 1980s and early 1990s, the Brazilian states and Argentine provinces were on unsustainable fiscal paths, however, they faced weak incentives to undertake politically painful adjustment because they believed the central government would ultimately step in with a bailout. The central government could not prevent them from continuing to undertake new borrowing and debt rollovers in the face of very precarious fiscal positions while explicitly waiting for federal bailouts. In both countries, the bailouts eventually materialized, and a very costly moral hazard problem played a major role in facilitating a series of fiscal crises. In Argentina, of course, the end result was the dramatic default of the federal government.

The European Monetary Union has fallen prey to exactly the same problem and seems to be failing in even more spectacular fashion. Member states and their creditors came to see the debts of the weaker member states as implicitly guaranteed by the stronger member states. Ireland and the Southern European countries were able to borrow at favorable rates, and ratings agencies were clearly bolstering their evaluations of the creditworthiness of the weaker member states by assuming an implicit guarantee. These bailout prophecies eventually became self-fulfilling. The dynamic game of incomplete information reached the final stage, and the European Union confirmed suspicions that it cannot tolerate outright default by a member state.

What are the lessons from these incidents? It is not surprising that these crises are interpreted as failures of market discipline. Unsustainable borrowing took place in part because market actors (correctly) interpreted the higher-level government's no-bailout commitment as non-credible.

It is just as appropriate, however, to interpret them as failures of hierarchy. As part of the Stability and Growth Pact, the European Union had a formalized Excessive Deficit Procedure, which, on paper, would have punished member states in the early stages of building unsustainable deficits or debt burdens. The Brazilian and Argentine federal systems also had elaborate procedures for monitoring and regulating the debts of the states and provinces.

Unfortunately, however, these regulations and procedures were undone by the politics of federalism. The European Excessive Deficit Procedure proved to be unenforceable. The largest countries had the political power to flout the rules, and smaller countries like Greece engaged in creative accounting without punishment. In Brazil, the Senate was responsible for approving and regulating the borrowing of the states, and representatives of insolvent states found that approval for unsustainable borrowing was relatively easy to obtain as part of the game of legislative horse trading.

These half-hearted efforts at hierarchical regulation inadvertently undermined market discipline by sending important signals about the central government's lack of credibility. If officials found it politically impossible to sanction Greece for its accounting abuses or Sao Paulo for its dubious loans from state-owned banks, how could it possibly summon the political fortitude to allow them to default? Moreover, the very act of attempting to regulate the borrowing of member states signals a certain level of responsibility. Weak or half-hearted regulations may have been worse than no regulations at all.

These failures of market discipline had another crucial common element: externalities associated with the banking system. One of the most important clues to the central government's credibility lies in the identity of the creditors of the lower-level governments, which is in turn shaped by the policies of the higher-level government. The Brazilian states were allowed to borrow directly from large commercial banks that they owned and controlled. Several of these were among the largest and most important banks in Brazil, and by the end, some of their largest "assets" were bad debts to their own state governments. It eventually became clear to everyone that a bailout of states would be necessary to save the banking system from collapse. The crisis of fiscal federalism in Brazil was thus in large part a failure in the organization of the banking system.

Something similar can be said about the European debt crisis. Data about the exposure of large European banks to insolvent member states are sparse, but it is quite clear that concern about bank failures was an important part of the logic of the bailouts of Greece, Ireland, and Portugal, which can be seen as bailouts of troubled German and French banks.

Large European banks invested not only in ill-fated real estate developments but also in bonds of member state governments. This was encouraged by European banking regulations that provide very strong financial incentives for banks to buy government debt. Banks are not required to set aside additional reserves when they buy government debt, which is officially viewed by the European Commission as risk free. This effectively lowers the price of government debt and distorts banks' decisions.

In other words, although the European Treaty contained a no-bailout clause, the European banking regulations explicitly provided a bailout assurance by signaling to market actors that the default risk of member states was zero. The signal was received not only by bankers but also by other creditors and by member state governments who came to understand that Germany implicitly guaranteed their debts.

The European and Latin American episodes demonstrate that in a decentralized federation characterized by strong representation for member states, both market and hierarchical forms of fiscal discipline can easily fail if institutions and incentives are not properly structured. A half-hearted hybrid of markets and hierarchy is unlikely to succeed.

IV. DEFAULT AND THE FOUNDATIONS OF MARKET DISCIPLINE

Although difficult, by no means is it impossible for a central government in a federation to make a credible no-bailout commitment. A very costly and credible signal is sent when a crisis arises, the bailout game reaches the final stage, and the central government simply turns its back and allows default. Such an event would send a strong signal to creditors and other governments, providing a firm foundation for market discipline going forward. This is the road not taken in Europe.

However, this is exactly what happened in the United States in the 1840s. After states had engaged in large-scale borrowing to build canals, railroads, and other internal improvements, a fiscal panic led to sudden reductions in revenues, and without reliable tax revenues, several states were unable to service their debts. Many of the creditors were British citizens, and Britain threatened military attack if the U.S. federal government did not assume the debts of the states (Ratchford 1941). A coalition of insolvent states assembled a bailout proposal, attempting to buy the support of less indebted states by offering to create a per capita transfer.

However, in a pivotal moment in the history of U.S. federalism, the bailout proposal failed in the legislature. Representatives of solvent states constituted a slim majority in the legislature (Wibbels 2003), and bailout opponents turned public opinion against the proposal in those states. Perhaps another important reason for the decision can be traced, once again, to the identity of creditors, most of whom were foreign individuals rather than important domestic constituencies.

Considerable uncertainty about the federal government's payoffs in the dynamic bailout game was resolved. Several states repudiated their debts, and the entire federation was cut off from international capital markets. State governments, citizens, and creditors learned a painful lesson: The U.S. states are sovereign debtors. To approach credit markets again, states made substantial reforms, including the introduction of direct taxation and the institution of various balanced budget requirements. Creditors learned to carefully assess the states' revenues and obligations.

This episode marked the beginning of a long period of successful market discipline among the U.S. states that was marred only by repudiations of debts of some Southern states in the aftermath of the Civil War. Unlike the political unions described, the U.S. federal government has not endeavored to limit the deficits or debts of the U.S. states; however, without any hierarchical oversight or regulation, in comparison with federated entities in most other federations, the deficits and debt burdens of the U.S. states have been quite low throughout the twentieth century, especially considering the very large role they play in providing basic public services and building infrastructure (see Rodden 2006).

The states typically adjust to revenue downturns rather quickly, and most likely because of their balanced budget rules, they do not smooth expenditures over the business cycle through borrowing. In fact, the revenues and expenditures of the U.S. states are both extremely pro-cyclical. Negative revenue shocks are met with rapid expenditure cuts (Rodden and Wibbels 2010). In the most recent downturns, these cuts have been so severe as to almost completely offset the impact of any federal government attempts at fiscal stimulus (see Aizenman and Pasricha 2011).

Empirical studies suggest that the balanced budget rules that emerged in the 1840s are an important part of the explanation for cross-state variation in the speed of adjustment (e.g., Poterba 1995). Although states have devised a variety of tricks and gimmicks to circumvent their balanced budget requirements, including delaying payments into the next fiscal year and underfunding pensions, these rules are probably part of the explanation for the fact that as a share of gross state product, general obligation bond debts of the states have been modest throughout the twentieth century.

State governments have been quite sensitive to credit ratings, and the need to keep debt burdens under control to keep borrowing costs down is an important part of the political discourse in the states. Credit downgrades are politically costly for governors. The empirical literature suggests that bond yields and credit ratings are quite sensitive to changes in states' debt burdens (see Bayoumi, Goldstein, and Woglom 1995; Rodden 2006), more so than in most, if not all, other federations.

In short, the United States is one of a very small number of federations, perhaps also including Canada and Switzerland, in which the central government has been able to convince market actors that the constituent units should be treated as sovereigns, and where fiscal decisions of the constituent units have been consistently constrained by credit markets for much of the twentieth century.

V. IMPLICIT BAILOUTS AND THE CHALLENGE TO MARKET DISCIPLINE

This optimistic story about market discipline with roots in the nineteenth century seems increasingly quaint and anachronistic in 2011. First, the U.S. federal system has centralized dramatically over the course of the twentieth century in ways that subtly undermine the central government's no-bailout commitment. Second, the fiscal crisis and the recent wave of bailouts in the private sector may have provided the coup de grace for the notion of market discipline.

Perhaps the central government was able to ignore the bailout demands in the 1840s in part because its powers and obligations relative to the states were so limited, as were the economic externalities linking the states. The federal government may have more at stake in allowing California to default today than it had in allowing Pennsylvania to default in 1840. Beginning with the New Deal, the states have increasingly become conduits for the delivery of government programs, like Medicaid, that are conceived and largely funded by the federal government.

Figure 6.1 depicts the growth of federal grants as a share of current state and local expenditures. Arguably, as grants become more important components of subnational budgets, and the books of the federal and lower-level governments become increasingly intertwined, the central government's no-bailout commitment loses credibility because it has become politically implicated in service provision in the states.

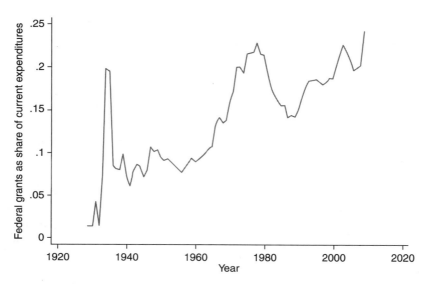

FIGURE 6.1. The growth of federal grants relative to state and local current expenditures.

When faced with a fiscal crisis requiring rapid and politically painful adjustment, elected officials in the states are tempted to avoid adjustment and call upon the central government for additional assistance. The political attractiveness of this strategy is shaped by their ability to make the case to voters that their troubles are not self-induced. This case is bolstered substantially by a plethora of grant-funded federal programs as well as unfunded mandates. Moreover, states can argue that matching provisions in some grant programs distort their incentives and discourage expenditure cuts that would enhance efficiency. The states can also shift blame for their fiscal problems by pointing out that intergovernmental grants, just like state tax revenues, are positively correlated with the business cycle, leaving them in difficult circumstances when revenues begin to dry up.

Thus, with each fiscal downturn in recent decades, the story is the same. Tax revenues and federal grants fall precipitously, and states are faced with an array of costly new expenditure programs and employee benefits that had been enthusiastically promulgated during the last boom. The states buy some time by borrowing to the extent allowed by their balanced budget rules, engaging in fiscal gimmicks, and crucially, neglecting to fund their pension programs.

However, these measures are usually not enough to avoid steep expenditure cuts. Declining expenditures in the states easily offset any federal efforts at fiscal stimulus, and a coalition for special assistance to the states begins to form in Washington. Of course, these are not referred to in polite company as "bailouts," but they are undeniably ad hoc, quickly negotiated transfers aimed at filling gaps in state budgets. In the most recent recession, these took the form of special short-term Medicaid supplements and pork-laden stimulus grants for shovel-ready infrastructure projects in the states.

In addition to the inefficiencies associated with delay and political bargaining, these implicit bailouts also send important signals to market actors that the federal government cannot allow states to cut expenditures, much less default on their bond obligations. In addition, they encourage state governments to believe that the political pain of adjustment might eventually be shifted to the federal government.

In 2009, the federal government also took the unusual step of formally subsidizing and presumably guaranteeing a special class of subnational debt known as Build America Bonds. It was extremely helpful for states to be able to borrow at subsidized rates, but a danger is that market actors view this as another signal of the federal government's ultimate responsibility for the obligations of states, another step along the way to a unitary-style system in which the center arranges the borrowing of the lower-level governments but without the concomitant hierarchical borrowing restrictions.

In sum, there is a danger that although a spectacular bailout like that of Greece has not yet happened, the federal government's no-bailout commitment is slowly eroding with each recession. In fact, some astute observers such as Nouriel Roubini[1] and Warren Buffett[2] have argued that the central government already provides a strong implicit guarantee, at least to the largest states. They argue that the political importance of California and the externalities associated with default are simply too great to imagine a world in which Congress and the president allow it to default. This argument is bolstered by the fact that the federal government has already revealed its taste for bailouts in the private sector.

VI. CAN MARKET DISCIPLINE SURVIVE?

When a string of states defaulted in the early 1840s, expectations of bailouts in future rounds of the game were somewhere near zero. The perceived

---

[1] "Who Will Default First: Greece or California?" *Wall Street Journal* March 24, 2010.
[2] "Buffett Says GM Rescue May Mean U.S. Can't Say No to States," *Business Week* May 5, 2010.

probability of bailouts is substantially higher today; however, the probability is also surely not equal to one. The crucial question is whether the perceived probability is sufficiently low as to provide incentives for states to adjust. Faced with the prospect of politically painful tax increases and expenditure cuts, are state governments willing to continue on an unsustainable fiscal path while placing their bets on a federal bailout? Are creditors willing to fund this?

If the answer is "no," market discipline can still survive.

First, let us put into proper perspective the growth of federal grants displayed in Figure 6.1. Along with the Canadian provinces and Swiss cantons, the U.S. states are among the most fiscally autonomous subnational entities in the world, and the vast majority of their expenditures are funded by taxes that they levy and collect themselves. It is not at all clear that a cynical strategy of courting disaster while waiting for bailouts would be politically wise for a governor.

It is also not clear that a bailout of selected insolvent states would receive a warm reception in Congress given the current political climate. In fact, it is plausible that voters' widespread anger about private sector bailouts would make a bailout of states politically challenging. Even efforts to raise the federal debt limit to avoid federal government default have been exceedingly rancorous and difficult.

Moreover, as in the nineteenth century, at the moment the states flirting with insolvency do not come close to constituting a legislative majority. In fact, although it is true that the most troubled states, like California and Illinois, are some of the largest and, hence, produce the largest externalities, they are dramatically underrepresented in the Senate.

Let us also return to a crucial variable in the analysis: the identity of the debt holders. Unlike the Latin American and European cases described, state defaults would not necessarily threaten the survival of the U.S. banking system. In fact, banks are relatively minor players as purchasers of state bonds. State bonds are attractive mostly to state residents because of their tax-exempt status, therefore, state debts are held largely by citizens of the state. Thus, compared with other political unions, externalities associated with default might be more limited, and hence, the center's commitment more credible because a significant share of the pain associated with default would be limited to state residents.[3]

---

[3] The impact of the bond insurance industry on bailout probabilities is unclear. One might argue that as long as the insurers are not viewed as "too big to fail," bond insurance reduces the probability of a bailout because it would be politically easier to impose losses

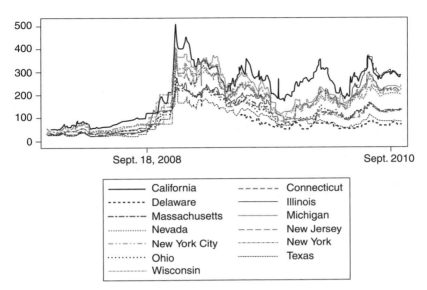

FIGURE 6.2. Credit default swaps for selected U.S. states.

Looking beyond the statements of Warren Buffett, how do other market actors assess the probability of federal bailouts? If creditors are increasingly reassured by the central government's implicit guarantee, bond yields, credit default swaps, and credit ratings should be converging.

Figure 6.2 displays data on credit default swaps (CDS) and reveals that the opposite is happening. In the wake of the crisis, markets are behaving as if there has been dramatically increased differentiation in the creditworthiness of the states.

Figure 6.3 provides CDS data for selected U.S. states and European member states. The initial precrisis clustering of U.S. states and EU member states does suggest a powerful critique of market discipline. Creditors seem to have underestimated the risks associated with these bonds, especially in Europe, where the policies described allowed creditors to believe that member state debt issues were guaranteed by other member states.

Even in the precrisis period, there was greater differentiation among U.S. states than EU member states. Moreover, the cost of insuring Greek debt did not surpass that of California debt until very late in the Greek

on insurers than on individual bondholders, many of whom are voters in the state. In any case, the bond insurance industry essentially collapsed in the wake of the fiscal crisis, and a very small percentage of new issues are now insured.

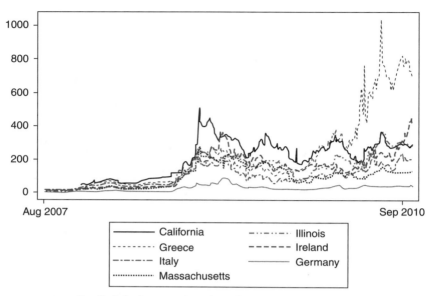

FIGURE 6.3. Credit default swaps for selected U.S. states and member states of the European Monetary Union.

crisis, in spite of a debt burden that was several times higher. Ireland and Illinois were neck and neck until the eve of the Irish bailout.

Although market actors may have been asleep at the wheel prior to the crisis, they appear to have awoken with a jerk. In both Europe and the United States, market discipline has returned with a vengeance. In Europe, the wake-up call appears to have come too late. Precisely because of panic at the discovery that bonds of EU member states were not risk-free instruments, the rapidly increasing spreads among member states depicted in Figure 6.3 forced the wealthier member states to step in to stave off Greek default and save their own banks.

In the United States, the increasing bond yields for troubled states did not create a panic, even in 2010 when breathless television analysts began predicting a wave of state defaults. Luckily, bond debt burdens of U.S. states were far lower than those of EU member states going into the crisis (see Figure 6.4).

Of course this does not mean that states are not in serious trouble. As explained in detail in other chapters in this volume, debt to gross economic product (GDP) ratios are manageable in part because balanced budget rules have created incentives to borrow from future public retirees rather than bond markets, and unrealistic accounting assumptions allowed states

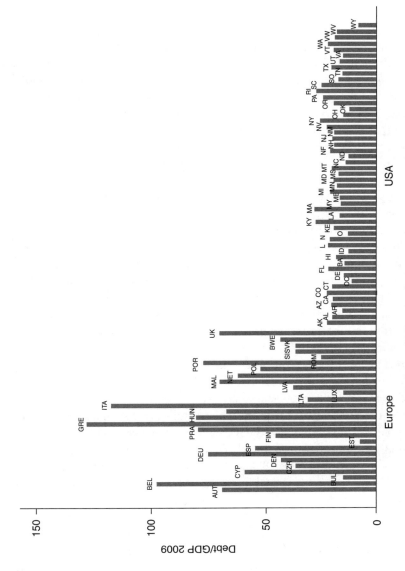

FIGURE 6.4. Debt-to-GDP ratios for European countries and U.S. states.

to hide from the problem. Many state pension programs are clearly on an unsustainable fiscal path, and painful reform is needed.

Another problem lies in the municipal sector, where the dynamic bailout game is played between the state and municipal governments. Although there is considerable cross-state heterogeneity, for the most part, state governments make rather weak no-bailout commitments to their municipalities. Municipalities have also gotten into serious trouble in the current crisis, and some face their own unsustainable debt burdens and unfunded pension liabilities. Faced with the prospect of a default of a large municipality, state governments often step in at the last minute with a conditional bailout, as happened with Harrisburg, Pennsylvania, in 2010. Thus, purchasers of state general obligation bonds must pay attention not only to the state's debt burden and its unfunded pension liabilities but also to those of its municipalities.

The same can be said for the proliferation of state and municipal bodies that have been created solely to issue debt in efforts to circumvent balanced budget requirements.

These are vexing and dangerous problems, but they need not spell the demise of market discipline. The costs of unfunded pension liabilities are finally coming into focus and are informing the assessments of creditors and rating agencies. States are under enormous pressure to find ways to shore up their pension programs. Moreover, it is straightforward for market actors to incorporate municipal and other potential indirect state liabilities into their analysis of state's creditworthiness.

Indeed, markets have punished the most troubled states, and they have faced burdensome and increasing borrowing costs. Credit default swaps for the most troubled U.S. states have surpassed Latvia and Hungary.

In short, state governments and their creditors may hope for an implicit federal guarantee and assess the probability of an eventual bailout as substantially greater than zero, but their hopes do not appear to be especially high. Governors and treasurers will complain loudly about dramatic cuts in federal assistance as the stimulus and Medicaid supplements run out, and they will continue to lobby for increased transfers.

However, there is no evidence that they are throwing up their hands, staying the course, and placing all of their bets on a federal bailout. On the contrary, state governments are making serious efforts at reform. Elected officials from both parties are risking their political careers by calling for hard choices. Both Democratic and Republican administrations are asking public employee unions for large concessions. Although they have a long way to go, some states are attempting to make structural changes to pension programs.

VII. TOWARD A REFORM AGENDA

The road ahead is extremely rocky. As illustrated by the large 2011 protests over the rights of public sector unions in Wisconsin, partisan recriminations and rancor are to be expected. In some states, the battles are between parties, but in others, efforts to achieve fiscal sustainability are creating fissures within rather than between parties. The intensity of these battles reveals that market discipline is functioning quite forcefully. In fact, in light of draconian and sometimes irrational expenditure cuts in vital areas like infrastructure and especially education, some might argue that it is working all too well.

In Chapter 2, Damon Silvers identifies many of the same structural problems with U.S. federalism discussed in this chapter. States implement a good deal of federally funded policy, especially in areas like welfare, education, and health, where one might hope for some insulation from the business cycle. However, these programs are funded with highly pro-cyclical revenue sources, and states are unable to smooth expenditures over the business cycle because of their balanced budget requirements. Thus, every recession is met with a combination of draconian cuts that fall disproportionately on the most vulnerable and calls for implicit bailouts while pension obligations go unpaid.

One might also add that booms are similarly accompanied by fiscal expansions, generous new contracts, and very little in the way of savings. The long-term result is inefficient and pro-cyclical spending, a growing debt burden, and insolvent pension programs.

In one view, market discipline and state sovereignty are the problems rather than the solutions. If the problem is a murky quasi-sovereignty for the states, the solution is hierarchy. In this view, Alexander Hamilton's deep skepticism about independent spending and borrowing by states was warranted, and it is time to implement his vision and turn the states into wards of the federal government. To return to the family analogy, the states should be viewed as children rather than adults. The Civil War and then the New Deal placed the United States on a path of fiscal centralization that was left incomplete because of the outmoded trappings of federalism. As the federal government expanded, the states were left with too much fiscal and political power, and the federal government was forced into an uncomfortable partnership with them.

In this view, the federal government should do the following. First, it should assemble wide-ranging new powers to regulate taxation, expenditures, and borrowing in the states, along the lines of a European central government vis-à-vis its municipal governments. Failing that, it should simply federalize existing programs that are implemented by states, which would presumably require a vast buildup of the federal bureaucracy throughout the country. Echoing Hamilton, some might even call for a clean slate beginning with a federal assumption of state debts and pension obligations.

Leaving partisan ideological debates aside, it is relatively clear that this type of solution is impractical. Above all, it is difficult to imagine such a far-reaching change to the constitutional order. It is not clear where the political impetus for such a major reorientation of American federalism would come from, or how it could possibly be achieved without constitutional change. In the current political climate, and with the federal government itself on a precarious debt path, it is also difficult to imagine a solution that relied on a dramatic expansion of the federal government.

The basic structure of American federalism is probably here to stay, and in any case, a hierarchical solution is not promising in such a large and diverse federation. When the higher-level government has just agreed to a large bailout and revealed to the world that it cannot tolerate defaults, as in the Latin American federations and the European Monetary Union, market discipline is impossible in the medium run, and hierarchy is the only viable option.

In the European case, there are good reasons for skepticism about the prospects for successful hierarchical control of member state budgets going forward. Europe has reached an unfortunate impasse in which Germany and the other wealthy member states guarantee the debts of the weaker member states. As such, it is crucial that the solvent member states gain new tools with which to control the fiscal decisions of the insolvent members; however, it is difficult to imagine what these tools might look like in a compact like the European Union. The history of the Excessive Deficit Procedure suggests the need for an independent enforcement process that is insulated from politics; however, it is difficult to imagine why the weaker member states would voluntarily agree to submit to such a process. Currently, the EMU can only threaten to withhold future tranches of bailouts, but given that it has already revealed that it cannot tolerate default, such threats have no credibility.

Fortunately, in contrast to the European Monetary Union or the Brazilian federation, the moment of imminent default has not arrived in the United States, and there is no need to explore second-best hierarchical solutions that would likely run into constitutional obstacles.

The lesson from other failed federations is that it is dangerous to rely on a half-hearted hybrid of markets and hierarchy. Given a choice between pure versions of these two strategies, the best option for the United States is also the most practical: bolster market discipline.

There are a number of ways in which a reform agenda can focus on bolstering market discipline while also addressing some of the persistent pathologies of U.S. federalism. One simple goal is to help states manage the business cycle by restructuring existing intergovernmental grant programs so that they are less pro-cyclical. Grants fall off during downturns along with state taxes, and then after a politicized, ad hoc scramble, some temporary and distortionary relief may or may not be provided by the federal government.

A better option would be for the federal government to develop a rules-based mechanism for smoothing intergovernmental grants over the business cycle, providing at least some counterweight to the boom-bust pattern of state public finance. This need not imply any change in the size of grants as a share of total state government revenue. This would help firm up the center's no-bailout commitment by putting an end to the ad hoc scramble for implicit bailouts and would help state governments make more rational expenditure decisions.

Market discipline could also be enhanced by efforts to disentangle the obligations of federal and state governments. Efforts to curb federal unfunded mandates would go a long way to enhance the flexibility of states to solve their budgetary problems, as would reforms to distortionary matching provisions in some federal grant programs.

Another interesting possibility is the institution of an orderly default procedure, perhaps along the lines of the proposals made in other chapters of this volume. The federal government can lay out some guidelines about how a default in a state would be handled. One reason why the rising bond yields of Greece and other EU member states quickly turned into a panic was that investors simply had no idea what might be coming next. Not only was there no formal bailout mechanism, but perhaps more importantly, there was also no sense of how a default or restructuring might be handled.

A good way to send a signal to market actors about the credibility of the central government's no-bailout commitment is to provide a formal set of rules and procedures for dealing with default. After the initial Greek bailout, the German government briefly attempted to propose an orderly default procedure in an effort to rekindle its no-bailout commitment, but this only served to fan the flames of the ongoing financial panic.

It is not too late in the United States. In fact, the timing might be quite good to clarify once and for all that states can and will default if they do not achieve fiscal sustainability and to clarify for market actors the rules under which default would take place. Quite simply, an orderly default is preferable to a disorderly default for everyone. By reducing fears of the latter, the federal government can enhance its no-bailout commitment.

As Levitin (2011) points out, it is insufficient to rely exclusively on an illusory no-bailout commitment in a modern market economy. Systemic risk cannot be avoided, and no matter how one structures incentives ex ante, a moment might come when the failure of a bank, or the default of a state, would have externalities that are clearly socially unacceptable. Sometimes the costs of allowing an entity to fail are unclear until the moment arrives. In a dynamic situation like the Lehman crisis, the revealed cost of allowing one unit to fail might make it clear that further failures would be unacceptable.

Absolute ex ante commitment may be impossible or undesirable, and the government may eventually find itself deeply involved in the process of loss allocation in the event of a crisis. As the European Monetary Union demonstrates, it is better to be prepared for that moment than to wish it away. By agreeing on a set of rules and procedures now, it might be possible to reduce the possibility of a panic in the future. To preserve market discipline, it is important that the loss allocation process be viewed by borrowers and creditors alike as inevitably very painful – something to be avoided under all but the most extreme circumstances.

Finally, reform efforts aimed at bolstering market discipline should focus on bad accounting practices and bad incentives associated with public sector pension programs. It might be possible to envision federally imposed accounting standards and information dissemination requirements, and perhaps even funding requirements, that would not send too strong a signal of federal responsibility.

The most likely path to improved fiscal discipline in the states, however, lies within the states themselves and requires that they be treated as adults who ultimately stand on their own. In the summer of 2011, the state governments are behaving far more like adults than the federal government. Their shallower pockets and lack of monetary authority have forced them to respond to market pressure and make hard decisions about how to balance their budgets that have eluded the federal government.

This process will continue to be painful, and we have probably not seen the last of street protests like those in Madison, Wisconsin; however, the 2011 protests in Madison are in many ways preferable to those that took place simultaneously in Athens, Greece. In Madison, a clash took place over very different approaches to the question of how the sovereign state of Wisconsin can achieve fiscal sustainability. In Athens, inchoate rage was directed in large part at austerity measures that were viewed as illegitimate foreign impositions from Germany, the EU, and the International Monetary Fund who had suddenly become responsible for Greek debt.

Although the U.S. system of federalism is under stress, it is in far better shape than the European Monetary Union. In spite of serious flaws, market discipline has worked in the past in the United States and can work in the future. Reform proposals that would enhance the perception of federal responsibility for state obligations should be resisted. If they are not, the current struggles of the states might look minor to future generations.

REFERENCES

Aizenman, Joshua and Gurnain Pasricha. 2011. Net Fiscal Stimulus During the Great Recession. NBER Working Paper 16779.

Bayoumi, Tamim, Morris Goldstein, and Geoffrey Woglom. 1995. Do Credit Markets Discipline Sovereign Borrowers? Evidence from the U.S. States. *Journal of Money, Credit, and Banking* 27(4):1046–1059.

Levitin, Adam. 2011. In Defense of Bailouts. *Georgetown Law Journal* 99:435–514.

Poterba, James. 1994. State Responses to Fiscal Crises: The Effects of Budgetary Institutions and Politics. *Journal of Political Economy* 102(4):799–821.

Ratchford, Benjamin. 1941. *American State Debts*. Durham, NC: Duke University Press.

Rodden, Jonathan. 2006. *Hamilton's Paradox: The Promise and Peril of Fiscal Federalism*. Cambridge: Cambridge University Press.

Rodden, Jonathan and Erik Wibbels. 2010. Fiscal Decentralization and the Business Cycle: An Empirical Study of Seven Federations. *Economics and Politics* 22(1):37–67.

Von Hagen, Juergen and Barry Eichengreen. 1996. Federalism, Fiscal Restraints, and European Monetary Union. *American Economic Review* 86(2):134–138.

Wibbels, Erik. 2003. Bailouts, Budget Constraints, and Leviathans: Comparative Federalism and Lessons from the Early U.S. *Comparative Political Studies* 36(5):475–508.

7

American States and Sovereign Debt Restructuring

ADAM FEIBELMAN

INTRODUCTION

The problem is easy enough to describe, if seemingly intractable: A large governmental entity is in acute financial distress or faces the possibility that without assistance of some sort it will be perilously hobbled for years to come by the weight of its obligations. If this governmental entity were a corporation, it would be an excellent candidate for reorganization under bankruptcy law. Ideally, reorganization would force its various stakeholders to compromise their claims and would return the government to financial well-being to everyone's benefit. However, this particular governmental entity is prohibited from filing for bankruptcy, and there is no other formal mechanism available to help it restructure its obligations.

This problem is newly salient for some American states, but it is a familiar dilemma for sovereign nations, especially those with emerging or developing economies. Sovereign financial crises occur with some regularity, and such crises often become debt crises as these sovereigns face acute liquidity constraints or unsustainable debt burdens or both. As with American states, there is no formal bankruptcy-type mechanism available to sovereigns.

These are parallel problems – states and sovereigns[1] in financial distress with no formal bankruptcy-type mechanism available to them – and the parallels run even deeper. States and sovereigns both incur obligations to provide public and social goods to their citizens. The path to financial

---

Thanks to Peter Conti-Brown, Lee Buchheit, Lisa Daniels, Jef Feibelman, Mitu Gulati, John Pontius, and Mark Weidemaier for helpful comments and conversation and to Justin Hebenstreit for research assistance. All errors are my own.

[1] Throughout this chapter, "states" refers to subunits of the United States and "sovereigns" refers to nations.

distress appears to be similar for both as well: low growth, diminishing revenues, overborrowing, some unexpected shock, or an interrelated combination of these. Granted, the comparison is complicated. For example, sovereign debt crises often stem from or are exacerbated by exchange rate crises or banking crises. States generally do not borrow in a different currency than their domestic one, and the costs of banking crises in America are borne primarily by the federal government and only indirectly by the states. Although such differences may affect the scope of comparison, the financial circumstances of states and sovereigns are similar enough that the experience of sovereigns in debt crises provides useful lessons for American states, their stakeholders, and their counterparties.

The most important lesson for states to draw from the realm of sovereign debt is that many government entities have been able to obtain meaningful debt relief in the absence of a formal bankruptcy regime or similar mechanism.[2] It is not a pretty lesson; sovereign debt-restructuring episodes are messy, costly, and contentious affairs, and they are usually predicated on the debtor facing acute financial crisis. Nonetheless, many sovereigns have successfully obtained debt relief from private and official creditors, including "standstills" on payment, debt rollovers, and debt exchanges that extend maturity, change the face value of debt, or change the interest rate. Generally speaking, these restructurings have been conducted with the voluntary consent of sovereigns' creditors. But "voluntariness" in this context is in the eye of the beholder, and the creditors involved often do not view their own choices as freely made, especially when negotiations occur against the backdrop of default or serious threat thereof.

A second important lesson is that sovereign debt restructuring generally does not eliminate the need for external official support or bailout. Debt relief, "involving" or "bailing-in" creditors, is often discussed as an alternative for bailing out a debtor,[3] and debt relief should reduce a sovereign's

---

[2] There have been approximately fifty to sixty restructurings in the modern era. *See* Lee C. Buchheit & G. Mitu Gulati, *How to Restructure Greek Debt*, working paper, at 7, April 10, 2010, available at http://papers.ssrn.com/sol3/papers.cfm?abstract_id=1603304 [hereinafter, *Greek Debt*]. This basic lesson is underscored by the recent willingness of a large portion of Greece's creditors to voluntarily rollover a significant portion of that sovereign's debt. And there is growing awareness that constraints on debt restructuring by a country like Greece are more political and financial than legal.

[3] *See, e.g.*, David Skeel, *Testimony Before the Subcommittee on TARP, Financial Services and Bailouts of Public and Private Programs*, Committee on Oversight and Government Reform, U.S. House of Reps., Feb. 9, 2011 ("We need a fire department for state fiscal crises that does not depend on using a major federal bailout as a backstop."); Steven Schwarcz, *A Minimalist Approach to State Bankruptcy*, working paper, at 3, available

need for official support to some extent. But sovereigns in debt crises generally need new money even if they are able to obtain debt relief. They often need to finance debt restructuring itself and, in any event, they continue to have acute financial needs during the period of restructuring and immediately after. Thus, the choice between bailout and bail-in tends to be a false one – resolving a sovereign debt crisis often involves some of both, and there is struggle over what the balance of each will be. The unfolding experience of Greece illustrates this dynamic. Greece's official creditors, including other Eurozone countries and the International Monetary Fund (IMF), are increasingly determined that some of Greece's private creditors restructure or roll over their claims against the sovereign before those official creditors commit to additional bailout or rescue funds. It is not clear, however, how much involving private creditors would ultimately reduce the amount of official support provided; perhaps a debt restructuring would just make the official rescue more effective.

None of the forgoing is meant as an argument that the current ad hoc approach to sovereign debt restructuring is ideal or that it is preferable to a formal mechanism. It is certainly possible that it is neither. Because the current approach generally requires that a sovereign be in acute crisis (unless, perhaps, is it is a heavily indebted, low-income sovereign[4]), it presumably excludes some sovereigns that are not yet in crisis or that might avoid crisis altogether with otherwise burdensome levels of indebtedness. Furthermore, the costs of ad hoc restructuring may be high enough that some sovereigns delay or forgo it even where restructuring would be more efficient for the sovereign and their various stakeholders.[5] Whether or not the availability of a formal mechanism would encourage more sovereigns to seek debt relief or to do so sooner, it might significantly reduce the costs of restructurings actually undertaken to the benefit of sovereigns, their creditors, and their citizens.

---

at http://scholarship.law.duke.edu/cgi/viewcontent.cgi?article=3006&context=faculty_scholarship&sei-redir=1#search=%22steven%20schwarcz%20minimalist%20approach%20state%20bankruptcy%22 [hereinafter, *A Minimalist Approach*].

[4] The official sector – sovereigns and multilateral institutions like the IMF and the World Bank – has adopted a separate and distinct approach to providing debt relief to heavily indebted low-income (or poor) countries. *See, e.g.*, IMF Factsheet, *Debt Relief Under the Heavily Indebted Poor Countries (HIPC) Initiative*, available at http://www.imf.org/external/np/exr/facts/hipc.htm. *See also, infra* note 53 (discussing the Paris Club's approach to debt relief for low-income debtors).

[5] *See* Anna Gelpern, *Mapping to Bankruptcy*, working paper (on file with author) ("In most cases, the debt restructuring option is invoked too late in hindsight ....").

Such concerns have fueled various proposals for a sovereign bankruptcy regime or a similar debt-restructuring mechanism. Here, too, the fate of these proposals and the content of debate over them provide some useful lessons for those considering extending bankruptcy protection to American states. Efforts to create a formal sovereign debt-restructuring mechanism or bankruptcy regime have faced numerous practical, political, and theoretical challenges, and none have gained much traction. There has been a flurry of interest in the topic again as Eurozone countries have faced debt crises and the need for debt restructuring. After some semi-serious discussion of creating a debt-restructuring mechanism for Eurozone countries, however, the idea has faded into the background once again. The preferred mode of resolving sovereign debt crises continues to be informal, ad hoc.

Some of the obstacles to extending bankruptcy protection to sovereigns could perhaps be avoided in the context of American states. Because Chapter 9 could easily be adapted to extend to states, the practical challenges and the negotiation costs at the design stage of a bankruptcy regime for states could be quite low compared to these costs of creating a sovereign bankruptcy regime. But challenges of political economy and theoretical concerns about making debt relief easier and less costly for sovereigns probably apply with equal or greater force in the context of American states.

In sum, while the debt of American states may appear "nearly impossible to restructure" absent bankruptcy protection,[6] the experience of sovereign debt restructuring suggests otherwise, although financial conditions may have to reach a real impasse before stakeholders are motivated to come to the table. Furthermore, the history of proposals and efforts to extend bankruptcy-type protection to sovereign debtors suggests that bankruptcy is not likely to supplant an ad hoc approach for American states. This chapter proceeds as follows. Section I compares the financial relationships of states and sovereigns and describes, among other things, how these relationships may affect their vulnerability to financial distress. Section II provides a quick summary and overview of patterns of sovereign debt restructuring over the last quarter-century. Section III discusses various proposals for sovereign bankruptcy-type mechanisms made in recent history and the debates surrounding such proposals. Sections II and III highlight some of the lessons

---

[6] See David Skeel, *A Bankruptcy Law – Not Bailouts – For the States*, WALL STREET JOURNAL, Jan. 18, 2011 (noting that state bond debt is "nearly impossible to restructure outside of bankruptcy").

that these experiences and debates offer to states and to those who would like to extend bankruptcy protection to them.

I. DEBT AND DISTRESS

Experiences involving sovereign debtors provide a useful comparison for American states only to the extent that states and sovereigns conduct similar financial activities, take on similar obligations, suffer distress for similar reasons, and face similar constraints in avoiding and resolving financial crises.

In fact, there are many fundamental similarities. At a broad level of generality, both sovereigns and states take on obligations to provide public goods, including infrastructure, regulation, education, social insurance and assistance, defense, utilities, and so on.[7] Sovereigns must fund a broader array of such public goods. States share the burden for some goods (some infrastructure, for example) with the federal government, and they bear little or no burden for some public goods made available to their citizens (national defense for instance).

Both types of governments generally finance their various expenditures from revenues, especially taxation of income, transactions, and wealth. But both also borrow from private creditors – sometimes from banks but generally by issuing bonds[8] – to finance some of the programs and services they provide and the infrastructure they build. They may borrow to smooth public expenditures when revenues dip or to finance fiscal deficits (states do this rarely compared to sovereigns),[9] but many of their obligations are

---

[7] See, e.g., Schwarcz, A Minimalist Approach, supra note 3, at 7 n. 31 (noting that state debt includes obligations of numerous state entities that perform a wide variety of functions). See also, Adam Feibelman, Federal Bankruptcy Law and State Sovereign Immunity, 81 Tex. L. Rev. 1381, 1384–1385 (2003) (noting the range of responsibilities of state governments).

[8] See, e.g., Buchheit & Gulati, Greek Debt, supra note 2, at 1; Schwarcz, A Minimalist Approach, supra note 3, at 7. Some state bonds are purchased by banks, although many state bondholders are retail investors or nonbank institutional investors. The term "bonds" here refers to a broader category of borrowing by sovereigns, which also includes bills, for example, and other short-term securities. See, e.g., Buchheit & Gulati, Greek Debt, supra note 2, at 1.

[9] It is generally true that states rarely borrow to cover operating expenses; most of their borrowing is for capital expenditures. However, instances of borrowing for operating expenses appear to be increasing, especially "revenue anticipation notes" issued by California and other states. These notes are repaid within the same fiscal year. Most notably, this kind of borrowing is apparently being done by states that are inching closest to acute financial distress.

incurred pro-cyclically, when times are good.[10] In addition to borrowing, states and sovereigns both tend to have ongoing obligations to provide benefits and assistance to public employees and citizens.

Furthermore, sovereigns and states can find themselves in financial distress for similar reasons. In the sovereign context, such distress is most often a result of a combination of some fundamental weakness in the economy and some unsustainable policies.[11] Weakness in the economy, the most predominant cause of sovereigns' financial distress,[12] may be caused by any number of factors that impact productive output and trade, reducing revenues. It may also be caused by external shocks (disasters, oil price spikes, market panic) or contagion from beyond the jurisdiction. Unsustainable policies may result in fiscal deficits, overborrowing, high debt-servicing costs, or overexposure to future liabilities and obligations.[13] Sovereign financial distress generally turns into a crisis when a government does not have the ability to pay obligations – especially debt-servicing payments – as they come due.[14]

The current financial problems of some American states appear to map onto some of these determinants and early signs of sovereign financial distress.[15] The general global financial crisis and the resulting economic environment has slowed output and sapped state revenues against a backdrop of mounting fiscal pressures on the spending side of the ledger. These pressures include significant levels of indebtedness, some of which will come due in the short- to medium-term and, in some states, large underfunded obligations to current and former public employees. These various obligations may be unsustainable by various metrics in the long run,[16] but they have not led to the kind of acute crisis in which a state was, for example, unable to make payments coming due or could not tap credit markets for necessary funds. Not yet, anyway.

---

[10] See Ugo Panizza, Federico Sturzenegger, & Jeromin Zettelmeyer, *The Economics and Law of Sovereign Debt and Default*, 47 J. ECON. LIT. 1, 14 (2009).

[11] See Panizza et al., *supra* note 10, at 17–20 (finding that 62% of sovereign defaults are due to output declines); NOURIEL ROUBINI & BRAD SETSER, BAILOUTS OR BAIL-INS, 32 (2004). But see Panizza et al., *supra*, at 19–20 (noting that it is often difficult to resolve the determinants of any particular debt crisis).

[12] See Panizza et al., *supra* note 10, at 17.

[13] See ROUBINI & SETSER, *supra* note 11, at 16, 32.

[14] See id. at 16.

[15] See e.g., Schwarcz, *A Minimalist Approach*, *supra* note 3, at 1.

[16] For discussions of how to define unsustainability in this context, see Adam Feibelman, *Contract, Priority, and Odious Debt*, 85 N.C. L. REV. 727, 734, n. 25 (2007) [hereinafter *Odious Debt*]; Gelpern, *Mapping to Bankruptcy*, *supra* note 5, at 10–12 (noting the "lack of a solvency metric" for sovereigns).

Beyond these general similarities, however, there are a number of important related differences between sovereigns and states as financial actors. First, sovereigns often incur significant amounts of debt denominated in another currency. Many private interests within those sovereigns may also incur debt denominated in a foreign currency.[17]

Second, and related, sovereigns generally have an array of domestic and external obligations that may be denominated in different currencies and that are subject to different legal treatment.[18] The distinction between domestic and external debt has become blurred in many respects, although the currency owed and the law governing an obligation are still important factors. A sovereign has significant potential control over obligations that are governed by its laws and denominated in its own currency.[19] The distinction between domestic and external creditors also remains very important.[20] A sovereign's relationship with domestic obligees is often very different than its relationship with external creditors, who often include other sovereigns and multilateral organizations. As Anna Gelpern and Brad Setser put it: "Residents and non-residents will strike fundamentally different political and economic bargains with the borrowing country ..."[21] American states have internal and external obligations, but external obligations do not give rise to exchange rate risk or to a significant difference in the applicable legal regime. Like sovereigns, however, states presumably do have different relationships with domestic and external obligees that may reflect important political crosscurrents.

Third, a potentially important difference with sovereigns and states is that the latter have significantly less control over their finances than

---

[17] This is one of the reasons why "sovereign debt" can include the external borrowing of domestic private firms, especially banks. *See, e.g.*, ROUBINI & SETSER, *supra* note 11, at 15. *See also*, Anna Gelpern, *Banks, Governments, and Debt Crises*, working paper, abstract available at http://papers.ssrn.com/sol3/papers.cfm?abstract_id=1736100 (exploring the deep connections between banking systems and government liabilities and the relationships between banking crises and government debt crises).

[18] For an excellent discussion of the evolving distinctions between domestic and foreign debt, see Anna Gelpern & Brad Setser, *Domestic and External Debt: The Doomed Quest for Equal Treatment*, 35 GEO. J. INT'L. L 795 (2004).

[19] *See, e.g.*, Buchheit & Gulati, *Greek Debt*, *supra* note 2, at 10–13.

[20] *See* Gelpern & Setser, *supra* note 18, at 795–796. The distinction between domestic and foreign debt was once clear. Domestic debt was held by residents, subject to local law, and denominated in local currency, whereas foreign debt was held by nonresidents, subject to foreign law and denominated in foreign currency. In the wake of global financial liberalization, however, sovereigns began to borrow in ways that combined every variation of these choices – residence of creditor, governing law, and currency.

[21] *See id.* at 798.

sovereigns do.²² Some of this difference is due to particular historical aspects of state finance. Under their own laws, states must generally obtain approval from their legislatures (and sometimes from state voters) before borrowing funds. Most states have some form of legal requirement that the state balance its operating budgets, although most of these laws leave the states some room to maneuver.²³ Another limitation on states' control over their finances stems from the basic fact that states are subunits of a national government.²⁴ States are constrained in various ways by that relationship. A national government imposes some costs and burdens on its states (e.g., unfunded or underfunded mandates) and confers some benefits as well. Perhaps most important, states have a narrower band of policy room for raising tax revenues than sovereigns.²⁵ A large portion of tax revenues generated within the United States is filtered through the federal government with cross-subsidization among states determined by national policy makers.²⁶ Because of the significant federal tax burden, the room for states to tax their citizens without reducing productivity or deterring transactions is likely smaller than it would be if the states were the primary taxing authorities.

Fourth, debt owed by sovereigns and states may enjoy different levels of formal legal enforceablility. Sovereign debt is generally considered to be very difficult to enforce through traditional legal mechanics.²⁷ Until the middle of the twentieth century, sovereign debt contracts were subject to "absolute" sovereign immunity.²⁸ Even if a creditor seeking to enforce an obligation against a recalcitrant sovereign could convince a foreign or

---

[22] Perhaps for this reason, states tend to borrow against specific revenue streams – through "revenue bonds" – more often than sovereigns. See Gelpern, *Mapping to Bankruptcy*, *supra* note 5, at 9.
[23] See *id.* at 10.
[24] See generally, *id* (noting the similarity between American states and Eurozone sovereigns).
[25] See, e.g., Schwarcz, *A Minimalist Approach*, *supra* note 3, at 5 (noting that states' power to tax is not unlimited).
[26] This cross-subsidization can be an important advantage for states as well because the federal government can direct resources from one state or region to another to help avoid or resolve crises. Sovereigns may enjoy some cross-subsidization, especially those in currency or monetary unions, but through international institutions as well. Potential exposure to involuntary cross-subsidization is arguably inversely related to degree of sovereignty. See *supra* note 24 and accompanying text.
[27] See Panizza et al., *supra* note 10, at 5.
[28] See W. Mark C. Weidemaier, *Contracting for State Intervention: The Origins of Sovereign Debt Arbitration*, 73 L & Cont. Probs. 335, 336 (2010). "[F]ormal legal enforcement was virtually unavailable to sovereign lenders during the early twentieth century." *Id.* at 338.

domestic court to exercise its jurisdiction over the sovereign, it still had to succeed on the merits and then find a way to collect assets of the sovereign not within the sovereign's control.[29] Sovereign obligations were sometimes enforced by military action, international sanctions, or formal legal intervention by creditors' home countries.[30]

Sovereigns' formal and informal immunity from enforcement has been eroded significantly.[31] Sovereigns do not generally enjoy immunity in U.S. federal courts from suits on claims related to commercial debts,[32] and they now generally waive sovereign immunity.[33] Thus, they have been increasingly subject to litigation and sometimes lose on the merits.[34] Although it is still extremely difficult to enforce a judgment against a recalcitrant sovereign through legal process, creditors have gotten more aggressive – and arguably more successful – in seeking ways to enforce judgments against sovereigns' assets abroad.[35]

> [T]here are some examples [*Elliott Associates v. Banco de la Nacion*, in particular] in which holdouts have been able to enforce [their] claims, or settle at substantially better terms than the average creditor. These settlements have occurred either because holdouts were able to credibly threaten to attach sovereign assets or interfere with international transactions or because of reputational concerns – debtor reluctance to defy court judgments at a time when they were regularizing their record as borrowers.[36]

State obligations may be more or less susceptible to litigation and enforcement than sovereign ones. States do enjoy broad immunity from suits for damages as a constitutional matter,[37] but this immunity does not extend

---

[29] *See id.* at 337–338.
[30] *See, e.g., id.* at 339. "For loans to Latin American and Caribbean borrowers in the early 1900s, U.S. military intervention was a very real possibility. In that context, early loan contracts employed arbitration as a means to both signal and justify heavy-handed, post-default intervention in the borrower's affairs. As the century wore on, private lenders had less reason to anticipate that creditor states would employ such direct means of controlling sovereign borrowers. Yet they had some reason to hope that creditor states might espouse their citizens' claims before international tribunals like the ICJ." *Id.* at 351.
[31] *See* Panizza et al., *supra* note 10, at 5–9; Weidemaier, *supra* note 28, at 341 (noting that the modern doctrine of sovereign immunity treats a sovereign's waiver as binding).
[32] *See* Gelpern, *Mapping to Bankruptcy*, *supra* note 5, at 7.
[33] *See* Weidemaier, *supra* note 28, at 341.
[34] *See* ROUBINI & SETSER, *supra* note 11, at 295–302; Panizza et al., *supra* note 10, at 5–9; Feibelman, *Odious Debt*, *supra* note 16, at 741 n.61.
[35] *See* Panizza et al., *supra* note 10, at 7–9.
[36] *Id.* at 9.
[37] *See* U.S. CONST., AMENDMENT 11 ("The Judicial power of the United States shall not be construed to extend to any suit in law or equity, commenced or prosecuted against one of the United States by Citizens of another State, or by Citizens or Subjects of any Foreign

to certain claims for injunctive relief.[38] Furthermore, the Contracts Clause of the U.S. Constitution prohibits states from, among other things, passing laws that modify their contractual obligations.[39] State sovereign immunity may bar suits for damages under this constitutional provision in state and federal courts,[40] but, again, suits for injunction relief pursuant to it may not be barred.[41] As with sovereign nations, states' waivers of immunity are generally enforced if initially valid.[42] It is unclear how often, and to what extent, states effectively waive their immunity from suit in their debt contracts, but it appears they often decline to do so at the contracting stage.[43] If a creditor successfully sues a state in federal court (whether through a

State."). This immunity has been construed to prohibit suits for damages against states in federal courts. See Seminole Tribe v. Florida, 517 U.S. 44 (1996). See also Schwarcz, A Minimalist Approach, supra note 3, at 15–17 (discussing state sovereign immunity in the context of state debt enforcement). Congress can only authorize such suits pursuant to its enforcement powers under Section 5 of the Fourteenth Amendment. See Feibelman, Federal Bankruptcy Law, supra note 7, at 1387. The Supreme Court has found that the doctrine of state sovereign immunity is broader than the Eleventh Amendment; for example, it can operate to bar suits for damages under federal statutes in state courts as well. See Alden v. Maine, 527 U.S. 706 (1999).

[38] For example, pursuant to the doctrine of Ex parte Young, 209 U.S. 123 (1908), private individuals can sue state officials for injunctive relief to remedy ongoing violations of federal law. See Idaho v. Coeur d'Alene Tribe of Idaho, 521 U.S. 261, 269 (1997); Feibelman, Federal Bankruptcy Law, supra note 7, at 1389–1390.

[39] Article 1, section 10 Clause 1, U.S. Constitution ("No State shall ... pass any ... Law impairing the Obligation of Contracts....").

[40] See Hans v. Louisiana, 134 U.S. 1 (1890); Alden, 527 U.S. at 732 (1999). See also infra note 179 and accompanying text.

[41] It is worth noting that many of the immunity issues implicated by a default or restructuring of state bonds have not been aggressively tested under current law. Where there is any room for creditors' counsel to maneuver, there would presumably be a serious legal challenge to a state bond default, which is often all a holdout creditor needs to obtain a higher payout. Even if these questions are resolved in states' favor in an initial episode of restructuring, the sovereign context suggests that states would end up waiving immunity more broadly in the future.

[42] See Feibelman, Federal Bankruptcy Law, supra note 7, at 1390–1391; Schwarcz, A Minimalist Approach, supra note 3, at 17.

[43] There is no available data on state practice regarding waiver of state sovereign immunity in this context across U.S. jurisdictions and over time. Given the large number and wide variety of state bond issues and the difficulty in determining when and to what extent a state has waived immunity, it would be very difficult to make meaningful generalizations about the current practice by states. It is important to note that it is possible for a state to waive immunity for claims arising from a bond in ways that could not be determined from the language of the bond. In any event, it is clear that at least some state bonds are silent about immunity and waiver. See, e.g., State of California 2010–11 Revenue Anticipation Bonds, Official Statement, Nov. 18, 2010 (available at http://emma.msrb.org/EA435680-EA338811-EA734651.pdf). Others expressly do not waive immunity. See, e.g., State of Tennessee, General Obligation Bonds, Official Statement, Oct. 13,

waiver of immunity or some other exception to the doctrine), however, it may have stronger footing for enforcing or settling that judgment than would a judgment creditor of a sovereign determined not to pay a foreign judgment.[44]

These various differences in states' and sovereigns' financial transactions and relationships in turn fuel some of the differences in how financial distress unfolds for sovereigns and how it would likely unfold for states. Most significantly, the fact that sovereigns and private firms within a sovereign may borrow in foreign currency means that exchange rate instability often plays a major role in sovereign debt crises.[45] Many sovereign debt crises stem from or cause an acute need for foreign currency and a lack of access to it.[46] Sovereigns with economic or financial troubles often face an increasing need for foreign currency driven largely by trade imbalances or fiscal deficit. If, as often happens, the value of sovereign's currency drops or is devalued, the level of indebtedness of – and within – the country can jump dramatically. At some point, access to foreign currency may dry up as foreign creditors retreat and refuse to extend more credit. Because they borrow in dollars, the domestic currency, American states are generally insulated from the direct effects of exchange rate instability. This may make them significantly less prone to acute crises than sovereigns.

Another significant difference between the financial exposure of sovereigns and that of states is the fact that sovereigns often effectively take over or internalize the obligations of private firms within the country, especially domestic banks.[47] This may happen because the sovereign must rescue domestic firms, essentially converting private debt into public debt. If crisis resolution has a deep impact on the banking sector because, say, banks own large amounts of bonds that are restructured, the banking industry may need recapitalization or other support from the sovereign to avoid a banking crisis.

2010. It is also worth noting that a state can waive immunity ex post at the time of a dispute with bondholders.

[44] It is true that such a judgment creditor will probably not be able to attach a state's assets if the state refuses to pay – *see* Gelpern, *Mapping to Bankruptcy*, *supra* note 5, at 7 – however, it may be more difficult for a state to refuse to pay (or settle) a federal court judgment than for a sovereign judgment debtor to refuse to pay a judgment from a foreign court.

[45] *See* ROUBINI & SETSER, *supra* note 11, at 18–19, 26.

[46] *See id.* at 16, 26. Until recently, sovereign debt crises were most frequently triggered by collapse of a currency peg or target. *See id.* at 25.

[47] *See id.* at 48–51. For emerging markets, currency collapses "usually are associated with severe banking, corporate, or sovereign payments crises." *Id.* at 26. *See also supra* note 17 and accompanying text.

American states generally do not have to internalize the losses of private firms within their jurisdictions in the same way or to the same extent as sovereigns do. Again, because states and debtors within states generally are not broadly exposed to significant exchange rate instability, one source of potential systemic failure of private firms within a state is absent. Furthermore, if a systemic bailout or broad-based public assumption of losses becomes necessary in the United States, it would generally occur at the federal, not state, level. This is most clearly true for the U.S. banking sector, probably the most systemically significant private sector. When banking losses or risks need to be absorbed or insured by the public in this country, they are absorbed or insured for the most part by arms of the federal government – especially the FDIC – or with expenditures by federal agencies, not by the states.[48] This is not to say that states would be unaffected by a banking crisis; they would certainly internalize some costs of a crisis, including the cascading effects of instability in the banking sector.

In sum, there are nontrivial differences in the financial profiles of states and sovereigns, in the nature of the transactions they conduct with their obligees, and in the financial risks they face. At the broadest level, however, sovereigns and states are both economic and financial actors that incur large obligations to provide important public goods. These obligations include debts to banks and bondholders that expose these governments to private and public markets for debt. Both states and sovereigns can become over-indebted or experience acute liquidity constraints, and yet neither has the ability to employ formal debt relief regimes available to individuals, business associations, and some smaller governmental units.

It is also worth emphasizing another fundamental similarity: Government debt always has some political dimension that private debt does not have, and government debt crises are always political episodes.[49] Public financial crises often stem from unwise but politically expedient policies or from other political forces and constraints. They inevitably have political consequences, often leading to political upheavals, and the policies adopted to resolve them always have some political calculus.

---

[48] This, of course, is not universally true. There are, for example, state insurance funds to cover some losses in that industry.
[49] See, e.g., Anna Gelpern, *What Iraq and Argentina Might Learn From Each Other*, 6 CHI. J. INT'L L. 391, 414 (2005) [hereinafter, *Iraq and Argentina*].

II. SOVEREIGN DEBT RESTRUCTURING

American states, unlike their municipalities, have no meaningful experience of default or restructuring in the modern era,[50] and there have been very few episodes of sustained financial or debt crises at the state level. Sovereigns, on the other hand, have a deep and long history of debt crises, default, and debt restructuring. This difference in vulnerability may be the result of some of the factors described above (e.g., sovereigns' exchange rate risk and exposure to the banking sector, legal restraints on state borrowing). In any event, the modern history of sovereign debt crises and sovereign debt restructuring provides a fruitful comparison for states and policy makers in the United States who are contemplating strategies for resolving financial crises at the state level.[51]

In the period since World War II, resolving sovereign debt crises has been an ad hoc process, but it has developed some familiar patterns. These patterns have been determined in large part by a handful of institutions. Creditor nations created the Paris Club in 1956 in the wake of an Argentine debt crisis, for example, to improve coordination of their debt restructuring and debt forgiveness.[52] The Paris Club codified its procedures and principles in the late 1970s. Since that time, it has tended to treat heavily indebted, low-income sovereign debtors differently than middle-income ones, often agreeing to extend some debt reduction to the former while generally rescheduling debts owed by the latter.[53] In recent years, however, the Paris Club has proven more willing to reduce the obligations of middle-income debtors owed to its members.[54] There are also private creditor clubs like the London Club, which was formed in the 1970s and was modeled after the Paris Club. The IMF, designed initially to provide surveillance of exchange rate policies, has come to play a central role in responding to sovereign financial crises and in helping develop a practice of sovereign debt restructuring. Because the IMF is a crucial source for meaningful financial

---

[50] Only one state, Arkansas, has defaulted on a general obligation in this century, and that was during the Great Depression. American municipalities, on the other hand, have defaulted on obligations on many more occasions in the modern era. Their defaults are often due to "over-expenditure." See Panizza et al., supra note 10, at 17.

[51] See Gelpern, Mapping to Bankruptcy, supra note 5, at 13 (making a similar point).

[52] See, e.g., Feibelman, Odious Debt, supra note 16, at n. 24.

[53] See Andrew Yianni & Lauren Malek, Seychelles Debt Restructuring: Restoring the Viability of the Public Finances, 25 J. INT'L BANKING L. & REG'N 330, 331 (2010). The Paris Club's practice of extending debt reduction to heavily indebted, low-income sovereigns is now parallel to the IMF and World Bank HIPC program. See supra note 4.

[54] See id. at 331–332.

assistance for sovereigns during a crisis, it often has significant leverage over sovereigns and other stakeholders in the restructuring process.[55]

The patterns of sovereign debt crises have also been affected by the changing composition of relevant stakeholders, especially creditors. In the initial postwar period, most private borrowing by sovereigns was in the form of bank loans. This shifted toward bonds in the late 1970s, and the shift accelerated dramatically in the 1980s.[56] Currently, marketable securities like bonds and short-term bills are the primary source for private sovereign borrowing, although there is still a significant amount of bank lending to some sovereigns.[57] Among other things, the switch to bonds improved the liquidity of the market for sovereign debt to the benefit of debtors and creditors, and it is thought to have reduced the cost of funding available to sovereigns. On the other hand, it is widely believed that the process of restructuring during the era of bank loans was easier because sovereigns had fewer creditors who could coordinate more easily[58] and with whom sovereigns may have had ongoing relationships. Bondholders can be radically dispersed, and many of them have no ongoing relationship with their debtor. In addition to bank and bond debt, sovereigns also generally have some amount of trade debt, and some sovereigns borrow significant amounts directly from the official sector, including other sovereigns (bilateral) and international financial institutions (multilateral).

Whatever the identity and the composition of relevant stakeholders, resolving sovereign financial crises generally involves a combination of policy adjustment and financial support.[59] The policy adjustments usually include reducing fiscal deficits and pursuing strategies to increase output and trade. Financial support is sometimes in the form of a bailout (usually a bilateral or multilateral loan)[60] or of restructuring and reducing

---

[55] In fact, IMF involvement in restructuring process has waxed and waned over the years. It began "lending into arrears" in 1989 and expanded this practice in 1998 to lend to sovereigns in arrears on their bonds. See Kenneth Rogoff & Jeromin Zettelmeyer, *Bankruptcy Procedures for Sovereigns: A History of Ideas, 1976–2001*, Int'l Monetary Fund working paper WP/02/133, at 11 (2002), available at http://papers.ssrn.com/sol3/papers.cfm?abstract_id=879911. IMF lending to sovereigns in arrears not only enables a sovereign to get funds while negotiating with its creditors, "it [gives] the IMF an instrument with which to exert leverage over a defaulting debtor." *Id.*

[56] See Panizza et al., *supra* note 10, at 21.
[57] See ROUBINI & SETSER, *supra* note 11, at 11.
[58] See Panizza et al., *supra* note 10, at 21 (discussing the role of bank advisory committees). But see *infra* notes 161–62.
[59] See ROUBINI & SETSER, *supra* note 11, at 17.
[60] See *id.* at 1–2 (noting that the IMF has made big loans to countries that did not restructure their debt, including Mexico, Thailand, Indonesia, Korea, Brazil, and Turkey). See

existing obligations (i.e., bail-in) or some combination of both, as is often the case.⁶¹ Sovereigns have restructured their obligations in a variety of ways, including payment standstills, debt rollovers, debt exchanges that effectively alter maturity, interest rate, or principal.⁶² In the absence of a formal bankruptcy-type mechanism, such relief requires some form of voluntary, quasi-voluntary, or coercive arrangement with creditors, obligors, and other affected stakeholders. The following discussion, summarizing highlights of recent episodes of sovereign debt restructuring,⁶³ describes some of these strategies.

Episodes

The Brady Plan. Named after Nicholas Brady, who was Secretary of the U.S. Treasury at the time, the Brady plan marked a major milestone in the modern history of sovereign debt restructuring. It had its roots in a financial and economic crisis that plagued numerous developing economies, especially those in Southern and Central America, including Argentina, Bolivia, Brazil, Chile, Costa Rica, the Dominican Republic, Ecuador, El Salvador, Guatemala, Jamaica, Mexico, Panama, Paraguay, Peru, Trinidad and Tobago, Uruguay, and Venezuela.⁶⁴ Some of these countries had recently defaulted on obligations, and others were in danger of doing so. Most of the external debt of these sovereigns was owed to foreign banks;

---

   also Gelpern & Setser, *supra* note 18, at 797 (discussing Turkey's decision not to restructure its obligations).
61   See ROUBINI & SETSER, *supra* note 11, at 17. Although debates about sovereign debt (like the current state debt debates) often focus on the policy choice between bailouts and bail-ins, most restructurings require significant new official financial support, and many bailouts end up simply forestalling debt relief. *See id.* at 19.
62   *See, e.g.*, ROUBINI & SETSER, *supra* note 11, at 148–156.
63   Although these "highlights" include some of the major restructuring events of the last twenty-five years or so, it should be noted that there have been numerous smaller episodes of restructuring during this period. In the last year or so, for example, Liberia, Jamaica, and Seychelles have restructured some of their obligations. *See* Buchheit & Gulati, *Greek Debt*, *supra* note 2, at 5 (Liberia), 6 (Jamaica) & 10 (Seychelles). In the case of Seychelles, for example, that country obtained exceptional debt reduction (for a middle-income sovereign) from Paris Club creditors and conducted a successful debt exchange for existing notes, bonds, and commercial loans. *See* Yianni & Makel, *supra* note 53, at 333–334. Liberia completed a multiyear restructuring and relief program in 2010. Among other things, official lenders supported an arrangement by which Liberia settled its debts to private creditors (at three cents on the dollar). Liberia then obtained significant relief from debts owed to these and other multilateral and bilateral lenders.
64   *See* Paolo Manasse & Nouriel Roubini, *"Rules of Thumb" for Sovereign Debt Crises*, IMF, working paper, 05–42, at 9 (2005).

consequentially, this crisis threatened these commercial banks in stronger economies.[65] The plan, conducted in 1989, allowed the banks to exchange their loans for dollar-denominated bonds that they could then trade or for instruments that required them to provide new credit (to a now less-indebted sovereign).[66] Most banks opted to exchange their obligations for the exit bonds[67] of which there were further options, including par bonds and discount bonds.[68] Notably, a large percentage of the Brady bonds were effectively collateralized with U.S. Treasuries held in escrow. The plan was financed with funding from the IMF and the World Bank.[69] In addition to influencing the practice of future debt restructurings, the Brady bonds represented an important moment in the shift from bank loans to bonds as the primary method of sovereign external finance.[70]

Russia. In August 1998, the financial crisis in Asia and resulting economic weakness among its trading partners triggered a crisis in Russia.[71] After a large bailout loan from the IMF and the World Bank, Russia allowed the ruble to depreciate and defaulted on some of its domestic debt, much of which was held by foreign investors.[72] After an initial exchange offer was rejected,[73] Russia offered holders of this debt cash, new short-term treasury bills, and new bonds of varying maturities in exchange for a steep discount in their scheduled payments.[74] Within a year of the proposed deal, approximately 90 percent of creditors had agreed to it,[75] despite the fact that foreign investors had to place the proceeds of the exchange in restrictive accounts for a period

---

[65] *See* Buchheit & Gulati, *Greek Debt, supra* note 2, at 6–7.
[66] *See id.*
[67] *See id.*
[68] As the names suggest, par bonds were at the same value as the exchanged obligation but at a lower coupon (interest) rate, and discount bonds had a lower face value and a higher coupon rate. There were other types of bonds offered in these exchanges as well, including past-due interest bonds. *See id.*
[69] *See* Rogoff & Zettelmeyer, *supra* note 55, at 9–10.
[70] After the collapse of the Soviet Union, Russia also negotiated (with the London Club, in this case) to exchange some of its Soviet-era bank loans for dollar-denominated bonds. *See* Federico Sturzenegger & Jeromin Zettelmeyer, *Haircuts: Estimating Investor Losses in Sovereign Debt Restructurings, 1998–2005*, Int'l Monetary Fund, working paper, WP/05/137, at 14, available at http://papers.ssrn.com/sol3/papers.cfm?abstract_id=888006.
[71] The Asian crisis exacerbated a festering set of problems in Russia, including low output, ongoing fiscal deficits, and an unsustainable fixed exchange rate.
[72] *See* Sturzenegger & Zettelmeyer, *supra* note 70, at 9; Gelper & Setser, *supra* note 18, at 799–804.
[73] *See* Sturzenegger & Zettelmeyer, *supra* note 70, at 9.
[74] *See id.*
[75] *See id.* at 13 (including 95% of domestic creditors in the restructured issues and 88.5% of foreign creditors).

of time.[76] Although it can be very difficult to measure the effect of a restructuring on the present value of creditors' claims,[77] the "haircut" for these investors is estimated to have been between 41 percent and 55 percent.[78]

In the meantime, the ruble's depreciation and Russia's default had fueled a banking crisis in that country, which in turn "led to servicing difficulties for Russian external debt payments."[79] More than 75 percent of holders of one bond issue of dollar-denominated external debt agreed to exchange their bonds for similar dollar-denominated bonds or for ruble-denominated bonds at a much higher interest rate.[80] Depending on which bonds were chosen by creditors in exchange for their original instruments, the haircut was either 63 percent or in a range between 41 and 54 percent.[81] Russian authorities then offered to exchange two other bonds (issued by a state-owned bank) representing slightly more than $30 billion in obligations (principal and past-due interest).[82] The offer closed with nearly 99 percent participation.[83] The haircuts on the two bonds restructured in this offering were 52 percent and 54 percent.[84]

---

[76] *See id.* at 13; Gelpern & Setser, *supra* note 18, at 802–803. Furthermore, "[n]on-residents who decided not to participate ... were repaid in full, but had to place their proceeds in [restrictive accounts] in combination with a 5-year repatriation restriction." Sturzenegger & Zettelmeyer, *supra* note 70, at 13. Thus, domestic institutional investors in the restructured obligations received a better deal at the outset, see Sturzenegger & Zettelmeyer, *supra* note 70, at 11; and many domestic investors received favorable treatment in opaque or secret transactions, see Gelpern & Setser, *supra* note 18, at 803. It was this default and restructuring that fueled the infamous Long-Term Capital Management (LTCM) hedge fund crisis. *See id.* at 801–803. Exacerbating the effect on hedge funds like LTCM was the fact that Russia prohibited domestic banks from paying out on hedging deals that they had made with the funds to provide protection against exchange rate risk. *See id.* at 803. Gelpern and Setser note that Russia decided against other policies to address the crisis, such as a steeper depreciation of the ruble, which would have impacted domestic creditors more heavily. *See id.* at 803.

[77] *See* Sturzenegger & Zettelmeyer, *supra* note 70, at 4–8. "[The] definition of 'haircuts,' which is often used by market participants – namely to measure investor losses with respect to the face value of the outstanding debt rather than its present value – tends to exaggerate the losses actually suffered by investors." *Id.* at 63. The estimates of haircuts throughout this chapter are those computed by Sturzenegger and Zettelmeyer.

[78] *See id.* at 10–11.

[79] *See id.* at 14.

[80] *See id.*

[81] *See id.* at 15.

[82] *See id.* at 16. In exchange for these bonds, Russia offered new 30-year bonds with smaller face values but higher interest rates, 10-year bonds to cover past-due interest, and some cash. *Id.* Furthermore, these new bonds were effectively given some greater priority than the bonds they replaced. *See id.* at 18.

[83] *See id.* at 16.

[84] *See id.* at 17.

Ukraine. The financial crisis in Russia spilled over to Ukraine, making it hard for that country to roll over its debt as it came due in 1998.[85] At that point, in addition to receiving financial assistance from the IMF,[86] it restructured treasury bills held by domestic banks and foreign investors and a bank loan placed through a foreign commercial bank.[87] Domestic commercial banks agreed to exchange approximately one-third of their treasury bills for new bonds with longer maturities and face values determined by the maturity of their bills at the time of the exchange and a floating interest rate after one year.[88] The haircut was small, estimated at between 5 percent and 10 percent.[89] Foreign holders of treasuries were offered dollar-denominated bonds representing a larger haircut, just over 50 percent.[90] The loan holders got 25 percent of the cash coming due to them and an amortizing loan for the balance. They received an estimated 30-percent haircut.[91]

After experiencing more debt-servicing challenges and restructuring another bond issue,[92] Ukraine's situation continued to deteriorate in 2000.[93] In February of that year, with prodding from the Paris Club as a condition of restructuring their claims,[94] Ukraine conducted a "comprehensive exchange offer involving all outstanding commercial bonds."[95] Many of these were coming due in 2000–2001.[96] The minimum threshold for participation was 85 percent, and nearly all bondholders participated.[97] Depending on the bonds exchanged, the haircuts were between 22 percent and 35 percent.

---

[85] *See id.* at 18
[86] *See id.* at 22.
[87] *See id.*
[88] *See id.*
[89] *See id.* at 19.
[90] *See id.* at 20. The size of the haircut depended on the maturity of treasuries exchanged and whether the holder had hedged currency risk. *See id.* at 19–21.
[91] *See id.* at 22.
[92] *See id.* Ukraine restructured this bond issue valued at $160 million by paying in 20% cash and exchanging old bonds for new ones with a longer maturity and slightly lower face value. The haircut was 38%. Holders of the bonds exchanged for foreign held treasuries in 1998 were also invited to participate in the exchange, and 50% of those bondholders did so. *See id.*
[93] *See id.* at 23.
[94] *See also, Involving the Private Sector in the Resolution of Financial Crises: Restructuring International Sovereign Bonds,* IMF staff report, at Jan. 6, 2001, available at http://www.imf.org/external/pubs/ft/series/03/IPS.pdf.
[95] *See* Sturzenegger & Zettelmeyer, *supra* note 70, at 23. Ukraine offered two amortizing bonds – one denominated in Euros, one in dollars – with a seven-year maturity. *See id.*
[96] *See id.*
[97] *See id.*

Pakistan. Pakistan experienced a debt crisis in 1999 fueled first by high levels of public debt and then a declining balance of payments caused by international sanctions related to the country's nuclear program.[98] Pakistan obtained assistance from the IMF and then from other official creditors via the Paris Club, which was conditioned upon it also seeking relief from its private creditors.[99] After negotiating a haircut for some commercial bank loans,[100] Pakistan made an exchange offer in November 1999 for three Eurobond issues with payments due within the next two years, effectively extending maturities before missing any payments.[101] The haircuts were approximately 33 percent, 31 percent, and 30 percent, respectively.[102]

Ecuador. Ecuador was among the countries that issued Brady bond's in exchange for bank loans in the early 1990s. A banking crisis there in 1999 in turn led to a currency crisis (because Ecuador's central bank had to provide liquidity to the banking system, weakening the currency). The declining currency made debt servicing difficult because its bonds were denominated in foreign currencies.[103] Ecuador sought and received help from the IMF, which insisted that the country obtain relief from its creditors as well.[104] Ecuador then defaulted on collateralized Brady discount bonds, then on Eurobonds, and then on its other Brady bonds,[105] "the first default on international sovereign bonds since the 1930s."[106] The IMF provided support for a bond exchange offer, made on July 27, 2000.[107] Bondholders were offered a variety of instruments in exchange for their existing bonds, including cash for the value of Brady bond collateral and for missed payments.[108] By August, there was over 97 percent participation in the exchange.[109] Haircuts depended on bonds being exchanged – bonds

[98] See id. at 25.
[99] See id.; IMF, *Involving the Private Sector, supra* note 94, at 5.
[100] See Sturzenegger & Zettelmeyer, *supra* note 70, at 25.
[101] See id. The offer was for a 6-year amortizing bond with no reduction in face value. See id. at 26.
[102] See id.
[103] See id. at 27.
[104] See id.
[105] See IMF, *Involving the Private Sector, supra* note 94, at 7. The other Brady bonds were par bonds, past-due interest bonds, and interest equalization bonds. *See id.*
[106] See Sturzenegger & Zettelmeyer, *supra* note 70, at 27. "[S]hort-term domestic dollar-denominated debt" was restructured at this time, providing for longer maturities and lower interest rates. *See id.*
[107] The exchange was for 30-year bonds with increasing interest rates at a face value based on the maturity of the defaulted bonds being exchanged. *See id.*
[108] See id.
[109] See id.

with longer maturities at the time of exchange took bigger haircuts than those with shorter ones, and collateralized bonds took smaller haircuts.[110]

Ecuador's restructuring introduced a number of innovations, including debt retirement commitments, "principal reinstatement" requiring new issuance of bonds upon a payment default within ten years, and exit consents.[111] Although they were controversial, the exit consents are thought to have been effective, and they have been employed in subsequent exchange offers. Ecuador's bond contracts allowed a requisite majority of bondholders to amend certain seemingly minor provisions of the bond contracts. As part of the exchange, bondholders voted to amend these terms of the bond issue they were exiting to make the old bonds less appealing to potential holdout creditors.

Argentina. Another Brady bond issuer, Argentina continued to struggle throughout the 1990s with ongoing fiscal problems, high debt, and then effects of financial crisis in Brazil. It was ultimately unable to obtain financing from the market or from official sources in late 2001. A protracted process of debt restructuring[112] began with a debt exchange for domestic creditors, especially domestic financial institutions.[113] The country's government fell shortly afterward, and the country defaulted on various obligations. The new government offered to exchange existing bonds for loans (not bonds, interestingly) with lower interest rates and longer maturities and guaranteed by revenues from a tax on financial transactions. The government threatened "an involuntary restructuring at worse terms if the exchange was not accepted,"[114] and there was nearly complete participation by domestic banks, pension funds, and residents.[115] The average haircut was around 40 percent.[116]

Then, chaos ensued. There was a bank run, followed by a bank deposit freeze, and then the new government fell. The subsequent government defaulted on all debt and then devalued the currency, a dramatic move because most of the country's debt was denominated in dollars, and there was a large amount of domestic dollar-denominated debt (including the

---

[110] *See id.* at 28–29.
[111] *See id.* at 29; IMF, *Involving the Private Sector, supra* note 94, at 8.
[112] For discussions of this episode, see Sturzenegger & Zettelmeyer, *supra* note 70, at 30–45; Anna Gelpern, *What Bond Markets Can Learn From Argentina*, IFLR, April 2005, available at http://www.iie.com/publications/papers/gelpern0405.pdf
[113] *See* Gelpern & Setser, *supra* note 18, at 805.
[114] *See* Sturzenegger & Zettelmeyer, *supra* note 70, at 30.
[115] Banks and pension funds were allowed to value their bonds at par, not at market values. *See id.* at 30.
[116] *See id.* at 37.

recently exchanged loans, which also lost their collateral at this point[117]). Most of this domestic debt was "pesified" in 2002 at a rate significantly lower than the exchange rate,[118] and interest rates on the debt were reduced.[119] The average estimated haircut from pesification was 45 percent, ranging between 30 percent and 65 percent.[120] Interestingly, however, Argentina continued to service the loans recently issued to domestic creditors, which provided a useful way to insulate domestic banks and other domestic institutions from the treatment of other bondholders.[121] At this point, Argentina still had $80 billion in international debt, most of which was held by foreigners. The government initially proposed restructuring this debt with a 75 percent haircut.[122] It then revised its offer and provided a range of options: par bonds, discount bonds, and quasi-par bonds.[123] Participation was 76 percent, and average haircuts were between 71 percent and 75 percent, with some significant variation across tendered bonds.[124] Argentina did not employ exit consents.[125] There has been a good deal of litigation by creditors who declined to participate in the exchange.[126]

Uruguay. In the wake of financial woes in Argentina and Brazil, Uruguay experienced acute financial and economic pressures, including output shocks, destabilizing bank deposit withdrawals, and a resulting banking crisis.[127] Its external debt was downgraded, helping to fuel a debt run. This and liquidity support by its central bank led to a currency crisis[128] and financial support from the IMF. Devaluation of its currency in turn led

---

[117] See Gelpern & Setser, *supra* note 18, at 806.
[118] See Sturzenegger & Zettelmeyer, *supra* note 70, at 37.
[119] Some domestic creditors who had exchanged their bonds before opting to get their old bonds back. Others refused, successfully fighting pesification after an extended dispute. See id.
[120] See id.
[121] See Gelpern & Setser, *supra* note 18, at 806–807. The government then also recapitalized the banking system. See id. at 807.
[122] See Sturzenegger & Zettelmeyer, *supra* note 70, at 40.
[123] Unpaid interest before default was paid in cash, but interest accrued between default and exchange was not paid – the only example of this during the period 1998–2005. See id.
[124] See id at 41. Initial domestic restructured bonds after pesification had a similar haircut, around 70%. See id. at 49.
[125] See Gelpern, *What Bond Markets Can Learn, supra* note 112, at 22.
[126] See supra notes 31–36 and accompanying text (discussing litigation of sovereign debt disputes).
[127] See, e.g., Carlos Steneri, *Voluntary Debt Reprofiling: Lessons From Experience*, 35 GEO. J. INT'L L. 731 (2004).
[128] See Sturzenegger & Zettelmeyer, *supra* note 70, at 49.

to an increase in debt obligations denominated in foreign currency, which exacerbated debt-servicing challenges. Uruguay then offered to exchange all of its traded debt (about half of total debt, including domestic, international, and Japanese bonds) for bonds that simply extended maturity or for bonds that had a longer maturity and lower interest rate but a higher face value.[129] The country employed exit consents as well.[130] Participation was high: 90 percent for international debt and 99 percent for domestic debt. The average haircut for external debt was 13 percent, with a range between 5 percent and 20 percent.[131] Domestic bonds took slightly higher haircuts: between 15 percent and 35 percent (floating rate) and 15 percent and 30 percent (short dated).[132]

Iraq. Iraq experienced one of the few major debt restructurings that have occurred since Argentina, and it did so in a unique fashion. In the wake of the fall of Saddam Hussein's government and a U.S.-led takeover of that country, there was widespread concern that the heavy debt that Hussein had incurred on the country's behalf would hobble its postwar recovery effort. A number of commentators, including some U.S. officials, initially floated the idea that Iraq's Hussein-era debt was "odious debt" and therefore not enforceable.[133] This invigorated an academic field and a debt-relief movement with ramifications that continue to unfold.[134] American officials backed off the odious debt route and orchestrated a restructuring of the Iraqi debt, securing a United Nations resolution that effectively stayed enforcement of obligations against Iraqi assets and helping Iraq negotiate relief from official and then private creditors.[135] As others have suggested,

---

[129] Some cash was given creditors for accrued interest, and collateralized Brady bonds got "present value of the principal repayment." *Id.* at 50. *See also* Felix Salmon, *Stop Selling Bonds to Retail Investors*, 35 GEO. J. INT'L L. 837 (2004) (arguing that this plan effectively discriminated against retail investors because they would opt for the shorter maturity even though those bonds were worth less). Nonetheless, Uruguay's restructuring is an example of a "soft" restructuring with only a slight reduction of net present value due to extending maturities. *See* Buchheit & Gulati, *Greek Debt*, *supra* note 2, at 8.

[130] *See* Sturzenegger & Zettelmeyer, *supra* note 70, at 50.

[131] *See id.* at 54.

[132] The haircut for floating rate bonds was between 20% and 35%; for short-dated bonds, the haircut was between 15% and 30%. *See id.*

[133] *See* Gelpern, *Iraq and Argentina*, *supra* note 49, at 403.

[134] *See* Lee Buchheit, Mitu Gulati & Robert Thompson, *The Dilemma of Odious Debts*, 56 DUKE L.J. 1201, 1203 (2007) ("The removal of Iraq's Saddam Hussein in 2003 sparked a resurgence of interest in this subject."). *See also* Feibelman, *Odious Debt*, supra note 16, at 728 n.1 (citing scholarship on the topic through 2007). For practical ramifications of the doctrine, see the discussion of Ecuador, *infra*.

[135] *See* Gelpern, *Iraq and Argentina*, *supra* note 49, at 394–96; Feibelman, *Odious Debt*, supra note 16, at 736–37.

this was arguably the closest the world has come to witnessing a sovereign bankruptcy process.[136]

Ecuador again. Emboldened by the new movement to allow forgiveness of odious or illegitimate debt, Rafael Correa ran for the Ecuadorean presidency in 2006 on a promise to repudiate Ecuador's external debt if elected.[137] He won and then created a debt commission, which determined that much of the country's debt was illegitimate because it had been incurred by repressive regimes and for the benefit of the Ecuadorean elite and foreign creditors.[138] Armed with this finding, the country defaulted on two of its bond issues. Interestingly, Ecuador did not conduct a bond exchange. Rather, after buying some of its bonds at depressed prices on the market before default, it offered to purchase the remaining defaulted bonds (at a 35 percent discount), which were trading at very low prices because of the default and the growing global financial crisis.[139] Approximately 91 percent of the holders of the defaulted bonds agreed to the repurchase.[140] What was especially notable about this move was that the country was not in a financial crisis and was not insolvent at the time of the default, although its level of debt was arguably a significant drag on the country's economic performance and hampered the government's ability to conduct basic functions.

Now, Europe. Currently, a number of European countries are in some degree of financial distress. This crisis in Europe has its roots in the global financial crisis that originated in the U.S. mortgage market and that has lowered global output, depressed asset values, and shrunken the credit markets that fueled expansion in these countries until recently. The problems in some places (like Greece) have stemmed from dangerously high levels of public debt; in other places (like Ireland and Iceland), the problems stemmed from private (bank) debt that has become, or is becoming, public through guarantees and other efforts to rescue, nationalize, or recapitalize domestic banks. These troubles are coming to a head in large part because of market pressure on traded debt and concerns about whether these countries will be able to roll over debt when it comes due or to borrow more in the near future for other purposes. It is worth noting that the Eurozone debt crises are generally not a function of exchange rate instability – these countries generally borrowed in their own currency,

---

[136] See Gelpern, *Iraq and Argentina, supra* note 49, at 394–396 (describing the episode, especially the U.N. action, as "backdoor bankruptcy").
[137] See Adam Feibelman, *Ecuador's Sovereign Default: A Pyrrhic Victory for Odious Debt?* 25 J. INT'L BANKING L. REV. 357, 358 (2010).
[138] *See id.* at 358–359.
[139] *See id.* at 359.
[140] *See id.*

and in any event, the value of the Euro has remained stable in relation to other currencies. In fact, these countries' inability to unilaterally devalue their currency may be a serious limit on their ability to resolve their current crises.[141]

Until very recently, the response to these emerging crises had been coordinated bailouts/rescues from other European countries and the IMF.[142] German officials have insisted that private creditors bear some of the cost of the crisis. During the summer of 2011, a number of European banks and other institutional investors expressed willingness to voluntarily roll over the bulk of their claims that mature within the next few years. Because most of Greece's creditors are domestic and European banks, a broader restructuring could lead to a banking crisis that would, in turn, require additional bailouts and might sow the seeds of future crises.[143] A mishandling of the debt crisis in the Eurozone could also undermine the stability of the Euro.[144] As discussed below in more detail, the prospect of debt restructuring in Europe has led to discussion among European policy makers about creating a formal debt restructuring mechanism.[145]

Summary. These restructuring episodes were messy, politically determined, and idiosyncratic affairs, but they reflect a prevailing pattern. According to this pattern, a sovereign reaches the point where it cannot make a debt payment as it comes due or cannot borrow when it needs funds (often to make a debt payment). It seeks help from the IMF, which generally extends some assistance. That is enough in some circumstances, but sovereigns that still cannot service their obligations or still face other symptoms of financial crisis may seek restructuring of obligations to official and private creditors, often with some nudging by the IMF.

Restructuring, when it comes, takes a number of forms, such as a negotiated standstill or a rollover of maturing debt.[146] Middle-income sovereigns with sizable debts are most likely to restructure their private obligations by exchanging old bonds or loans for new bonds, the effect of which is to extend maturity, reduce principal, adjust interest payments, or some combination of these approaches.[147] The new bonds may feature

---

[141] *See, e.g.,* Gelpern, *Mapping to Bankruptcy, supra* note 5.
[142] *See* Lee C. Buchheit & G. Mitu Gulati, *Greek Debt – The Endgame Scenarios*, working paper, at 2, April 8, 2011, available at http://papers.ssrn.com/sol3/papers.cfm?abstract_id=1807011 (noting also support from the European Central Bank in buying the bonds of EU countries in crisis).
[143] *See* Buchheit & Gulati, *Greek Debt, supra* note 2, at 7.
[144] *See id.*
[145] *See infra* note 220 and accompanying text.
[146] *See* ROUBINI & SETSER, *supra* note 11, at 161.
[147] *See* Buchheit & Gulati, *Greek Debt, supra* note 2, at 7–9.

some type of "credit enhancement" – perhaps in the form of collateral or partial guarantees – sometimes provided or funded by other official sponsors.[148] Whatever exchange or other type of debt relief or restructuring that emerges from the crisis will be the product of some consultation or negotiation with various groups of creditors.[149]

The details of each sovereign debt-restructuring episode are largely a function of the composition of the sovereign's obligations. A middle-income sovereign's debt generally includes obligations to official creditors, as well as bonds and other securities like treasury bills, bank loans, and trade credit. Within each of these categories there will likely be further variations; for example, a sovereign may have numerous bond issues outstanding with different maturities, denominated in different currencies, subject to different laws. Perhaps most significantly, these obligations will be owed to a variety of categories of creditors – institutional and retail, domestic and external. Experience has shown that sovereigns generally have significant formal and informal latitude to alter the relationships and functional priorities between and among these obligations, especially if the restructuring proceeds through different stages over time, as it did in Russia and Argentina.[150] Thus, political and financial constraints will inevitably shape a restructuring process and may affect the status of an obligation more than contractual language would suggest.[151]

Creditor haircuts in the major sovereign debt restructurings since the 1990s have generally ranged between 25 percent and 35 percent, with variation between 13 percent and 73 percent.[152] Case by case, as the forgoing discussion suggests, there was a large variation in size of haircuts across exchanges[153] as well as significant variation in the haircuts suffered within

---

[148] See id. at 9–10. See also, Yianni & Makel, supra note 53, at 336 (noting that Seychelles' recent bond exchange "benefitted from the support of a partial credit guarantee from the African Development Bank").

[149] See Buchheit & Gulati, Greek Debt, supra note 2, at 9 (noting that the IMF requires some consultation as part of its policy of "lending into arrears").

[150] See Gelpern & Setser, supra note 18, at 797 ("[T]he effective status of a single obligation relative to others could change several times in its lifetime as the sovereign dilutes, elevates, and subordinates instruments to suit.").

[151] See Buchheit & Gulati, Greek Debt, supra note 2, at 8. "Governments rarely allow the legal features of their instruments to drive core restructuring decisions. The desire to limit legal liability is one of many government concerns, and rarely the dominant one. The desire to curry favor with powerful political groups, to avoid a bank run, to stem the outflow of foreign exchange, or to preserve access to future financing may drive government policy." Gelpern & Setser, supra note 18, at 797.

[152] See generally Sturzenegger & Zettelmeyer, supra note 70.

[153] See id. at 58.

the same exchange.[154] Aside from political considerations, these variations have generally depended on the instruments surrendered and the ones received, especially if there were various options under the exchange. Generally, Brady bondholders did better than others – due primarily to compensation for collateral.[155] It is hard to make a general observation about the difference in treatment of residents and foreign investors across episodes; sometimes residents were treated better than foreigners and sometimes perhaps less so.[156] It was often the case, however, that at least some domestic creditors were treated better than others and better than foreign creditors.[157]

In general, the restructurings that took place had relatively high participation rates. The participation rates may reflect some coercive action by sovereigns. According to one study, however, it does not appear that sovereign debtors have been more coercive in recent decades than when most sovereign creditors were banks.[158] Participation rates may reflect that sovereigns made attractive offers, sometimes including cash payments, to avoid holdouts and litigation.[159] There are notable examples of exchange offers being withdrawn, perhaps reflecting that consent can indeed be withheld by creditors in some circumstances. Furthermore, most restructurings had some holdouts, and there has been an increase in litigation related to sovereign debt.[160] According to one study, litigation appears to have delayed restructuring in 7 out of 90 cases since 1980.[161] Finally, although commentators and scholars have tended to assume that bond debt is harder to restructure than a smaller number of bank loans, there have been a significant number of defaults and restructurings in recent years, and they have taken less time to resolve than restructurings took in the bank-loan era.[162]

Costs and Consequences

Most theoretical discussions of sovereign defaults and debt restructuring begin with or circle around a background question: Given that sovereign

---

[154] See id. at 61.
[155] See id. at 62.
[156] See id.
[157] See generally Gelpern & Setser, supra note 18.
[158] See Panizza et al., supra note 10, at 23–25.
[159] See id. at 22.
[160] See supra notes 31–36 and accompanying text.
[161] See Panizza et al., supra note 10, at 22 (citing Christoph Trebesch, Delays in Sovereign Debt Restructuring: Should We Really Blame the Creditors? unpublished).
[162] See id. at 22.

obligations can be difficult or impossible to enforce, either de jure or de facto,[163] why do sovereigns ever pay their obligations at all?[164] Or, put another way, why does anyone extend credit to a sovereign borrower? In theory, there must be some nonlegal factors that compel sovereigns to meet their obligations and repay their debts. Presumably, these nonlegal factors are costs related to default. Thus, scholarship on the topic has explored whether sovereigns repay because they will be excluded from credit markets[165] or face higher borrowing costs if they default,[166] because they will suffer other more direct penalties,[167] or because they will suffer various types of "collateral damage" from default.[168]

There is evidence that sovereigns do incur financial and economic costs as a result of defaulting on and restructuring their obligations. They appear to suffer some market exclusion and increased borrowing costs during their default period, but they quickly regain access to credit, and their borrowing costs quickly return to the status quo ante.[169] Furthermore, sovereign defaults appear to be associated with loss in trade and tend to be "costly for export oriented industries," although "the channel linking default to trade remains a mystery."[170] Evidence suggests that the most significant cost of sovereign default is a drop in domestic output,[171] which can have long-lasting effects.[172] Finally, it is worth noting that default may cause noneconomic losses for the politicians and governments who trigger them, which may go a long way to explain why sovereigns generally repay their debts.[173]

In sum, default and restructuring is costly for sovereigns in various ways. This helps explain why sovereigns take their financial obligations

---

[163] See *supra* note 30 and accompanying text.
[164] See ROUBINI & SETSER, *supra* note 11, at 80–83.
[165] See Panizza et al., *supra* note 10, at 9–10.
[166] See id. at 11–12.
[167] See id. at 10–11.
[168] See id. at 12–13.
[169] See id. at 25–27, 33–35. "Except in the short run, the effects of defaults on borrowing costs seem small, and eventually disappear." *Id.* at 27.
[170] See id. at 28–29 (citing evidence that "countries that trade more can contain higher levels of debt").
[171] See id. at 29–31 (citing evidence that "the costs of default are mainly domestic"). "If anything, defaults appear to be deterred by the domestic 'collateral damage' that tends to accompany debt crises, rather than punishments from the outside." *Id.* at 42. *See also id.* at 37–38.
[172] See id. at 38 ("[T]here is not reason to think that they are compensated by higher growth after the crisis.").
[173] See id. at 32. Where political economy runs the opposite direction – as in Ecuador, perhaps – that may help explain default.

seriously, and it suggests that even sovereigns with inefficient levels of debt or acute liquidity constraints will delay or avoid defaulting or seeking relief, further increasing the costs of financial distress. If so, and if sovereigns will still suffer these basic consequences of restructuring under a formal mechanism for debt restructuring, this weighs against claims that extending bankruptcy protection would significantly reduce the overall costs of sovereigns' financial distress.

Lessons for States

There is one overriding lesson for American states from the experience of sovereign debt restructuring: Throughout recent history, many sovereigns have successfully restructured their obligations even though there is no formal mechanism for doing so. The modern approach to debt restructuring, when it has been conducted, effectively achieves most of the functions of a bankruptcy regime.[174] Ad hoc sovereign debt restructuring has developed a type of "hardware," if not a formal mechanism.[175] Even as creditors have grown more aggressive, and arguably more adept, in formally enforcing sovereign obligations, sovereigns and their lawyers have been very successful in finding ways to effect a restructuring of, or obtain relief from, a wide array of claims – including bank loans, trade credit, and bonds[176] – and to reduce the effectiveness of holdout creditors. Participation rates for numerous voluntary debt exchanges have generally been high, even in Argentina, which imposed a relatively large haircut and faced a significant number of holdouts.[177]

Beyond this basic lesson, there are a few other factors and qualifications that are worth emphasizing. First, with one arguable exception – Ecuador's restructuring of 2009 – sovereigns have only restructured their obligations in the midst of a clear and acute crisis. In general, in the days, or weeks, or months preceding these episodes, it became clear that the sovereigns' obligations were unsustainable or that they were facing a liquidity crisis

---

[174] As Nouriel Roubini and Brad Setser put it: "A de facto – though not de jure – Chapter 11 debt reorganization process for sovereigns' international debt already exists." See ROUBINI & SETSER, *supra* note 11, at 290. *See also* Gelpern & Setser, *supra* note 18, at 798 (noting that the modern approach to restructuring, which encompasses and affects a broad array of sovereign obligations, "is much closer to firm bankruptcy than to a traditional sovereign restructuring").

[175] ROUBINI & SETSER, *supra* note 11, at 338.

[176] *See id.* at 120 ("[B]onds – including those that lack collective action clauses – can be restructured in a wide range of circumstances."). *See also id.* at 162, 166–167.

[177] *See id.* at 166–67.

(or both) and that insisting on full enforcement might reduce the value of existing claims against the sovereign. We should hope that no American state reaches such a point of acute crisis, but if a state is not in crisis, its stakeholders may not have sufficient incentive to be willing to agree to restructure their claims. But again, introducing a formal mechanism would not necessarily change this; states might also resist employing a formal mechanism until they were in acute distress.

Second, a little coercion goes a long way.[178] Sovereigns must presumably offer a minimally appealing exchange to encourage voluntary participation by claimants, but they can stack the deck by threatening default, effectively imposing a standstill, using exit consents, or diluting the claims of potential holdouts, among other tactics. It is possible that sovereign immunity will save states from significant holdout problems and effectively provide a stay on enforcement actions against the states.[179] As noted earlier, however, state sovereign immunity may not provide an impenetrable wall, and state waivers of immunity may become more common now that state default and bankruptcy can be discussed in polite company.[180] It stands to reason that states will have to negotiate with their creditors to restructure their obligations and to obtain other relief in much the same way that sovereigns do.

Third, the details of sovereign debt restructurings tend to be determined in large part by the composition of instruments and, more importantly, the composition of creditors.[181] Some domestic creditors may have significant political clout, for example. Creditor banks, whether domestic or foreign, may command attention because of the destabilizing effects that restructuring has on them that might cascade further. Furthermore, foreign creditors, especially but not exclusively official ones, might have geopolitical importance or might represent a needed source for future finance. These and similar issues will be relevant for states. Steven Schwarcz has noted, for example, that state obligations generally include multiple bond issues by different state agencies, which might command different degrees

---

[178] *See id.* at 120–121, 143–145, 163–164.
[179] *See* Schwarcz, *A Minimalist Approach, supra* note 3, at 4.
[180] *See supra* note 41 and accompanying text.
[181] *See* Gelpern & Setser, *supra* note 18, at 797 ("[W]hen a government runs out of money, it often treats domestic and foreign creditors differently.") "[D]espite important concerns about inter-creditor equality, the ability to treat domestic and foreign creditors differently is a necessary policy option for governments in financial crises." *Id.* at 796. They may do so ex post, after restructuring, by recapitalizing domestic banks and not providing similar support to other creditors, for example. *See id.* at 799.

of attention from state officials.[182] To the extent that banks hold state debt, state officials may be concerned about the effect on the banking system of restructuring bank claims even though states do not have to internalize all, perhaps not even most, of the costs of a banking crisis. Federal officials would certainly be concerned about banks holding bonds of a state in financial distress, and any state in such a condition could not be unconcerned about the interests of the federal government.

Fourth, the choice between a bailout and a debt restructuring is often something of a false one. At the very least, "the official sector has an important role to play in the restructuring of debts owed to private creditors"[183] and has helped sovereigns and stakeholders coordinate restructurings.[184] Official creditors often voluntarily restructure their own claims against sovereigns in crisis, whether by rolling over debt or taking haircuts.[185] Increasingly, they insist on private sector involvement as a condition to their extending new money or reducing their own claims. Furthermore, most restructurings require some financial support from the official sector.[186] This support is sometimes needed to provide cash payments to some creditors as part of a debt exchange (to pay past-due interest, for example) to fund government operations and services during a restructuring, or to stave off further crisis. A sovereign debtor may not be able to tap private markets for financing during or in the immediate wake of a restructuring.[187] States would very likely face a similar problem if they restructured their debt or were able to file for bankruptcy, and any restructuring or bankruptcy process would likely need to provide for financial support during and immediately after any debt restructuring.[188] This strongly suggests that the federal government would help finance any state debt restructuring

---

[182] See Schwarcz, *A Minimalist Approach*, supra note 3, at 26–28.

[183] ROUBINI & SETSER, supra note 11, at 121; see also id. at 141–142 (discussing official sector support during bail-ins). See also Buchheit & Gulati, *Greek Debt*, supra note 2, at 1 (abstract) (noting that Greece would still need financial support from the official sector even if it restructures its debt – "But it may change how some of the funds are spent (for example, backstopping the domestic banking system as opposed to paying off maturing debt in full)").

[184] See ROUBINI & SETSER, supra note 11, at 162. See also id. at 164–166 (calling on the official sector to provide more coordination).

[185] See id. at 162–163.

[186] See id. at 12.

[187] See id. at 19–20 (noting IMF policy to backstop sovereigns' domestic banks and proposing that the IMF increase its lending to countries while they undergo debt restructuring).

[188] See, e.g., Schwarcz, *A Minimalist Approach*, supra note 3, at 28–29 (suggesting that the private market could provide such funding but that the federal government might need to do so).

or support a state's activities during and after a restructuring and would, therefore, likely have some significant and direct leverage in the details of the restructuring.

Fifth, states should anticipate that unpleasant policy adjustment will be part of any approach to resolving a crisis.[189] Creditors agreeing to restructure sovereign obligations rely on this, and the official sector, especially the IMF, demands it as a condition of financial assistance. Here again, Greece provides a salient example. The IMF and its EU partners were unwilling to release portions of their rescue package until, among other things, Greece's parliament adopted a very unpopular austerity package.

III. PROPOSALS FOR SOVEREIGN BANKRUPTCY REGIMES

Dissatisfied with the existing practice of sovereign debt restructuring, a number of writers and policy makers have contemplated creating a bankruptcy regime or some other formal debt-restructuring mechanism for sovereigns. Interest in this topic began to gather momentum in the 1980s, but the idea long predates this period.[190] The precise details and motivations for these proposals have differed somewhat over the years, but the range of design possibilities for a bankruptcy-type framework for sovereigns has generally been consistent over time. In many respects, these proposals and the debate they have engendered mirror the proposals and debate over allowing states to obtain bankruptcy relief. Perhaps because this movement has not borne fruit, the debate over sovereign bankruptcy also yields some meaningful lessons for commentators who are interested in the possibility of extending bankruptcy protection to American states.

Motivations

Proposals to create a formal sovereign bankruptcy-type mechanism have aimed to address interrelated underlying concerns with the existing ad hoc process of sovereign debt restructuring. First, there is a widespread belief that the current approach to debt restructuring is too costly[191]; however,

---

[189] *See id.* at 30 (proposing that some form of adjustment or conditionality could be included in a state bankruptcy process).

[190] *See, e.g.*, Anne O. Krueger, *Sovereign Debt Restructuring Mechanism – One Year Later*, address at the European Commission, Dec. 10, 2002, available at https://www.imf.org/external/np/speeches/2002/121002.htm (noting a conference on the topic of an international agreement regarding sovereign debt disputes in 1874).

[191] *See* ROUBINI & SETSER, *supra* note 11, at 291.

there is not agreement in the literature about why it is too costly or about the consequences of these costs. One possibility is that the process of restructuring is too cumbersome for sovereigns and, especially, for creditors who face basic coordination or collective-action problems.[192] According to this view, the shift to bond financing made debt restructuring more difficult in this regard and thus more expensive, in part because it makes it easier for creditors to hold out for private gain at the expense of other creditors and sovereign debtors. Recent developments in sovereign debt litigation and enforcement of judgments against sovereign debtors have amplified these concerns[193] and fueled interest in sovereign bankruptcy and other strategies for eliminating holdouts, like collective-action clauses.[194] It is possible that these and other direct and indirect costs to sovereigns of the existing process of restructuring are high enough that some sovereigns in distress or approaching distress may not seek timely debt relief, and those that do seek relief do not get enough.

Second, and related, proponents of sovereign bankruptcy argue that if debt restructuring is too costly or difficult or otherwise unappealing for sovereigns and other stakeholders, it is more likely that sovereigns experiencing financial distress will seek and obtain bailouts.[195] At the point of acute financial distress, if no other relief is feasible, it is extremely hard for policy makers to refuse a rescue or bailout. This, in turn, could exacerbate the moral hazard problem of financial rescue – if sovereigns and their creditors know that bailouts are available, they may not make as much of an effort to avoid actions that could lead to financial distress for the sovereign. Thus, the official sector increasingly wants to "involve" the private sector in financial bailouts to force them to internalize more of the risk and consequences of sovereign debtors' financial distress.

Third, and also related, the prevailing approach to sovereign debt restructuring generally excludes sovereigns that are not facing financial crisis but are nonetheless heavily indebted, some with debts that are potentially odious or illegitimate. Ecuador's remarkable recent restructuring is an exception that proves this general rule. Although some sovereigns may

---

[192] *See* Rogoff & Zettelmeyer, *supra* note 55, at 28–32.
[193] *See id.* at 8.
[194] *See* Panizza et al., *supra* note 10, at 21–22. *See infra* notes 211–217 and accompanying text.
[195] *See, e.g.*, Rogoff & Zettelmeyer, *supra* note 55, at 34; Steven Schwarcz, *Facing the Debt Challenge of Countries that are Too Big to Fail*, in ROBERT W. KOLB, ED., SOVEREIGN DEBT: FROM SAFETY TO DEFAULT, 2 (forthcoming) ("[A]n orderly resolution procedure for troubled countries can bypass the need for a bailout.").

be able to obtain debt relief under the Heavily Indebted Poor Countries (HIPC) program or from the Paris Club, this relief has arguably been modest and difficult to obtain, and it is limited to low-income sovereigns. A sovereign bankruptcy mechanism might provide a credible mechanism for over-indebted countries, however defined, to obtain more robust debt relief without forcing them to slide first into acute financial distress. It could also provide an explicit provision for discharging debt on equitable grounds.

These concerns about the costs, limits, unfairness, and inefficiency of sovereign debt restructuring have fueled a rich and interesting history of ideas about sovereign bankruptcy. As Panniza, Sturzenegger, and Zettelmeyer write, "[t]he main policy message from [the sovereign debt] literature is that there is indeed room for public intervention that would both reduce the costs of debt crises ex post and improve efficiency ex ante."[196] That view may not be universally held, yet the topic has shifted from the fringes of conventional wisdom to well within the mainstream.[197] Events in Europe and the prospect of sovereign debt crisis there have led to the most recent, and perhaps one of the most serious, discussions of the topic.

Proposals

Most proposals for a sovereign bankruptcy regime or a formal debt-restructuring mechanism have aimed to provide one or more of three basic functions of a bankruptcy system: stopping collection efforts against the debtor during restructuring (the stay); enabling creditor coordination by allowing for majority or supra-majority of creditors to bind holdouts; and creating a mechanism to encourage some creditors to provide new money during and immediately after the restructuring. These proposals tend to fall along a spectrum of thick institutional structure to thin, featuring a variety of international legal mechanisms and varying roles for the IMF.

Perhaps the first serious attempt to advance a formal sovereign debt-restructuring institution was made in 1979 by a group of countries with developing economies. They proposed creating an international debt commission to address a wave of debt crises that were brewing in a number of countries across the developing world.[198] The commission would entertain requests for relief from sovereign debtors, examine the debtors' circumstances, make recommendations for debt relief and new official sector

---

[196] *See* Panizza et al., *supra* note 10, at 40.
[197] *See* Rogoff & Zettelmeyer, *supra* note 55, at 34.
[198] *See id.* at 5.

support, and then convene all of the parties necessary to achieve these recommendations. Presumably, the strength of such a commission would depend on its legal authority and its ability to bind various stakeholders, but the formal basis and institutional design of this proposed commission were never fleshed out.

Shortly thereafter, Christopher Oechsli proposed that over-indebted developing sovereigns have access to something like Chapter 11 bankruptcy, the reorganization chapter of the U.S. Bankruptcy Code.[199] The proposal focused on the benefits of bankruptcy's formal triggering process, its use of creditor committees, and the third-party function of a court, trustee, or examiner. It envisioned that the IMF could serve as the equivalent of a bankruptcy court but argued that contractual agreements to arbitrate under International Centre for Settlement of Investment Disputes (ICSID) or some similar framework could also serve this function.

In 1984, Whitney Debevoise proposed that the existing legal framework under IMF's Articles of Agreement could provide formal authority for a stay on collection,[200] a crucial aspect of any bankruptcy system.[201] According to this proposal, Article VIII could provide legal basis for the IMF to formally authorize a sovereign member of the IMF to stop paying its debt obligations. If this analysis is correct, then the IMF's Articles, an international treaty with nearly universal force, could provide a legal tool for staying creditor enforcement against sovereigns as they tried to restructure their obligations.[202] An effective payment standstill – or stay on collection – can be a very useful form of debt relief, functionally equivalent to direct emergency financial assistance.[203]

In the years after the debt crises of the 1980s and before the Mexican financial crisis of the mid-1990s, there was a flurry of interest in extending some type of bankruptcy protection to sovereigns.[204] The literature from that time included various proposals for a new institution – independent from the IMF, although perhaps affiliated with it – to be created by treaty

---

[199] Christopher G. Oeschli, *Procedural Guidelines for Renegotiating LDC Debts: An Analogy to Chapter 11 of the U.S. Bankruptcy Reform Act*, 21 VA. J. IN'TL L. 305 (1981); Rogoff & Zettelmeyer, *supra* note 55, at 5.
[200] Whitney Debevoise, *Exchange Controls and External Indebtedness: A Modest Proposal for a Deferral Mechanism Employing Bretton Woods Concepts*, 7 HOUSTON J. INT'L L. 157 (1984).
[201] *See, e.g.*, Douglas G. Baird & Randal C. Picker, *A Simple Noncooperative Bargaining Model of Corporate Reorganizations*, 20 J. LEGAL STUD. 311, 312 (1991).
[202] *See* Rogoff & Zettelmeyer, *supra* note 55, at 12.
[203] *See* ROUBINI & SETSER, *supra* note 11, at 97–98.
[204] *See* Rogoff & Zettelmeyer, *supra* note 55, at 13–17.

that would have legal authority to force negotiations, preclude litigation against the sovereign by holdout creditors, enforce negotiated terms, and require policy adjustments by the sovereign debtor.²⁰⁵ Other proposals from this time period included a mechanism (either the IMF or an independent institution) triggered by a sovereign's debt load and a fund to insure payments by sovereigns that fell under the debt load trigger.²⁰⁶

In 1995, Jeffrey Sachs gave a big boost to the idea of sovereign bankruptcy by suggesting in very general terms in a lecture that the IMF could effectively serve as a bankruptcy court and a lender of last resort.²⁰⁷ As the sovereign debt crises of the following decade unfolded, and especially as holdout creditors were increasingly perceived to be complicating efforts to restructure sovereign debt, the idea began to attract increasing attention. The early 2000s saw a number of prominent proposals, including one by Andy Haldane and Mark Kruger, which proposed a thin process run by the IMF or some other independent international entity that would (informally) authorize a payment standstill, arrange for seniority for new financial support to the sovereign, and coordinate negotiations between the sovereign and its creditors.²⁰⁸

---

²⁰⁵ *See id.*; Barry C. Barnet, Sergio Galvis, & Chislain Gouraige, Jr., *On Third World Debt*, 25 HARV. INT'L L.J. 83 (1984); Benjamin Cohen, *A Global Chapter 11*, 75 FOR. POL'Y 109 (1989); Kunibert Raffer, *Applying Chapter 9 Insolvency to International Debts: An Economically Efficient Solution With a Human Face*, 18 WORLD DEV. 301 (1990). Cohen's proposal would have allowed the institution to bind non-consenting creditors to an agreement assented to by a majority. *See* Rogoff & Zettelmeyer, *supra* note 55, at 14–15. Raffer's proposal was essentially modeled after Chapter 9 of the U.S. Bankruptcy Code (which is available to American municipalities).

²⁰⁶ *See* Rogoff & Zettelmeyer, *supra* note 55, at 15–17 (citing a speech by Daniel Kaeser in 1990).

²⁰⁷ *See* Jeffrey Sachs, *Do We Need an International Lender of Last Resort?* Frank D. Graham Lecture at Princeton Univ., available at http://www.earth.columbia.edu/sitefiles/file/about/director/pubs/intllr.pdf; Rogoff & Zettelmeyer, *supra* note 55, at 17–20 ("Although it was never formally published, Sachs' lecture probably did more to popularize the idea of international bankruptcy than all of the literature that preceded him"). As it turns out, the IMF was simultaneously studying the possibility of creating a sovereign bankruptcy mechanism that it would operate that would be based on the Chapter 9 model. *See id.* at 19. John Chun elaborated Sachs' argument by proposing the creation of an institution that would be modeled on Chapter 9 – e.g., automatic stay, priority for new financing, and authority to bind holdout creditors – that would be an independent affiliate of the IMF. *See* John H. Chun, *"Post-Modern" Sovereign Debt Crisis: Did Mexico Need an International Bankruptcy Forum?* 64 FORDHAM L. REV. 2647 (1996).

²⁰⁸ *See* Andy Haldane & Mark Kruger, *The Resolution of International Financial Crises: Private and Public Funds*, Bank of Canada, working paper, 2001–2020 (2001). Other influential proposals made during this period include Barry Eichengreen, *Can the Moral Hazard Caused by IMF Bailouts be Reduced?* Geneva Reports on the World Economy (2000) (proposing the use of a standstill mechanism coupled with contractual collection

Subsequently, in the midst of the unfolding debt crisis in Argentina, Anne Krueger, then acting as first deputy managing director of the IMF, authored the most prominent sovereign bankruptcy-type mechanism proposal to date.[209] Krueger's Sovereign Debt Restructuring Mechanism (SDRM), as it has come to be known, would ideally be authorized by treaty (perhaps as an amendment of the IMF's Articles of Agreement). Although the proposal set forth a number of design alternatives, it clearly advocated a mechanism operated by the IMF that would have authority to impose a stay on creditor enforcement activities, to coordinate negotiation toward a restructuring plan that could be binding on some non-consenting creditors, and to ensure priority for new financial support to the sovereign. Although it attracted much attention and spurred debate, Krueger's SDRM proposal did not take hold. There was apparently a lack of support from U.S. officials, but there were other objections from other quarters that might have proven fatal as well.[210]

As it became clear that the SDRM was not going to happen anytime soon, there was a corresponding spike in enthusiasm for more informal solutions, including contractual alternatives to bankruptcy-type protections and, especially, collective-action clauses.[211] As noted earlier, sovereign bond contracts allow for a majority or supermajority of bondholders to alter various terms of the contract on behalf of all creditors. Bonds issued under English law have long included such clauses

action clauses); Adam Lerrick & Allan Meltzer, *Blueprint for an International Lender of Last Resort* (unpublished, discussed in Rogoff & Zettelmeyer, *supra* note 55, at 26–27) (proposing a structure similar to Haldane & Kruger, with brief unconditional lending by the IMF to support the price of the sovereign's debt); Steven Schwarcz, *Sovereign Debt Restructuring: A Bankruptcy Reorganization Approach*, 85 CORNELL L. REV. 101 (2000). Schwarcz proposed a treaty to implement a "minimal" bankruptcy that would essentially ensure priority of new financing to the sovereign and provide that a supermajority of creditors could formally bind all creditors. *Id*. Negotiations toward a reorganization plan would ideally be conducted by ICSID or a tribunal modeled after it. *Id*.

[209] Anne O. Krueger, *A New Approach to Sovereign Debt Restructuring*, IMF (2002), available at http://www.imf.org/external/pubs/ft/exrp/sdrm/eng/sdrm.pdf. See also IMF, *Proposed Features of a Sovereign Debt Restructuring Mechanism*, available at http://www.imf.org/external/np/pdr/sdrm/2003/021203.htm. The Krueger/IMF proposal spurred additional commentary and scholarship on the topic. See, e.g., Patrick Bolton & David A. Skeel, Jr., *Inside the Black Box: How Should a Sovereign Bankruptcy Framework Be Structured?* 53 EMORY L.J. 763 (2004).

[210] *See, e.g., Sovereign Debt Restructuring Mechanism: Who Opposes it and Why?* available at http://www.cilae.org/publicaciones/SDRM.pdf (describing concerns of borrowers, creditors, and others).

[211] See Rogoff & Zettelmeyer, *supra* note 55, at 23. *See also* Anna Gelpern & Mitu Gulati, *Public Symbol in Private Contract: A Case Study*, 84 WASH. U. L. REV. 1627 (2006); Eichengreen, *supra* note 207.

that allow less than unanimous approval to change even fundamental terms regarding payments, principal, and interest. Bonds issued under New York law traditionally only allowed less than unanimous consent to more minor changes. After Argentina, it became conventional wisdom that expanding the inclusion and use of collective-action clauses could significantly improve the existing process for sovereign debt restructuring.[212] At least some observers believed that doing so was preferable to creating a more formal sovereign bankruptcy mechanism. Other observers were skeptical that these changes would make it easier to avoid or resolve sovereign debt crises,[213] viewing them as an improvement but not a necessary one.[214] After much advocacy and nudging from the official sector, bonds issued under New York law began to include broader collective-action clauses in recent years. Policy makers in Europe have proposed that they should be included in bonds issued by members of the Eurozone.[215] As the current crisis reveals, however, collective-action clauses may be of limited value in resolving a full-blown debt crisis.[216] It is worth noting that initial reports suggest that state bonds do not contain collective-action clauses relating to payment terms, but there are not yet reliable data on this question.[217]

Thus, throughout the last decade, the debate over reforming sovereign debt restructuring has traveled in the space between contractual approaches and bankruptcy-type approaches.[218] The contract approach appears to have won the day after the demise of the SDRM but has proven to be an insufficient, partial solution at best. Not surprisingly, as the threat

---

[212] See W. Mark C. Weidemaier & Mitu Gulati, *How Markets Work: The Lawyer's Version*, working paper (on file with author) ("Reading the sovereign debt literature, and listening to the pronouncements of public officials, one sometimes gets the sense that CACs have near-magical properties.").

[213] See, e.g., ROUBINI & SETSER, *supra* note 11, at 11.

[214] See id. at 11–12, 167–169, 309; Buchheit & Gulati, *Greek Debt*, *supra* note 2, at 9 (noting that there is "no reason not to use" collective action clauses); Schwarcz, *A Minimalist Approach*, *supra* note 3, at 9–10 (discussing the limitations of collective action clauses).

[215] See Weidemaier & Gulati, *supra* note 212, at 2.

[216] See id. ("It may seem far-fetched to suggest that a contract term can prevent global financial crisis or make future bailouts unnecessary. (It seems so to us.)").

[217] See Schwarcz, *A Minimalist Approach*, *supra* note 3, at 8 (finding that a small random sample of municipal bonds required unanimous consent to change payment terms). As discussed in *supra* note 43, given the large number and wide variety of state bond issues, any claims about contracting practices must be viewed as highly tentative until the practice has been empirically investigated.

[218] See Rogoff & Zettelmeyer, *supra* note 55, at 34.

of a full-blown sovereign debt crisis reemerges, this time across Europe, there have been new calls for new approaches to sovereign debt crises and debt restructuring.[219] Most notably, German and French officials proposed early in the crisis to create a Berlin club of sorts, a "mechanism" that would be run by the Eurozone members providing for financial support that would be conditional on policy adjustment and, perhaps, on private creditor involvement.[220] This appears to signal an appetite for something more formal than the existing approach to resolving debt crises, and it is widely reported that some German officials prefer something in this direction. Nonetheless, the recent agreement to expand the scope of the European Financial Stability Facility reflects a preference for informality and flexibility. European officials may end up recreating the current informal, ad hoc model on a regional scale, perhaps substituting a European Union institution or facility for the IMF. Anne Krueger and coauthors proposed a European sovereign debt restructuring mechanism, a regional version of the SDRM. It is essentially the SDRM model for the European context with two institutions playing the role initially envisioned for the IMF under the SDRM – one to serve the function of a bankruptcy court (perhaps the European Court of Justice) and the other to coordinate economic assistance to the sovereign debtor.[221] Although the proposal apparently has some official support in Europe, it does not appear to be gaining any more traction than previous proposals. Meanwhile, Greece has already begun to muddle its way through an ad hoc debt restructuring, with more likely on the way.

Obstacles and Objections

As discussion about allowing American states to obtain bankruptcy relief gathers steam, it is worth exploring why sovereign bankruptcy has not escaped the conceptual realm. First, consider the practical political obstacles. What appear to be the most far-reaching proposals require some form of international agreement, presumably in the form of new treaties or

---

[219] See, e.g., Schwarcz, supra note 195.
[220] See Lee C. Buchheit & G. Mitu Gulati, *Endgame Scenarios, supra* note 142, at 2; *Paris and Berlin Near Mechanism Deal*, Financial Times, Nov. 25, 2010, available at http://www.ft.com/intl/cms/s/0/9f9fd0f6-f8d3-11df-b550-00144feab49a.html#axzz1S9kWIGfT.
[221] See Francois Gianviti, Anne O. Krueger, Jean Pisani-Ferry, & Andre Sapir, *A European Mechanism for Sovereign Debt Restructuring: A Proposal*, working paper, available at http://www.indiana.edu/~econdept/workshops/Fall_2010_Papers/EMSDR_191010.pdf.

amendments to existing ones. The required treaty-making process would be extremely difficult and time-consuming to orchestrate in the best of circumstances, absent a current crisis. At the very least, skepticism about the viability or the effect[222] of any sovereign bankruptcy regime will make it difficult to convince policy makers to tackle the treaty-making process or the process of obtaining ratification back home. And why would policy makers want to expend the time and resources to tackle these practical challenges when there is not an immediate or acute need to do so? Anything worth the trouble may be too difficult to get adopted in economic peacetime.[223]

Once there is an immediate or acute need, then a different set – and different type – of practical and political problems emerge. Most obviously, at that point, there may simply not be time for lawmaking or institution building, and general substantive concerns with sovereign debt relief become extremely salient and particularized. The winners and losers then have names and faces. At such a moment, negotiation over institutional design details may become outcome oriented and fraught – designing a mechanism could easily become the battleground over how to resolve the crisis of the moment.

Furthermore, there is deeper resistance to sovereign bankruptcy regime from some scholars and policy makers who disapprove of any mechanism that makes it easier for sovereigns to obtain debt relief. Some are concerned that, as with bailouts, improving the process of obtaining debt relief may create moral hazard, making sovereigns and their counterparties less hesitant to accept risks of the sovereign's financial distress and more willing to default strategically.[224] As Panizza and coauthors write, "Intervention could be costly or it could backfire. ... Simply lowering the costs of renegotiation across the board ... will not do ...."[225] If extending bankruptcy protection increases moral hazard for sovereigns, then it would presumably increase the cost of credit to sovereigns. There is significant debate, however, about whether this would happen.[226]

---

[222] See ROUBINI & SETSER, *supra* note 11, at 324–325 (suggesting that a sovereign debt restructuring mechanism would not "radically change the behavior" of sovereigns or the IMF).

[223] *See id.* at 323–324.

[224] *See id.* at 73–76.

[225] *See* Panizza *et al.*, *supra* note 10, at 40.

[226] *See* Schwarcz, *A Minimalist Approach*, *supra* note 3, at 19. *See* Stephen J. Choi, G. Mitu Gulati, & Eric Posner, *Pricing Terms in Sovereign Debt Contracts: A Greek Case Study with Implications for the European Crisis Resolution Mechanism*, working paper, available at http://papers.ssrn.com/sol3/papers.cfm?abstract_id=1713914 (2011) (finding

Ideally, any sovereign debt-restructuring mechanism should be available only for countries with "excusable" defaults,[227] but creating a mechanism that can successfully distinguish excusable from inexcusable in practice is tricky, to say the least.

There is a countervailing view that if defaults and restructuring were easier, it would discourage overborrowing because creditors would be less likely to extend credit or be more careful in doing so.[228] This is a compelling point. However, as noted earlier, there is evidence that sovereigns are already hesitant to seek debt relief when they could do so, perhaps because of economic or political costs. If sovereigns anticipate suffering large costs from any default or restructuring, they may be unwilling to use any mechanism or approach, however well designed. If so, any disciplining effect or moral hazard from making bankruptcy available would likely be reduced.

Relevance for States

The history of the idea of sovereign bankruptcy holds little promise for those who want to extend bankruptcy protection to American states. It does seem likely that the practical constraints of extending bankruptcy protection to states are less forbidding than those in the sovereign context. If the question is limited to whether states should be able to file for bankruptcy under Chapter 9 of the Bankruptcy Code,[229] then there is no need to design a regime from scratch and surmount all of the negotiations that would be required to do so in the sovereign context. The regime is already designed; the question would simply be whether to extend it to states. Doing so could be accomplished with very easy amendments to Chapter 9. In other words, the logistics of enabling states to file for bankruptcy could be much easier and less costly to resolve than those of creating a sovereign bankruptcy regime from scratch.

Logistics aside, however, many of the political obstacles to sovereign bankruptcy exist in the state context as well. The history of the sovereign bankruptcy proposals suggests that if there is no clear immediate or acute need to extend Chapter 9 to states, then policy makers will not want to

---

evidence that factors relevant to potential restructuring – in this case the choice of law provisions of Greek sovereign bonds – affect the value/price of the bonds).

[227] *See* Panizza et al., *supra* note 10, at 41.
[228] *See* ROUBINI & SETSER, *supra* note 11, at 84–87.
[229] *But see* Schwarcz, *A Minimalist Approach*, *supra* note 3 (proposing a "minimalist" restructuring scheme as opposed to extending Chapter 9).

expend whatever political capital is needed to push through a new regime that might not be necessary. State officials have thus far been decidedly unenthusiastic about the prospect of amending U.S. law to allow states to file for bankruptcy.[230] Furthermore, if a state reaches crisis point, then the question of amending Chapter 9 will be wrapped up in debates about how to resolve that crisis – voting to reform Chapter 9 will be seen as a vote in favor of letting that particular state file for bankruptcy, impose a haircut on particular bondholders, and renegotiate particular agreements with particular stakeholders (who vote).

Finally, the underlying theoretical issue of whether it is efficient (ex ante or ex post or both) to rationalize the debt relief process also applies in the context of states. There is no solid evidence at this point for the claim that extending to states the ability to file for bankruptcy would reduce the incidence or the scope of bailouts. If the option of bankruptcy makes debt relief more available, American policy makers will have to convince themselves that enabling states to obtain debt relief or renegotiate agreements with public employees will not increase the chances that states will spend and borrow more than they should, make promises they cannot keep, and thereby experience financial distress in the first place.

CONCLUSION

American states and sovereign nations are comparable financial actors in many fundamental respects. Despite the fact that they can and do become heavily indebted and experience financial distress, there is no formal mechanism for facilitating the efficient restructuring of their obligations if that becomes necessary or desirable. The history of sovereign debt crises and debt restructuring reflects that much can be done in the absence of a formal mechanism and provides some lessons for states. The experience of sovereign debtors suggests that if a state experiences an acute financial crisis, it will likely find a way to encourage its counterparties to agree to restructure or reduce their claims even if they have no legal obligation to do so and have some legal basis for objecting. It may be suboptimal to force a state to reach the point of acute crisis before it can gain its creditors' full attention, and the overall costs of ad hoc restructuring may be higher for states and their creditors (or the federal government) than those of reorganization in bankruptcy. Whatever the merits of extending bankruptcy to states,

---

[230] See id. at 11–12.

however, the history of efforts to promote a sovereign bankruptcy regime or a sovereign debt-restructuring mechanism is instructive. It suggests that even if there is room for improvement over an ad hoc approach, there is unlikely to be much of an appetite among policy makers for adopting a more formal mechanism.

PART III

Evaluating Solutions

8

State Bankruptcy from the Ground Up

DAVID A. SKEEL, JR.

INTRODUCTION

The nineteenth-century English poet William Wordsworth famously defined poetry as the "spontaneous overflow of powerful feelings ... recollected in tranquility."[1] By this definition, there is something a little poetic about the recent debate as to whether Congress should enact a bankruptcy law for states. In late 2010, as the extent of the fiscal crisis in many states became clear, a handful of commentators and politicians proposed that Congress enact a bankruptcy law for states.[2] "If Congress does its part by enacting a new bankruptcy chapter for states," one advocate concluded with a somewhat hyperbolic flourish, California governor "Jerry Brown will be in a position to do his part by using it."[3] These proposals met immediate, passionate resistance. One law professor denounced state bankruptcy as a "terrible idea."[4] "[I]f we in fact create ... a state bankruptcy chapter," another critic testified to Congress, "I see all sorts of snakes coming out of that pit," as "[b]ankruptcy for states could – would cripple bond markets.'"[5]

After a brief, high-profile debate, the state bankruptcy proposals dropped from sight in Washington, apparently knocked out by a left-right combination: Because the proposals were perceived as a tool to punish

---

[1] Wordsworth offered this definition in his preface to the *Lyrical Ballads*. William Wordsworth, *Preface*, in WILLIAM WORDSWORTH & SAMUEL TAYLOR COLERIDGE, LYRICAL BALLADS, WITH A FEW OTHER POEMS (1800).
[2] *See, e.g.*, Jeb Bush & Newt Gingrich, *Better Off Bankrupt*, L.A. TIMES, Jan. 27, 2011; David Skeel, *Give States a Way to Go Bankrupt*, WEEKLY STD, Nov. 29, 2010, at 22; David Skeel, *Bankruptcy – Not Bailouts – for the States*, WALL ST. J., Jan. 18, 2011, at A17.
[3] Skeel, *Give States a Way to Go Bankrupt*, *supra* note 2, at 24.
[4] *See* Matt Miller, *The World Wonders: Can States Go Bankrupt?* THE DEAL, Feb. 18, 2011, at 30, 32 (quoting University of Texas Law Professor Jay Westbrook).
[5] Quoted in Jonathan S. Henes & Stephen E. Hessler, *Deja Vu, All Over Again*, N.Y.L.J., June 27, 2011.

public employee unions, Democrats opposed them from the beginning. Many Republicans turned against the proposal after bond market representatives warned that state bankruptcy could hurt the bond markets.[6]

With the initial passions having cooled, at least for a time, we can now consider state bankruptcy, as well as other responses to states' fiscal crisis, a bit more quietly and carefully. That is precisely what I hope to do in this chapter. Although my analysis will not be mistaken for poetry, it may benefit from reflection outside the passions of the initial public debate.

I begin the chapter by discussing the often-neglected threshold question of what "bankruptcy" is. I then summarize the case for state bankruptcy as I see it. Because I have defended state bankruptcy at length in companion work,[7] I keep the defense comparatively brief. My particular concern here is, as the title suggests, to develop the basic scaffolding for a comprehensive state bankruptcy framework, working from the ground up. After outlining the foundational principles for state bankruptcy and assessing two more limited alternatives, I work my way through seven key components: the threshold requirements; the initiator; proposing a reorganization plan; the role of a stay, reachback provisions, and confirmation rules; the possibility of "guillotines" or "checks" tailored to the state bankruptcy context; financing; and the structure of the bankruptcy court.

I. WHAT DO WE MEAN BY BANKRUPTCY?

The term "bankruptcy" is often treated as if it were self-explanatory. But of course, it is not. The warrant for using this particular language can be found in the Constitution itself, which gives Congress the power to make uniform laws on the subject of bankruptcies.[8] Over the past 200 years, the Supreme Court has periodically been called upon to clarify just what bankruptcy means. In its most important early case, *Sturges v. Crowninshield*, the Court made clear that the Bankruptcy Clause gives Congress the power to marshal some or all of the debtor's assets to pay its creditors and to discharge some or all of the debtor's obligations.[9] Interestingly, the Court did

---

[6] A key moment in bond-market inspired resistance came when House majority leader Eric Cantor announced that he would not support any state bankruptcy proposal. *See, e.g.,* James Pethokoukis, *When States Go Bust*, WEEKLY STD, Feb. 14, 2001 (noting that Cantor "brushed off the idea" on January 24, 2011).

[7] David A. Skeel, Jr., *States of Bankruptcy*, U. CHI. L. REV. (forthcoming, 2012).

[8] CONST. ART. I, § 8.

[9] 17 U.S. (4 Wheat.) 122, 193 (1819). In *Sturges*, the Court defined bankruptcy to include both bankruptcy laws, which historically had discharged a debtor after his assets were distributed to creditors, and insolvency laws, which released a debtor from prison.

not state in this case, and has never explicitly held since, that insolvency is a prerequisite for bankruptcy. Over time, bankruptcy has come to include nearly any reasonably comprehensive framework for adjusting a debtor's obligations, providing for payment of creditors, and giving the debtor a discharge.[10]

The precise label does not matter, of course. Any restructuring framework that has the qualities just described is a bankruptcy law, even if Congress calls it something else. Even experts sometimes get tripped up on this point. In a 2011 hearing, a bankruptcy lawyer condemned state bankruptcy as unworkable, then went on to advocate that Congress consider adopting a framework modeled on the Sovereign Debt Restructuring Mechanism (SDRM) proposed by the International Monetary Fund in the early 2000s.[11] The difference between what he was praising and what he was condemning was not clear. The SDRM proposed a stay on collection under some circumstances and envisioned that creditors would file claims and vote on a restructuring.[12] Under any ordinary conception of bankruptcy, state SDRM would thus be "state bankruptcy," even if it did not carry this label.

Given the tendency of many to recoil at the mere mention of the word bankruptcy, there is something to be said for using a different term for any state-restructuring framework. My preference might be: State Debt Adjustment Framework. But the framework, at least as I envision it, will be just as much a bankruptcy law as it would be if it bore that label, just as Chapter 9 – whose formal title is "Adjustment of Debts of a Municipality" – is bankruptcy.

---

[10] For a short and still useful discussion of the Supreme Court's expanding interpretation of the Bankruptcy Clause, see Frank R. Kennedy, *Bankruptcy and the Constitution*, in BLESSINGS OF LIBERTY 131, 137–38 (ALI/ABI Comm'n on Continuing Prof'l Educ. ed., 1988) (characterizing the case law as "com[ing] close to permitting Congress complete freedom in formulating and enacting bankruptcy legislation"). For the most complete treatment of Congress's bankruptcy authority, see Jonathan C. Lipson, *Debt and Democracy: Towards a Constitutional Theory of Bankruptcy*, 83 NOTRE DAME L. REV. 605 (2008) (developing constitutional theory of bankruptcy).

[11] *The Role of Public Employee Pensions in Contributing to State Insolvency and the Possibility of a State Bankruptcy Chapter: Hearing of the Subcomm. of Cts., Comm'l, and Adminst. Law of the H. Comm. on the Judiciary*, 112th Cong. 1, 13 (2011) (prepared statement of James Spiotto, Partner, Chapman and Cutler LLP).

[12] Ann Krueger outlined the original proposal in a 2002 speech, and it was developed into a much more elaborate framework thereafter. See INT'L MONETARY FUND, PROPOSED FEATURES OF A SOVEREIGN DEBT RESTRUCTURING MECHANISM (2003), *available at* http://www.imf.org/external/np/pdr/sdrm/2003/021203.pdf.

II. A CASE FOR STATE BANKRUPTCY

Scholarly critics of state bankruptcy have argued that state fiscal difficulties are "political," not "financial."[13] The financial predicaments faced by states like California and Illinois can be traced to taxing and spending problems, the reasoning goes, and to a political tendency to borrow to fund current expenditures without fully considering the long-term costs. Bankruptcy is not designed to address these kinds of problems. Unlike in an ordinary Chapter 11 case, bankruptcy would not shift decision-making authority to a new or different decision maker. (For those who are not bankruptcy afficionados, Chapter 11 is the provisions that are designed principally for corporate reorganization; Chapter 7 provides for liquidation. Chapter 9, which is similar to Chapter 11 in many respects, governs municipal bankruptcy.) Moreover, the other standard benefits of bankruptcy – its ability to halt the "grab race" by creditors that can dismember an otherwise viable firm – would not apply if the creditor is a state rather than a private entity.

If we shift the frame of reference from corporate to personal bankruptcy, the limits of these objections quickly become clear. Like a state, a consumer debtor cannot be liquidated, and the same decision maker – the debtor herself – will remain in this role even after bankruptcy. Although consumers are not biased in precisely the same ways as political decision makers, there are obvious similarities; most importantly, both tend to focus more on the short-term benefits of borrowing than its long-term costs. With both consumers and states, bankruptcy can address the problem of debt overhang – debt that may make it impossible for the debtor to fund even the most promising investments.[14] In both contexts, the prospect that debt may be discharged also enlists creditors as monitors, giving them an incentive to discourage overborrowing by increasing interest rates or cutting off funding for profligate debtors.[15]

States differ from consumer debtors in some respects. The question of who will file the bankruptcy petition is more complicated, for instance, and states may need interim financing to fund the bankruptcy case.[16] But

---

[13] Adam Levitin makes this argument with vigor in his contribution to this volume.

[14] The classic analysis of debt overhang is Stewart C. Myers, *Determinants of Corporate Borrowing*, 5 J. FIN. ECON. 147 (1977).

[15] *See, e.g.,* THOMAS H. JACKSON, THE LOGIC AND LIMITS OF BANKRUPTCY LAW 249 (1986) (highlighting this effect in the consumer bankruptcy context).

[16] In this sense, states resemble the nineteenth-century railroads. Although the railroads theoretically could be liquidated, perceived public interest and the interests of every

the similarities suggest a broad analogy between consumer bankruptcy and the potential role of bankruptcy for states.

Even if persuaded that state bankruptcy can be justified in theoretical terms, some still might harbor doubts about its efficacy in practice. Perhaps the most frequent objection is that bankruptcy is unnecessary because states already have the tools to deal with their financial distress. The wave of recent state efforts to scale down their obligations to public employees – quite controversially in Wisconsin but with fewer fireworks in New York and Rhode Island – could be seen as initial confirmation of this argument. By reining in spending and/or adjusting taxes, as well as renegotiating problematic agreements, states can address their problems without any bankruptcy option.[17] According to critics, state bankruptcy could interfere with these ad hoc adjustments: The bankruptcy alternative might create an excuse to leave things as they are, relieving pressure to fix the state's finances out of bankruptcy.

Yet bankruptcy is at least as likely to encourage restructuring as to dissuade states from it. The threat of bankruptcy would give states more leverage in their negotiations outside of bankruptcy. Indeed, one of the most attractive features of state bankruptcy is the extent to which its benefits would arise even if no state ever filed for bankruptcy.

State bankruptcy also would provide tools that are not available to state lawmakers outside of bankruptcy, such as the ability to restructure pension obligations or bond debt. Although it may be true that every state will survive the current crisis without these tools, it is also possible that the crisis will get worse or that another will soon follow. If there were lessons in the 2008 crisis, surely one was the risk of ignoring a remote but potentially devastating possibility.

A second concern is moral hazard. In the sovereign debt context, critics frequently argue that the existence of a bankruptcy framework would prove too tempting to debtor nations, tempting them to evade their obligations rather than making a sustained effort to repay them. Perhaps even more with a state than a nation, moral hazard seems unlikely. A governor whose state filed for bankruptcy would be subject to extensive new oversight and would pay a substantial reputation price for having been the state's chief executive in a bankruptcy. At least under a traditional bankruptcy framework – as contrasted with the streamlined alternatives

---

relevant constituency favored reorganization because railroad track was worth virtually nothing apart from connecting track.

[17] See, e.g., E.J. McMahon, *State Bankruptcy is a Bad Idea*, WALL ST. J., Jan. 24, 2011.

I also will discuss below[18] – the moral hazard danger is likely to be quite limited.

A third major objection is that enactment of a state bankruptcy option would devastate the market for state bonds, which currently are viewed as safe investments.[19] As a result of the bond market contagion, the argument goes, even fiscally responsible states would be punished. Contagionists tend to conflate the enactment of a bankruptcy law with an actual default by a state. Simply putting a law in place would not paralyze the bond markets. Indeed, we already have a municipal bankruptcy law, yet these markets continue to function (contrary to the dire, vaguely familiar warnings voiced by critics in the 1930s when it was first enacted).[20] Recent bond prices – which have been significantly lower for California and Illinois than for less troubled states – suggest that the markets distinguish between good credit risks and poor ones. Moreover, to the extent a bankruptcy law might lead to slightly lower bond prices and slightly higher interest rates, this would not necessarily be problematic. States currently have too great an incentive to borrow because the proceeds can be used now and much of the cost will be borne by future taxpayers. Higher borrowing costs might curb this tendency, at least on the margin.

A final objection is that a state's financial structure is too complex for bankruptcy courts to handle. Nicole Gelinas has pointed out, for instance, that New York state has several hundred special districts and other entities[21]; this complexity is a familiar feature of bankruptcy. The WorldCom and Lehman bankruptcies, for instance, involved a large number of entities. The capacity to determine the extent of a debtor's guarantees and other obligations – and thus to address the complexity – is in fact a signal benefit of bankruptcy. Often this is resolved through negotiation. But the bankruptcy court has the authority to resolve any uncertainties about the parties' entitlements.[22]

---

[18] See *infra* notes 34–41 and accompanying text.
[19] See *supra* note 5 and accompanying text.
[20] The dissenters from the original 1934 municipal bankruptcy law predicted that "the very novelty of the thing will adversely affect the municipal bond market" and that "the presence of the law on the statute books would ... cost investors and solvent municipalities millions of dollars." Quoted in Henes & Hessler, *supra* note 5.
[21] Gelinas argues that this complexity would make state bankruptcy implausible. *Hearing on State and Municipal Debt: The Coming Crisis? Before Subcomm. on TARP, Financial Services, and Bailouts of Public and Private Programs of Comm. on Oversight and Government Reform*, 113th Cong. 1–2 (2011) (prepared statement of Nicole Gelinas, Manhattan Institute).
[22] See 11 U.S.C. § 502(a) (court authority to determine claims).

III. THE GENERAL FRAMEWORK

To paraphrase a famous line by Felix Frankfurter, saying that state bankruptcy (or a state debt adjustment framework) would be desirable only begins the inquiry.[23] We still need to determine what the framework could or should look like. Given the parallels between state and municipal bankruptcy, one might easily rework Chapter 9 into a state bankruptcy framework, making adjustments as appropriate. This approach has several shortcomings, however. Because Chapter 9 is seriously flawed, it is not the best role model. Starting with a fully formed framework also would obscure many of the key decisions that must be made in determining how to structure the bankruptcy regime. I will begin at a more foundational level, asking what features lie at the heart of an effective state bankruptcy framework. This will enable me to develop the basic scaffolding for a state bankruptcy framework.

Although a variety of other key features will be discussed, the edifice rests on five core principles. The first is the importance of providing a coherent priority scheme, starting with the recognition of property rights. Second, similarly situated creditors should receive comparable treatment. Third, the debtor should be given the power to terminate or assume its ongoing ("executory") contracts. Fourth, the creditors in a particular class should be subject to a restructuring if it is endorsed by an appropriate majority of the claims in the class. Finally, the framework should discharge the debtor's pre-bankruptcy obligations.

Start with property rights and other priorities.[24] Not only is recognition of property rights compelled by the Takings Clause of the Constitution but establishing and honoring priorities also brings important benefits even outside of bankruptcy. Well-ordered priorities can reduce credit costs by facilitating monitoring and clarifying creditors' status in the event of insolvency.[25] This is particularly important for states because state priorities are quite unclear and can often be subverted outside of bankruptcy. If one class of claims is thought to be entitled to special treatment, for instance,

---

[23] Frankfurter said that determining that someone is a fiduciary "only begins analysis." S.E.C. v. Chenery Corp., 318 U.S. 80, 85–86 (1943).
[24] Under existing bankruptcy law, the principal priorities are established in the first instance by 11 U.S.C. § 725 (property rights) and 11 U.S.C. § 726 (other priorities).
[25] This benefit is the subject of a long literature. Some years ago, Alan Schwartz proposed first-in-time priority for unsecured debt to obtain some of these benefits even within the class of general unsecured claims. Alan Schwartz, *A Theory of Loan Priorities*, 18 J. LEG. STUD. 209 (1989).

a state can subvert the special status by targeting it, but not other claims, for restructuring.

A second key principle is that similarly situated creditors should receive comparable treatment.[26] If a state has two similar classes of bonds, it should not be able to promise one class 90 percent of what it is owed when giving the other only 10 percent. Similarly, bondholders should not receive 90 percent when state employees' contracts are scaled down closer to 10 percent.

The first two principles are closely related, and together they give rise to an important corollary: The sacrifice entailed in a state's bankruptcy should be distributed equitably among all constituencies, not just borne by one or two constituencies. A state's financial distress is a common disaster, as Bob Scott argued about corporate reorganization several decades ago, and the bankruptcy framework should reflect this – in contrast to nonbankruptcy restructuring efforts, which often do not.[27]

Third, bankruptcy should give the state the power to assume or (often more importantly) to terminate its executory contracts.[28] This is a feature of personal, corporate, and municipal bankruptcy in the United States, and it is particularly important for a financially troubled state. In the nineteenth century, when state default was last a pervasive concern, executory contracts would not have featured prominently in a state's distress. Governmental functions were far more limited, and state bond debt was the principal concern. In the current crisis, by contrast, unsustainably generous public employee contracts have been a major component of most troubled states' woes. Lawmakers have considerable incentives to award generous contacts to state employees, both because state employees are an important voting block and because lawmakers themselves may be direct or indirect beneficiaries of the contracts. The ability to restructure these contracts is an essential component of an effective state bankruptcy framework.

---

[26] This principle has long been a central objective of American bankruptcy law. It is reflected in the general distribution scheme in a Chapter 7 liquidation, as well as in provisions such as 11 U.S.C. § 1129(b), which forbids "unfair discrimination" in a nonconsensual Chapter 11 reorganization.

[27] Scott first outlined his "common disaster" conception in Robert E. Scott, *Through Bankruptcy with the Creditors' Bargain Heuristic*, 53 U. CHI. L. REV. 690 (1986). Under Scott's conception, creditors' priorities would be honored, but even secured creditors would be expected to help bear the burden in some respects (such as forgoing the right to immediately seize and sell their collateral).

[28] To simplify slightly, an executory contract is a contract that has not yet been fully performed by either side. An agreement with a supplier is an executory contract, whereas bond debt is not (because the investor completes her performance when she pays). Current bankruptcy law addresses executory contracts in 11 U.S.C. § 365.

Bankruptcy also should provide for a binding vote of each class of creditors on any proposed restructuring plan. In the absence of voting provisions, holdout creditors might thwart or significantly complicate a state's restructuring efforts in an effort to secure greater payments for themselves.[29] A binding vote removes this difficulty by compelling dissenting creditors to accept the terms agreed to by a majority of their peers.[30]

The holdout problem can be surmounted even without voting provisions. In the late nineteenth century, railroad reorganizers persuaded courts to set an "upset price" that would be paid to dissenting bondholders in the reorganization. If the upset price was low, as it generally was, it discouraged holdouts.[31] More recently, corporations and countries have restructured their bonds through exchange offers that included "exit consents" that are designed to punish bondholders that reject the restructuring.[32] Although each of these devices is a substitute for voting provisions, both carry baggage. Paying the upset price to dissenters was quite costly, and dissenting bondholders are still entitled to full payment, at least in theory, after a contemporary exchange offer. In the exchange offer, the state might also be forced to limit the extent of its restructuring to minimize holdouts. Voting provisions avoid these problems and can facilitate a more effective restructuring.

The final requirement is discharge. Whatever terms are agreed to or imposed on a creditor as a result of the bankruptcy should be permanent. As bankruptcy advertisements put it, the debtor's obligations should be erased.

---

[29] The disruption caused by holdout creditors has been a major concern in the sovereign debt context. Starting with Mexico in 2003, the United States led an effort to persuade sovereign debtors to include voting provisions in the bonds they issue to avoid this problem. See, e.g., Anna Gelpern & G. Mitu Gulati, *Forward: Of Lawyers, Leaders, and Returning Riddles in Sovereign Debt*, 73 L. & CONTEMP. PROB. i, vi (2010) (forward to symposium on "A Modern Legal History of Sovereign Debt") (describing the intervention).

[30] When corporate reorganization was first codified in the United States in 1933 and 1934, providing a binding voting rule was the principal objective of the new statute. See, e.g., Robert T. Swaine, *Corporate Reorganization Under the Bankruptcy Power*, 19 VA. L. REV. 317 (1933) (emphasizing the need for binding votes).

[31] See, e.g., Joseph Weiner, *Conflicting Functions of the Upset Price in a Corporate Reorganization*, 27 COLUM. L. REV. 132, 145 (1927) (noting the use of low upset prices to minimize holdouts).

[32] See, e.g., John C. Coffee, Jr. & William A. Klein, *Bondholder Coercion: The Problem of Constrained Choice in Debt Tender Offers and Recapitalizations*, 58 U. CHI. L. REV. 1207 (1991) (describing strategies used to pressure bondholders to participate).

These five principles, together with the obligation to devote some of the state's assets in some way for payment to its creditors, as noted earlier,[33] are the foundation for an effective state bankruptcy framework.

IV. A SIMPLER ALTERNATIVE?

One can imagine a much simpler state bankruptcy framework than the one I have begun to sketch out. Consider two possible alternatives and the limitations of each.

An Immediate Discharge

Under one approach, all of the state's obligations would simply be discharged when it filed for bankruptcy.[34] This is how Chapter 7 works for consumer debtors. When a debtor files for bankruptcy, she turns over all over her nonexempt assets so that the trustee can distribute them to creditors. In practice, the vast majority of consumers do not have any nonexempt assets.[35] As a result, they simply file for bankruptcy and receive an almost immediate discharge. Given that state bankruptcy plays much the same role as consumer bankruptcy, this approach would simply follow the analogy all the way down.

The immediate discharge would not be quite so radical a departure from a traditional bankruptcy as at first appears. Although everything would be discharged – from the state's collective bargaining agreements to its bonds and its contracts with suppliers – a state no doubt would wish to reaffirm some of these obligations; the state might renegotiate its bonds and collective bargaining agreements, offering to pay something less than the original obligations. With consumer bankruptcy, bankruptcy law permits a debtor to reaffirm debts that would otherwise be removed but requires that the reaffirmation be approved by a court.[36] An analogous provision would be warranted for states, although for a somewhat different purpose.[37] Whereas the court polices consumer reaffirmations

---

[33] See supra notes 9–10 and accompanying text.
[34] Barry Adler suggested this approach at a recent conference. State and Municipal Default Workshop, Hoover Institution, June 15–16, 2011.
[35] See, e.g., Michelle J. White, *Abuse or Protection? Economics of Bankruptcy Reform Under BAPCPA*, 2007 U. ILL. L. REV. 275, 284 (no nonexempt assets in 96% of consumer Chapter 7 cases).
[36] 11 U.S.C. § 524(c).
[37] As Barry Adler also has suggested.

to ensure they are voluntary and do not impose an undue hardship on the debtor, the concern with a state is to ensure that the state does not treat similar obligations radically differently.

Notice where this leaves us. Although the discharge is prompt and automatic, a state might well negotiate the terms of a restructuring with many of its creditors, much as it would in a more elaborate restructuring framework. How, then, would the immediate discharge differ from the structure whose core principles were outlined earlier? The largest distinction might come in the nature of the bargaining. In an ordinary bankruptcy framework, bargaining between the state and a particular group of creditors is a bilateral monopoly: Each party may be the other's only realistic contracting party, which makes the outcome uncertain and may reduce the likelihood of a thoroughgoing restructuring. Immediate discharge would break the impasse by inviting the state to dictate the terms of any bargain. The distinction should not be overstated. Under the principles described earlier for the framework advocated in this chapter, for instance, the state would have leeway to terminate existing contracts, such as collective bargaining agreements with its unions. An immediate discharge would, however, sharply expand this leverage and would reduce the need for judicial oversight.

The increased restructuring leverage also would bring a potentially serious risk: the prospect that the immediate discharge would prove *too* tempting. In part, this is a standard moral hazard issue. If bankruptcy is especially attractive, a debtor may invoke it even if the debtor is capable of repaying its obligations. This moral hazard would be counteracted by the risk that precipitously filing states would be punished by the credit markets and by pressure against filing from interest groups that would be affected by the state's bankruptcy. Even if these forces discouraged unnecessary bankruptcy filings under most circumstances, however, they might not prevent state decision makers from triggering bankruptcy on a whim. Suppose that lawmakers threatened to file for bankruptcy unless the state's public employees agreed to sharp reductions in their collective bargaining agreements. If the negotiations reached an impasse, the state might make good on its threat, despite not needing bankruptcy relief. The odds of a precipitous filing would not be great, but this would be a much larger risk than with a fuller bankruptcy framework. At the very least, this would call for more stringent restrictions on initiation than I advocate for the framework developed in this chapter.

Immediate discharge also would not avoid many of the most difficult issues in a bankruptcy case. Absent a settlement, the court would still need to determine just what has in fact been discharged. This would require rulings on whether and to what extent a creditor was protected by a property right, for instance, and what obligations the state had to special districts, pension funds, or local governments whose obligations it may have guaranteed. These determinations would of course be many orders of magnitude more complex than in a consumer bankruptcy case.

Overall, the benefits of the immediate discharge do not seem great enough to justify forgoing the protections of a more elaborate framework. It is a plausible alternative, however, and hints at the wide-ranging options for structuring a state bankruptcy framework.

A Simple Voting Framework

Under a second strategy, bankruptcy would center on the fourth of the core objectives, establishing binding voting provisions. "A minimalist legal framework incorporating across-the-board supermajority voting," as its principal advocate puts it, "is all that would be required to help states solve the creditor-holdout problem. Such a framework would not need to bring in other bankruptcy baggage."[38] Although the voting provisions could take different forms, one approach would follow roughly the pattern of corporate bankruptcy law, allowing the state to group creditors into as few or as many classes as it wishes, so long as the claims in the class are substantially similar.[39]

The voting approach differs from a more complete framework in at least two respects. First, it would omit the third objective, termination of executory contracts. Bankruptcy therefore would not provide a tool to alter collective bargaining agreements and other contracts. This presumably would preclude adjustments to a debtor's pension obligations, although the implications here are somewhat unclear. If the extent of the pension beneficiaries' property interests were in doubt, for instance, the court would need to determine what portion should be treated as a priority obligation and what portion would be unsecured.

Second, the voting approach would not explicitly require that similarly situated creditors receive comparable treatment. Creditors could not be lumped with dissimilar creditors, and a class of creditors would be more likely to vote no if a proposed plan treated them worse than a group of seemingly similar creditors. But the debtor would not be precluded

---

[38] Steven L. Schwarcz, *A Minimalist Approach to State 'Bankruptcy,'* 59 UCLA L. REV. (forthcoming 2011), manuscript at 10.
[39] *Id.* at 14.

from offering radically different treatment to two classes of similar creditors. Indeed, the debtor might restructure one group of creditors but not another.[40]

As with the immediate discharge, the voting framework would appreciably reduce the need for judicial oversight but would not go altogether by itself. Many of the decisions required by a more elaborate framework also would arise with a voting framework, except to the extent the debtor excluded the creditors in question from restructuring. A court would need to estimate or fix the creditor's claim, for instance, to determine how large a vote the creditor had.

The voting framework would resemble a prepackaged corporate bankruptcy in scope.[41] As with a prepackaged bankruptcy, the voting framework would be most beneficial if the debtor's problems can be solved with a simple restructuring of its balance sheet. For states with more complex problems, the voting framework would be less effective.

Although each of these more limited approaches has attractive qualities, neither addresses all of the core objectives described earlier. For this, we need a more comprehensive framework. The remainder of this chapter considers the key dimensions of a comprehensive state bankruptcy law.

V. INITIATION REQUIREMENTS

The terms of initiation are a particularly sensitive issue for the bankruptcy of a sovereign or quasi-sovereign entity. If initiation is difficult, bankruptcy's benefits may be difficult or impossible to achieve. If initiation is easy, bankruptcy may be too tempting – at least under a self-executing framework such as the immediate discharge.

Current municipal bankruptcy law is particularly instructive on this dilemma. To enter Chapter 9, a municipality must show that the state has authorized a filing, that the municipality is insolvent, and that it has negotiated in advance with its creditors unless negotiation is impracticable.[42] Chapter 9 also assumes that the filing decision will be made through the

---

[40] This was a concern with the IMF's SDRM, which was similar to, although much more elaborate than, the simple voting framework. *See, e.g.,* Patrick Bolton & David A. Skeel, Jr., *Redesigning the International Lender of Last Resort*, 6 CHI. J. INT'L. L. 177, 184 (2005) (describing danger that priorities can be undermined).

[41] In a prepackaged bankruptcy, the debtor files a reorganization plan along with its bankruptcy petition in the expectation that the plan will be confirmed within the first few weeks of the case.

[42] 11 U.S.C. § 109(c).

ordinary political process, which often means agreement by the mayor and the city council. The stringent preconditions apparently were included primarily to ensure that the Chapter 9 would not be struck down as an unconstitutional interference with state sovereignty. In practice, the preconditions have made it difficult to use Chapter 9.

The most nettlesome requirement is the obligation to show that the municipality is insolvent, which is defined to mean that the municipality is "generally not paying its debts as they become due" or is "unable to pay its debts as they become due."[43] When Bridgeport, Connecticut, filed for bankruptcy several decades ago, the case was eventually tossed out because the court was not persuaded that Bridgeport had exhausted all of its options for meeting its obligations – it had not yet been cut off by potential lenders, for instance, and had not run out of cash.[44] If the same "unable to pay its debts as they become due" standard applied to state bankruptcy, the interference would be far greater. Because a state can always raise taxes or borrow, objectors would have a plausible challenge to any filing, no matter how dire the state's financial condition. As McConnell and Picker put it in the municipal bankruptcy context, "At a certain point, raising tax rates ceases to raise tax revenues, but identifying the tax-maximization point on this implicit 'Laffer Curve' is not a simple proposition."[45]

Our checkered experience with Chapter 9 suggests that state bankruptcy should avoid imposing so stringent an insolvency requirement. It is possible that state bankruptcy could omit this requirement altogether, as corporate bankruptcy does.[46] Given the difficulty of reaching a state's assets, however, a bankruptcy framework that omitted any insolvency requirement might be challenged as exceeding Congress's bankruptcy powers. This suggests that, although the insolvency requirement needs to be relaxed, it should not be excluded altogether. One plausible candidate comes from an unlikely source: the Dodd-Frank Act's resolution rules for systemically important financial institutions. The Dodd-Frank Act's

---

[43] 11 U.S.C. § 101(32)(c).
[44] In re City of Bridgeport, 129 Bankr. 332, 336–338 (Bankr. D. Conn. 1991). The court's application of the insolvency standard may have been colored by the state's staunch resistance to the filing, although the court held that the filing was authorized by state law. The *Bridgeport* decision is pointedly criticized in Michael McConnell & Randal C. Picker, *When Cities Go Broke: A Conceptual Introduction to Municipal Bankruptcy*, 60 U. CHI. L. REV. 425, 456 (1993).
[45] McConnell & Picker, *supra* note 44, at 466.
[46] In a corporate bankruptcy case, insolvency comes in only indirectly, as a possible objection to the good faith of the filing (if the debtor is clearly solvent) or as a possible objection by the debtor to an involuntary case. 11 U.S.C. § 303(h).

insolvency requirement focuses on whether the institution is "in default" or "in danger of default."[47] This standard would satisfy the need for some showing of insolvency but would be much less stringent than the Chapter 9 insolvency requirement.

VI. WHO CAN INITIATE?

Because state bankruptcy would involve an exercise of its bankruptcy powers, Congress should be able to decide which state decision maker would have the authority to initiate a bankruptcy case. If this is correct – and I acknowledge that the issue is not free from doubt – Congress would not need to defer to the state to the extent Chapter 9 does with municipalities. Consider three possible decision makers. First and most obviously, Congress could require a joint decision by the governor and legislature. This, of course, is how ordinary legislation is enacted. Second, Congress could vest the authority in the governor alone. Initiation by the governor would simplify the decision-making process and accords with the powers that executives and the executive branch are sometimes given in other contexts.[48] Finally, Congress could authorize the citizens of a state to trigger a bankruptcy filing by referendum, thus relying on direct democracy. The referendum approach is the most radical, but authorizing citizens to make the bankruptcy decision is not dramatically different than the powers they have in referendum states such as California.

In my view, the governor should be given the authority to file for bankruptcy, perhaps after mandatory consultation with the leaders of the two legislative branches (or branch, in a unicameral system). Under ordinary corporate bankruptcy, the board of directors makes this decision, not the chief executive.[49] Given the similarity between the board and a state

---

[47] Dodd-Frank Wall Street Reform and Consumer Protection Act, Pub. L. No. 111–203, § 203(b) (2010).

[48] The scope of the president's authority has the source of considerable debate in recent years. For a historical critique of the "unitary executive" thesis, which lies at the heart of much of the debate, see Stephen Skowronek, *The Conservative Insurgency and Presidential Power: A Developmental Perspective on the Unitary Executive*, 122 HARV. L. REV. 2070 (2009).

[49] It is interesting to note that this is, in a sense, a practical accommodation of corporate and bankruptcy law to the realities of bankruptcy. Major corporate decisions usually require both directorial approval and a shareholder vote. See, e.g., DEL. CODE ANN. Tit. 8 § 251 (shareholder vote on mergers). Requiring a shareholder vote on bankruptcy would be cumbersome, however, and (more importantly) shareholders' decision-making incentives are suspect when the firm is insolvent.

legislature, one could argue that the legislature should have a formal role. However, the governor and legislature do not operate as a single coherent team in the way that a chief executive and her corporate board often do. The legislature is also a far more cumbersome decision-making body than a corporate board, which generally has less than twenty directors.

The case for making voters the exclusive decision maker is much weaker. If voters triggered a bankruptcy filing over the objections of the state's governor, the likelihood that the restructuring effort would be pursued with vigor would be relatively small. It is possible, however, that a governor would be prodded into action by the wishes of a majority of the state's citizens. This suggests that it might be a mistake to exclude the possibility of voter involvement altogether. To leave an opening for voter involvement, Congress could vest the principal authority elsewhere – in the governor, I have argued – but invite the state to enact legislation also giving voters this authority.

The requirements I have described – a petition by the state's governor, based on a showing that the state is in default or in danger of default – should be the only prerequisites for initiating a state bankruptcy requirement. The risk of a precipitous bankruptcy filing is exceedingly small, given the consequences to the state of being in bankruptcy.

VII. PROPOSING A REORGANIZATION PLAN

Initiation does not end the tricky political issues posed by state bankruptcy. The other major issue is who should propose a reorganization plan on behalf of the state.

Chapter 9 assumes that a municipality's reorganization plan will be proposed by the body that has decision-making authority under state or local law. Much as the board of directors acts on behalf of a corporate debtor, the municipal council as a whole generally proposes a plan on behalf of the municipality. The case for adopting a similar approach for state bankruptcy – and thus involving both the governor and the legislature – is stronger in two respects in this context than with initiation. First, time is less likely to be of the essence. In most cases, the reorganization negotiations will have unfolded over a period of months, and legislative approval could be included as part of the voting process. Second, a process that provided for full legislative approval could include measures such as tax adjustments that might not otherwise be possible.

Despite these advantages, the more simplified approach proposed for initiation seems appropriate for the plan process as well. Allowing the governor to propose a plan after consultation with legislative leaders would avoid the danger that legislative resistance might derail any proposed plan. To be sure, this would preclude the plan from including provisions like new or different taxes that would require formal legislative approval. In practice, however, a governor would likely insist on legislative approval of tax increases (or other adjustments that require legislative approval) prior to or at the same time as the creditor vote on a proposed plan if tax increases were necessary to facilitate the restructuring. In this context, the governor's authority would function quite similarly to a requirement that both the governor and the legislature devise the reorganization plan. Vesting the formal authority to propose a plan exclusively in the governor would provide more flexibility, however, particularly with plans that did not call for tax increases or other legislative changes.

VIII. OTHER PROVISIONS

Three key provisions provide much of the framework for ordinary corporate reorganization: the automatic stay, which halts creditor collection efforts; the reachback rules that enable the trustee to retrieve pre-bankruptcy preferences and fraudulent conveyances; and the rules for confirming a reorganization plan.[50] The automatic stay gives the debtor a "breathing space" by preventing creditors from dismembering an otherwise viable corporation, while both the reachback and confirmation rules help, among other things, to ensure the equal treatment of similarly situated creditors.[51]

In contrast to corporate bankruptcy, in which the stay and reachback rules are essential, neither is strictly necessary for state bankruptcy. Because creditors have few mechanisms for forcing a recalcitrant state to pay or for attaching its assets, the "grab race" that figures so prominently in corporate bankruptcy is far less important for a state. With few exceptions, the state could simply stop paying its creditors after it filed for bankruptcy. This suggests that, at most, a limited stay would be needed as a part of a state bankruptcy framework.[52] The stay could halt litigation against the

---

[50] These rules are found in 11 U.S.C. § 362 (automatic stay), 11 U.S.C. § 547 and 548 (preference and fraudulent conveyance provisions), and 11 U.S.C. § 1129 (plan confirmation requirements).

[51] The preference provision requires a creditor that has received preferential payments to disgorge these payments if no safe harbor applies; this restores the creditor (to the extent of the payment) to the same status as other general unsecured creditors. The confirmation rules require equal treatment unless a class of creditors agrees to different treatment.

[52] Interestingly, the stay seems less necessary for state bankruptcy than it would be for sovereign bankruptcy. Sovereigns often have assets outside their borders that can potentially be attached. States do not seem to have extraterritorial assets to the same extent.

state, for instance, but not interfere with the state's creditors in any other way. A stay on litigation would channel any fights over the state's use of funds during the bankruptcy case into the bankruptcy court and would prevent creditors from attempting to obtain non-bankruptcy rulings on issues such as the extent of the state's responsibility for the obligations of special districts and other entities.

Although one can imagine a role for reachback rules – states may make preferential transfers to creditors before bankruptcy, just as other debtors do – these rules could be omitted altogether from a state bankruptcy framework. At most, as with the stay, a strictly limited version of the reachback rules would be in order.[53] Extensive reachback rules would add significant complexity to the bankruptcy process, and the benefit of pursuing the recipients of preferential payments would likely be limited. With a state, politics is likely to be a more cost-effective corrective to favoritism than is the traditional litigation process. In egregious cases – where state assets are sold to an insider for a pittance – the recipients can be pursued through the criminal process.

Unlike stay and reachback provisions, the voting and confirmation rules would be essential to the state bankruptcy process. For municipalities, Chapter 9 largely incorporates the confirmation rules from corporate bankruptcy.[54] Although this is probably the most sensible strategy, Chapter 11-style voting rules are not quite as effective for sovereign entities as for corporations. Because states do not have owners and cannot be liquidated, it is more difficult to impose a cramdown – that is, a nonconsensual reorganization – in the event that one or more classes of creditors vote against the debtor's proposed plan. In the sovereign debt context, a coauthor and I proposed a two-step process to address this problem.[55] Creditors would first vote on the extent of the haircut necessary – how much of the debt load needs to be reduced – to give the debtor a more manageable debt load. They then would vote on the debtor's proposed treatment of each class of

---

[53] Lawmakers could use a version of the "Hotchpot" rule that applies in some European countries as an alternative to full-blown reachback rules. *See, e.g.*, IMF, SDRM DESIGN, *supra* note 40, at 35–37 (explaining and adopting Hotchpot rule for proposed SDRM). Under the Hotchpot rule, the recipient of a preference is not required to give back the preferential payment, but the amount of the preference is offset against any claim the creditor has.

[54] In large part. Chapter 9 incorporates specified subsections of § 1129(a) and (b) pursuant to 11 U.S.C. § 901(a).

[55] Patrick Bolton & David A. Skeel, Jr., *Inside the Black Box: How Should a Sovereign Bankruptcy Framework be Structured?* 53 EMORY L.J. 763 (2004). The two-step process is outlined in *id.* at 796–799.

creditors. If each class approved the proposed treatment, this plan would be confirmed. If one or more classes voted no, on the other hand, the court would automatically impose the agreed-on haircut, starting with the lowest priority creditors. Although one could plausibly adopt this approach for states, the two-step approach is most effective if the debtor's liabilities consist primarily of bond debt or similarly fungible obligations. Bonds are a much smaller portion of most states' obligations than they are with sovereign debtors such as Greece or Argentina. Employee contracts and pension obligations, which do not lend themselves as easily to the two-step approach, figure much more prominently. This suggests that the single vote used in Chapter 9 and Chapter 11 probably should be retained for state bankruptcy as well.

IX. CHECKS AND GUILLOTINE PROVISIONS

Under a bankruptcy framework that incorporated the kinds of provisions I have outlined in this chapter, the state would negotiate with its creditors over the terms of a restructuring plan, which would be put to a creditor vote. The state could assume any valuable contracts and terminate those that are not beneficial. Although I have focused on the basic scaffolding of state bankruptcy, more innovative provisions could easily be added. Two possible strategies – one to ensure adjustments and another to limit them – will illustrate.

Start with the concern to ensure adjustments. One of the most sensitive issues for a financially distressed state is its collective bargaining agreements with its public employees. Renegotiating the state's collective bargaining agreements may be particularly fraught, as it will usually be imperative to restructure the contracts. Yet state officials are loathe to simply cancel them.[56] Congress could preempt the possibility of an impasse, and also limit the need for a court to decide whether the contracts can be terminated, by providing for automatic adjustments under specified conditions. If the state and its employees failed to reach agreement within six months, for instance, the provisions might automatically reduce wages and benefits by 20 percent. The automatic adjustment would serve as a guillotine in the event of an impasse.[57]

[56] If there were any doubt about frictions involved, the recent battles over collective bargaining agreements in Wisconsin, Ohio, New Jersey, and elsewhere put these questions to rest.

[57] See generally George G. Triantis, *The Interplay of Liquidation and Reorganization in Bankruptcy: The role of Screens, Gatekeepers and Guillotines*, 16 INT'L REV. L. & ECON. 101 (1996) (describing role of guillotine provision in Canadian bankruptcy).

Congress also could limit the extent of restructuring by including a provision constraining the depth of permissible cuts. Although such a provision sounds counterintuitive – why limit a restructuring? – its relevance became clear during the debates over state bankruptcy. One of the major objections was, as we have seen, a concern that enacting a bankruptcy framework would prompt a devastating bond market run. Although the concern seems overblown,[58] it could be assuaged by conditioning any restructuring of the bond debt on a determination by the bankruptcy court that the restructuring was not likely to have destructive spillover effects in the bond markets.

One state recently adopted an analogous strategy for the municipal bankruptcy context. In 2011, anticipating a bankruptcy filing by Central Falls, Rhode Island enacted legislation that purports to provide priority for bonds over other obligations.[59] If upheld, the legislation will ensure that municipal bonds are likely to be paid in full in any municipal bankruptcy.

The provisions I have described would automatically reduce the state's collective bargaining obligations and limit the restructuring of its bond debt. Lawmakers could, of course, do precisely the opposite: They could hardwire automatic adjustments for bond debt into the bankruptcy law and constraints on the restructuring of public employee contracts. In my view, neither version of these provisions is necessary. But they illustrate some of the ways state bankruptcy could be tailored to the particular issues raised by financially troubled states.

X. FINANCING THE BANKRUPTCY PROCESS

Through its taxes and other revenues, even the most distressed state has significant sources of income. As a result, a state is appreciably less likely than an ordinary corporation to need fresh financing to fund the bankruptcy process. This is especially so if the state stops paying its debts during the bankruptcy process. Nevertheless, new financing will sometimes be essential, which raises the issue of how financing might be addressed in the bankruptcy framework.

The simplest approach would be to simply borrow the debtor-in-possession financing rules that already apply to corporations and

---

[58] See supra notes 19–20 and accompanying text.
[59] See, e.g., Paul Burton, *Chapter 9 in Rhode Island Sparks Questions*, THE BOND BUYER, Aug. 3, 2011, available at http://www.bondbuyer.com/issues/120_148/central-falls-bankruptcy-1029588-1.html.

municipalities.⁶⁰ Under these rules, a debtor has a series of options, from borrowing on an unsecured basis, to borrowing that is given administrative expense priority in the case, to borrowing secured by a lien on assets of the debtor. Although loans in a state bankruptcy would likely look different than traditional debtor-in-possession loans – secured lending is more difficult with a state – the range of options is as appropriate for a state as for other debtors in bankruptcy.

This much is straightforward. Things get stickier, however, when we consider the question of *who* is likely to provide the financing. One likely candidate – perhaps *the* one likely candidate – is the federal government. Should the federal government be permitted to play this role? In a related context, a coauthor and I proposed a financing model that would rely more on private than public sector funding.⁶¹ In theory, it might be possible to limit federal government involvement by, for instance, permitting federal government funding only if private sector funding is not available.⁶² Even if such a restriction were plausible, however, it might simply push the rescue funding forward in time, inducing the state to refuse to file for bankruptcy until the federal government first agreed to provide pre-bankruptcy funding. If federal funding were permitted in bankruptcy, by contrast, as I believe it should be, the federal government could credibly refuse to step in until the state filed for bankruptcy. The government also could impose restrictions on its disbursements,⁶³ and the prospect of a bankruptcy restructuring would significantly reduce the amount of funding needed as compared to a pure bailout. To be sure, there are risks to federal involvement, as reflected in the government's picking of winners and losers in the

---

⁶⁰ 11 U.S.C. § 364 (debtor-in-possession financing); § 903 (incorporating § 364(c)-(f) into Chapter 9).

⁶¹ Bolton and I proposed that the IMF coordinate and approve bankruptcy funding, rather than serving as its sole source. Patrick Bolton & David A. Skeel, Jr., *Redesigning the International Lender of Last Resort*, 6 CHI. J. INT'L L. 177, 196–199 (2005).

⁶² This proposal is made for systemically important financial institutions in a white paper authored by Tom Jackson for a Hoover Institution working group. Resolution Project Subgroup of Working Group on Economic Policy, Hoover Institution, *Bankruptcy Code Chapter 14: A Proposal* (April, 2011), at 14 [hereinafter cited as Chapter 14 Proposal]. I am a member of the subgroup.

⁶³ There is, in fact, precedent for federal involvement on something like these terms. During New York City's financial crisis in 1975, Congress agreed (after President Ford initially refused) to make $1.5 billion in "seasonal loans" to New York, with each new installment conditioned on evidence of progress in New York's restructuring. *See, e.g.*, SEYMOUR P. LACHMAN & ROBERT POLNER, THE MAN WHO SAVED NEW YORK: HUGH CAREY AND THE GREAT FISCAL CRISIS OF 1975 at 164–165 (2010) (describing enactment of the rescue package).

Chrysler and GM cases. But there also are benefits, and the government could not realistically be excluded altogether from providing funds.

XI. THE BANKRUPTCY COURT

State bankruptcy would put a great deal of pressure on the bankruptcy court, given the magnitude of the issues and the state's status as a party in interest. A comprehensive bankruptcy framework would remove much of the pressure by relying on negotiations between the state and its creditors to resolve most issues, enabling the court to serve more as umpire than as decision maker. On some issues, such as a proposal by the state to terminate its collective bargaining agreements, however, the court would be the principal decision maker.

The bankruptcy of a state introduces another ticklish issue as well: Where should the case be held? If a state were analogous to other debtors, the logical locale would be the state itself. Holding the case in the state would be awkward. The judge or judges would not be officials of the state itself; they would be federal judges. But a more neutral location would be preferable.

Given the stakes and the distinctive posture of the case, state bankruptcy cases should not simply be funneled into the judicial framework that applies to other bankruptcy debtors. This would put enormous pressure on a single bankruptcy judge in the state itself. It would also mean vesting oversight in a non-Article III judge, which would limit the jurisdictional reach of the court in ways that might complicate the case.[64]

Under one possible approach for addressing these concerns, each circuit court would designate a small number of Article III district court judges who have bankruptcy expertise, and the judges would be included on a nationwide panel of judges. If a state filed for bankruptcy, a three-judge panel would be randomly selected to oversee the case. The logical venue for the case would be the District Court for the District of Columbia. This framework, which echoes other existing or proposed special courts in important respects,[65] would distribute the pressure of the case across three shoulders rather than one; it would provide a logical venue; and it would give full Article III scope to the proceedings.

---

[64] The jurisdictional limitations of the bankruptcy court were recently underscored by a major Supreme Court decision. Stern v. Marshall, 131 S.Ct. 2594 (2011).

[65] The special court established by the Foreign Intelligence Surveillance Act of 1978 (FISA) is picked from a panel of district and circuit court judges appointed for seven-year terms

The most obvious concern is the distance of the court from many of the state's creditors and other parties in interest. During a controversy over venue in the 1990s, which has recently reemerged, critics of the corporate bankruptcy venue rules have objected strongly to venue outside the debtor's domicile on these grounds.[66] The importance of geographical convenience was debatable for the simple reason that the vast majority of small creditors do not participate in the case and distance is not a problem for large creditors. However, some small creditors might be more inclined to raise issues and appear in person in a bankruptcy involving a state. The best solution to this concern is to make it as simple as possible to participate. The court could allow participation by video link in major hearings, for instance, and broadcast court sessions on CNN or the Internet. It also could hold informational hearings in the state.

CONCLUSION

In this chapter, I have sought to make a case for state bankruptcy, to identify its core objectives, and then to outline its key contours. State bankruptcy would involve political decision makers, rather than simply private actors. As a result, it raises a number of issues that are not present, or are less ticklish, in ordinary bankruptcy cases. In answer to the questions of who should initiate the case and who should be given authority to propose a reorganization plan, I argued that these decisions should be made by the governor in consultation with state legislative leaders. An effective framework need only include a limited stay, would not have reachback rules, and could use a streamlined confirmation process. I also have argued that the federal government should be permitted to help finance the process and that the judge could be selected from a panel of district court judges in the event of a state bankruptcy filing. The framework is likely to work best if it is as simple as possible and is tightly focused on the core objectives outlined at the beginning of the chapter.

---

by the Chief Justice of the Supreme Court. The Chapter 14 proposal drafted by Tom Jackson for a Hoover Institution working group would assign systemically important financial institution bankruptcies to a judge (one of a group preselected by the Chief Justice of the Supreme Court based on financial institution expertise) in the Second or DC Circuit. Chapter 14 Proposal, *supra* note 62, at 6–7.

[66] The lightning rod in the earlier debate was a Federal Judicial Center report that raised the inconvenience issue. Federal Judicial Center, *Report to the Committee on the Administration of the Bankruptcy System*, Chapter 11 *Venue Choice by Large Public Companies* (Jan. 9–10, 1997).

9

Fiscal Federalism and the Limits of Bankruptcy

ADAM J. LEVITIN

The latest round of state fiscal crises has engendered a proposal by Professor David Skeel,[1] echoed by prominent Republican politicians,[2] to permit states to file for bankruptcy based on the model of Chapter 9 bankruptcy for municipalities. In this Chapter, I argue that states' fiscal problems are a structural-political problem that bankruptcy cannot be expected to fix. Bankruptcy is not a solution to every debt problem.

Cyclical state budget crises are the inevitable outcome of fiscal federalism, the fiscal relationship between the federal and state governments. The U.S. fiscal federalism arrangement means that economic downturns place unusual financial strains on the states, which may be exacerbated by political agency problems – elected official pursuing private benefits, including reelection, rather than the public interest. These are ultimately problems with political structures, rather than with finances, and that necessitates political rather than financial restructuring. Accordingly, bankruptcy makes sense only as a political tool, rather than a financial-legal restructuring tool.

Bankruptcy is ill-equipped to accomplish political restructuring, however. It is not a forum in which fiscal federalism can be renegotiated. At best, it is a convening and negotiating tool, but it is of limited use because

---

Thanks to Anna Gelpern for her feedback on this chapter. © 2011, Adam J. Levitin.

[1] David Skeel, *A Bankruptcy Law – Not Bailouts – for the States*, WALL ST. J., Jan. 18, 2011; David Skeel, *Give States a Way to Go Bankrupt*, THE WEEKLY STANDARD, Nov. 29, 2010. *See also* Steven L. Schwarcz, *A Minimalist Approach to State "Bankruptcy,"* 59 UCLA L. REV. (forthcoming 2011) (including model federal statute for state debt restructuring). Skeel has subsequently developed these ideas in much more detail. See David A. Skeel, Jr., *States of Bankruptcy*, U. CHI. L. REV. (forthcoming 2012); David A. Skeel, Jr., *State Bankruptcy from the Ground Up*, this volume.

[2] Jeb Bush & Newt Gingrich, *Better Off Bankrupt*, L.A. TIMES, Jan. 27, 2011.

it cannot bring all of states' stakeholders to the table. All it offers is procedural assistance with creditors, a subset of stakeholders, and even then bankruptcy offers even less procedural assistance than it does for individuals or firms because central bankruptcy principles such as a liquidation baseline[3] and absolute priority[4] are inapplicable to the states.

Furthermore, bankruptcy has never been a tool to deal with a business's structural problems, and fiscal federalism is, for states, an inherently structural problem. Bankruptcy can reduce financial leverage and restructure debts, but it cannot fix bad business models. Bankruptcy similarly cannot fix the structural-political problem underlying states' budgets any more than it can make a buggy whip maker or brick-and-mortar video rental store profitable. Not surprisingly, state bankruptcy proposals simply do not engage with the sources of state budget problems.

At best, bankruptcy might mitigate some of the political agency costs that exacerbate state budget problems, but it could also easily be used as a partisan political tool. The politics of state budget gaps is fundamentally a debate between tax hikes and service/benefits cuts. Bankruptcy can be used to force service and benefits cuts that cannot happen in the normal realm of state politics. Under a Chapter 9 model, however, bankruptcy cannot be used to force tax hikes. Thus, Republican politician Newt Gingrich expressed his support for a state bankruptcy option as a tool for enabling the renegotiation of public employee unions' contracts:

> I ... hope the House Republicans are going to move a bill in the first month or so of their tenure to create a venue for state bankruptcy, so that states like California and New York and Illinois that think they're going to come to Washington for money can be told, you know, you need to sit down with all your government employee unions and look at their health plans and their pension plans and, frankly, if they don't want to change, our recommendation is you go into bankruptcy court and let the bankruptcy judge change it, and I would make the federal bankruptcy law prohibit tax increases as part of the solution, so no bankruptcy judge could impose a tax increase on the people of the states.[5]

---

[3] The liquidation baseline, known as "best interests," is the principle that creditors must receive at least as much in a restructuring as in a liquidation.
[4] "Absolute priority" means that senior creditors are paid in full before junior creditors or equity holders receive any recovery.
[5] Doug Halonen, *Gingrich Seeks Bill Allowing State Bankruptcy to Avert Bailouts*, PENSIONS AND INVESTMENTS, Jan. 10, 2011, at http://www.pionline.com/article/20110110/PRINTSUB/301109976 (quoting a Nov. 11, 2010, speech given by Newt Gingrich before the Institute for Policy Innovation).

The possibilities for a state bankruptcy regime are hardly bounded by Newt Gingrich's vision; one could imagine a different type of bankruptcy regime in which tax hikes would be possible or even mandatory or in which there are protections for collective bargaining agreements.[6] Part of the appeal of a Chapter 9-modeled state bankruptcy regime, however, is clearly as a sword for one side of the tax hike versus austerity cut debate, making it a Republican partisan tool. Rather than addressing the causes of state budget crises, proposals for state bankruptcy dangle the false hope of fiscal solutions to political crises and offer cover for partisan agendas. Current state bankruptcy proposals leave the root causes of state fiscal distress unaddressed, setting the stage for serial filings by states, much as in the airline industry, where massive cuts in labor costs have been unable to fix a tenuous business model that depends heavily on fuel costs and consumer spending.

How to reform the fiscal federalism arrangement is a topic far beyond the scope of this chapter, but that is where we must look, rather than to bankruptcy, to find real solutions to state budget crises.

This chapter proceeds as follows. Section I considers the fiscal federalism sources of state financial distress. Section II addresses whether bankruptcy is a tool that can fix state's fiscal problems. Section III considers bankruptcy's use as a political tool. The last section concludes.

I. FISCAL FEDERALISM AND STATE FINANCIAL DISTRESS

Every state has its idiosyncratic budget problems, but cyclical state fiscal crises are the inevitable outcome of fiscal federalism – the budgetary relationship between state and federal governments. The current U.S. fiscal federalism arrangement is hardwired to create cyclical state financial distress. The extent of this distress will vary among states during cyclical downturns. States as a whole, however, cannot escape budget crises when there is an economic downturn because of the lopsided burdens placed on them by fiscal federalism.

Under the current fiscal federalism arrangement, states are saddled with countercyclical spending obligations – both explicit obligations and those implicit in the political compact. As a result of budgetary prohibitions of their own design, however, they lack the borrowing power required to

---

[6] *Cf.* Clayton P. Gillette, *Political Will and Fiscal Federalism in Municipal Bankruptcy*, U. CHI. L. REV. (forthcoming) (proposing that bankruptcy courts be allowed to impose tax increases in municipal bankruptcies to neutralize strategic behavior of local officials).

support these obligations.[7] The result of this structural mismatch are budget crises, as states struggle to come up with spending cuts and tax hikes to close their budget gaps.

The states have countercyclical spending obligations because they are the primary providers of many services to citizens, including education, corrections, health care, disability, and unemployment benefits. Much of this spending is a result of unfunded or partially funded federal mandates – costs that the federal government legally or functionally requires the states to incur.[8]

These federal mandates range from education to environmental protection, with welfare and health care programs being the most expensive. Demand for welfare and state-funded health care is also cyclical with the general economy. For example, as unemployment rises so too do demands on the states for partially state-funded welfare benefits[9] such as unemployment insurance; Temporary Assistance to Needy Families (TANF, the successor to Aid to Families with Dependent Children or AFDC)[10]; Supplemental Nutrition Assistance Program/Employment and Training (SNAP/ET, formerly known as the Food Stamp Program)[11]; the Children's Health Insurance Program (CHIP); and, most importantly, Medicaid, which accounted for 21% of state spending in fiscal year 2009.[12]

---

[7] *See* JOHN MAYNARD KEYNES, THE GENERAL THEORY OF EMPLOYMENT INTEREST AND MONEY ch. 22 (1936). *See also* David A. Super, *Rethinking Fiscal Federalism*, 118 HARV. L. REV. 2544, 2605–2611 (2005) (discussing the pre-Keynesian nature of state budgets).

[8] Although few of these costs are truly mandated, they are often the consequence of states participating in intergovernmental programs, and the costs might be lower than if the states attempted to provide the service alone. *See* Robert D. Behn & Elizabeth K. Keating, *Facing the Fiscal Crises in State Governments: National Problem; National Responsibilities*, Kennedy School of Govt. Research Working Paper No. 04–025, at http://ssrn.com/abstract=5631362, at 3.

[9] *See, e.g.*, Marshall J. Vest, *The Effects of the Economic Cycle on Government Revenue*, at http://ebr.eller.arizona.edu/Arizona_fiscal_issues/economic_cyclicality%20_government_revenues.asp.

[10] TANF is funded through federal block grants, but requires matching state maintenance of effort (MOE) funds to retain block grant eligibility. Roughly half of TANF expenditures are from state funds. Nat'l Ass'n of State Budget Officers, Fiscal Year 2009 State Expenditure Report 30, *at* http://www.nasbo.org/LinkClick.aspx?fileticket=w7RqO74llEw%3d&tabid=79 (hereinafter the National Association of State Budget Officers (NASBO) 2009 Report).

[11] The SNAP component of SNAP/ET is funded directly by the federal government, but the states have a 50% matching contribution requirement for the ET component. The states also share administrative costs for SNAP with the federal government.

[12] NASBO 2009 Report, *supra* note 10, at 10, tbl. 5. States are also vulnerable to changes in federal budgeting. *See* Michael Cooper, *No Matter How Debt Debate Ends, Governors See More Cuts for States*, N.Y. TIMES, July 15, 2011, at A8.

States, however, cannot simply increase their spending to meet the demand for welfare services. Unlike the federal government, every state in the country except Vermont and Wyoming has a balanced-budget requirement,[13] and most states also have debt limits of various types.[14] Many states also have constitutional tax limitations that constrain their ability to raise revenue.[15] Although states have found numerous ways to circumvent these requirements,[16] the circumventions are at best short-term rather than long-term fixes.[17]

[13] Wyoming does not have a balanced budget requirement, but Wyoming "is required to balance in practice." *See* GEN. ACCOUNTING OFFICE GAO/AFMD-93-58BR, BALANCED BUDGET REQUIREMENTS: STATE EXPERIENCES AND IMPLICATIONS FOR THE FEDERAL GOVERNMENT 3 & n.3 (1993); Peter R. Orszag *The State Fiscal Crisis: Why It Happened and What to Do About It*, MILKEN INSTIT. REV. 3d Q. 2003, at 21; Institute for Truth in Accounting, *The Truth About Balanced Budgets: A Fifty State Study*, Feb. 2009, at 25, *at* http://statebudgetwatch.org/50_State_Final.pdf. For a listing of the constitutional and statutory citations of state balanced budget requirements, *see* Yilin Hou & Daniel L. Smith, *A Framework for Understanding State Balanced Budget Requirement Systems: Reexamining Distinctive Features and an Operational Definition*, PUB. BUDGETING & FIN. 22, 31–33 (fall 2006). There is significant variation in state balanced-budget requirements. In forty-four states, the governor must submit a balanced budget. James M. Poterba & Kim S. Rueben, *Fiscal News, State Budget Rules, and Tax- Exempt Bond Yields*, 50 J. URBAN ECON. 537, 547 (2001). Only 37 states, however, require the legislature to enact a balanced budget, but revenues and expenditures may vary from it. *Id.* Six of these states require unexpected deficits to be corrected the next fiscal year, whereas twenty-four prohibit deficits to be carried forward. *Id.* at 547–548. This means that deficits can be run both in the states that only require the submission of a gubernatorial budget (IL, LA, MA, NH, NV, NY) and in those that do not require deficits to be accounted for in future budgets (AK, CA, CT, MD, MI, PA, WI). *See* Steven M. Shiffrin, *State Budget Deficit Dynamics and the California Debacle*, 18 J. ECON. PERSPECTIVES 205, 206–207 (2004).
[14] ROBERT S. AMDURSKY & CLAYTON GILLETTE, MUNICIPAL DEBT FINANCE LAW: THEORY AND PRACTICE § 4.2 (1992). *See also* Robert Krol, *A Survey of the Impact of Budget Rules on State Taxation, Spending, and Debt*, 16 CATO J. 295 (1997) (counting twenty-three states with tax or expenditure limitations).
[15] *See* Richard Briffault, *The Disfavored Constitution: State Fiscal Limits and State Constitutional Law*, 34 RUTGERS L. J. 907, 915–925 (2003).
[16] *See* Institute for Truth in Accounting, *supra* note 13, at 26–30 (detailing ways in which states evade balanced budget requirements).
[17] The empirical political science literature has shown that budgetary institutions influence fiscal policies. *See, e.g.*, Signe Krogstrup & Sébastian Wälti, *Do Fiscal Rules Cause Budgetary Outcomes?* 136 PUB. CHOICE 123 (2008) (examining impact of fiscal rules in Swiss sub-federal jurisdictions); H. Abbie Erler, *Legislative Term Limits and State Spending*, 133 PUB. CHOICE 479 (2007) (finding higher state spending in states with legislative term limits); James M. Poterba, *Do Budget Rules Work?* NBER Working Paper No. 5550 (1996); James M. Poterba, *Capital Budgets, Borrowing Rules, and State Capital Spending*, 56 J. POL. ECON. 165 (1995); James E. Alt & R. C. Lowry, *Divided Government and Budget Deficits: Evidence from the States*, 88 AM. POL. SCI. REV. 811 (1994) (finding that states with harder balanced-budget rules react more promptly to revenue or spending shocks); James M. Poterba, *State Responses to Fiscal Crises: The*

The result is that states cannot engage in countercyclical deficit spending to stimulate the economy when private sector spending falls off. Instead, when demands on the federally mandated parts of states' budgets grow during economic downturns, states must either raise taxes and/or cut non-mandated (discretionary) spending – expenditures on state programs other than for existing debts.

Both responses are politically unpopular and economically counterproductive. Tax hikes and spending cuts both exacerbate economic downturns by reducing aggregate demand.[18] Higher taxes reduce the funds citizens have to spend, thereby contributing to economic contraction.[19]

Similarly, spending cuts mean layoffs, canceled contracts, reduced benefit payments, and lower payments to businesses and nonprofits that provide direct services.[20] This means that citizens – either as direct benefit recipients or as employees of the state or affected firms – receive less money from the state and, thus, have reduced consumption ability. What is more, many state expenditures are tied to federal matching funds. Therefore, cutting expenditures reduces state services more than it reduces state costs. For example, cutting a dollar of Medicaid expenses will only net a state between 12 cents and 44 cents of savings, but it will deny the state's residents a dollar's worth of Medicaid-covered services.[21] Both tax increases and spending cuts can exacerbate economic woes.

The combination of countercyclical spending obligations without matching borrowing capacity means that state budgets are inevitably stressed whenever there is a national economic downturn. Balanced-budget requirements are simply inconsistent with Keynesian (deficit) spending obligations. Thus, at the root of states' budget problems is a structural problem stemming from the fiscal federalism arrangement. This is not a

---

Effects of Budgetary Institutions and Politics, 102 J. POL. ECON. 799 (1994) (same); Jürgen von Hagen, *A Note on the Empirical Effectiveness of Formal Fiscal Restraints*, 44 J. PUB. ECON. 199 (1991) (finding that state budget rules effect the level and composition of state debts). *See also* Dale Bails & Margie A. Tieslau, *The Impact of Fiscal Constitutions on State and Local Expenditures*, 20 CATO J. 255, 257–258 (2000) (discussing conflict in political science literature between "public choice" view and "institutional irrelevance" views of state budget institutions).

[18] Orszag, *supra* note 13, at 22.
[19] *Id.* Both spending cuts and tax hikes might affect savings rates before consumption levels, but given the low savings rate for most of the population, spending is likely to be rapidly affected.
[20] Elizabeth McNichol et al., *States Continue to Feel Recession's Impact*, Ctr. for Budget Pol'y and Priorities, June 17, 2011, at 7.
[21] Jeremy Gerst & Daniel Wilson, *Fiscal Crises of the States: Causes and Consequences*, FED. RESERVE BANK OF S.F. ECON. LETTER, 2010-20, June 28, 2010, at 3.

problem of state overleverage per se but rather a mismatch between spending duties and borrowing capacity.

This problem suggests a need to revisit the current fiscal federalism arrangements. U.S. fiscal federalism does have an insurance function that provides a partial stabilizing safety net for states against asymmetric revenue shocks via tax and transfer flows.[22] It also accomplishes significant interstate and interregional redistribution.[23]

It is simply not tenable, however, for states to have both federal spending mandates and balanced-budget requirements. Either states need to jettison their balanced-budget requirements and be willing to deficit spending, making them true Keynesian entities, giving real effect to their sovereignty, or they have to be recognized as mere administrative subdivisions of the federal government, which would obligate federal spending to kick in to fund federally mandated state obligations when the demand for state services rises.[24]

---

[22] See, e.g., Jacques Mélitz & Frédéric Zumer, *Regional Redistribution and Stabilization by the Center in Canada, France, the UK and the US: A Reassessment and New Tests*, 86 J. PUB. ECON. 263 (2002) (fiscal federalism accounts for 10% regional stabilization in the United States); Kenneth Kletzer & Jürgen von Hagen, *Monetary Union and Fiscal Federalism*, tbl. 1, THE IMPACT OF EMU ON EUROPE AND THE DEVELOPING WORLD (CHARLES WYPLOSZ, ED., 2001) (table summarizing literature's estimates for redistribution and insurance effects of intranational transfers in the United States); Tamim Bayoumi & Paul R. Masson, *Fiscal Flows in the United States and Canada: Lessons for Monetary Union in Europe*, 39 EUR. ECON. REV. 253 (1995) (estimating fiscal federalism stabilization effect of 30 percent); Eric van Wincoop, *Regional Risksharing*, 39 EUR. ECON. REV. 1545 (1995); Charles E. A. Goodhart & Stephen Smith, *Stabilisation*, in THE ECONOMICS OF COMMUNITY PUBLIC FINANCE, 5 European Economy Reports and Studies 417 (1993) (estimating fiscal federalism stabilization effect of 13 percent); Jürgen von Hagen, *Fiscal Arrangements in a Monetary Union – Some Evidence From the US*, in FISCAL POLICY, TAXES, AND THE FINANCIAL SYSTEM IN AN INCREASINGLY INTEGRATED EUROPE 337–359 (DON FAIR & CHRISTIAN DE BOISSIEUX, EDS., 1992) (estimating fiscal federalism stabilization effect of 10 percent); Jeffrey Sachs & Xavier Sala-i-Martin, *Fiscal Federalism and Optimum Currency Areas: Evidence for Europe from the United States*, in ESTABLISHING A CENTRAL BANK: ISSUES IN EUROPE AND LESSONS FROM THE US 195–219 (VITTORIO GRILLI, MATTHEW CANZONERI & PAUL MASSON, EDS., 1992) (estimating that U.S. fiscal federalism produces combined short-term stabilization and long-term redistribution effect between 33 and 40 percent).

[23] See Kletzer & von Hagen, *supra* note 22, tbl 1 (summarizing estimates of redistribution effect of U.S. fiscal federalism, ranging from 7 cents to 47 cents); von Hagen, *supra* note 22 (emphasizing distinction between short-term stabilization and long-term redistribution). Relative to other fiscal federalism arrangements, the United States does not engage in substantial interregional redistribution. German fiscal federalism has a complex, constitutionally mandated redistribution requirement. See Ralf Hepp & Jürgen von Hagen, *Fiscal Federalism in Germany: Stabilization and Redistribution Before and After Unification*, working paper, August 30, 2010, at http://faculty.fordham.edu/hepp/vHH_MZ02_Paper_2010_0830_web.pdf.

[24] The Federal government did toss a Keynesian bone to the states in the form of the American Recovery and Reinvestment Act of 2009 (also known as "the stimulus"),

Although eliminating balanced budget requirements could serve as a simple solution to the problem – liberating states to spend themselves into Keynesian oblivion if they wish – there are good reasons to have balanced-budget requirements for subnational entities. As a general matter, balanced-budget rules function as both a commitment and a signaling device. They increase credibility with creditors, who know that future discretionary spending will be cut or future revenue increased to pay the obligations owed to them.

Furthermore, balanced-budget requirements for subnational entities help guard against the moral hazard of state profligacy in reliance on a federal bailout. If states have to first make the expenditure cuts or tax increases to balance their budget before turning to the federal government for assistance, they might be less likely to see federal bailouts as attractive insurance for unwise profligacy.[25]

In short, there are good reasons for subnational entities to have balanced-budget rules, but they come at the price of loss of ability to engage in fiscal stabilization over the economic cycle. In a federal system in which the federal government fills the fiscal stabilization role, this is not a problem. When federal stabilization is unreliable or insufficient, however, there will be an inevitable economic strain on subnational governments.

States' fiscal problems are brought on by a deep structural problem but are often exacerbated by political agency problems. There is a vast literature on the political economy of budget deficits.[26] Although it identifies many political economy factors that may contribute to deficits, it has identified political agency problems as a particular cause, as politicians seeking private benefits and subject to limited electoral discipline run up state spending without corresponding revenue increases.[27]

---

mainly in the form of increased Medicaid funding and a State Fiscal Stabilization Fund. That aid helped states weather budget shortfalls in 2009–2011, but there are few funds remaining for disbursement in 2012 and forward. McNichol *et al.*, *supra* note 20, at 7.

[25] Relatedly, balanced budget rules are a way of addressing political agency costs, as they force greater fiscal discipline by limiting politicians' ability to seek private benefits through spending without corresponding revenue increases.

[26] For an excellent overview of the theoretical literature on budget deficits, *see*, Alberto Alesina & Roberto Perotti, *The Political Economy of Budget Deficits*, 42 IMF Staff Papers No. 1, 1 (1995).

[27] *See, e.g.*, Roland Hodler, *Elections and the Strategic Use of Budget Deficits*, 148 PUB. CHOICE 149 (2011) (model in which a conservative incumbent with preferences for low public spending strategically running a budget deficit to prevent the left-wing opposition candidate from choosing high public spending if elected, and possibly also to ensure his own reelection); John F. Cogan, *The Dispersion of Spending Authority and Federal Budget Deficits*, in THE BUDGET PUZZLE: UNDERSTANDING FEDERAL SPENDING

II. WHAT BANKRUPTCY CANNOT DO: CURE BAD BUSINESS MODELS

If state fiscal problems are structural (albeit exacerbated by political agency problems), can bankruptcy help? The answer is no. Bankruptcy is a remarkably successful tool for dealing with collective action problems,[28] preserving going-concern value, getting rid of debt overhang,[29] and

---

[16] (JOHN F. COGAN, TIMOTHY J. MURIS & ALLEN SCHICK, EDS. 1994); Alberto Alesina & Guido Tabellini, *A Positive Theory of Fiscal Deficits and Government Debt*, 57 REV. ECON. STUDIES, 403 (1990) (modeling two parties that disagree about spending priorities, but not spending levels, in which both parties are encouraged to issue debt strategically); Guido Tabellini & Alberto Alesina, *Voting on the Budget Deficit*, 80 AM. ECON. REV. 37 (1990); Torsten Persson & Lares E. O. Svensson, *Why a Stubborn Conservative Would Run a Deficit: Policy with Time-Inconsistent Preferences*, 104 Q. J. ECON. 325 (1989) (modeling two parties that disagree about spending levels, but not priorities, which encourages the low-spending party to issue debt to constrain the high-spending party in the future); Kenneth Rogoff, *Equilibrium Political Business Cycles*, 80 AM. ECON. REV. 21 (1990) (observing how election cycles can drive expenditure decisions); Alberto Alesina, *Politics and Business Cycles in Industrial Democracies*, 8 ECON. POL'Y 54 (1989) (observing how election cycles can drive expenditure decisions); Alberto Alesina & Jeffrey Sachs, *Political Parties and the Business Cycle in the United States*, 20 J. MONEY CREDIT & BANKING 62 (1988) (observing how election cycles can drive expenditure decisions); Kenneth Rogoff & Anne Sibert, *Elections and Macro-Economic Policy Cycles*, 55 REV. ECON. STUDIES 1 (1988) (observing how election cycles can drive expenditure decisions); JAMES M. BUCHANAN, CHARLES K. ROWLEY, & ROBERT D. TOLLISON, DEFICITS (1986) (noting that politicians will run deficits in a recession, but not surpluses when the recession ends because fiscally illuded voters reward this behavior); Barry R. Weingast, Kenneth A. Shepsle, & Christopher Johnsen, *The Political Economy of Benefits of Costs: A Neoclassical Approach to Distributive Politics*, 89 J. POL. ECON. 642 (1981) (noting the common pool problem of the "Law of $1/n$" that spending increases with the number of legislators when there is geographic representation); Duncan McRae, *A Political Model of the Business Cycle*, 85 J. POL. ECON. 239 (1977) (observing how election cycles can drive expenditure decisions); JAMES M. BUCHANAN & RICHARD E. WAGNER, *Democracy in* DEFICIT: THE POLITICAL LEGACY OF LORD KEYNES (1977) (noting how Keynesianism contributes to excessive deficits because of politicians exploiting fiscally illuded voters for personal benefits of reelection); Richard E. Wagner, *Revenue Structure, Fiscal Illusion and Budgetary Choice*, 25 PUB. CHOICE 45 (1976) (opportunistic politicians seeking reelection for their personal benefits exploit this misapprehension by raising spending more than taxes to curry favor with the "fiscally illuded" voters); William D. Nordhaus, *The Political Business Cycle*, 42 REV. ECON. STUDIES 169 (1975) (observing how election cycles can drive expenditure decisions).

[28] *E.g.*, THOMAS H. JACKSON, THE LOGIC AND LIMITS OF BANKRUPTCY LAW 10–19 (1986) (describing bankruptcy as a response to a common pool problem).

[29] *E.g.*, Paul R. Krugman, *Financing vs. Forgiving a Debt Overhang*, 29 J. DEVELOPMENT ECON. 253 (1988) (debt overhang problems in developing countries); DOUGLAS G. BAIRD, ELEMENTS OF BANKRUPTCY 30 (2010) (explaining the fresh start rationale for individual debtors); Thomas H. Jackson, *The Fresh-Start Policy in Bankruptcy Law*, 98 HARV. L. REV. 1393 (1985).

providing social insurance.[30] If a firm's problems are merely financial – that is, if the firm is overleveraged or illiquid but solvent – bankruptcy provides an excellent forum for restructuring the firm's capital structure to preserve going-concern value or, if there is none, to provide for an orderly liquidation. Moreover, bankruptcy provides a backdrop against which private orderings can occur, both when the initial decision to extend credit is made and when outstanding debt needs to be restructured.

Bankruptcy, however, is not, a panacea for all problems that enterprises face. Bankruptcy can cure financial problems but not operational problems. Bankruptcy can help enterprises get out of burdensome contracts[31] and can slough off extra leverage. But bankruptcy cannot fix a bad business model.

If a firm's business is selling whale oil, slide rules, floppy disks, cassette tapes, 8-tracks, or books in a brick-and-mortar store, bankruptcy cannot help it beyond providing an orderly way to redeploy the assets and a dignified funeral. At best, bankruptcy can buy an enterprise the financial breathing room to undertake an operational restructuring, but nothing in bankruptcy law – understood broadly, with a small "b," as any type of debt restructuring regime rather than necessarily in the model of Title 11 of the U.S. Code – can fix a bad business model.

In Chapter 11, bankruptcy provides a forum for creditors to make a collective decision about the viability of a firm. If they do not think that its business model will work even when restructured, they can try and block a reorganization plan and liquidate the firm. The creditors' collective viability decision is only meaningful, however, because of the liquidation option.

For a state, there is no liquidation option. (For municipal corporations, such an option technically exists, but it is hard to imagine it being applied to any sizeable municipality, and federal bankruptcy law does not provide a right to convert a Chapter 9 bankruptcy to a Chapter 7 liquidation.)[32] Therefore, even if the state's business model is fundamentally flawed – as it necessarily is given the problems with the current fiscal federalism arrangement – creditors would be stuck with a financially reorganized, but nonviable, entity.

---

[30] *See, e.g.,* Adam Feibelman, *Defining the Social Insurance Function of Consumer Bankruptcy*, 13 AM. BANKR. INST. L. REV. 129 (2005); Jean Braucher, *Consumer Bankruptcy as Part of the Social Safety Net: Fresh Start or Treadmill*, 44 SANTA CLARA L. REV. 1065 (2004).
[31] *See* 11 U.S.C. § 365 (rejection of unexpired leases and executory contracts).
[32] Michael W. McConnell & Randall C. Picker, *When Cities Go Broke: A Conceptual Introduction to Municipal Bankruptcy*, 60 U. CHI. L. REV. 425, 481–483 (1993).

Existing Chapters of the U.S. Bankruptcy Code attempt to deal with this problem with a (vague) plan feasibility requirement.[33] None of them, however, contemplate the bankruptcy of a class of entity where there is an inherent risk of serial filing as a result of structural problems. There is nothing that prevents states from being serial bankruptcy filers just as Argentina and Mexico have been serial defaulters.[34] Indeed, even within the handful of municipalities that have filed for Chapter 9 bankruptcy, there are several serial filers.[35]

Bankruptcy cannot fix the underlying cyclical structural problem in states' budgets stemming from the confluence of unfunded federal mandates and balanced-budget requirements. At most, then, bankruptcy might be able to mitigate some of the political agency problems that exacerbate state budget problems, as state political actors may pursue private gains at the expense of the public interest. As Section III argues, however, bankruptcy is a perilous tool to use to solve political problems.

III. BANKRUPTCY AS A POLITICAL TOOL

Bankruptcy could serve as a tool for addressing the political agency problems that exacerbate (but do not cause) state budget problems. Bankruptcy could function as a political tool in several ways. It could serve as a political discipline mechanism; provide cover for politically unpopular decisions; serve as a convening mechanism to facilitate negotiations; and facilitate negotiations by setting baseline rules and alternatives.

Bankruptcy could serve as a political discipline mechanism, in that a state's bankruptcy plan could impose discipline on the state's budget politics. State bankruptcy, then, could function as a form of "second-order rationality,"[36] as it gives states' politicians the tools to tie their hands because they know they lack the political willpower otherwise. There is no ability, however, for courts to prevent states from going right back to their old habits once they are out of bankruptcy, so any second-order rationality benefits might be short-lasting.

---

[33] 11 U.S.C. §§ 943(b)(7); 1129(a)(11), 1225(a)(6), 1325(a)(6).

[34] See Carmen M. Reinhart, et al., *Debt Intolerance*, 34 BROOKINGS PAPERS ON ECON. ACTIVITY 1 (2003) (discussing states that are in serial default).

[35] Six of the forty-two Chapter 9 filings by municipalities or counties (as opposed to hospital or sanitary districts or other entities) since 1980 were repeat filings. PACER records and author's analysis.

[36] See Richard Epstein, *Second-Order Rationality*, in BEHAVIORAL PUBLIC FINANCE 355 (EDWARD J. MCCAFFREY & JOEL SLEMROD, EDS. 2006) (explaining that second-order rationality refers to a range of rational responses to cognitive biases).

Bankruptcy could also provide politicians with the cover to undertake deals that are opposed by their constituents. It is impossible to say, however, whether this enables politicians to look out for the commonwealth rather than to be beholden to narrow rent-seeking interests or merely gives politicians the ability to reach deals of personal convenience without regard to their constituents' interests.

Bankruptcy also provides a convening and negotiating mechanism that can bind non-consenting holdouts to a deal. Its usefulness, however, is limited in the case of the states. As a convening tool, bankruptcy brings all claimants together into a single proceeding and settles, Godfather-like, (nearly) all claims.[37]

In Chapter 11, this works by bringing together creditors, employees, and equity holders. For states, however, a major set of stakeholders is absent – voters. Court-mandated austerity measures (or tax increases) require the acquiescence of voters because the politicians involved in reaching deals on austerity measures are responsive to voters. The exclusion of other stakeholders may make creditors, in turn, reluctant to cut deals because of a concern as to whether the deals will stick without the assent of the absent stakeholders. Thus, bankruptcy's convening power is limited for states.

What is more, bankruptcy power as a negotiating mechanism for creditors is diminished because of the lack of a viable liquidation threat and absolute priority distribution baseline. Two fundamental principles of bankruptcy law are that absent creditors' consent, creditors must receive more in a restructuring than in a liquidation (the "best interests" test) and that senior creditors must be paid in full before junior creditors realize any recovery.

For firms and individual debtors, bankruptcy forces claimants to come to the negotiating table, lest they be locked out of a legally binding deal. The convening power's real value is that it is coupled with a negotiating mechanism that relies on two implicit threats:

1. You'd better reach a deal, or else you'll get just liquidation value.
2. If everyone else reaches a deal, you'll be forced to go along.

These threats vanish in the case of states because there is no liquidation option (with absolute priority applied) and, thus, no "best interest test" baseline to protect non-consenting creditors. Bankruptcy is only able to

---

[37] As Michael notes to Carlo at the conclusion of Godfather, Part I, "Today I settle all family business."

bind non-consenting creditors by giving them at least liquidation value and making the deal in their "best interests."[38]

Bankruptcy can bring states' creditors together, but it lacks the leverage to encourage deals. The alternative facing a creditor in a state bankruptcy would not be liquidation but whatever the creditor would get outside bankruptcy. Thus, creditors that think they will fare better in the normal course of state politics will be reluctant to deal in bankruptcy. Creditors' own liquidity concerns may encourage deal making in order to get paid,[39] but this is a much weaker threat than liquidation value.

The inherent benefits of bankruptcy as a political tool are uncertain. Unfortunately, bankruptcy could also serve as a mechanism for carrying out partisan agendas under the cover of judicial robes. Traditionally, bankruptcy courts have not had the power to order tax increases or even rate increases for public utilities.[40] Indeed, there is no analog in a Chapter 11 bankruptcy – the court cannot order the debtor to increase prices on the goods and services it sells. At most, a bankruptcy court can approve a plan of reorganization that makes such changes, but operational decisions are not in the court's hands. Instead, courts simply supervise cuts in existing obligations.

This imbalance in the powers of bankruptcy courts raises serious concerns that a state bankruptcy regime would be used as a partisan political device to balance state budgets through cuts to employees' compensation, services, and benefits – austerity in the form of service cuts but not tax increases.[41] Bankruptcy, then, would be an end-run around democratic checks and balances on distributional decisions rather than a way of enabling tough political decisions.

---

[38] 11 U.S.C. §§ 1129(a)(7); 1225(a)(4)-(5); 1325(a)(4)-(5).

[39] Cf. Sarah Woo, *Regulatory Bankruptcy: How Bank Regulation Causes Fire Sales*, 99 Geo. L.J. 1615 (2011) (observing that liquidity concerns can encourage creditors to seek liquidation).

[40] *But see Meriwether v. Garrett*, 102 U.S. 472, 518 (1880) ("When creditors are unable to obtain payment of their judgments against municipal bodies by execution, they can proceed by mandamus against the municipal authorities to compel them to levy the necessary tax for that purpose, if such authorities are clothed by the legislature with the taxing power; and such tax, when collected, cannot be diverted to other uses."). Meriwether was not a bankruptcy case and is arguably no longer applicable law, but the possibility of a mandamus remedy was noted in dicta by the Supreme Court as recently as 1990. *Missouri v Jenkins*, 495 U.S. 33, 56–58 (1990) (considering whether a federal district court judge could use a writ of mandamus to raise property taxes as part of a remedial scheme for past segregation).

[41] *See supra* note 2.

Bankruptcy can thus be either a means of forcing states to make unpleasant choices, or it can provide cover for politicians to make those choices (which may be a good or bad thing). Bankruptcy can enable deals, or force bad deals. The virtues of bankruptcy as a political tool are hardly certain; it carries with it the possibility of being abused to carrying out partisan agendas.

It is possible to envision, however, a state bankruptcy system in which the court would have the power to direct tax increases. Leaving aside questions of constitutionality, such an arrangement would mitigate the danger of bankruptcy being used as a factional device. (It is nonetheless hard to imagine a court ever ordering a tax increase.) If we were to fantasize about such a system, would it be a good one? Put differently, are courts the proper body for making decisions about tax increases and spending cuts?

Robert Amdursky and Clayton Gillette have noted that it is unclear whether courts have any institutional advantage over other bodies, like legislatures, in balancing conflicting interest of government debtor constituents.[42] They also observe some reasons to prefer judicial second-guessing, such as the concern that legislatures will cater to the interests of voters over debt holders.[43]

Amdursky and Gillette's concern is well taken but actually has broader application than could have been recognized when they wrote it. Different fora are more or less favorable to different interest groups. Bankruptcy courts, for example, are a forum that is more favorable to secured creditors and less favorable to creditors with ongoing contracts, such as vendors and labor, because of the ability to reject executory contracts. In particular, in Chapter 9 bankruptcy, which is cast as the model for a state bankruptcy regime, collective bargaining agreements and retiree benefits are not subject to the extra protections that exist in Chapter 11.[44]

Courts' qualities as decision-making bodies cannot be divorced from the legal framework in which they operate; courts' discretion is circumscribed by legislatures, just as legislatures' discretion is circumscribed by constitutions. Thus, the relative appeal of courts for making distributional decisions depends heavily on the distributional rules that courts must follow. If bankruptcy courts could raise taxes, but not cut services, their appeal as a

---

[42] ROBERT S. AMDURSKY & CLAYTON GILLETTE, MUNICIPAL DEBT FINANCE LAW: THEORY AND PRACTICE § 1.3.1 (1992).
[43] Id.
[44] 11 U.S.C. §§ 1113–1114. Cf. NLRB v. Bildisco & Bildisco, 465 U.S. 513 (1984) (permitting, before the enactment of 11 U.S.C. §§ 1113–1114, collective bargaining agreement to be rejected under 11 U.S.C. § 365).

forum would be different than if they could only cut services but not raise taxes or if they could both cut services and raise taxes. Accordingly, the same factors that should make us concerned about legislative outcomes should also concern us about judicial outcomes.

Whether one prefers legislatures or courts making budget-balancing decisions is, of course, a normative matter. But the long-standing normative choice embodied in the structure of American government and law is that distributional decisions beyond a constitutionally mandated baseline – the ultimate political choice – should be made by electorally responsive bodies. This is where state sovereignty fundamentally collides with bankruptcy law. There is a fundamental difference between transferring governance rights to creditors from shareholders and transferring them to creditors from voters. The individual shareholder has opted into a financial relationship that is subject to this transfer of governance rights. The individual voter has not. The former is part of the change of control that can occur during a business bankruptcy. The latter is an abandonment not just of sovereignty but of democracy.

CONCLUSION

State bankruptcy proposals offer a financial restructuring solution to a political problem. Even if bankruptcy were to function as a positive political tool and mitigate political agency problems, however, it would do nothing to fix the underlying conundrum of state finances. Rather than fixing state political dysfunction, state bankruptcy proposals are likely to result in bankruptcy being used to carry out a partisan vendetta behind the cover of judicial robes. Bankruptcy is simply not a device for negotiating the fiscal federalism problems that drive state budget crises.

10

Extending Bankruptcy Law to States

MICHAEL W. MCCONNELL

As a matter of federal statutory law, municipalities may declare bankruptcy, but states may not.[1] The principal advantage of bankruptcy, under current fiscal circumstances, is to allow cities and counties to force renegotiation of contractual obligations such as pay, retirement, pensions, and health care. Often these future obligations would be untouchable as a matter of state constitutional law and, thus, cannot be brought into line with current financial resources except by means of federal law, and especially Chapter 9 of the Federal Bankruptcy Code. As some states come to face gargantuan fiscal shortfalls, scholars and public policy analysts have proposed that federal bankruptcy law be amended to include states within its ambit.

It has long been assumed that it would be unconstitutional to subject states, which are sovereign entities, to the kind of federal judicial control that conventional bankruptcy entails; however, that assumption has come under question. If city and county governments can avail themselves of bankruptcy, why not states? In addition, if states consent to bankruptcy – no one is proposing involuntary bankruptcy for states – why does that not satisfy any federalism concerns? These arguments are substantial and might well carry the day. My purpose here is not to refute them but to point out some difficulties and identify more precisely the constitutional questions that would arise if Congress amended the Bankruptcy Code to include states. In doing so, I will accept as a given, for present purposes, the precedents set by the Supreme Court in connection with municipal bankruptcy.

Prior to 1934, bankruptcy law applied only to private persons and companies. Congress extended bankruptcy law to cities and special districts in

---

[1] 11 U.S.C. § 109(a).

My thanks to Randall Picker and David Skeel for helpful comments.

1934, at the behest of municipal governments overwhelmed with bonded indebtedness, which they were unable to service.[2] In *Ashton v. Cameron County Water Improvement District*, the Supreme Court struck this law down on federalism grounds.[3] According to the five-Justice majority, "If obligations of states or their political subdivisions may be subjected to the interference here attempted, they are no longer free to manage their own affairs; the will of Congress prevails over them... And really the sovereignty of the state, so often declared necessary to the federal system, does not exist."[4] Significantly for our purposes today, the Court posed the rhetorical question: "If federal bankruptcy laws can be extended to respondent, why not to the state?"[5]

Congress passed a new statute in 1937,[6] only cosmetically changed from the prior version.[7] This time, the Supreme Court approved. In *United States v. Bekins*, the Court reasoned that

> [t]he statute is carefully drawn so as not to impinge upon the sovereignty of the State. The State retains control of its fiscal affairs. The bankruptcy power is exercised in relation to a matter normally within its province and only in a case where the action of the taxing agency in carrying out a plan of composition approved by the bankruptcy court is authorized by state law. It is of the essence of sovereignty to be able to make contracts and give consents bearing upon the exertion of governmental power.[8]

In other words, the statute did not interfere with state sovereignty because it was drawn to ensure that the state retained control of its fiscal affairs and because the state consented to the bankruptcy proceeding.

The arguments for and against the constitutionality of state bankruptcy today are similar to the arguments about municipal bankruptcy in the 1930s. Opponents argue that bankruptcy for states would interfere with state sovereignty. Proponents have three main arguments for the constitutionality of state bankruptcy: (1) state bankruptcy is justified by the same constitutional logic that justifies municipal bankruptcy; (2) state bankruptcy would not interfere with the state's governmental powers; and (3)

---

[2] Pub. L. No. 251, 48 Stat. 798 (1934).
[3] 298 U.S. 513 (1936).
[4] Id. at 531.
[5] Id. at 530.
[6] Pub. L. No. 302, 50 Stat. 653 (1937).
[7] 304 U.S. 27 (1938). For a comparative discussion of the two statutes, see Michael W. McConnell & Randall C. Picker, "When Cities Go Broke: A Conceptual Introduction to Municipal Bankruptcy," 60 *U. Chi. L. Rev.* 425, 450–454, (1993).
[8] 304 U.S. at 815.

bankruptcy would be a voluntary exercise of state authority to waive its sovereign immunity.[9] Let us consider each of these arguments.

I. WHAT IS THE SIGNIFICANCE OF THE FACT THAT STATES ARE SOVEREIGN WHEREAS MUNICIPALITIES ARE NOT?

The argument that state bankruptcy can be justified along the same lines as municipal bankruptcy overlooks traditional constitutional differences between municipalities and states. Municipalities have traditionally not been understood as sovereign entities. As Justice Cardozo put the point in his dissent in *Ashton*:

> There is room at least for argument that within the meaning of the Constitution the bankruptcy concept does not embrace the states themselves. In the public law of the United States a state is a sovereign or at least a quasi sovereign. Not so a local governmental unit, though the state may have invested it with governmental power. Such a governmental unit may be brought into court against its will without violating the Eleventh Amendment. It may be subjected to mandamus or to equitable remedies. "Neither public corporations nor political subdivisions are clothed with that immunity from suit which belongs to the state alone by virtue of its sovereignty."[10]

The basis for this difference lies in the old common-law understanding that cities were municipal corporations formed by their residents for particular purposes that were neither wholly public nor wholly private. Cities were not understood to be sovereign governments in any formal sense of the term and so lacked some typical governmental prerogatives. As Justice Cardozo pointed out and remains true, Eleventh Amendment sovereign immunity does not apply to cities.[11] Under civil rights law, for instance, cities can be sued when states cannot.[12] Antitrust law does not treat cities the

---

[9] See David A. Skeel Jr., "Give States a Way to Go Bankrupt: It's the Best Option for Avoiding a Massive Federal Bailout," *Cal. J. Pub. Pol'y*, 2011.

[10] *Ashton*, 298 U.S. at 542 (Cardozo, J., dissenting) (internal citations omitted) quoting *Hopkins v. Clemson Agricultural College*, 221 U.S. 636, 645 (1911).

[11] *Id.* See, for example, *Alden v. Maine*, 527 U.S. 706, 756 (1999) ("[Sovereign immunity] bars suits against States but not lesser entities. The immunity does not extend to suits prosecuted against a municipal corporation or other governmental entity which is not an arm of the State").

[12] 42 U.S.C. § 1983; *Monell v. Department of Social Services*, 436 U.S. 658, 690 (1978) ("Local governing bodies, therefore, can be sued directly under § 1983 for monetary, declaratory, or injunctive relief where, as here, the action that is alleged to be unconsti-

same way it treats states.¹³ At the same time, however, cities are regarded as governments for important purposes. Cities may be the creatures of states,¹⁴ but that means that they enjoy some part of the constitutional status of states. In *National League of Cities v. Usery*, for example, the Court regarded cities as having the same status as states for purposes of the Tenth Amendment and general federalism principles.¹⁵ For purposes of qualified immunity, city officials and state officials stand on the same footing. The state action doctrine applies to cities and states in the same way. Cities are thus amphibious creatures: governmental but not sovereign.

The New Deal Congress evidently shared this conception. The 1937 bankruptcy act applied to cities and special districts, which are municipal corporations, but not to counties, which were classified by the common law as a subdivision of the state and therefore as partaking of sovereignty. It was only in 1946 that Congress amended the statute to include counties,¹⁶ and that extension has never been tested in the Supreme Court.

To the extent that the constitutionality of the 1937 Act rested on the non-sovereign character of municipal corporations, as suggested by Justice Cardozo's *Ashton* dissent, an extension to the states would be unconstitutional. Only if the constitutionality of the 1937 Act rested on other rationales could state bankruptcy be a viable constitutional path.

II. HOW MUCH DOES BANKRUPTCY INTRUDE INTO SOVEREIGN POWERS?

The second theory of the constitutionality of state bankruptcy, which dates back to the briefs and opinion in *Bekins*, argues that an extension of the bankruptcy code would not interfere with the sovereign authorities of the jurisdictions to which it applies. Unlike ordinary bankruptcy

---

tutional implements or executes a policy statement, ordinance, regulation, or decision officially adopted and promulgated by that body's officers").

[13] *Lafayette v. Louisiana Power & Light Co.*, 435 U.S. 389, 416 (1978) ("[W]hen the State itself has not directed or authorized an anticompetitive practice, the State's subdivisions in exercising their delegated power must obey the antitrust laws").

[14] See, 1 William Blackstone, *Commentaries on the Laws of England*, Bk. I, Ch. 1, at 123 (11th ed. 1791) ("Persons also are divided by the law into either natural persons, or artificial. Natural persons are such as the God of nature formed us: artificial are such as created and devised by human laws for the purposes of society and government; which are called corporations or bodies politic"); *Reynolds v. Sims*, 377 U.S. 533, 535 (1964) ("[Cities] have been traditionally regarded as subordinate governmental instrumentalities created by the State to assist in the carrying out of state governmental functions").

[15] 426 U.S. 833 (1976).

[16] 60 Stat. 409 (1946). See McConnell & Picker, at 453 (cited in note 2).

in the private context, municipal bankruptcy is completely voluntary. In addition, under the 1937 Act the Federal Bankruptcy Court was not entitled to create its own plan, force a city to raise taxes, or require a city to reduce specific expenditures. The role of the bankruptcy court was limited to approving or disapproving a plan drawn up by the city and presented to the court. This theory understands the function of the court not as interfering with the city's sovereignty but rather as empowering the city to act on its sovereign interests. As the *Bekins* court said, in submitting to bankruptcy, "[t]he State acts in aid, and not in derogation, of its sovereign powers."[17] In effect, under this theory, extension of federal bankruptcy law is best understood as the Federal government lending to cities and states its power to impair contracts, a power otherwise reserved under the Constitution for the Federal government.[18] As the court said: "The natural and reasonable remedy through composition of the debts of the district was not available under state law by reason of the restriction imposed by the Federal Constitution upon the impairment of contracts by state legislation. The bankruptcy power is competent to give relief to debtors in such a plight."[19] This line of argument was especially prominent in the brief for the Solicitor General in support of the act.

If this theory holds water, it would be a strong argument for the constitutionality of state bankruptcy. Unfortunately for state bankruptcy, it is a quite unrealistic way of thinking about the consequences of bankruptcy. Although the bankruptcy court does not have formal authority to write its own plan, it does have the ability to attach conditions and to refuse to accept a plan unless the state satisfies certain demands.[20] Additionally, particular to the statute there are two points at which state sovereign interests will surely be affected. The first is the requirement that the jurisdiction be insolvent. To determine the solvency of a governmental entity, which owns little attachable property and whose revenues are taxes, the court must evaluate the tax rate, along with the state's obligations and expenses.[21] If the court is not satisfied that the state has exhausted its ability to raise revenue and reduce spending, presumably the court will not find the state

---

[17] *Bekins*, 304 U.S. at 54.
[18] See Michael W. McConnell, "Contract Rights and Property Rights: A Case Study in the Relationship between Individual Liberties and Constitutional Structure," 76 *Cal. L. Rev.* 267 (1988).
[19] *Id.*
[20] Clay Gillette, "Lessons and Implications from Public Default: Local, State, National," Stanford Law School. Stanford, 13 May 2011.
[21] *Id.*

insolvent. This determination of solvency effectively gives the court supervening authority over two of the most important and fundamental sovereign powers of the jurisdiction. The power of taxation is as much at the core of sovereignty as anything could possibly be: The American Revolution was fought over the proposition of no taxation without representation.

Second, in addition to the insolvency standard, there is the best-interest-of-the-creditors standard, which in private bankruptcy means that creditors will be better off under the plan than they would be in case of liquidation. In the case of state bankruptcy, liquidation is not an option. In the legislative history of the 1937 Act, the best-interests standard was defined by reference to two prior decisions, both based on the concept that the city had not exhausted its taxing capacity. Thus, viewed realistically, state bankruptcy would cut deeply into the inherently sovereign powers of the state over taxation and expenditure. It is not genuinely possible for a court to say, as the Supreme Court did in *Bekins*, that "[t]he State retains control of its fiscal affairs."[22] Bankruptcy would transfer that control to the court.

III. IS THE VOLUNTARY NATURE OF STATE BANKRUPTCY ENOUGH TO MAKE IT CONSTITUTIONAL?

The third argument for state bankruptcy's constitutionality relies on the voluntary nature of the process. States are permitted to waive their sovereign immunity under the Eleventh Amendment; why should they not be permitted to waive their sovereign immunity against the intrusion of bankruptcy courts?[23] This argument raises a fundamental question: What is federalism for? If federalism protects states' rights, then it follows that an entity that has rights ought to be able to waive those rights. Indeed, the ability to waive a right in exchange for valuable consideration is often seen as part of its value. Alternatively, if federalism diffuses power and thus provides a check against tyranny and oppressive centralized authority, then the state should not be able to waive this central structural aspect of federal constitutionalism.

The Supreme Court considered an analogous question in *New York v. United States*.[24] This case concerned a radioactive waste disposal law,

---

[22] *Bekins*, 304 U.S. at 51.
[23] David A. Skeel Jr., "The States in Crisis: Political Dimensions," Stanford Law School, Stanford, 13 May 2011.
[24] 505 U.S. 144 (1992).

which imposed certain mandates on state governments that the Court concluded were beyond the powers of Congress. The Court's ruling is striking because the objecting state, New York, and other states had actually lobbied in favor of the legislation. How could the Court possibly rule the law unconstitutional as a violation of federalism when it was what the state wanted? The Supreme Court answered:

> The Constitution does not protect the sovereignty of States for the benefit of the States or state governments as abstract political entities, or even for the benefit of the public officials governing the States. To the contrary, the Constitution divides authority between federal and state governments for the protection of individuals. State sovereignty is not just an end in itself: "Rather, federalism secures to citizens the liberties that derive from the diffusion of sovereign power." ... State officials thus cannot consent to the enlargement of the powers of Congress beyond those enumerated in the Constitution.[25]

If that logic were applied to the extension of bankruptcy to state governments, the extension would be in trouble.

This view of federalism – as a structural protection for citizens rather than a set of "states' rights" for the benefit of state governments – is increasingly dominant today. In *Bond v. United States*, the Court recently stated in ringing tones: "Federalism is more than an exercise in setting the boundary between different institutions of government for their own integrity."[26] It went on to explain that "[t]he limitations that federalism entails are not therefore a matter of rights belonging only to the States. States are not the sole intended beneficiaries of federalism."[27]

On the other hand, the pragmatic perspective of the *Bekins* court could still exert a pull. Like cities, many states made profligate promises in the past that now are binding on future taxpayers under the Contracts Clause, squeezing out vital public expenditures on currently valuable services. It is difficult to see why states as employers should be less able than private employers to reorganize their financial affairs to operate effectively in the future. Taxpayers, and even courts, may be inclined to ask whether the sovereign interests of the public might not be better served by breaking the stranglehold of old contracts, even at the cost of submission to the scrutiny of federal bankruptcy judges.

---

[25] *New York*, 505 U.S. at 181–182 (internal quotations omitted).
[26] 131 S. Ct 2355, 2364 (2011).
[27] *Id.*

CONCLUSION

Under modern economic circumstances, access to the bankruptcy laws is primarily a benefit to the bankrupt entity, rather than a form of external discipline. This is especially true of governmental entities, which by their nature cannot be liquidated and which have few, if any, assets that can be sold for the benefit of creditors. For governmental entities, bankruptcy provides a means of shedding or reducing contractual obligations, such as collective bargaining agreements with public employees, overly generous pension promises, and health and other employment benefit arrangements that no longer can be afforded. In the few instances when cities have sought federal bankruptcy protection, it has been an effective bargaining tool for a restructuring of these obligations. Scholars have raised the question whether the Bankruptcy Code should be extended to encompass state governments.

Whether such an extension is constitutional is not obvious either way. There long has been a distinction between cities, which are a species of corporation, and states, which are sovereign or quasi-sovereign entities. The more important point, however, may be that as long as bankruptcy is voluntary, its availability does not invade the sovereignty of the state but instead gives the state greater flexibility to restructure its contractual commitments. The process must ensure, however, that the democratic process and not the judiciary retains control over the states' fundamental taxing and spending decisions. This might be achieved by departing from Chapter 9's insolvency and best-interests-of-the-creditors standards, which currently invest bankruptcy courts with the practical ability to overrule decisions about taxation and expenditures. If these provisions were replaced by objective triggers, or even by a complete voluntariness standard, extension of bankruptcy to states might well be consistent with the Constitution. That, of course, does not resolve whether it would be prudent public policy to do so.

11

Bankruptcy For the States and By the States

GEORGE TRIANTIS

INTRODUCTION: BANKRUPTCY FOR STATES

The financial crisis of 2008 and the ensuing economic recession imposed considerable stress on the fiscal health of U.S. states. Although state governments took steps to control spending, reduce commitments, and raise revenues, some scholars and politicians[1] worried that these steps were insufficient to address the severe challenge facing states such as Illinois and California. These commentators proposed that the U.S. Congress enact a formal debt restructuring or "bankruptcy" process for states, similar to the municipal bankruptcy process governed by Chapter 9 of the U.S. Bankruptcy Code. The proposed state-bankruptcy process would not interfere with state sovereignty because the state government would have sole authority to initiate bankruptcy. Perhaps more importantly, its proponents argued, a statutory state-bankruptcy framework would facilitate out-of-court adjustments in its shadow.

Some of the justifications for a state-bankruptcy process echo the familiar goals of bankruptcy law in the commercial context. In particular, bankruptcy clarifies priorities to allocate losses in an orderly and reasonably predictable manner. By restoring solvency and financial health,

---

[1] E.g., David Skeel, *Give States a Way to Go Bankrupt*, The Weekly Standard, Nov. 29, 2010, at 22; Grover G. Norquist and Patrick Gleason, *Let States Go Bankrupt*, Politico, Dec. 24, 2010 (http://www.politico.com/stories/1210/46777.html); David Skeel, *A Bankruptcy Law – Not Bailouts – for the States*, Wall St. J., Jan. 18, 2011, at A17; Jeb Bush and Newt Gingrich, *Better off Bankrupt*, Los Angeles Times, Jan. 27, 2011 (http://articles.latimes.com/print/2011/jan/27/opinion/la-oe-gingrich-bankruptcy-20110127). Professor Skeel developed his arguments in David A. Skeel, Jr., *States of Bankruptcy*, U. CHI. L. REV. (forthcoming, 2012) and David A. Skeel, Jr., *State Bankruptcy from the Ground Up* (this volume).

I am grateful for discussions with John Manning and the valuable research and comments provided by Will Dreher (Harvard Law Class of 2013).

it relieves the overhang of debt that would otherwise drive capital (and taxpayers themselves) out of the jurisdiction. In addition, it mitigates the problem of holdouts in restructuring efforts by imposing equitable adjustments – approved by a majority of a class of creditors – on dissenting claimants. The ideal of bankruptcy law is that, by addressing these goals, the formal process creates a surplus shared among the creditors in a manner that leaves no creditor worse off than if there were no bankruptcy process.

The proponents of a bankruptcy chapter for states add two objectives to this list. First, bankruptcy would give distressed states further power to address the "bloated, broken and underfunded pension system[s]", as well as the "lucrative pay and benefit packages" that they have conceded to the unions of public employees.[2] Second, the availability of bankruptcy would relieve the pressure on Congress to bail out states in dire financial condition. The promise of bailouts undermines states' fiscal discipline (the problem of moral hazard) [3] and shifts the cost of financial rescue, in an ad hoc manner, onto taxpayers outside the state itself. State bankruptcy, in contrast, would ensure that losses are shared in a systematic and predictable manner among the various creditors (such as bondholders or employees) of the distressed state.

The proposal met quickly with strong criticism from various groups and subsequently drifted from the attention of Congress and the press. Unions were concerned that bankruptcy would increase the power of state governments to terminate collective bargaining agreements and compromise the claims of employees in bankruptcy. The Center on Budget and Policy Priorities and the Manhattan Institute for Policy Research each issued a report analyzing the financial condition of states, recommending fiscal reform, and criticizing the state-bankruptcy proposal.[4] Congressional hearings on the subject generated little support for the idea, and the House

---

[2] Bush and Gingrich, *supra* note 2.

[3] Skeel, *Give States a Way to Go Bankrupt*, *supra* note 2 ("The appeal of bankruptcy-for-states is that it would give the federal government a compelling reason to resist the bailout urge."); Bush and Gingrich, *supra* note 2 ("Federal bailouts must come to an end. Federal taxpayers in states that balance their budgets should not have to bail out the irresponsible, pandering politicians who cannot balance their budgets. Congress must allow a safe, orderly way under federal bankruptcy law for states to reorganize their finances").

[4] Iris J. Lav and Elizabeth McNichol, *Misunderstandings Regarding State Debt, Pensions, and Retiree Health Costs Create Unnecessary Alarm Misconceptions Also Divert Attention from Needed Structural Reforms*, Center on Budget and Policy Priorities, Jan. 20, 2011, at http://www.cbpp.org/cms/index.cfm?fa=view&id=3372 (short-term budget gaps are not the problem; long-term structural deficits are. Federal bankruptcy is not a solution).

Majority Leader and the Chairman of the House Judiciary Committee each rejected the proposal.[5]

State government officials were overwhelmingly opposed to the idea. This was perhaps surprising: Although states typically react strongly against federal attempts to interfere with their fiscal policy, any federal statutory process for state bankruptcy would necessarily have respected state sovereignty. Most proposed statutory frameworks, for example, would give state governments the sole authority to initiate a bankruptcy proceeding and to propose a restructuring plan and the bankruptcy court no authority over matters of state governance. Nevertheless, the National Governors Association and the Conference of State Legislatures issued a statement strongly opposed to the idea.[6] The states maintained that a federal bankruptcy chapter for states was unnecessary and counterproductive. They argued that the fresh start promise of bankruptcy would itself be a source of moral hazard and would delay fiscal reforms by states. They claimed that the mere prospect of such legislation would raise their financing costs in capital markets. In light of these sentiments, this chapter proposes a solution likely more amenable to state leaders: that states legislate their own restructuring or bankruptcy regime tailored to their political and economic circumstances.

During the current economic recession, state governments have taken a range of significant measures to narrow their current and future budget deficits: They have laid off or furloughed public employees, frozen wages, reduced pension benefits, and increased the share of health insurance premiums paid by workers.[7] The federal fiscal stimuli of the past three years,

---

[5] "State and Municipal Debt: The Coming Crisis?" Congressional hearings before the House Oversight and Government Reform subcommittee of TARP, Financial Services and Private Programs, February 9, 2011, at http://oversight.house.gov/index.php?option=com_content&view=article&id=1101%3A2-9-11-qstate-and-municipal-debt-the-coming-crisisq&catid=34&Itemid=39; "State and Municipal Debt: The Coming Crisis? (Part II)," March 15, 2011, at http://oversight.house.gov/index.php?option=com_content&view=article&id=1198%3A3-15-11-qstate-and-municipal-debt-the-coming-crisis-part-iiq&catid=34&Itemid=39.

[6] See *NGA Statement Regarding Bankruptcy Proposals for States*, Jan. 25, 2011, at http://www.nga.org/cms/home/news-room/news-releases/page_2011/col2-content/main-content-list/nga-statement-regarding-bankrupt.html; *NGA/NCSL Bankruptcy Letter*, Feb. 3, 2011, at http://www.ncsl.org/default.aspx?tabid=22155.

[7] See NGA Center for Best Practices, *State Government Redesign Efforts 2009 and 2010*, October 18, 2010, at http://www.nga.org/files/live/sites/NGA/files/pdf/1010STATEGOVTREDESIGN.PDF; Pew Ctr. On the States, *The Trillion Dollar Gap: Underfunded State Retirement Systems and the Road to Reform* (February 2010) (review of pension deficits in states); Pew Ctr. On the States, The Widening Gap: The Great Recession's Impact on State Pensions and Retiree Health Care Costs (April 2011).

the stabilization of capital markets, and the (albeit sputtering) economic recovery have also mitigated the financial distress of states. The risk of default by even the most distressed of states remains low, and for the time being, the need for a formal restructuring process is small.[8] Nevertheless, the events of the past several years alert us to the possibility that states – even the United States as a country – might become so financially distressed as to prevent economic recovery. A broad financial restructuring of outstanding liabilities may be necessary in the future to address the dual problems of debt overhang and creditor hold-out, to give the states a fresh start. Thus, the proponents of a bankruptcy regime for states may be justified in arguing for a formal restructuring process in such circumstances of "catastrophic failure."[9]

This chapter suggests that bankruptcy legislation, however designed, should be encouraged at the state government, rather than federal, level.[10] Indeed, the federal government should refrain from legislating in this area – or should produce a set of default, rather than mandatory, rules – to give states the space and incentive to do so for themselves. Of course, state legislation might invite the federal government to play a role as a lender, perhaps even with the type of control it enjoyed as debtor-in-possession lender in the GM or Chrysler bankruptcies. As in those corporate cases, however, the state court with jurisdiction over the case would be required to authorize any such control. States should legislate their own bankruptcy regimes, to tailor them to their respective economic and financial circumstances, as well as their respective political preferences. States are subject

---

[8] Nat'l Governors Ass'n & Nat'l Ass'n of State Budget Officers, *The Fiscal Survey of States*, Spring 2011, at http://www.nga.org/files/live/sites/NGA/files/pdf/FSS1106.PDF; Testimony of Robin Prunty, Managing Director, Ratings Services, S&P Financial Services, Committee on Oversight and Government Reform, Subcommittee on TARP, March 15, 2011, at http://docs.noodls.com/viewDoc.asp?filename=50914\EXT\0F921037263B47A93939A9551C0CB8347EA5D31A_DB2DAEE5AB3AC0AA8279E6368BE326AE0DE93558.PDF.

[9] Skeel, *State of Bankruptcy*, supra note 2, at 5 ("The likelihood that most states can muddle through does not justify ignoring the very low probability of a catastrophic failure").

[10] The U.S. Constitution grants to the federal government the jurisdiction to enact bankruptcy laws for corporations and individuals. U.S. Const. art. 1, §8, cl.4. However, there are sound policy reasons why states would be better equipped to legislate in this area. After all, states regulate contractual relations, including debtor-creditor laws outside of bankruptcy. David Skeel, currently the leading academic proponent of federal bankruptcy for states (see *supra* note 2), wrote almost twenty years ago that states should regulate corporate bankruptcy, just as they regulate corporate law. David Skeel, *Rethinking the Line Between Corporate Law and Corporate Bankruptcy*, 72 TEX. L. REV. 471 (1994).

to financial discipline in doing so because they would pay a premium in their contracts to reflect the implicit insurance provided by their creditors in their respective bankruptcy regime. In the current as well as past financial crises, states have unilaterally amended many contracts, particularly with employees. Such an ad hoc adjustment of obligations would likely continue even if a federally legislated bankruptcy process were available because states would be reluctant to file under a federal regime. They would be more likely to invoke their own bankruptcy legislation, and this would promote a more structured and predictable restructuring of obligations than the current ad hoc practice.

A state-bankruptcy regime would be incorporated implicitly in all future contracts and, in this respect, would not meet significant legal hurdles. To the extent that it modifies contracts existing at the time the law is enacted, bankruptcy law's retroactive effect would raise potential political, economic, and legal issues. This chapter argues that retroactivity does not impose significant economic costs in this case and that obstacles in the federal and in state constitutions can be overcome by meeting the balancing tests employed in the judicial interpretation of each pertinent constitutional provision. In brief, a state-legislated restructuring process is likely to pass constitutional muster if it satisfies three requirements: (a) the state can invoke the process only under unforeseen and catastrophic conditions; (b) it is subject to judicial oversight; and (c) the court conditions its approval of the adjustment of creditor claims on the finding that the non-consenting creditors are economically no worse off than if they sought to recover their claims in full from a defaulting state debtor. The second and third requirements are prominent under the existing federal bankruptcy regime for private debtors. The first condition, in contrast, is the product of U.S. Supreme Court jurisprudence indicating that conditions that are either moderate or foreseeable will not justify the impairment of state obligations.

I. STATE OR FEDERAL LEGISLATION (OR BOTH)?

The state-bankruptcy process should be enacted by state legislation for the following reasons: (1) Each state's circumstances and political preferences vary, and state-by-state legislation would permit each state to tailor its bankruptcy process; (2) the state would internalize the cost of issuing debt under the bankruptcy regime of its choice, and this would reduce the rent-seeking distortions in the legislative process; (3) a state is more likely to initiate its own bankruptcy mechanism than one legislated by the federal government, and this would reduce the unpredictability of ad hoc unilateral adjustments currently implemented by the states; and (4) a state-by-state approach would minimize the pressures for a federal bailout, particularly if combined with federal legislation that expressly sets a default bankruptcy regime from which the states can opt out.

To most advocates of a state-bankruptcy process for sovereign entities, the primary goal is to provide a fresh start for distressed states. The prospect of a fresh start statute effectively adds an insurance provision to each contract of the debtor, which might be efficient if the creditors can better diversify the risk of distress in their portfolios. There are countervailing incentive costs of insurance, particularly moral hazard. However, the moral hazard of debt financing under a fresh start regime may be less severe than the moral hazard, mentioned earlier, that is raised by the prospect of a federal bailout. Moreover, forcing the states to pay for insurance in their debt contracts may be more reliable politically than hoping that state governments refrain from cutting taxes or increasing spending when good economic conditions produce surpluses.

State legislatures could tailor their legislation to their economic and political circumstances, whereas federal legislation would provide one-size for all.[11] Bankruptcy allocates risk and losses among groups of creditors, which is partly a function of political considerations, such as the perceived importance of protecting the contract rights of public employees and pensioners. These considerations may vary by state, and state-specific legislation may be more successful in accounting for these variations. Further, state-specific bankruptcy legislation that is a bargain between the major political influences within a state is likely to be deemed more legitimate by that state than is a federal bankruptcy regime imposed upon the states. The state regime is accordingly more likely to be invoked than a federal scheme in times of distress. If a formal process for restructuring is valuable because it increases predictability and mitigates hold-out obstacles, state-legislated bankruptcy is more likely to yield these results in practice.

The political process of legislating bankruptcy is, however, also fraught with rent seeking, as each constituency strives to shift losses onto the others. Their efforts are largely wasteful and can distort the final product

---

[11] This alternative has an analog in some scholarly literature that advocates a contractual approach to bankruptcy and debt restructuring. Under this normative approach, a corporation would design, or choose from a menu, its own bankruptcy regime and identify it in its charter. See, e.g., Robert A. Haugen and Lemma W. Senbet, *Bankruptcy and Agency Costs: Their Significance to the Theory of Optimal Capital Structure*, 23 J. Fin. & Qu. Analysis 27, 29–31 (1988); Robert K. Rasmussen, *Debtor's Choice: A Menu Approach to Corporate Bankruptcy*, 71 Tex. L. Rev. 51 (1992).

in the legislation. Federal legislators would be susceptible to these influences because they can externalize costs to the states, and bankruptcy law lacks the salience to bring broad attention or coverage by the news media. After all, their decisions would affect the cost of the states' debt and not the federal debt. State legislators, in contrast, would internalize the cost of bankruptcy legislation borne by some constituencies because the market for state debt, as well as for workers, would "price" each state's bankruptcy choice. This would improve the incentives of state legislators who would seek to minimize the adverse effects of bankruptcy on the cost of capital. To the degree that the legislation granted the state a fresh start, the market would price the implicit insurance written by the bondholders. In the language of scholarship describing the merits of state-level corporate law, this may promote a "race to the top," as each state tries to promote its political objectives while minimizing its cost of capital.

State-bankruptcy legislation would also reduce the pressure for a federal bailout. Each state would have access to its own restructuring process, enjoying greater sovereignty in its fiscal affairs and facing market discipline. The markets would compel the states to pay the insurance premiums implicit in their bankruptcy statute. Each state would be encouraged, thereby, to pre-commit to a narrower set of circumstances under which it can compel the adjustment of its debt. For example, bankruptcy might be limited to cases in which a court rules that the state suffered great distress as a result of unforeseen and dramatic exogenous shocks (for example, a natural disaster).

As noted earlier, proponents of a federal bankruptcy regime for states argued that federal legislation would mitigate the political pressures on Congress to bail out insolvent states. However, a distressed state might hesitate to authorize a filing under a federal bankruptcy process in the hope of receiving federal assistance. This is unlikely to attract much sympathy at the federal level, and the federal government might condition assistance on filing. Under a state-legislated bankruptcy regime, the federal government might similarly require a filing under the state-run process. However, an insolvent state might decline to enact a bankruptcy regime, perhaps strategically, to avoid paying the premium to bondholders and to preserve the prospect of a bailout. David Skeel points to this as a weakness of the state-by-state approach,[12] but Congress could anticipate this problem by providing incentives to promote state legislation before the crisis hits. Under one approach, the federal government might enact a bankruptcy regime

---

[12] Skeel, *States of Bankruptcy*, supra note 2, at 29.

for states that is expressly a default: That is, states would be authorized to legislate their own statute and could otherwise resort to the federal process. This would ensure that the state's authority to pass its own restructuring legislation would not be preempted, even as a result of the federal government's dormant jurisdiction over bankruptcy.

II. THE POLICY IMPLICATIONS OF RETROACTIVITY

The application of new bankruptcy legislation to prospective liabilities of the state is straightforward: The bankruptcy provisions are simply incorporated in the terms of all new contracts. The legislation is transparent so that future consensual creditors can adjust the price they charge the state. This is not the case with liabilities that are incurred before the enactment of bankruptcy: The laws would have a retroactive effect. Retroactive laws redistribute wealth and raise concerns about fairness of winners and losers. The effect may be small because, to some degree, creditors routinely adjust their prices to anticipate unknown risks of government action, as well as market shocks. Some of those risks impose costs, and others create windfalls.[13] Bankruptcy, in particular, is based on a theoretical premise that it promotes collective action to resolve debt overhang and thereby creates value that is shared among the various creditors. In other words, there may be only winners and no losers.

The U.S. Bankruptcy Code is designed to ensure that no creditor is worse off than if it had exercised its individual enforcement rights in a world without bankruptcy. Bondholders of states have very limited legal remedies if the state chooses not to pay these obligations. Bondholders are unlikely to be able to sue in federal court[14] and will have difficulty enforcing a state law claim. They cannot seize assets or garnish revenues of the state debtor, and a mandamus order compelling a state official to collect revenues is of limited effect.[15] Sovereign states typically pay because of concerns about their standing in capital markets rather than legal enforcement. The limited recourse to legal enforcement, however, helps sovereign states wrest consent to reduced debt claims even without bankruptcy.

Labor unions have expressed concern that a bankruptcy process would enable the states to revise their collective bargaining agreements and to

---

[13] Louis Kaplow, *An Economic Analysis of Legal Transitions*, 99 Harv. L. Rev. 509 (1986).
[14] See *Hans v. State of Louisiana*, 134 U.S. 1 (1890).
[15] Robert S. Amdursky and Clayton P. Gillette, *Municipal Debt Finance Law: Theory and Practice* 1.2 (1992).

alter the contract rights of their workers and pensioners. However, state governments already have significant capacity to unilaterally modify these contracts even outside of bankruptcy, provided that they do not violate the Contracts Clause of the U.S. Constitution. As described later in the chapter, the courts apply a balancing test under which states can demonstrate that the modification is reasonable and necessary to achieve an important public purpose. States have been far more inclined to unilaterally reduce worker entitlements than those of bondholders or other creditors. Therefore, the burden on public employees might be less under a bankruptcy regime that ensures equal treatment of similarly situated creditors. As suggested earlier, a state is more likely to invoke its own bankruptcy regime than one legislated at the federal level. It follows then that public workers may be better off under a state-legislated than a federal bankruptcy regime.

In theory, however, no one need be worse off in bankruptcy than without it. Professor Randall Kroszner's study of the market reaction to the government's nullification of the gold clause in contracts is interesting in this respect. In 1933, the United States devalued the dollar to address the economic depression. Anticipating this possibility, many long-term public and private financial contracts had included a gold clause, which effectively indexed the obligations to the dollar value of gold. Congress acted to nullify such clauses in both public and private contracts, which reduced the nominal value of obligations in these contracts by 69 percent. The U.S. Supreme Court upheld the legislation in a 5–4 split decision.

Kroszner found that the prices of equity and debt of leveraged corporations rose in response to the decision. "The equity and debt of low rated and heavily-indebted firms experienced the greatest increase in value, thus firms closest to bankruptcy benefited the most from the decision. However, government bonds with the gold clause, where there was little question of the ability to repay ... fell in value."[16] Kroszner theorized that the creditors themselves were better off because of the quick coordinated debt forgiveness plan that lifted debt overhang among the most troubled firms, without the uncertainty, delay, or cost of complex debt renegotiations. He highlighted the importance of a one-time transparent government action, which was legitimized by a court, particularly in a jurisdiction of otherwise strong property rights enforcement.

---

[16] Capital Ideas, *Is it Better to Forgive than Receive* (2006), at http://www.chicagobooth.edu/capideas/feb06/4.aspx, summarizing Randall S. Kroszner, *Is it Better to Forgive than Receive? Repudiation of the Gold Indexation Clause in Long-Term Debt During the Great Depression* (U. Chic. Business Sch. working paper 1998).

III. OVERCOMING CONSTITUTIONAL OBSTACLES TO RETROACTIVE BANKRUPTCY

Federal and state constitutions constrain some (but not all) types of retroactive legislation. The web of general and specific constitutional provisions at both levels and the related judicial doctrine in this area are complex.[17] Courts are inclined to use a balancing test in applying these provisions, weighing the adverse burden of legislation on existing entitlements against the necessity and reasonableness of the legislation in serving a public interest. By way of example, the following discussion focuses on the constitutional obstacles to a state's restructuring of its general obligation bonds, namely: (A) the requirement in state constitutions (as well as state statutes) that the state pledge its faith and credit to the repayment of the state's debts, which is typically reaffirmed in the legislation authorizing the issuance of debt (as well as the contract itself), and (B) the Contracts Clause of the U.S. Constitution. The legality of unilateral state adjustments to worker entitlements – including job security, wages, pension rights, and health benefits – under these provisions is similar.[18]

The States' Faith and Credit Pledge

Most states – by constitution as well as by statute – pledge their faith and credit to the repayment of principal and interest on general obligation bonds. Revenue bonds, in contrast, are payable from funds or revenue streams pledged specifically in the bond contract. Some state constitutions explicitly require the state to pledge its faith and credit to the payment of other contract debts as well. This pledge impedes the adjustment of a debt claim against the state without the creditor's consent. However, constitutional law also prevents states from surrendering future discretion in the exercise of their police power. In enforcing the pledge, therefore, courts

---

[17] Under the Federal Constitution, the takings clause of the 5th Amendment and the Contracts Clause in Article 1, Section 10. For the broader range of provisions at the state level, see Morrison & Foerster, LLP & Greeneham Doll & McDonald PLLC, *Index by States: Extent of Protection of Pension Interests*, Sept. 15, 2007, at http://finance.ky.gov/NR/rdonlyres/275A2978-5DDE-4138-A7F5-AF02D17D7F97/0/statebystatememo10.pdf; Darryl B. Simko, *Of Public Pensions, State Constitutional Protection, and Fiscal Constraint*, 69 Temp. L. Rev. 1059 (1996).

[18] For a recent analysis of Contracts Clause jurisprudence concerning unilateral alteration of collective bargaining agreements, see Stephen F. Befort, *Unilateral Alteration of Public Sector Collective Bargaining Agreements and the Contracts Clause*, 59 Buff. J. Int'l. L. 1, 9–14 (2011).

balance the faith and credit pledge against the constitutional protection of the state's police power.

Perhaps the best-known appellate opinion applying the faith and credit clause arose during New York City's financial distress in the mid-1970s.[19] The City issued and offered new long-term revenue bonds in exchange for its outstanding short-term notes; The bonds and notes had the same principal amount. To encourage the holders of the notes to consent to the exchange, the City imposed a three-year moratorium on enforcement actions against the holders who declined to exchange, even if payment became due. Flushing National Bank held short-term notes and challenged the constitutionality of the moratorium. Under the state constitution of New York, the municipality was required to pledge its faith and credit for the payment of the principal and interest. In its defense, the City argued that the moratorium was a constitutional exercise of its police power under emergency conditions.

The moratorium was upheld in the Special Term and Appellate Division of the New York courts, but the Court of Appeals of New York reversed this holding. Writing for a five-judge majority,[20] Judge Breitel interpreted the constitutional requirement as obliging the City to pay and *in good faith* use its revenue powers to produce funds to make the payments when due. Both the majority and dissent agreed that the good faith standard reflected the constitutional balance between the faith and credit pledge, on the one hand, and the power reserved to the sovereign state to secure the health, safety, and welfare of its people, on the other. They differed, however, in the standard to be applied and their respective application to the facts of the case.[21] The dissent of Judge Cooke was more deferential to the political

---

[19] *Flushing National Bank v. Municipal Assistance Corporation for the City of New York*, 40 N.Y.2d 731 (1976).

[20] Cooke, J., dissented and affirmed the lower court. Judge Cooke interpreted the faith and credit clause as requiring "no more than that the city make a good faith effort to use its resources, credit and powers to pay its indebtedness. This effort must be measured in the light of the city's over-all financial condition and its over-all obligations to its citizens and others... Every step [in the record presented by the City] exhibits the city's good faith." *Id.*, at 747.

[21] The dissent suggested that the balancing test is the same for the faith and credit requirement of the state constitution, as for the contracts clause of the federal constitution. So, it relied on the then-leading Supreme Court opinion in *Home Bldg. & Loan Ass'n v. Blaisdell*, 290 U.S. 398 (1934). "The manner in which the Supreme Court has analyzed the Federal contract clause in similar situations should now serve as a stare decisis precedent to be followed in our analysis in respect to our own State constitutional provisions when those provisions might be interpreted as limiting police power." *Flushing, supra* note 17, at 755.

decision maker and he accepted the City's argument that its condition went beyond "difficult economic circumstances" and had reached "grave public emergency" and "imminent danger... to the health, safety and welfare of [the City's] inhabitants."

Judge Breitel held that the moratorium was unconstitutional because it thrust the burden of resolving the heavy debt of the City on the short-term note holders, who were being coerced to exchange under a "fugitive recourse to the police power of the State."[22] He thereby left open the possibility that a more equitable allocation of the burden might satisfy the requirement of good faith and comply with the constitutional pledge of faith and credit.

Judge Breitel also noted that this faith and credit pledge requirement is designed to protect debt-holder rights in difficult economic circumstances. He found that the difficulties of New York City were "envisioned" at the time the notes were issued.[23] Therefore, the state's faith and credit pledge prevented it from justifying the moratorium on the grounds of difficulties that were (or ought to have been) anticipated at the time of the creation of the indebtedness. This approach is reminiscent of the contract law doctrine of commercial impracticability, which hinges on factual findings as to the severity of the intervening occurrence and its unforeseeability.[24]

After finding the moratorium to be unconstitutional, however, the majority declined to award any remedy to the note holders. It left to the legislature the task of rectifying the violation. Judge Breitel wrote:

> In order to minimize market and governmental disruptions which might ensue it would be injudicious at this time to allow the extraordinary remedies in the nature of injunction and preemptory mandamus sought by plaintiff. Plaintiff and other noteholders of the city are entitled to some judicial relief free of throttling by the moratorium statute, but they are not entitled immediately to extraordinary or any particular judicial measures unnecessarily disruptive of the city's delicate financial and economic balance.[25]

---

[22] "The city has an enormous debt and one that in its entirety, if honored as portions become due, undoubtedly exceeds the city's present capacity to maintain an effective cash flow. But it is not true that any particular indebtedness of the city, let alone the outstanding temporary notes, is responsible for any allocable insufficiency. In short, what has happened is those responsible have made an expedient selection of the temporary noteholders to bear an extraordinary burden." *Id.*, at 736.

[23] *Id.*, at 736.

[24] E.g., Restatement Contracts (2d); Uniform Commercial Code 315. It should be noted that excuse for impracticability does not apply to debt contracts.

[25] *Flushing*, supra note 17, at 741.

Indeed, as noted earlier, the enforcement rights of creditors against sovereign states are of questionable value. As a result, the practical value of debt claims against the state may be much less than their face amount. Therefore, bankruptcy restructuring that adjusts the face value does not necessarily compromise the expected value. The effect would be a question of fact for a court to determine.

The Contracts Clause

The Contracts Clause of the U.S. Constitution prohibits states from impairing their contractual obligations.[26] Similar clauses are present in a subset of state constitutions as well. In this limited respect, the federal government has an advantage in enacting a restructuring regime under its bankruptcy power. Nevertheless, there is a good deal of case law interpreting the Contracts Clause. Although there is some variation among the treatment of the state constitution clauses among the states and of the federal clause by the U.S. Supreme Court,[27] two of the leading Supreme Court cases in the modern era suggest how states might enact bankruptcy legislation for their own debt without running afoul of the clause. The prevailing test asks whether the challenged legislation imposes a substantial impairment on a contractual obligation, and if so, whether the legislation is reasonable and necessary to serve an important public purpose.[28] The judicial deference to legislation is lower when the affected contract is an obligation of the state.[29] As in the application of the faith and credit provisions of state constitutions, the Contracts Clause doctrine applies a standard that looks to the parties' understanding at the time of contracting, the intervening circumstances that prompted the challenged modification, and the necessity of the modification in light of these circumstances.

Home Bldg. & Loan Ass'n v. Blaisdell, 290 U.S. 398 (1934),[30] is a leading case establishing that the standard for Contracts Clause violations balances the constitutional protection of contracts and the sovereign power of the states to safeguard the welfare of their citizens. The Court upheld modifications to home loan agreements to provide relief from foreclosure because they addressed the financial crisis of the Great Depression.

---

[26] U.S. CONST.art I, § 10, cl.1.
[27] See Whitney Cloud, *Comment, State Pension Deficits, the Recession, and a Modern View of the Contracts Clause*, 120 Yale L.J. 2199, 2203–2206 (2011).
[28] *U.S. Trust Company of New York v. State of New Jersey*, 431 U.S. 975 (1977).
[29] *Id.*
[30] *Home Bldg. & Loan Ass'n v. Blaisdell*, 290 U.S. 398 (1934).

The majority opinion in the modern case of *U.S. Trust Company of New York v. State of New Jersey*, 431 U.S. 975 (1977) was less deferential to the judgment of the state government, largely because the modified contracts were obligations of the state itself.[31]

In *U.S. Trust*, an investor in Port Authority bonds challenged legislation in New York and New Jersey that repealed a covenant in the bonds that had been created by earlier statutes in each of the two states. The covenants had restricted the ability of the Port Authority to subsidize rail passenger transportation from revenues and reserves of the Authority (from which the bonds obligations were being paid). The Supreme Court reiterated the settled law that the Contracts Clause does not prohibit the states from repealing or amending the terms of its own contracts if it is exercising an essential attribute of its sovereignty. Justices Brennan, White, and Marshall, in dissent, found that the purpose in this case – promoting rail transit – was a lawful exercise of the state's police powers and would have been more inclined to defer to legislative policy decisions.

The majority held that the laws impairing the contract must be "reasonable and necessary to serve an important public purpose," and that court must conduct its own inquiry beyond the state legislature's pronounced purposes. The majority further held that the repeal of the covenant was neither necessary nor reasonable because a less severe modification would have been effective. The court found that the conditions were not sufficiently dire or extreme to justify the repeal of the covenants in question. Moreover, in holding that the repeal was also not reasonable, the court noted that the need to support mass transportation was well known at the time of the statutory covenant. It was neither unforeseen nor unintended. Indeed, Chief Justice Burger also observed in a concurring opinion that the covenant was intended to protect the reserves against the possibility that they might be used for such purposes. This focus on the foreseeability of the event creating the need for modification is similar to that used in the good faith test under the constitutional pledge of faith and credit of states, as well as the doctrine of impracticability in commercial law.

U.S. Trust cited approvingly the earlier case *Faitoute Iron & Steel v. City of Asbury Park*, 316 U.S. 1129 (1942), which is worth noting because the state action in *Faitoute* was a restructuring of bond debt and directly pertinent to the constitutionality of a state-legislated bankruptcy regime. New Jersey passed a statute in the early 1930s to authorize state control

---

[31] *U.S. Trust, supra* note 25, at 26 ("a complete deference to a legislative assessment of reasonableness and necessity is not appropriate because the State's self-interest is at stake").

over insolvent municipalities. The statute allowed a plan for adjustment of the non-principal claims of creditors against an insolvent municipality to be made binding on all creditors. If 85 percent of the creditors, the municipality, and the relevant state commission approved of the plan, and a court reviewed the plan to ensure, inter alia, that it was in the best interest of all creditors, then it would be binding. Bondholders challenged the statute under the Contracts Clause.

The Supreme Court recognized that states had the power to restructure their debt to address unforeseen financial distress, and it upheld the New Jersey statute.[32] The Court identified several other features that were significant in their finding of constitutionality. First, the statute required that the plan be scrutinized and authorized by the state court before it could be imposed on a nonconsensual creditor. Second, the Court found that the restructuring plan did not leave the bondholders worse off. This criterion is reminiscent of the best-interests test under the current Bankruptcy Code. In finding that the bondholders were not harmed by the adjustment, the Court stated that

> the practical value of an unsecured claim against the city is inseparable from its reliance upon the effectiveness of the city's taxing power. The only remedy for the enforcement of such a claim is mandamus to compel the levying of authorized taxes. The experience of the two modern periods of municipal defaults, after the depressions of '73 and '93, shows that the right to enforce claims against the city through mandamus is the empty right to litigate.[33]

It is interesting to compare this statement with the New York state appellate court's opinion in *Flushing National Bank* discussed earlier, which gave judgment to the challenging bondholders but no remedy.

Although the Supreme Court focused on the constitutionality of contract modifications in this case and others, it also invoked from time to time a contractual approach that considers the implied terms of the bargain. This was implicit in the courts' attention to foreseeability in the two other cases discussed here (*U.S. Trust* and *Flushing National Bank*). The Court also referred to it in *Faitoute*. One of the reasons given by the court to hold that the practical value of the debt holder's remedy was limited is that the states could withdraw the authority of a municipality to levy taxes even to pay debts, particularly in the face of unforeseen conditions. "The necessity compelled by unexpected financial conditions to modify an

---

[32] The holding in *Faitoute* was reversed by Congress' amendment to Chapter 9.
[33] *Faitoute, supra* note 28, at 1133.

original arrangement for discharging a city's debt is implied in every such obligation for the very reason that thereby the obligation is discharged, not impaired."[34]

In sum, the constitutionality of a state-legislated bankruptcy process is a transitional issue. As obligations are satisfied, replaced, renewed, or refinanced, the bankruptcy regime will be incorporated into the state's contracts that follow. In the short term, however, existing creditors might challenge the retroactive effect of the legislation when it is enacted, if the enactment leads to a decrease in the value of their rights or claims against the state (such as a drop in the market price of the state's bonds). The foregoing analysis suggests that a state's bankruptcy regime can survive such challenges under either state or federal constitution if the state can invoke the process only in severe and unforeseen distress, the statute provides for the oversight by the state courts, and the regime promotes the usual bankruptcy objective of creating a surplus while ensuring that no creditor is worse off than if it pursued its individual remedies in a world without bankruptcy. These conditions are not difficult to satisfy, and indeed, they are also congenial to the design of an effective regime. The political and economic benefits of state-enacted bankruptcy over a federal regime that are raised earlier in this chapter might provide further justification for upholding the state-bankruptcy regime.

CONCLUSION

Inspired by the recent debate over a proposed federal bankruptcy statute for states, this chapter argues in favor of allowing states to legislate their own bankruptcy regimes. Economic and political considerations militate strongly in favor of enactment at the state level. Either federal or state efforts to legislate a state-bankruptcy regime would face a distinct set of constitutional obstacles. Under the preliminary analysis presented in this chapter, a state-enacted statute could be designed to survive constitutional challenge. To the extent that the debate over the merits of a bankruptcy process for states continues, the alternative of legislation by states should be seriously considered.

---

[34] *Id.* at 1134.

12

Labor and the States' Fiscal Problems

CATHERINE FISK AND BRIAN OLNEY

INTRODUCTION

The highly publicized efforts of Republican governors and Republican-controlled legislatures in Wisconsin and several other states to eliminate collective bargaining rights for public sector workers have sparked a flurry of interest in the question of whether unionization of public employees contributes to the budget deficits in many states. Although the political discussion has suggested that government employees' pay and benefits are the cause of the budget problem and that elimination of collective bargaining will help solve it,[1] the data show otherwise. As to pay, holding education and other human capital factors constant, government employees are paid on average slightly less than their private sector counterparts. Nor are pension costs the cause of the states' fiscal problems: On average, pension contributions by states account for only about 1.9 percent of their annual budgets.[2] The unfunded pension liabilities are a result of the massive economic downturn in 2008–2009, will shrink as the stock market recovers,

---

[1] For a survey of the recent political discourse, see Joseph E. Slater, *The Assault on Public Sector Collective Bargaining: Real Harms and Imaginary Benefits*, The American Constitution Society, at 4–5 (June 2011), *available at* http://www.acslaw.org/sites/default/files/Slater_Collective_Bargaining.pdf.

[2] Calculated by dividing "Government contributions: From state government" in U.S. Census Bureau, *Table 2a. Revenues of State and Local Public Employee Retirement Systems by State and Level of Government: Fiscal Year 2008* (March 23, 2010), *available at* http://www.census.gov/govs/retire/2008reto2a.html., by "Expenditure: State government amount" in *State and Local Government Finances by Level of Government and by State: 2007–08* (July 7, 2010), U.S. Census Bureau, *available at* http://www.census.gov/govs/estimate/. This figure includes only state government (i.e. taxpayer) contributions, and does not include contributions by employees or by local governments.

and in most states can be funded over many years through reasonable measures.³

After surveying the law of public employee collective bargaining, we examine the data on state budgets and state labor costs, showing that across all fifty states and the District of Columbia there is no correlation between the size of a state's budget problems and whether or the extent to which it provides its government employees the right to bargain collectively.⁴ Some states with no public employee bargaining rights have severe budget problems; other states with expansive bargaining rights do not have substantial budget problems. We then examine in greater detail the budget situations and the public employee bargaining rights of three states – California, Nevada, and Texas – each of which has a severe budget shortfall, but each of which has dramatically different law regarding public employee bargaining. Through this in-depth examination, we explain the sources of each state's budget crisis and show that the crisis has nothing to do with the labor law rights of its government employees.

Having demonstrated that public employee collective bargaining is not the cause of state fiscal problems, we suggest ways in which collective bargaining could nevertheless facilitate the search for solutions. After first dispelling the notion that states could solve their budget crises by slashing public sector compensation through repudiating existing labor agreements or seeking to discharge them in bankruptcy, we offer examples of ways in which public employees, through their unions, have partnered with governments to reduce costs and suggest other ways in which they could do so.

In the end, however, we argue that the contemporary debate over the labor rights of government employees is really a debate about fundamental values. It is important to move beyond the politicized debate about public sector bargaining, which tends to take individual cases of public sector employees earning six-figure salaries or pensions or having the right to retire

---

³ Most public pension funds use "asset smoothing" to phase in over several years the effect of large changes in the value of a fund's assets. For this reason, unfunded liabilities will continue to increase in coming years as plans continue to recognize the impact of the market decline during the recession but will likely show improvements after 2013 as they begin to recognize the substantial market rebound that occurred between 2009 and 2010. Elizabeth McNichol and Iris J. Lav, *A Common-Sense Strategy For Fixing State Pension Problems in Tough Economic Times*, Center on Budget and Policy Priorities, at 5–6 (May 12, 2011), *available at* http://www.cbpp.org/cms/index.cfm?fa=view&id=3492.

⁴ The data and law discussed in this chapter are current as of July 21, 2011. As discussed in this chapter, state and local laws and budget projections are subject to change and thus particular laws or budget situations discussed here may have changed by the time this chapter is published.

in their fifties as examples of a broken system needing fixing, and focus instead on what level of pay and benefits for government employees is just.[5] In Wisconsin, for example, the new law eliminating or curtailing collective bargaining did so for teachers but not for police officers and firefighters.[6] The line drawn by that new law is not because teacher pay and pensions caused the state's budget issues, and public safety officers' compensation did not. In Wisconsin, as in many other states, public safety employees (police, prison guards, and firefighters) have more generous pension benefits and lower retirement ages than do teachers and office workers,[7] and in any event, the Wisconsin public pension plan was in sound financial shape and was not the source of the state's budget issues.[8] One suspects the line drawn may be political: Teachers and public safety officers tend to support different political parties. We can have a debate about what public school teachers, park rangers, police, or firefighters should get paid and at what age and with what pension they should be permitted or required to retire if they can no

---

[5] Charles Duhigg, *Public Unions Take on Boss to Win Big Pensions*, N.Y. Times, June 22, 2011, at A1.

[6] 2011 Wisconsin Act 10 (Mar. 25, 2011). *See State of Wisconsin ex rel. Ozanne v. Fitzgerald*, 798 N.W.2d 436 (Wis. 2011) (process for enacting statute repealing collective bargaining rights did not violate state constitution). For a summary of new and proposed laws in Wisconsin and several other states, see Slater, *The Assault on Public Sector Collective Bargaining*, at 10–14.

[7] In Wisconsin, "protective" workers (police, firefighters, etc.) receive a higher multiplier than other public workers (2.0%, or 2.5% for positions not covered by Social Security, vs. 1.6%). This figure is multiplied by the average of an employee's three highest years of earnings and multiplied again by the employee's years of service to determine the pension payment. Protective workers also receive an earlier retirement age (fifty years vs. fifty-five years). State of Wisconsin Department of Employee Trust Funds, *2009 Comprehensive Annual Financial Report*, at 113 (November 11, 2010), *available at* http://etf.wi.gov/about/2009_cafr.pdf. Public safety officers also receive more generous retirement benefits in other states. In California, for example, as the nonpartisan legislative analyst explained in analyzing proposed changes to the state pension system, recently hired state office workers are eligible to receive a pension at age sixty equal to 2% of their highest average monthly pay during any thirty-six consecutive months of employment, times their years of service. State teachers can retire at age sixty and are eligible for a similar 2% times the highest average annual pay over thirty-six consecutive months, times their years of service. However, state prison guards with five or more years of service are eligible to retire at age fifty with a benefit equal to 3% of their highest annual salary times their years of service. California Legislative Analyst's Office, *Report on Proposed Constitutional Initiative A.G. File No. 11–0007, Amdt. #1NS*, (Apr. 29, 2011).

[8] Pew Center on the States, *The Trillion Dollar Gap: Underfunded State Retirement Systems and the Roads to Reform* (2010); Center on Wisconsin Strategy, *The Wisconsin Retirement System Is One of the Healthiest in the Country* (March 2011) (both studies reporting that the Wisconsin pension plan is 100% funded and that state and local contributions to the fund are only 1.35% of state and local budgets, less than the 3% average among other states).

longer safely perform their job. Reducing or eliminating collective bargaining rights for these workers, however, will not solve the budget problems of their states, and it will not contribute to a sensible policy discussion.

I. LABOR COSTS AND PUBLIC SECTOR COLLECTIVE BARGAINING

Public Sector Labor and Employment Law

Unionization of state and local government employees in the early twentieth century was motivated by the same good government concerns that spurred the development of civil service protections.[9] Government reformers believed that government employees should be hired and evaluated on merit rather than on the basis of patronage or bribery, and that protections against arbitrary discipline or discharge would attract a higher caliber of person into public service.[10] The demand for collective bargaining was also motivated by the same concerns about pay and working conditions that drove unionization of all workers. In particular, as tax revenues plummeted in the Depression of the early 1930s, government employees were laid off or furloughed, paid in scrip or government warrants, or worked without pay for months at a time. In Chicago, for example, the Board of Education began paying in scrip in January 1931. After a court invalidated the scrip system, teachers and other school employees were paid nothing at all. By the end of 1932, according to the leading history of government employee unionization, Chicago owed its employees $40 million in back wages.[11] These phenomena repeated themselves in later economic downturns, as governments facing fiscal crises in the 1970s and 2009 also furloughed employees or paid them in IOUs.[12]

---

[9] Joseph E. Slater, *Public Workers: Government Employee Unions, the Law and the State, 1900–1962*, at 17, 127 (Ithaca, NY: ILR Press, 2004).

[10] The first civil service protection, the Pendleton Act of 1883, was intended to protect the federal government from the corruption and incompetence that were thought to flow from the spoils system. Slater, *Public Workers: Government Employee Unions, the Law and the State, 1900–1962*, at 91; Martin Malin, Ann Hodges, and Joseph Slater, *Public Sector Employment: Cases and Materials*, at 134–135 (2d ed. 2011). Teacher tenure laws, which were adopted in many states at the same time as civil service protections, were likewise intended to attract professionally prepared teachers and also to attract a larger number of men into an occupation that advocates hoped to professionalize. Malin, Hodges, and Slater, at 163.

[11] Slater, *Public Workers: Government Employee Unions, the Law and the State, 1900–1962*, at 102.

[12] Stephen F. Befort, *Unilateral Alteration of Public Sector Collective Bargaining Agreements and the Contracts Clause*, 59 Buffalo L. Rev., at 1, 10–11 (2011).

Prior to the enactment of civil service and public sector bargaining laws and the application of state and federal antidiscrimination law to government employment, state and local government officials, including mayors, school boards, and the heads of police and fire departments, unilaterally issued rules governing employment. Courts generally upheld the power of government officials to dictate working conditions. Under this judge-made labor relations law, employees had few rights and could be hired and fired, and paid or not paid, on the whim of department heads. Governments could even abrogate employment contracts with impunity because judicially created rules of sovereign immunity made it difficult to sue governments to enforce their promises.[13] Officials exercised their power to hire for reasons of race, gender, political affiliation, patronage, or union membership, and court challenges typically failed because public service was considered a privilege that could be conditioned on the waiver of constitutional rights. As Justice Holmes famously said in holding that a police officer could be fired for exercising freedom of speech, the government employee "may have a constitutional right to talk politics, but he has no constitutional right to be a policeman."[14] Eventually, courts held that public employment could not be conditioned on the employee's relinquishing federal constitutional rights of speech and association, including the right to join a union.[15] Thus, subject to civil service laws limiting their political activity and to appointments to high-level political offices (for example, speechwriters and policy-making positions), government employees in the 1960s gained constitutional rights to be free from retaliation at work based on political, religious, or union activity or affiliation.[16]

---

[13] Slater, *Public Workers: Government Employee Unions, the Law and the State, 1900–1962*, at 149.

[14] *McAuliffe v. Mayor of New Bedford*, 155 Mass. 216, 220 (1892); accord, *AFSCME Local 201 v. City of Muskegon*, 369 Mich. 384 (1963) (upholding a bar on public sector unionization because there is no constitutional right to public employment). The notion that public employment is a privilege that can be conditioned on the relinquishing of constitutional rights was repudiated, and the famous Holmes dictum of *McAuliffe* was disapproved, in later cases, including *Garrity v. New Jersey*, 385 U.S. 493 (1967).

[15] *American Federation of State, County & Municipal Employees, AFL-CIO v. Woodward*, 406 F.2d 137 (8th Cir. 1969) (city employees have First Amendment right to join union and may sue under 42 U.S.C. § 1983 to challenge firing for union activities); *Atkins v. City of Charlotte*, 296 F. Supp. 1068, 1077 (W.D.N.C. 1969) (striking down North Carolina statute prohibiting government employees from joining unions); cf. *Keyeshian v. Board of Regents*, 385 U.S. 589, 609 (1967) (striking down New York law prohibiting state university employees from belonging to the Communist Party).

[16] *Smith v. Arkansas State Highway Employees, Local 1315*, 441 U.S. 463 (1979) (although First Amendment prohibits retaliation against government employees based

Although public sector employees had no legal rights to unionize or bargain collectively until the 1960s, many employees joined unions anyway. In 1956, three years before public sector workers first acquired statutory bargaining rights, 915,000 government employees were union members (out of an estimated 7.3 million public sector workers).[17] Public sector unions negotiated informal agreements with many government entities; in 1957, the American Federation of State, County, and Municipal Employees (AFSCME) said it had agreements for 445 local unions (out of more than 1,500 locals).[18] The agreements operated based on voluntary compliance.[19] Even today in states without bargaining rights, some government employees join unions and bargain.[20] Once government workers gained statutory rights to bargain, they joined unions in droves, and today they have higher rates of union membership than do private sector workers. In 2010, the union membership rate for public sector workers was 36.2 percent, whereas the union membership rate for private industry workers was 6.9 percent.[21]

Today, the collective bargaining rights of government employees are determined by federal law for federal employees and by the law of states and municipalities for state and local employees. Most, but not all, federal employees have a statutory right to unionize and to bargain collectively.[22] The rights of state and local employees vary, as summarized in the Appendix. Although every government employee has a federal constitutional right to

on membership in organizations, including labor unions, it does not compel the government to respond to grievances filed by union on behalf of its members in the absence of a statute compelling bargaining); *Wieman v. Updegraff*, 344 U.S. 183 (1952); *Keyeshian*, 385 U.S. 589 (1967); *Branti v. Finkel*, 445 U.S. 507 (1980) (assistant public defender cannot be discharged solely because of political party affiliation); *Rutan v. Republican Party of Illinois*, 497 U.S. 62 (1990) (extending prohibition on discrimination based on political party to decisions about hiring, promotion, transfer, and recall from layoff).

[17] Slater, *Public Workers: Government Employee Unions, the Law and the State, 1900–1962*, at 162.
[18] *Id.*, at 163.
[19] *Id.*
[20] Ann C. Hodges, *Lessons from the Laboratory: The Polar Opposites on the Public Sector Labor Law Spectrum*, 18 Cornell. J.L. & Pub. Pol'y, at 735, 752 (2009) (describing the various nonbinding memoranda of agreement between governments and public sector unions in Virginia, a state where public sector collective bargaining agreements are unenforceable); Felker, Griffith, and Durant, *Public Sector Unionization in the South: An Agenda for Research*, 13 J. Collective Negotiations Pub. Sector 1 (1984).
[21] Bureau of Labor Statistics, Dep't of Labor, USDL-11-0063: News Release: Union Members – 2010 (January 21, 2011), available at http://www.bls.gov/news.release/archives/union2_01212011.pdf.
[22] Title VII of the Civil Service Reform Act of 1978 now governs the collective bargaining rights of federal government employees. 5 U.S.C. § 7101 et seq.

join a union, whether a state or local employer is obligated to recognize or bargain with the union is generally determined by statute or other state or local law.[23] In a few states, it is illegal for government employers to bargain with an employee union, and a collective bargaining agreement is void.[24] In several states, some employees have a statutory right to bargain, and others do not.[25] In some states, most state and local employees have a right to bargain.[26] In other states, there is no statutory authorization for bargaining, but court decisions have held that governments may validly bargain in the absence of enabling legislation.[27] Even in states with statutory prohibitions on public sector bargaining, however, some employees have joined unions and have obtained nonbinding collective bargaining agreements.[28]

Most state statutes and local ordinances granting collective bargaining rights to public sector employees are patterned loosely on the National

[23] The Florida, Hawaii, and Missouri state constitutions recognize a state constitutional right to bargain collectively, although the scope of the right to bargain differs among these jurisdictions. Fl. Const. Art. I, § 6; Hi. Const. Art. XIII, § 2; *Chiles v. United Faculty of Florida*, 615 So. 2d 671 (Fla. 1993); *United Public Workers, AFSCME Local 646 v. Yogi*, 101 Haw. 46 (2002); *Independence-National Educ. Ass'n v. Independence School Dist.*, 223 S.W.3d 131 (Mo. 2007). In most jurisdictions, however, bargaining rights are determined by statute.

[24] These states include North Carolina (N.C. Gen Stat. §§ 95–98); Virginia (*Commonwealth v. County Bd. of Arlington County*, 232 S.E.2d 30 (Va. 1977); Va. Code Ann. §40.1-57.2); and, to a certain extent, Texas (Tex Rev. Civ. Stat. Ann. Art. 5154c-1).

[25] For example, Arizona permits public safety employees to bargain. Ariz. Rev. Stat. § 23–1411. Tennessee has no general authorization for bargaining. Until recently, it allowed education professionals and transit workers to bargain, but in 2011, it repealed the law allowing exclusive representation and bargaining for education professionals. In its place, the Tennessee Professional Educators Collaborative Conference Act provides that, if at least 15% of the teachers submit a written request for collaborative conferencing between October 1 and November 1, the school board must appoint a committee consisting of equal numbers of board members and professional employees to conduct a confidential poll of the employees. If a majority of employees vote for collaborative conferencing, then the school board appoints a committee of between seven and eleven representatives, and the teachers appoint an equal number. The representatives thus selected remain in place for three years at which point the process begins anew with a new poll conducted by a new joint school board–employee committee. Tenn. Code Ann. § 49-5-605.

[26] As explained more fully in Part II, California is such a state.

[27] *Littleton Education Ass'n v. Arapahoe County School Dist.*, 191 Colo. 411 (1976) (upholding bargaining in the absence of statutory authorization); *Miller v. Montezuma-Cortez School Dist.*, 841 P.2d 237 (Colo. 1992) (rejecting right of public employees to strike in absence of statutory authorization).

[28] See Hodges, *Lessons from the Laboratory*, 18 Cornell J.L. & Pub. Pol'y, at 751 (describing Virginia public sector bargaining and noting that several unions – especially among teachers and firefighters – have negotiated memoranda of understanding with which employers generally comply).

Labor Relations Act (NLRA), the federal statute granting collective bargaining rights to private sector employees.[29] Like the NLRA, the statutes typically grant employees the right to form, join, or assist a union, or to refrain from doing so, they impose on employers the obligation to bargain in good faith with the representative chosen by their employees, and they establish an administrative agency to enforce the law.[30]

However, public sector labor laws differ from the NLRA in important respects. First, they often require political approval for collective bargaining agreements (in the form of or in addition to legislative appropriation of funds) once they are negotiated by the employing agency.[31] Second, many statutes limit the subjects on which employees may bargain and reserve to government broader powers to unilaterally set policies or to change the terms of the contract in response to political needs.[32] Third, many (although not all) explicitly forbid public sector employee strikes.[33] In lieu of the strike, public sector labor statutes tend to rely on some combination of mediation, fact-finding, and/or arbitration to resolve negotiating disputes.[34]

In the absence of, or in addition to, collective bargaining governing wages, hours, benefits, and working conditions, the employment rights of government employees are covered by specific statutes setting pay, benefits, and pensions, civil service laws (covering most government employees in most jurisdictions), teacher tenure laws (in many jurisdictions), and by a range of federal and state laws, many of which also apply to private sector workers.[35] A bewildering array of state and local constitutional or charter provisions, statutes, and administrative rules specify pay, benefits,

---

[29] 29 U.S.C. § 151 *et seq.*
[30] *See,* e.g., Cal. Gov't Code § 3515; N.Y. Civ. Serv. Law § 202; Ore. Rev. State. § 243.662.
[31] Clyde Summers, *Bargaining in the Government's Business: Principles and Politics,* 18 Univ. Toledo L. Rev., at 265 (1987).
[32] Malin, Hodges, and Slater, at 465–468 (contrasting multiple state statutory provisions delineating the scope of the duty to bargain); Befort, *Public Sector Bargaining: Fiscal Crisis and Unilateral Change,* 69 Minn. L. Rev., at 1221 (surveying the laws in many states allowing governments unilaterally to alter terms of public employee collective bargaining agreements and urging that law gives governments too much power to change terms without bargaining).
[33] Malin, Hodges, and Slater, at 557.
[34] A recent study found that there is no significant difference in the wage increases obtained by police and firefighters who have a right to use interest arbitration to resolve bargaining disputes as opposed to those who have only a right to use fact-finding. Thomas A. Kochan, et al., *The Long Haul Effects of Interest Arbitration: The Case of New York State's Taylor Law,* 63 Indus. & Lab. Rel. Rev., at 570 (2010).
[35] *See generally,* Malin, Hodges, and Slater, chap. 3.

and pensions for government workers by job category. In Los Angeles, for example, pensions for police officers and firefighters are set by the city charter, which can be amended only by legislative referendum put to the voters.[36] In Tennessee, a state statute sets longevity pay for public employees, with special provisions for teachers, "wildlife officers" of the state wildlife resources agency and others, and special exemptions for certain officials.[37] Typical civil service and teacher tenure laws provide that employees must be hired and promoted on the basis of merit, and specify that, after serving a probationary period, covered employees enjoy procedural and substantive just cause protections in matters of discipline or discharge. Civil service laws often cover the specifics of personnel administration, including leaves, holidays, and the handling of grievances.[38] In addition, federal and state laws prohibit employment discrimination on the basis of race, religion, gender, national origin, age, disability, and other statuses.[39] Laws also prohibit discrimination against veterans but allow discrimination in their favor.[40] In sum, collective bargaining, in the states that allow it, is only one aspect of a complex web of law that, in every state, regulates compensation and working conditions for public employees. Lawmakers wield many of the same tools with regard to managing public employee compensation packages as they do in setting other budget priorities, and legislative change remains an important means of adjusting priorities.

Labor Costs in Government Budgets

Labor costs consume a relatively larger share of revenues in the public sector than in the private sector.[41] Private sector businesses spent, on average,

---

[36] L.A., Ca. City Charter, Vol. II (1999), *available at* http://www.amlegal.com/nxt/gateway.dll/?f=templates&fn=default.htm.

[37] Tenn. Code Ann. § 8-23-206(5)(A).

[38] *See generally*, Joseph R. Grodin, June Weisberger, and Martin Malin, *Public Sector Employment: Cases and Materials*, at 70–79 (2004).

[39] Title VII of the Civil Rights Act, 42 U.S.C. § 2000e; Age Discrimination in Employment Act, 29 U.S.C. § 630(b).

[40] *See*, e.g., *Personnel Administrator v. Feeney*, 442 U.S. 256 (1979) (rejecting a sex discrimination challenge to a state veterans' preference statute, finding that although veterans' preference laws favor men because more men than women are veterans, such statutes are not motivated by the intent to discriminate against women and are therefore lawful); *Roberto v. Dep't of Navy*, 440 F.3d 1341 (Fed. Cir. 2006) (under the Veterans' Preference Act, an eligible federal employee who has lost his job is entitled to reemployment priority rights).

[41] Labor costs may be analyzed as either a proportion of total revenues or of total expenditures. Both analyses provide a common-size measurement that allows comparisons

19.6 percent of revenues on employee compensation (including benefits) in 2007.[42] By contrast, state and local governments spent, on average, 36.5 percent of revenues on employee compensation including benefits.[43] Relative expenditures were much higher among local governments (49.5 percent) than state governments (18.9 percent), and expenditures as a percentage of revenue were actually lower in state governments than in the private sector.[44] Among state governments, spending on employee compensation ranged from a low of 11.8 percent in Maine to a high of 42.0 percent in Delaware.[45]

---

between business and among industries. Here, we have analyzed public and private sector labor costs as a proportion of revenues because this is the most recent data available, provided by the 2007 Economic Census. This analysis likely overstates the difference between the public and private sector because only the latter earns a profit, meaning revenues will generally exceed expenditures in the private sector (except for unprofitable businesses) but not in the public sector.

[42] Calculated by dividing the Census data category "Annual Payroll" by the category "Sales, Shipments, Receipts, Revenue, or Business Done." U.S. Census Bureau, Dep't of Commerce, *2007 Economic Census* (July 6, 2011), *available at* http://factfinder.census.gov/servlet/IBQTable?_bm=y&-geo_id=&-ds_name=EC0700CADV1&-_lang=en. We adjusted for the cost of benefits using data provided by the Bureau of Labor Statistics, Dep't of Labor, *Employer Costs for Employee Compensation, December 2007* (March 12, 2008), *available at* http://www.bls.gov/news.release/archives/ecec_03122008.pdf. Although there is some ambiguity in the Census Bureau data as to whether its definition of salary and wages includes paid leave and supplemental pay, we assume the data include them and adjust the Employer Costs for Employee Compensation data accordingly. *See* David Madland and Nick Bunker, Center for American Progress Action Fund, *State Budget Deficits Are Not an Employee Compensation Problem*, n. 20 (March 10, 2011), *available at* http://www.americanprogressaction.org/issues/2011/03/state_budget_deficits.html.

[43] Calculated by averaging labor costs for the 2007 and 2008 fiscal years, which are calculated by dividing the Census data category "Salaries and Wages Expense" by the category "Revenue." U.S. Census Bureau, Dep't of Commerce, *State and Local Government Finances by Level of Government and by State: 2006–07* (table revised July 14, 2010) and *State and Local Government Finances by Level of Government and by State: 2007–08* (July 7, 2010), both *available at* http://www.census.gov/govs/estimate/. We averaged two years of data to more closely conform the reporting period for this data, which is based on state fiscal years (ending June 30 for all but four states) to that of the 2007 Economic Census data, which uses a calendar year. We adjusted the data to include the cost of benefits for each year using data from the Bureau of Labor Statistics, Dep't of Labor, *Employer Costs for Employee Compensation, December 2007* (March 12, 2008), *available at* http://www.bls.gov/news.release/archives/ecec_03122008.pdf and *Employer Costs of Employee Compensation, December 2008* (March 12, 2009), *available at* http://www.bls.gov/schedule/archives/ecec_nr.htm. Figures cited are the average of individual state totals for all state and local government spending in each state.

[44] *Id.*

[45] *Id.*

A major reason for the differences in overall labor costs between the private and public sectors, and within the public sector between state and local governments, is that the industries and occupations they include are not comparable, and government tends to provide more labor-intensive services.[46] For example, manufacturing and sales account for a large portion of the private sector workforce but are rare in the public sector.[47] By contrast, education services account for just 0.5 percent of total employment in the private sector but 59.0 percent of local government employment.[48] In fact, occupations accounting for 31 percent of the public workforce have no equivalent in the private sector.[49]

One fact that has gone largely unmentioned in the debate over what relationship, if any, exists between public employee collective bargaining rights and state budget crises is that local governments, not states, employ the overwhelming majority of nonfederal government employees. In 2010, state governments employed 6.3 million workers, whereas local governments employed an additional 11.0 million workers, nearly two-thirds (64 percent) of the total.[50] Local government workers also constitute the majority of nonfederal public employee union membership, which includes

---

[46] The proportion of revenues or expenses spent on labor costs varies considerably among different industries and is typically higher in labor-intensive industries that require lower levels of capital. For example, in the home health care services industry, labor costs account for 64.7% of revenues, whereas in the utilities industry they account for just 13.4%. These figures were calculated by dividing the category "Personnel Costs" by the category "Revenue," as reported by the U.S. Census Bureau, Dep't of Commerce, *Service Annual Survey 2009* (February 2011), *available at* http://www.census.gov/services/index.html. Home Health Care Services is NAICS code 6216 and Utilities is NAICS code 22.

[47] Bureau of Labor Statistics, U.S. Dep't of Labor, *Employer Costs for Employee Compensation*, March 2011 (June 8, 2011), *available at* www.bls.gov/news.release/pdf/ecec.pdf.

[48] Figures are calculated using industry and total employment figures taken from the U.S Census. Private employment figures are taken from *Educational Services*, NAICS code 61, 2007 Economic Census, *available at* http://factfinder.census.gov/servlet/IBQTable?_bm=y&-geo_id=&-ds_name=EC0700CADV1&-_lang=en. State and local employment figures are taken from U.S. Census Bureau, Dep't of Commerce, *Government Employment and Payroll* (accessed July 6, 2011), *available at* http://harvester.census.gov/datadissem/index.aspx.

[49] Keith A. Bender and John S. Heywood, *Out of Balance? Comparing Public and Private Sector Compensation over 20 Years*, Center for State and Local Government Excellence, National Institute on Retirement Security, at 5 (April 2010), *available at* http://www.slge.org/index.asp?Type=B_BASIC&SEC={22748FDE-C3B8–4E10–83D0–959386E5C1A4}&DE={BD1EB9E6–79DA-42C7-A47E-5D4FA1280C0B}.

[50] Bureau of Labor Statistics, Dep't of Labor, *Union Affiliation of Employed Wage and Salary Workers by Occupation and Industry* (January 21, 2011), *available at* http://www.bls.gov/news.release/union2.t03.htm. Data are for 2010.

2.2 million state workers (30 percent) and 5.1 million local government workers (70 percent).[51]

Public Sector Employees Are Paid Less Than Comparable Private Sector Employees

Political debate has focused recently on whether public workers are paid more than private sector workers. Several studies have concluded that public employees earn higher compensation by comparing unadjusted data from the U.S. Bureau of Labor Statistics (BLS) or other government agencies showing public sector workers receive higher average gross hourly compensation than private sector workers,[52] $40.54 versus $28.10 according to the most recent data available (Figure 12.1).[53] However, these conclusions are incorrect because they derive from analyses that fail to account for the substantial differences between public and private sector jobs. This use of the data is surprising because even the BLS cautions against using its data in such direct comparisons as a result of differences between the public and private sectors in work activities and occupational structures.[54] Several studies compare compensation by adjusting for these differences between the public sector and private sector workforces.[55] All

---

[51] *Id.*

[52] See, e.g. Chris Edwards, *Public-Sector Unions*, Cato Institute (March 2010), available at www.cato.org/pubs/tbb/tbb_61.pdf (comparing unadjusted data from the BLS showing public workers earn hourly wages 45% higher than private sector workers); Dennis Cauchon, *Wisconsin One of 41 States Where Public Workers Earn More*, USA Today, March 2, 2011, available at http://www.usatoday.com/news/nation/2011-03-01-1Apublicworkers01_ST_N.htm (comparing unadjusted data from the Bureau of Economic Analysis showing public workers earn higher total compensation than private workers in forty-one states, an average of 4.5% for the nation but reaching as high as 35.0% in Nevada).

[53] Bureau of Labor Statistics, U.S. Dep't of Labor, *Employer Costs for Employee Compensation, March 2011* (June 8, 2011), available at http://www.bls.gov/news.release/pdf/ecec.pdf.

[54] *Id.* at 4.

[55] See Jeffrey Keefe, *Debunking the Myth of the Overcompensated Public Employee*, Economic Policy Institute (September 15, 2010), available at http://www.epi.org/publications/entry/debunking_the_myth_of_the_overcompensated_public_employee; see also Jeffrey Keefe, *Desperate Techniques Used to Preserve the Myth of the Overcompensated Public Employee*, Economic Policy Institute (March 10, 2011) (rebutting methodological criticisms of "Debunking the Myth" and finding including California's cost of retiree health care does not significantly change the finding that public employees in California are neither overpaid nor underpaid), available at http://www.epi.org/publications/entry/desperate_techniques_used_to_preserve_the_myth_of_the_overcompensated_publi/; Bender and Heywood; John Schmitt, *The Wage Penalty for*

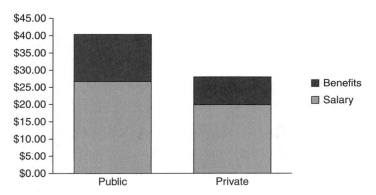

FIGURE 12.1. Unadjusted Hourly Compensation – Public and Private Sector Compared: 2011.
Source: Bureau of Labor Statistics, *Employer Costs for Employee Compensation, March 2011* (June 2011).

reach the same conclusion: Government workers on average earn slightly less than comparable workers in the private sector (Figure 12.2).[56]

Data show that wages for government employees tend to be higher than in the private sector for those employees without college educations and lower for those employees with college or postgraduate degrees. This is true even when controlling for the fact that public employees tend to work fewer hours than private sector workers, especially among higher educated workers.[57] Data also show, however, that governments tend to pay more generous health care and retirement benefits than private sector employers do.[58] Nevertheless, depending on the state, holding education and other human capital factors constant, total compensation (wages plus benefits) is about equal for private and public sector employees.

State and Local Government Employees, Center for Economic and Policy Research (May 2010), available at http://www.cepr.net/index.php/publications/reports/wage-penalty-state-local-gov-employees/.

[56] Slater, *The Assault on Public Sector Collective Bargaining*, at 5–8 (summarizing studies showing public sector workers earn slightly less than comparable private sector workers).

[57] Keefe, *Debunking the Myth of the Overcompensated Public Employee*, at 2.

[58] David Lewin, et al., *Getting it Right: Empirical Evidence and Policy Implications from Research on Public Sector Unionism and Collective Bargaining* (Employment Policy Research Network, Labor and Employment Relations Association) (March 2011), available at http://ssrn.com/abstract=1792942 (reporting results of several empirical studies finding that, nationally, public employees earn approximately 11% lower base pay than their private sector counterparts, but get better benefits, and that adding the two forms

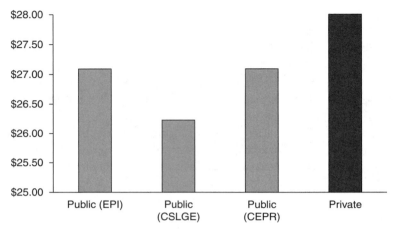

FIGURE 12.2. Adjusted Hourly Compensation – Public and Private Sector Compared: 2011.

Sources: Economic Policy Institute, Center for State and Local Government Excellence, Center for Economic and Policy Research, Bureau of Labor Statistics. Private sector compensation is reported by the BLS. Public sector compensation figures are calculated to reflect the percentage differentials from private sector compensation, as reported by the studies cited in this chart.

Comparing private sector and public sector compensation is challenging for a number of reasons. Larger employers pay better wages, and government tends to be a larger employer, which skews government wages higher.[59] Government employees tend to be more highly educated, and education level is the best predictor of wages.[60] Full-time workers tend to be paid better than part-time workers, and a large number of government jobs are full-time only. Public sector employees are more likely to be older,[61] and age is correlated with higher compensation. Public employees are also

of compensation together reveals that public sector workers are underpaid compared to private sector).

[59] Kenneth Troske, *Evidence on the Employer Size Wage Premium from Worker-Establishment Matched Data*, 81 Rev. of Economics and Statistics, 15 (1999); Walter Oi and Todd Idson, "Firm Size and Wages," in 3 *Handbook of Labor Economics* 2166 (Orly Ashenfelter and David Card, eds., 1999).

[60] Zahira Torres, *Republic Education Cuts Would Further Dash Family Incomes*, The El Paso Times (February 25, 2011) (quoting Steve Murdock), *available at* http://www.txstatedemocrats.org/?p=1786.

[61] In 2008, the mean age was 44.1 years for state workers and 43.7 years for local government workers, compared to 39.8 years for private sector workers. Bender and Heywood, at 7.

more likely to be female (57 percent compared to 43 percent in the private sector), and African American (14 percent compared to 12 percent).[62] The fact that makes comparisons most difficult is that many government jobs have no private sector analog, such as prison guards, police, firefighters, and park rangers. Even school teachers are difficult to compare, as private and parochial schools typically offer dramatically different working conditions than public schools.

Public sector workers are considerably more educated than private sector workers, and educational level is the single most important predictor of earnings.[63] Compared to workers who have not completed high school, high school graduates earn 28 percent more, and college graduates earn 84 percent more.[64] It is, therefore, highly significant that more than half (54 percent) of all public sector workers hold a college degree compared to just over one-third (35 percent) of private sector workers.[65] The studies comparing unadjusted gross earnings are thus no more meaningful than concluding NASA workers are overpaid because they earn more than employees at Wal-Mart.

Numerous studies that control for these factors show that public sector workers earn less than their private sector counterparts. In one recent study, the Economic Policy Institute (EPI) analyzed data gathered by the BLS and the U.S. Census Bureau.[66] It examined compensation levels by controlling for education, experience, hours of work, organizational size, gender, race, ethnicity, and disability. EPI found total compensation for full-time public sector workers is 3.7 percent less than for comparable private sector workers.[67] The compensation penalty was greater for state employees (7.6 percent less) than for local government workers (1.8 percent less).[68] In addition, the compensation penalty was greatest among the most highly educated employees, although a higher wage floor in the public sector meant workers with high school educations earned slightly more.[69]

The EPI conducted a follow-up study in which it extended its analysis to address various issues critics suggested had biased its earlier findings.[70]

---

[62] Keefe, *Debunking the Myth of the Overcompensated Public Employee*, at 9.
[63] *Id.*, at 4.
[64] *Id.*, at 5.
[65] *Id.*, at 4.
[66] See *Id.*
[67] *Id.*, at 1.
[68] *Id.*
[69] *Id.*, at 2.
[70] Jeffrey Keefe, *Desperate Techniques Used to Preserve the Myth of the Overcompensated Public Employee*, Economic Policy Institute (March 10, 2011),

The new study reaffirmed the initial study's key finding even when part-time workers were included or when organizational size was excluded. EPI also found claims that public employees benefited from a job stability wage differential because they experience lower turnover rates did not withstand scrutiny because it was not observable across other industries. In addition, EPI included the cost of retiree health care in an analysis of California public employees and found it added approximately 1 percent to total compensation, which was insufficient to alter the core conclusion that California public employees are neither overpaid nor underpaid relative to their private sector counterparts.[71]

Although national averages may sometimes mask regional differences, EPI also conducted similar state-level studies in a number of states with permissive public sector collective bargaining laws and high levels of public sector unionization. The same finding emerged again and again: Public sector employees earned slightly less when controlling for the aforementioned characteristics. Specifically, public employees earned 4.8 percent less than their private sector counterparts in Wisconsin,[72] 5.9 percent less in New Jersey,[73] 2.9 percent less in Michigan,[74] 3.5 percent less in Ohio,[75] 7.9 percent less in Minnesota,[76] and 7 percent less in California.[77]

The Center for State and Local Government Excellence (CSLGE) reached a similar conclusion in a study commissioned by the National Institute for Retirement Security.[78] CSLGE applied the "people approach" in its study of BLS data, which involves standardizing known earnings determinants such as education, training, age, and experience, which differ

---

available at http://www.epi.org/publications/entry/desperate_techniques_used_to_preserve_the_myth_of_the_overcompensated_publi/.

[71] Id., at 7.

[72] Jeffrey H. Keefe, *Are Wisconsin Public Employees Over-compensated?* Economic Policy Institute (February 10, 2011), available at http://www.epi.org/publications/entry/6759/.

[73] Jeffrey H. Keefe, *Are New Jersey Public Employees Overpaid?* Economic Policy Institute (July 30, 2011), available at http://www.epi.org/publications/entry/BP270.

[74] Jeffrey H. Keefe, *Are Michigan Public Employees Over-compensated?* Economic Policy Institute (February 3, 2011), available at http://www.epi.org/publications/entry/6713/.

[75] Jeffrey H. Keefe, *Are Ohio Public Employees Over-compensated?* Economic Policy Institute (February 10, 2011), available at http://www.epi.org/publications/entry/6758/.

[76] Jeffrey H. Keefe, *Are Minnesota Public Employees Overcompensated?* Economic Policy Institute (March 30, 2011), available at http://www.epi.org/publications/entry/6833/.

[77] Sylvia A. Allegretto and Jeffrey Keefe, *The Truth About Public Employees in California: They are Neither Overpaid nor Overcompensated,* Center on Wage and Employment Dynamics, Institute for Research on Labor and Employment, University of California, Berkeley (October 2010), available at http://www.irle.berkeley.edu/cwed/wp/2010-03.pdf.

[78] Bender and Heywood.

dramatically between the public and private sectors. It found that total compensation for public employees, including wages and benefits, has fallen relative to comparable private sector workers since the early 1990s and is now 6.8 percent lower for state employees and 7.4 percent lower for local government employees.[79] This national pattern was also present in a number of states with high levels of public unionism, including California, New York, Pennsylvania, Illinois, and Michigan.[80]

These findings were also echoed by the Center for Economic and Policy Research (CEPR), which found government workers earned 3.7 percent less than comparable private sector workers when controlling for age, education, gender, race, and region.[81] The wage penalty was smaller for women (1.9 percent) than for men (6.0 percent).[82] CEPR analyzed relative differences in compensation at different compensation levels and found low wage government workers earn more than comparable private sector workers. Employees at the lowest compensation decile are paid 5.9 percent more in the public sector than in the private sector. At the second-lowest decile (the 20th), they are paid 3.4 percent more, and at the 30th decile, 1.2 percent more. Beyond that, government employees are paid increasingly less than in the private sector; those in the highest decile earn 11.3 percent less.[83] Public employers distribute compensation differently than the private sector, with a higher wage floor and lower compensation at the high end of the wage scale. There is, thus, a smaller difference between the lowest and highest paid employees in government employment than in the private sector.

Other studies show that public sector compensation has not kept pace with the private sector. Since 1991, total compensation in the public sector, adjusted for inflation, increased just 11.4 percent, compared to 12.4 percent in the private sector.[84] Differences are far greater within specific occupations, such as teachers. Between 1979 and 2010, weekly earnings for teachers fell by 10.5 percent relative to comparable workers, with most of the change occurring between 1996 and 2001.[85] Among female teachers, weekly earnings declined 28 percent relative to comparable workers

[79] Id., at 3.
[80] Id., at 17.
[81] Schmitt, at 5.
[82] Id.
[83] Id., at 8.
[84] Madland and Bunker, at 6.
[85] Sylvia A. Allegretto, Sean P. Corcoran, and Lawrence Mishel, *The Teaching Penalty: An Update Through 2010*, Economic Policy Institute, at 2 (March 30, 2011), *available at* http://www.epi.org/publications/entry/the_teaching_penalty_an_update_through_2010/.

between 1960 and 2000.[86] As a result, in 2010 public school teachers earned 9 percent less in total compensation than comparable workers with similar education and work experience.[87]

The Issue of Pensions and Benefits

Attempts to link public employee compensation to state budget problems frequently focus on public employee legacy costs, specifically employee pensions. Although public employees are more likely than private sector employees to have access to defined benefit plans, this focus is misguided for several reasons. First, the real challenges facing public pension funding levels are nowhere near as dire or as widespread as many critics argue. Second, ensuring pensions are adequately funded is a long-term issue that is distinct from the short-term need to balance state budgets. Third, there is no correlation between collective bargaining rights and the magnitude of pension problems. States without collective bargaining rights for public employees actually make larger payments into plans that are less adequately funded. Fourth, the sensational headlines about certain highly paid public employees bear no relationship to the average government employee, who receives a modest retirement benefit ($22,653 per year) after a lifetime of service. Fifth, defined benefit pensions are the most efficient method of financing retirement. The debate our society needs to have is how to stabilize defined benefit pension plans and make them available to all working Americans.

Pension Benefits and Coverage in the Public Sector: An Overview

Government employees are more likely than private sector employees to have employer-provided retirement benefits. In 2007, 89 percent of public sector workers had access to retirement benefits,[88] whereas only 61 percent of private industry workers had retirement coverage.[89] Government employees are also more likely to participate in defined benefit retirement plans, as compared to a defined contribution retirement plan (or no

---

[86] *Id.*, at 3.
[87] *Id.* For a detailed discussion of the authors' methodology, *see* Sylvia A. Allegretto, Sean P. Corcoran, and Lawrence Mishel, *The Teaching Penalty: Teacher Pay Losing Ground*, Economic Policy Institute (2008), *available at* http://www.epi.org/publications/entry/book_teaching_penalty/.
[88] Bureau of Labor Statistics, *Dep't of Labor, Summary 08–01: National Compensation Survey: Employee Benefits in State and Local Governments in the United States, Sept. 2007* (March 2008), *available at* http://www.bls.gov/ncs/ebs/sp/ebsm0007.pdf.
[89] *Id.* For private industry workers, "retirement coverage" is defined as "at least one type of retirement coverage."

retirement plan at all).⁹⁰ A defined benefit plan is a pension plan that promises a specified monthly benefit at retirement, such as $100 per month or 1 percent of the employee's average salary for the last five years for every year employed.⁹¹ Virtually all workers who participate in defined benefit plans have retirement benefits calculated on the basis of their preretirement earnings.⁹² In contrast, a defined contribution plan lets employers or employees or both invest specified sums annually on participants' behalf and offers a benefit based on the total contributions plus (or minus) earnings (or losses) but does not guarantee any specified benefit.⁹³ Examples include 401(k) plans, 403(b) plans, employee stock ownership plans, and profit-sharing plans.⁹⁴ A defined benefit plan places the risk of investment loss, or the risk that an employee will outlive expectations and will need retirement income over a longer period, on the employer. In contrast, a defined contribution plan places the risk of investment loss or longevity on the employee. Although defined benefit plans used to be the norm in the private sector, over the last three decades many private sector employers have converted their defined benefit plan to a defined contribution plan.⁹⁵ In 2007, 83 percent of public sector workers had access to defined benefit plans.⁹⁶ Of those, 93 percent were in plans that remained open to new employees, and 81 percent could participate immediately after getting hired.⁹⁷ In the same year, 29 percent of all government workers and 43 percent of state government workers had access to defined contribution plans, often in addition to defined benefit plans.⁹⁸ Defined benefit plans have higher participation rates than defined contribution plans. Of the workers with access to defined benefit plans, 96 percent chose to participate.⁹⁹ Of the workers with access to defined contribution plans, 63 percent chose to participate.¹⁰⁰

[90] *Id.*
[91] Employee Benefits Security Admin., *Dep't of Labor, Frequently Asked Questions about Pension Plans and ERISA*, available at http://www.dol.gov/ebsa/faqs/faq_compliance_pension.html. (Look under "What are defined benefit and defined contribution pension plans?")
[92] Bureau of Labor Statistics, *Dep't of Labor, Summary 08–03: National Compensation Survey: Retirement Benefits in State and Local Governments in the United States, 2007* (May 2008), *available at* http://www.bls.gov/ncs/ebs/sp/ebsm0008.pdf.
[93] Employee Benefits Security Admin., *Dep't of Labor, Frequently Asked Questions about Pension Plans and ERISA*.
[94] *Id.*
[95] Colleen Medill, *Introduction to Employee Benefits Practice*, at 121–123 (3d ed. 2011).
[96] Bureau of Labor Statistics, *Dep't of Labor, Summary 08–01.*
[97] Bureau of Labor Statistics, *Dep't of Labor, Summary 08–03.*
[98] Bureau of Labor Statistics, *Dep't of Labor, Summary 08–01.*
[99] *Id.*
[100] *Id.*

Because a defined benefit plan typically promises benefits for the life of the plan participants, sound actuarial practice requires plan sponsors to contribute enough to cover promised future liabilities; many experts recommend that the plan be funded at least at 80 percent of its future liabilities.[101] The federal law regulating private sector pension plans requires employers to fund plans at a specified level, but it does not apply to state and local government benefit plans.[102] Some governments have underfunded their pension plans, effectively pushing onto future government officials the task of raising revenue to fund the pension promises of the past.

In general, public sector workers can retire earlier than private industry workers.[103] Some government public safety jobs require early retirement.[104] Some government pension programs allow early retirement although a number of recent amendments have increased the retirement age to reduce pension expense.[105] Other government pension programs reward early retirement. In 2007, 82 percent of government workers participating in defined benefit plans were covered by some kind of early retirement provisions.[106] Although early retirement incentives have changed as concerns about pension costs have increased, in the 1990s, pension plans often rewarded early retirement, typically by providing the maximum economic benefits to those who retired as soon as they became eligible to receive a pension.[107]

---

[101] Government Accountability Office, *State and Local Government Retirement Benefits: Current Funded Status of Pension and Health Benefits* (January 2008), *available at* http://www.gao.gov/products/GAO-08-223.

[102] Employee Retirement Income Security Act, 29 U.S.C. §§ 301–306, Internal Revenue Code, 26 U.S.C. § 412; *See* John Langbein, Susan Stabile, and Bruce Wolk, *Pension and Employee Benefit Law*, at 206–219 (explaining the minimum funding standards imposed by federal law on private pension plans).

[103] Arlene Dohm, *Gauging the Labor Force Effects of Retiring Baby-Boomers*, Monthly Lab. Rev., at 17, 20–21 (July 2000), *available at* http://filer.case.edu/stl3/Mgmt%20395/Final/Retire.pdf.

[104] The federal Age Discrimination in Employment Act generally prohibits mandatory retirement, but an exception allows governments to set age limitations both for hire and for discharge after age fifty-five for people employed "as a firefighter or as a law enforcement officer," a category that courts have construed expansively to allow mandatory early retirement for a wide variety of public safety workers. *See* 29 U.S.C. § 623(j); *Jones v. City of Cortland Police Dep't*, 448 F.3d 369 (6th Cir. 2006); *EEOC v. State of Illinois*, 986 F.2d 187 (7th Cir. 1993).

[105] Dohm. In 1994, two-thirds of government workers had pension plans that let them retire at fifty-five or younger, as long as they had met a minimum years-of-service requirement (usually thirty years). *Id.*

[106] Bureau of Labor Statistics, *Dep't of Labor, Summary 08–03*.

[107] Dohm.

The Solvency of Government Pension Funds and Their Impact on State Budgets

Public sector pension plans are not responsible for state budget problems. There are several important points to highlight to explain why arguments to the contrary are incorrect. First, the problems facing public pension plans are far less severe than the dire predictions filling recent headlines.[108] Nearly the entire aggregate estimated shortfall for all state and local plans is explained by the collapse of the housing bubble and the resulting downturn in the economy and the stock market, and not by benefits negotiated by public employee unions.[109] Public pension assets fell $0.9 trillion in 2008 from their 2007 peak of $3.2 trillion as a result of the collapse of the financial markets but have already regained most of the losses and were back to $2.9 trillion in 2010.[110]

The problem of underfunding of pension plans varies from state to state, but in the aggregate is not nearly as catastrophic as headlines would suggest. One of several measures used to understand the financial health of pensions is the funded ratio, which compares the actuarially accrued benefit liability to the actuarial value of a plan's assets at a specific moment in time.[111] The funded ratio for state and local pension plans was 79 percent in 2009 and estimated to be 77 percent in 2010.[112] This is only slightly below the 80-percent level recommended by many experts as sufficient for public plans.[113] Although it is true that certain plans are significantly underfunded, these are outliers and include both states with collective bargaining rights, like Illinois (51 percent funded), and states without, like West Virginia (56 percent funded).[114]

---

[108] See e.g. Duhigg; Roger Lowenstein, *The Next Crisis: Public Pension Funds*, N.Y. Times, June 25, 2010, at MM9.A1.
[109] Dean Baker, *The Origins and Severity of the Public Pension Crisis*, Center for Economic and Policy Research, at 1 (February 2011), *available at* http://www.cepr.net/documents/publications/pensions-2011-02.pdf.
[110] McNichol and Lav, at 5. These figures are the market value and not the actuarial value of plan assets.
[111] Government Accountability Office, at 2.
[112] Alicia H. Munnell, Jean-Pierre Aubry, Josh Hurwitz, Madeline Medenica, and Laura Quinby, *The Funding of State and Local Pensions in 2010*, Center for Retirement Research, at 1–2 (May 2011), *available at* http://crr.bc.edu/briefs/the_funding_of_state_and_local_pensions_in_2010.html. Even though the value of plan assets substantially increased from 2009 to 2010, the funded ratio declined because accounting rules require these gains to be phased in over several years. See McNichol and Lav, note 3.
[113] Government Accountability Office, at 3.
[114] Pew Center on the States, *The Widening Gap: The Great Recession's Impact on State Pension and Retiree Health Costs*, at 3 (April 2011), *available at* http://www.pewcenteronthestates.org/uploadedFiles/Pew_pensions_retiree_benefits.pdf.

Conventional estimates of the total state and local pension shortfall range from $700 billion[115] to roughly $1 trillion.[116] Some analyses have estimated the shortfall to be as much as $3.2 trillion.[117] The estimates vary so much because they employ different "discount rates," which carry different assumptions about the investment returns pension funds can expect to earn. The lower estimates follow the recommendations of the Governmental Accounting Standards Board (GASB) and assume pension funds will continue to earn the same return they have historically earned, about 8 percent.[118] By contrast, the larger estimates assume that in the future pension fund investments will only grow at the "risk-free rate" of the safest investments like Treasury bonds, around 4 percent.[119] Numerous studies have criticized the use of the risk-free rate as actuarially mistaken[120] and bad policy.[121]

Second, in considering the impact of pension underfunding on state budgets, it is important to remember that, unlike state budget shortfalls, which must be entirely resolved every year (or every two years in the case of biennial budgets), sometimes requiring drastic measures, pension shortfalls may be resolved over many years, and this often allows a more

---

[115] Congressional Budget Office, *The Underfunding of State and Local Pension Plans*, at 1 (May 2011), *available at* http://nunes.house.gov/UploadedFiles/05-04-Pensions.pdf.
[116] Baker, at 1.
[117] Robert Novy-Mark and Joshua D. Rauh, *The Liabilities and Risks of State-Sponsored Pension Plans*, 23 J. Economic Perspectives, at 191–210, 192 (2009), *available at* http://www.kellogg.northwestern.edu/faculty/rauh/research/JEP_Fall2009.pdf.
[118] McNichol and Lav, at 6. On July 8, 2011, GASB released a proposal to retain use of the historical rate of return for liabilities covered by the plan's assets, and to apply the risk-free rate, pegged to a tax-exempt, high-quality, 30-year municipal bond, only to any unfunded liabilities. Governmental Accounting Standards Board, GASB Proposes Major Improvements for Pension Reporting (July 8, 2011), *available at* http://www.gasb.org/cs/ContentServer?site=GASB&c=GASBContent_C&pagename=GASB%2FGASBContent_C%2FGASBNewsPage&cid=1176158722789. Legislation introduced in Congress in 2011 to require use of the risk-free rate for all liabilities has received only limited support. H.R. 567 would effectively circumvent GASB by requiring public pension plans to disclose all liabilities based on discount rates tied to bonds or lose access to the benefits of tax-free bonds. http://thomas.loc.gov/cgi-bin/query/D?c112:91:./temp/~c112BlmqqP::.
[119] McNichol and Lav, at 7.
[120] Baker, at 4 (arguing Novy-Marx and Rauh incorrectly equate the risk tolerance of a state or local government with that of an individual investor, despite the lower magnitude of potential declines in income for state and local governments and their greater tolerance for market volatility due to their longer time horizons).
[121] McNichol and Lav, at 8–9 (arguing using a risk-free discount rate will lead pension funds to become overfunded, which may impel policy choices with negative long-term consequences).

measured approach. Pension shortfalls do not pose an immediate crisis for states under budgetary pressures for the same reason a home owner need not pay the entire balance of her mortgage together with the month's bills. Current accounting rules allow states to specify an extended period (typically thirty years) to pay off or "amortize" liabilities.[122] State and local governments can fully fund their pension plans by increasing their annual contributions from the current average of 3.8 percent of their total spending to 5.0 percent over the next thirty years.[123] The size of the projected shortfalls also appears less daunting when viewed in the context of the state economies. In most states, unfunded liabilities for state plans represent just 0.2 percent of future income.[124]

Alternatively, states can address shortfalls through modest changes to employee contributions or benefits, as the majority of states have already done. A record number of states passed pension reform legislation in 2010 (twenty-one states)[125] and in 2011 (twenty-five states as of June 30, 2011).[126] Overall, thirty-nine states enacted legislation in at least one year, and several states did so in both years.[127]

Third, all states have public retirement plans, and there is no correlation between collective bargaining rights and either the financial health of the plans or the size of the state's annual contributions to fund the plan. In 2009, the median funding level for state pension plans in states that grant bargaining rights to all public sector employees ("all") was 76.0 percent, above the median for states with bargaining rights for no employees ("none") (74.0 percent) and slightly below the median for states with bargaining rights for only some employees ("some") (76.5 percent)

---

[122] *Id.*, at 17.
[123] Alicia H. Munnell, Jean-Pierre Aubry, and Laura Quinby, *The Impact of Public Pensions on State and Local Budgets*, Center for Retirement Research at Boston College, at 1 (October 2010), *available at* http://crr.bc.edu/briefs/the_impact_of_public_pensions_on_state_and_local_budgets.html. This represents the average increase necessary to address the aggregate underfunding. Contributions would need to be increased by larger amounts in states with the most severely underfunded pensions. These contribution rates differ from those discussed elsewhere in this chapter and which only include state government contributions but not local government contributions or employee contributions. *See, e.g., supra* note 2; *infra*, note 130.
[124] Baker, at 15.
[125] Ron Snell, *State Pension Reform in 2010 and 2011*, National Conference of State Legislators (April 2011), *available at* http://www.ncsl.org/documents/fiscal/2010-2011PensionsReport_Apr2011.pdf.
[126] Ron Snell, *Pensions and Retirement Plan Enactments in 2011 State Legislatures as of June 30, 2011*, National Conference of State Legislatures (June 30, 2011), *available at* http://www.ncsl.org/LinkClick.aspx?fileticket=ty70-VuYhz4%3d&tabid=22763.
[127] *Id.*

(Figure 12.3).[128] One of the best-funded state pension plans in the country in 2009 was Wisconsin, which was funded at 100 percent.[129] These findings are especially significant because the median state contribution to fund the plan was the same for "all" states as for "none" states (1.4 percent of state expenditures).[130] It is also important to note that public pension eligibility and benefit rules are generally established by statute rather than solely by collective bargaining agreement and that funding levels are (or could be) regulated by statute and not by collective bargaining.[131] So the existence, benefit levels, and financial health of the plan are not necessarily determined exclusively by bargaining.

Fourth, sensational headlines decrying high pensions for certain public employees do not remotely describe the modest benefits most public employees actually receive.[132] The average state and local pension benefit is $22,653 per year.[133] Further, a significant number (28 percent) of public employees are not eligible for Social Security.[134] One study found this resulted in $15.6 billion in savings that state and local governments would have otherwise paid to Social Security,[135] offsetting nearly one-fifth (19 percent) of all taxpayer pension contributions in 2008.[136]

---

[128] Pension funding data is taken from The Pew Center on the States, *The Widening Gap*, at 6. Collective bargaining data is derived from Bureau of Nat'l Aff., *Public Sector Bargaining – State Laws* (accessed July 21, 2011), *available at* http://laborandemploymentlaw.bna.com/lerc/2445/split_display.adp?fedfid=1480271&vname=lecbnlaw&fcn=1&wsn=501 128000&fn=1480271&split =0. For a list of the states in each category, together with a summary of public sector collective bargaining rights in every state, see Appendix.

[129] The Pew Center on the States, *The Widening Gap*, at 6.

[130] Calculated by dividing "Government contributions: From state government" in U.S. Census Bureau, *Table 2a. Revenues of State and Local Public Employee Retirement Systems by State and Level of Government: Fiscal Year 2008* (March 23, 2010), *available at* http://www.census.gov/govs/retire/2008reto2a.html., by "Expenditure: State government amount" in *State and Local Government Finances by Level of Government and by State: 2007–08* (July 7, 2010), U.S. Census Bureau, *available at* http://www.census.gov/govs/estimate/.

[131] National Conference of Public Employee Retirement Systems, *State Constitutional Protections for Public Sector Retirement Benefits* (2001) (fifty-state survey of laws regulating public retirement benefits).

[132] *See, e.g.*, Duhigg; Lowenstein, *supra* note 106.

[133] Iris J. Lav, *Testimony Before the House Ways and Means Committee Subcommittee on Oversight Hearing on the Transparency and Funding of State and Local Pensions*, at 2 (May 5, 2011) (citing Census data), *available at* http://waysandmeans.house.gov/UploadedFiles/Lav_Testimony.pdf.

[134] Bender and Heywood, at 16.

[135] National Association of State Retirement Administrators, *State and Local Government Spending on Public Employee Retirement Systems*, at 1.

[136] Total taxpayer contributions are taken from state and local government contributions, U.S. Census Bureau, *Table 2a. Revenues of State and Local Public Employee Retirement*

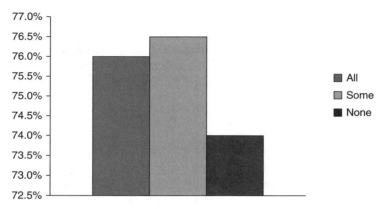

FIGURE 12.3. Public Pension Plan Funding Ratios by Extent of Collective Bargaining Rights: Fiscal Year 2009.
Sources: Pew Center on the States, *The Widening Gap: The Great Recession's Impact on State Pension and Retiree Health Costs* (April 2011); Bureau of National Affairs, *Public Sector Bargaining – State Laws*.

Fifth, defined benefit pension plans are the most efficient method of financing retirement. State and local governments bear only a small portion of the total cost, as employer contributions make up just one-quarter (27 percent) of public pension revenues. Employees contribute 13 percent, and the balance (60 percent) comes from investment earnings on the pooled contributions.[137] Compared to defined contribution plans, traditional pension plans benefit from professional management and superior investment returns, better management of longevity risk, and the ability to maintain a balanced portfolio throughout an individual's lifetime. One study found these advantages enabled defined benefit plans to deliver retirement income at 46 percent lower cost than defined contribution plans.[138]

The ability to deliver higher retirement payments, made possible by the lower cost of defined benefit pension plans, also provides two ancillary benefits for state and local governments. First, pension benefits generate spending by retirees that stimulates the economy and generates tax revenue, and one study quantified the value at $2.36 in total economic output

Systems by State and Level of Government: Fiscal Year 2008 (March 23, 2010), available at http://www.census.gov/govs/retire/2008reto2a.html.
[137] McNichol and Lav, at 3.
[138] Beth Almeida and William B. Fornia, *A Better Bang for the Buck*, National Institute on Retirement Security, at 1 (August 2008), available at http://www.nirsonline.org/index.php?option=content&task=view&id=121.

for every pension dollar paid.[139] Second, pension income plays a substantial role in reducing poverty among the elderly and thus the need for safety net services, which one study calculated saved $7.3 billion in public assistance not counting Medicaid expenditures.[140]

II. PUBLIC SECTOR BARGAINING DOES NOT CAUSE STATE AND LOCAL BUDGET CRISES

Although the Great Recession technically ended in June 2009,[141] nearly every state continues to face crushing budget deficits.[142] Every state except Vermont has a law requiring a balanced budget, and budget gaps must be closed through some combination of spending cuts, tax increases, or a drawdown of reserves.[143] The deficits are largely owed to short-term cyclical shortfalls brought on by the recession and its aftermath, which depressed revenues while increasing demand for public services. Between 2008 and 2010, state revenues fell by 12 percent.[144] Increased federal funds provided by the American Recovery and Reinvestment Act of 2009 filled part of this hole but decreased dramatically in fiscal year 2012.[145] In addition, many states also face long-term structural imbalances between revenues and expenditures brought on by earlier policy choices or their failure to adapt to changes in the economy.[146]

---

[139] Ilana Boivie, Beth Almeida, *Pensionomics: Measuring the Economic Impact of State and Local Pension Plans*, National Institute on Retirement Security, at 1 (February 2009), *available at* http://www.nirsonline.org/index.php?option=com_content&task=view&id=189&Itemid=48.

[140] Frank Porell and Beth Almeida, *The Pension Factor: Assessing the Role of Defined Benefit Plans in Reducing Elder Hardships*, National Institute on Retirement Security, at 1 (July 2009), *available at* http://www.nirsonline.org/index.php?option=com_content&task=view&id=285&Itemid=48.

[141] The National Bureau of Economic Research, Business Cycle Dating Committee (September 20, 2010), *available at* http://www.nber.org/cycles/sept2010.html.

[142] Elizabeth McNichol, Phil Oliff, and Nicholas Johnson, *States Continue to Feel Recession's Impact*, Center on Budget and Policy Priorities, at 1 (June 17, 2011), *available at* http://www.cbpp.org/cms/?fa=view&id=711; forty-one states and the District of Columbia experienced budget shortfalls in FY 2012, and already twenty-three states are projecting shortfalls for FY 2013.

[143] McNichol, Oliff, and Johnson, at 2.

[144] National Association of State Budget Officers, *2009 State Expenditure Report*, at 2 (Fall 2010), *available at* http://nasbo.org/LinkClick.aspx?fileticket=w7RqO74llEw%3D&tabid=79.

[145] *Id.*

[146] Matthew Murray et. al., *Structurally Unbalanced: Cyclical and Structural Deficits in California and the Intermountain West*, Brookings Mountain West, at 1–4 (January 2011), *available at* http://www.brookings.edu/papers/2011/0105_state_budgets.aspx

To understand the effect of collective bargaining on labor costs and, hence, on budget problems in various states, we compare the budget deficits of the states to the collective bargaining rights of government employees. We categorized every state and the District of Columbia into one of three categories: states providing collective bargaining rights to substantially all public employees ("all"), states providing collective bargaining rights to some public employees ("some"), and states that do not provide collective bargaining rights to virtually any public employees or who expressly forbid it ("none").[147] The all group comprised twenty-seven states and D.C., the some group comprised eleven states, and the none group comprised twelve states. We then compared median budget gaps between these three groups, focusing in particular upon the all and none groups, which we would expect to display the greatest differences if any correlation exists.[148]

The data show unequivocally that there is no correlation between public sector bargaining rights and state budget gaps. Indeed, states with expansive public sector bargaining rights tend to have smaller budget deficits than those with no public employee bargaining. According to the most recent data available, the median 2012 budget gap for the states with expansive bargaining rights is 11.5 percent, below the median for the states with no bargaining rights, which is 12.3 percent. The median for the some states falls below both, at 8.6 percent (Figure 12.4).[149]

Because state budget gaps fluctuate from year to year, we repeated this analysis for each of the three prior fiscal years to ensure the robustness of our analysis. The findings did not change. The all states had median budget gaps slightly above the none states in 2011 but the same in 2010 and below them in 2009 (Figure 12.5).

We next examined the size and cost of state workforces to see if larger and more expensive workforces correlated with states providing broad collective bargaining rights. No correlation was evident. In 2009, the median size of the state workforce, measured as a percentage of the total state civilian workforce, was 4.8 percent for all states, 5.6 percent for some states, and 7.2 percent for none states (Figure 12.6).[150]

---

[147] Bureau of Nat'l Aff., *Public Sector Bargaining – State Laws*. For a list of the states in each category, together with a summary of public sector collective bargaining rights in every state, see Appendix.
[148] *See* McNichol, Oliff, and Johnson.
[149] We also examined average budget gaps to see if this altered the findings. It did not. The average 2012 gap for the all states was 12.8%, slightly above the average for the none states of 12.6%, but below the average for the some states of 14.5%.
[150] Schmitt, at 16.

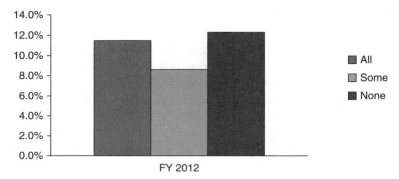

FIGURE 12.4. Median Budget Gap by Extent of Collective Bargaining Rights: Fiscal Year 2012.
Source: Center on Budget and Policy Priorities, *States Continue to Feel Recession's Impact* (June 2011); Bureau of National Affairs, *Public Sector Bargaining – State Laws*.

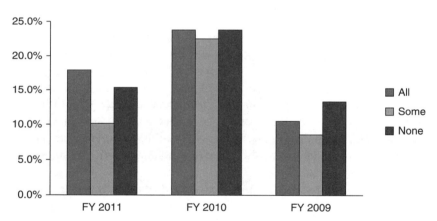

FIGURE 12.5. Median Budget Gaps by Extent of Collective Bargaining Rights, Fiscal Years 2009–2011.
Source: Center on Budget and Policy Priorities, *States Continue to Feel Recession's Impact* (June 2011); Bureau of National Affairs, *Public Sector Bargaining – State Laws*.

Nor was there any correlation between collective bargaining rates and the relative cost of the state employee workforce. In 2009, the median amounts states spent on salaries and wages for state employees, as a percentage of total state expenditures, were 18.5 percent for

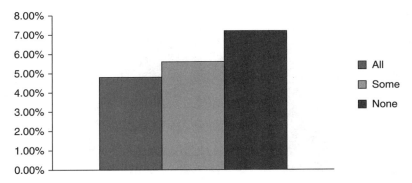

FIGURE 12.6. Median State Workforce as a Percentage of Total Workforce by Extent of Collective Bargaining Rights: 2009.
Source: Center for Economic and Policy Research, *Wage Penalty for State and Local Government Employees*; Bureau of National Affairs, *Public Sector Bargaining – State Laws*.

all states, 18.3 percent for some states, and 19.8 percent for none states (Figure 12.7).[151]

Finally, it is worth noting that state worker labor costs did not even increase in the years leading up to the Great Recession, but rather fell below historical averages during this period. In 2009, state spending on total labor costs, including benefits, averaged just 19.6 percent, below the average of 20.7 percent between 1992 and 2009.[152] This finding further undermines the argument made by Republican-elected officials in Wisconsin and elsewhere attributing recent budget shortfalls to runaway labor costs created by unions.

The aggregate data show no correlation between collective bargaining rights and state fiscal problems. To understand why the lack of correlation reveals an absence of causation, we examine the nature and causes of the budget crises in three states in detail. We chose California, Nevada, and Texas for in-depth analysis because they represent three points on the spectrum of different public sector labor regimes. California provides collective

[151] Calculated from data provided by the U.S. Census Bureau, *State Government Finances: 2009, available at* http://www.census.gov/govs/state/. Calculated by dividing the category "Salaries and Wages" by the category "Total Expenditure." This analysis did not take into account benefit costs but assumed each state spends a consistent proportion on benefits for its state employees. State-level data on public employee benefit costs are unavailable.
[152] Madland and Bunker, at 4.

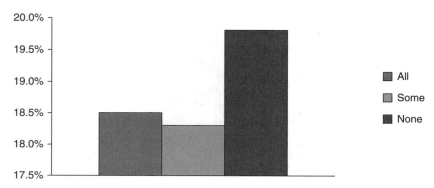

FIGURE 12.7. Median State Labor Expense as a Percentage of State Budget by Extent of Collective Bargaining Rights: Fiscal Year 2009.
Source: U.S. Census Bureau, *State Government Finances 2009*; Bureau of National Affairs, *Public Sector Bargaining – State Laws*.

bargaining rights for most public sector employees. Nevada allows collective bargaining only for local government employees. Texas provides almost no collective bargaining rights for any public sector employee. Other than these differences in the public sector labor regime, the states are similar in pertinent ways. All three have severe budget crises. All three experienced rapid growth in the 1990s and 2000s and experienced a real estate boom.

California

California adopted a statute broadly granting public employees bargaining rights in 1961 and had previously adopted special legislation for labor relations for firefighters and employees of various transit districts.[153] Today, California grants all public sector employees rights to unionize and bargain collectively. A number of different state statutes and local ordinances regulate the bargaining rights of public sector employees.[154] All of them

[153] Joseph R. Grodin, *Public Employee Bargaining in California, The Meyers-Milias-Brown Act in the Courts*, 50 Hastings L.J., at 717 (1999).
[154] The Meyers-Milias Brown Act grants bargaining rights to employees of local governments. Cal. Gov't Code § 3500 et seq. The State Employer Employee Relations Act grants similar bargaining rights to employees of state government. Cal. Gov't Code § 3512 et seq. The Higher Education Employer Employee Relations Act grants bargaining rights to employees of public colleges and universities. Cal. Gov't Code § 3560 et seq. The Education Employment Relations Act provides collective bargaining rights for elementary and secondary public school employees. Cal. Gov't Code § 3540 et seq.

resemble, to a greater or lesser degree, the federal NLRA. All recognize the right of employees to join a union and to bargain collectively over specified subjects. All are enforced by a five-member Public Employment Relations Board. California grants most public sector employees a right to strike, although public safety officers (police and firefighters) are specifically forbidden to strike.[155] California, like other states, sets compensation for civil service employees through an administrative process that considers comparable pay ranges in the public and private sector.[156] California also stipulates some terms of government employment, including retirement and pension rules, by statute, by regulation, and in the case of Los Angeles city employees, by city charter.[157]

California has struggled with some of the largest budget shortfalls of any state. In 2009, the Golden State faced a budget gap equal to 36.7 percent of its general fund, the second largest in the nation. In 2010, the deficit ballooned to 52.8 percent, fell to 20.7 percent in 2011, and climbed back to 27.2 percent in 2012. The state projects a 12.2 percent deficit for 2013.[158]

Experts agree that California's budget deficit is a product of structural features of its tax system. Although California's budget per capita is not large, falling just below the median among states at $5,289 per capita,[159] tax revenues are insufficient to support the state's spending programs. This "structural budget deficit" began in 1978 when Proposition 13 imposed strict limits on local property taxes and thus deprived local governments of funding for such services such as schools, health and mental health care, and law enforcement. The state responded by taking responsibility for funding these programs. Proposition 13 also required a two-thirds vote to raise taxes.[160] As property tax receipts declined, California became

---

[155] *County Sanitation Dist. v. SEIU Local 660*, 38 Cal.3d 564 (1985) ("strikes by public employees are not unlawful unless or until it is clearly demonstrated that a strike creates a substantial and imminent threat to the health and safety of the public" but noting that the legislative prohibition of all strikes by firefighters remains valid); *City of Santa Ana v. Santa Ana Police Benevolent Ass'n*, 207 Cal. App. 3d 1568 (1989) (police work stoppages are illegal irrespective of whether they endanger public health or safety).

[156] Cal. Gov't Code § 19826.

[157] L.A., Ca. City Charter, Vol. II (1999), http://www.amlegal.com/nxt/gateway.dll/?f=templates&fn=default.htm.

[158] McNichol, Oliff, and Johnson.

[159] Kaiser Family Foundation, *Total State Expenditures per Capita*, SFY2009 (last visited July 9, 2011), *available at* http://www.statehealthfacts.org/comparemaptable.jsp?ind=32&cat=1.

[160] California Department of Finance, *Governor's Budget 2008–09 Proposed Budget Summary: Origin of the Structural Deficit*, available at http://2008–09.archives.ebudget.ca.gov/BudgetSummary/INT/32270914.html.

increasingly dependent upon income taxes, which are far more volatile than property or even sales taxes.[161] By 2005, property taxes as a share of state and local revenue had fallen to just 12.6 percent from 27.7 percent in 1977.[162] Today, personal income taxes provide 52.4 percent of California's general fund, and corporate income taxes provide 11.5 percent, far above national averages of 40.3 percent and 6.8 percent, respectively.[163] Income tax receipts soared during the tech bubble of the late 1990s, driven by growth in capital gains.[164] The state used the windfall to increase spending on K-12 education, to provide health insurance to 1 million working poor and their children, and to roll back tax increases enacted in response to the recession of the early 1990s.[165] Then the tech bubble burst, and personal income taxes plummeted 25.5 percent in 2001–2002, opening the floodgates to a sea of red ink.[166] The state has the second highest unemployment rate in the nation.[167] It was also hit particularly hard by the mortgage crisis. Home prices in Los Angeles, San Diego, and San Francisco all more than doubled during the housing bubble and, as of October 2010, still remained nearly 40 percent off their prerecession peaks.[168]

California's inability to reorganize its finances to close its structural deficit has several causes. First, California's permissive initiative process has led to passage of many other propositions that have placed further limits on the legislature's ability to allocate funds.[169] Second, the two-thirds

[161] Gary C. Cornia and Ray D. Nelson, Federal Reserve Bank of St. Louis, *State Tax Revenue Growth and Volatility* Vol. 6, No. 1 (2010), *available at* http://research.stlouisfed.org/publications/red/2010/01/Cornia.pdf.
[162] Robert W. Wassmer, *California's State and Local Revenue Structure after Proposition 13: Is Denial an Appropriate Way to Cope?* (May 14, 2008), *available at* http://www.csus.edu/indiv/w/wassmerr/denial.pdf.
[163] National Association of State Budget Officers, *2009 State Expenditure Report*.
[164] Phil Spilberg and Lori Alexander, *The California Budget Crisis: Factors Leading to the Current Budget Deficit and a Discussion of Certain Proposed Solutions*, National Tax Journal (September 2003), *available at* http://www.entrepreneur.com/tradejournals/article/109581636.html.
[165] John W. Ellwoood, *A Daunting Task: California's Problems in Dealing With Its Budget Deficit*, *available at* http://www.ucdc.edu/faculty/California_Election/EllwoodTalk-Final.ppt.
[166] Spilberg and Alexander.
[167] Bureau of Labor Statistics, Dep't of Labor, *Regional and State Employment and Unemployment Summary* (June 17, 2011), *available at* http://www.bls.gov/news.release/laus.nro.htm
[168] Standard & Poor's, *S&P/Case-Shiller Home Price Indices: 2010, A Year In Review* (January 2011), *available at* http://www.standardandpoors.com/indices/sp-case-shiller-home-price-indices/en/us/?indexId=spusa-cashpidff–p-us––.
[169] For a comprehensive list of important fiscal initiatives passed since Proposition 13, *see* Wassmer, at 6–7.

supermajority required by Proposition 13 to raise taxes has effectively deprived legislators of a key tool to manage its increased fiscal obligations. California is not alone in this regard; states with supermajority requirements average 8 percent lower state tax revenues per capita.[170] Third, the ability of state lawmakers to draw their own districts has led to a well-documented decline in competitive general election races. The resulting polarization among legislators (who are now most concerned with an electoral challenge in primary elections in which voters in the extreme of each party tend to dominate) makes tax increases and spending cuts difficult to enact.[171] Fourth, the imposition of term limits in 1990 undermined legislative expertise and, therefore, legislators' abilities to deal with complex issues like the state budget and enhanced the power of lobbyists.[172]

Despite its comprehensive collective bargaining laws, California's state employee workforce does not appear to play an outsized role in the budget crisis because the public workforce is smaller than most states and even less expensive. California ranks thirty-eighth among states in terms of the size of its workforce; state government employees account for just 4.3 percent of all employees ages eighteen to sixty-four.[173] However, it ranks just forty-third in labor costs for state workers, measured as a percentage of total state expenditures, which total 20.2 percent.[174] California's state pension plan is reasonably well funded; it has assets to cover 81 percent of its projected liabilities, which is just above the 80-percent funding level recommended by experts. By the measure of the adequacy of assets to cover liabilities, the California pension fund ranks fifteenth among all states.[175] The state's contributions to state pension plans are near the median (1.9

[170] Timothy Besley and Anne Case, *Political Institutions and Policy Choices: Evidence from the United States*, Journal of Economic Literature, Vol. XLI, 7–73 (March 2003), available at http://links.jstor.org/sici?sici=0022–0515%28200303%2941%3A1%3C7%3 APIAPCE%3E2.0.CO%3B2–8.

[171] Anthony York, *California Passes Prop. 20, Redistricting Reform*, L.A. Times, November 2, 2010, available at http://latimesblogs.latimes.com/california-politics/2010/11/california-passes-prop-20-redistricting-reform.html. In November 2010, California voters passed Proposition 20, which takes the power to draw legislative districts away from state lawmakers and gives it to an independent commission.

[172] Public Policy Institute of California, *How Have Term Limits Affected the California Legislature?* (November 2004), available at http://www.ppic.org/main/publication.asp?i=563.

[173] Schmitt, at 16. Rankings for this metric include the District of Columbia.

[174] Calculated by dividing "Salaries and Wages" by "Total Expenditure," as reported by the U.S. Census Bureau, *State Government Finances: 2009* (January 13, 2011), available at http://www.census.gov/govs/state. Adjusted to include benefit expense. Bureau of Labor Statistics, *Employer Cost for Employee Compensation, December 2009*.

[175] Pew Center on the States, *The Widening Gap*, at 6.

percent of state expenditures), and California ranks twenty-second on this measure.[176] However, California ranks sixth as measured by total state and local government contributions to all public pension plans, which account for 3.8 percent of total state and local expenditures.[177]

Nevada

Since 1969, Nevada has provided statutory collective bargaining rights only for employees of local governments and political subdivisions, including school districts.[178] The Nevada Local Government Employee-Management Relations Act, which is patterned on the National Labor Relations Act, was enacted after a wave of union organizing among public school teachers and University of Nevada staff.[179] It was amended in 1973 to limit the scope of mandatory bargaining to twenty specified topics, including wages, benefits, leave, and working hours. The 1973 amendments exclude a duty to bargain on the right to hire, direct, assign or transfer except as discipline (which is bargainable) and the right to lay off employees because of "lack of work or lack of funds," appropriate staffing levels and the quantity, quality, and methods of offering services.[180] Effective July 1, 2011, the statute was amended again to require parties to bargain over reopening a collective bargaining agreement "during periods of fiscal emergency."[181] A three-member agency, the Local Government Employee-Management Relations Board, enforces the statute.[182] Bargaining disputes are resolved first through mediation and, if mediation fails, through fact-finding.[183] Strikes are forbidden.[184] For classified executive branch employees not represented by a union, compensation is set, as in California and other states,

---

[176] Calculated by dividing state government contributions, reported by U.S. Census Bureau, *Table 2a*, by total state expenditures, reported by U.S. Census Bureau, *2008 State and Local Government Finance Summary Report*, available at http://www.census.gov/govs/estimate/. All data are for fiscal year 2008.

[177] National Association of State Retirement Administrators, *State and Local Government Spending on Public Employee Retirement Systems* (January 2011), available at http://www.nasra.org/resources/ERContributions.pdf. Ranking for this metric includes the District of Columbia.

[178] Nev. Rev. Stat. § 288.150.

[179] R. Hal Smith, *Collective Bargaining in the Nevada Public Sector*, 11 State & Local Gov't Rev., at 95, 95 (1979).

[180] *Id.*, at 96. Nev. Rev. Stat. § 288.150.

[181] S.B. 98, to be codified as Nev. Rev. Stat. § 288.150(w).

[182] Nev. Rev. Stat. § 288.080.

[183] Nev. Rev. Stat. §§ 288.190–.201.

[184] Nev. Rev. Stat. § 288.230.

by the relevant governmental department, under the authority of the state personnel system, based on surveys of comparable work in the public and private sector in Nevada and nearby states and based on other factors, including the difficulty of recruiting and compensation paid to employees in similar job classifications.[185]

Nevada's budget gap, already among the country's largest in 2009 at 19.9 percent of its general fund, exploded to 46.8 percent in 2010, larger than every other state except Arizona and California.[186] Nevada has the dubious distinction of having the country's largest budget gap for 2011 (54.5 percent) and 2012 (37.4 percent), and the most recent projections suggest it will remain in pole position even through 2013 (37.4 percent).[187] In 2011, the state also led the nation in unemployment,[188] bankruptcies, and foreclosures.[189] Nevada's budget is exceptionally lean and is smaller than every state except Florida, measured in spending per capita ($3,420).[190]

Nevada's budget deficit, unlike California, is almost entirely owed to the cyclical effect of the economic downturn. Permanent tax increases introduced since the onset of the recession helped reduce its structural deficit from 5 percent in 2009 to just 1 percent in 2010 and 2011.[191] Nevada's tax system and the structure of its economy left it especially vulnerable to an economic downturn, which hit harder in Nevada than in any other state. Nevada's tax structure is among the least diversified in the country.[192] The state's constitution specifies the sales tax rate and prohibits a personal income tax.[193] Neither is there a corporate income tax.[194] As a result, 69 percent of Nevada state general fund revenues are generated by discretionary consumer activity,[195] including 25.3 percent from gaming taxes and

---

[185] Nev. Rev. Stat. § 284.175.
[186] McNichol, Oliff, and Johnson.
[187] Id.
[188] Bureau of Labor Statistics, U.S. Dep't of Labor, *Regional and State Employment and Unemployment Summary* (June 17, 2011), available at http://www.bls.gov/news.release/laus.nr0.htm.
[189] Heather Hill Cernoch, *Nevada Leads Nation in Bankruptcy Filings*, DSNews.com (June 7, 2011), available at http://www.dsnews.com/articles/nevada-leads-nation-in-bankruptcy-filings-2011-06-07.
[190] Kaiser Family Foundation, *Total State Expenditures per Capita, SFY2009*, available at http://www.statehealthfacts.org/comparemaptable.jsp?ind=32&cat=1 (last visited July 9, 2011).
[191] Murray, at 7.
[192] Id., at 15.
[193] Id., at 9.
[194] National Association of State Budget Officers, *2009 State Expenditure Report*.
[195] Andrew Clinger and Janet Rogers, *The Impact of the 2007–2010 Financial Crisis on the State of Nevada*, Presentation to the Financial Crisis Inquiry Commission, Las Vegas,

31.4 percent from sales tax.[196] As of September 2010, inflation-adjusted sales tax receipts had fallen 46.8 percent from their peak in December 2005 and were still falling.[197] Gaming fee receipts also plunged as a result of the decline in consumer activity and tourism and the growth of gaming competition in other states.[198]

Nevada is suffering from the most severe housing collapse in the country. Home prices rose faster and then fell faster and farther than in any other state, according to Standard & Poor's Case-Shiller Home Price Index.[199] The housing bubble, together with the development of new casinos, turbocharged the construction sector in the years leading up to the recession. Nevada had a larger proportion of high-paying construction-related jobs than in any other state. When the housing bubble burst, the Nevada construction industry was devastated.[200] The number of building permits for single-family homes issued annually declined to levels not seen since the 1980s.[201] Nevada now leads the nation in the percentage of homes worth less than their mortgages (two-thirds) and foreclosures (four times the national average).[202]

Although Nevada's state workforce lacks collective bargaining rights, it is more costly than most states' even despite its very small size. The number of state employees, as a percentage of the entire civilian workforce, is the fourth smallest of any state at 3.4 percent;[203] however, the state ranks twenty-first in the share of state spending on labor costs.[204] Nevada's state pension plan is 72 percent funded, ranking thirty-first among state plans.[205] The state ranks twenty-fifth among all states with regard to the share of the state budget spent on pension contributions (1.6 percent),[206] but ranks

Nevada (September 8, 2010), *available at* http://fcic-static.law.stanford.edu/cdn_media/fcic-testimony/2010-0908-Clinger.pdf.

[196] National Association of State Budget Officers, *2009 State Expenditure Report*.
[197] Clinger and Rogers.
[198] *Id.*
[199] *Id.*
[200] *Id.*
[201] *Id.*
[202] *Id.*
[203] Schmitt. Nevada ranks fifth counting the District of Columbia.
[204] Calculated from data provided by the U.S. Census Bureau, *State Government Finances: 2009*, *available at* http://www.census.gov/govs/state/. Calculated by dividing "Salaries and Wages" by "Total Expenditure."
[205] Pew Center on the States, *The Widening Gap*, at 6.
[206] Calculated by dividing state government contributions, reported by U.S. Census Bureau, *Table 2a*, by total state expenditures, reported by U.S. Census Bureau, *2008 State and Local Government Finance Summary Report*, *available at* http://www.census.gov/govs/estimate/. All data are for fiscal year 2008.

first when local expenditures are included (totaling 5.4 percent).[207] These high costs may be owed to the fact that plan participants are not covered by the federal Social Security program, and government contributions for most employees include an equal payment made on behalf of employees, in exchange for lower salaries.[208]

Texas

Texas adopted civil service protections for police and firefighters in 1947 – the same year it enacted a prohibition on collective bargaining by all government employees. The prohibition, which has not been amended since 1947, prohibits a political subdivision from recognizing a union as the bargaining agent for a group of public employees or entering into a collective bargaining agreement regarding wages, hours, or conditions of employment of public employees and establishes that any such agreement is void.[209] Notwithstanding the general prohibition, Texas allows police, firefighters, and emergency medical service personnel to bargain collectively but does not compel municipalities to recognize their unions absent a special election in which the issue of recognition is put to the voters.[210] They are forbidden to strike. Texas has enacted a so-called right to work law, which makes it unlawful to deny employment on the grounds of membership or nonmembership in a union; hence, a law that is generally enacted for the purpose of and which has the effect of making it more difficult to form unions does protect the rights of workers, including public sector workers, to join unions.[211] Texas, in common with California, Nevada, and other states, has enacted a regime that sets compensation for government employees according to a position classification system.[212] Like other states, it has also enacted a number of specific statutory provisions regulating the hours and working conditions of police, firefighters, and emergency medical service personnel.[213]

---

[207] National Association of State Retirement Administrators, *State and Local Government Spending on Public Employee Retirement Systems*.
[208] *Id.*
[209] Tex. Rev. Stat. Ann. Gov't Code § 617.002.
[210] Tex. Loc. Gov't Code § 174.001, 174.023, 174.051; EMS Personnel: Tex. Loc. Gov't Code § 142.155; Firefighters: Tex. Loc. Gov't Code § 142.108; Police: Tex. Loc. Gov't Code § 142.058.
[211] Tex. Labor Code § 101.052.
[212] Tex. Gov't Code § 654.011.
[213] Tex. Loc. Gov't Code § 141.031 (base salary for firefighters and police officers).

Although recently touted by conservatives as a paragon of state fiscal policy and economic success,[214] Texas has since encountered budget problems that are among the most severe in the nation. In 2009, Texas was one of just five states with no budget gap.[215] Its fiscal health then quickly deteriorated. Texas encountered a budget gap totaling 10.7 percent of its general fund in 2010. Estimates of Texas's shortfall for its 2011–2012 biennium ranged from $15 billion to maintain expenditures at current levels to as much as $27 billion to maintain services at current levels when factoring in expected growth in student enrollment and the Medicaid population.[216] Final figures indicate budget shortfalls of 20.9 percent in 2011 and 20.5 percent in 2012, the fifth highest shortfall of any state.[217] In addition, Texas is already projecting the nation's third largest budget gap for 2013, at 20.5 percent of its general fund.[218]

Experts attribute just one-third of Texas's revenue shortfall to the recession and the balance to a structural deficit created by the state's decision to overhaul its business tax structure and to reduce local property taxes in 2006.[219] After the Texas Supreme Court held that the statewide property tax was unconstitutional, the state changed its method of financing schools by lowering property taxes and restructuring its business tax.[220] However, the state comptroller warned that the new business tax was inadequate and would fall $23 billion short over the next five years.[221] Her projections have proved accurate. In January 2011, the State Comptroller's Office testified before the Senate Finance Committee that a $10 billion biennial

[214] See, e.g., Arthur B. Laffer, Stephen Moore, and Jonathan Williams, *Rich States, Poor States*, American Legislative Exchange Council (2009), available at http://www.alec.org/AM/Template.cfm?Section=2009_Rich_States_Poor_States.
[215] McNichol, Oliff, and Johnson, at 11.
[216] Standard & Poor's, *Texas' Budget Challenge: Structural Changes Are Key To Avoid Persistent Deficits* (February 16, 2011), available at http://www.tasbo.org/files-public/publications/other/texas_budget_challenge.pdf.
[217] McNichol, Oliff, and Johnson, at 5, 9.
[218] *Id.*, at 6.
[219] James C. McKinley Jr., *After Years of Cost Cuts, Texas Tries to Find More*, N.Y. Times, at A12 (April 8, 2011), available at http://www.nytimes.com/2011/04/09/us/09texas.html?pagewanted=1&_r=3&sq=Texas%20budget&st=cse&scp=1; Standard & Poor's, *Texas' Budget Challenge: Structural Changes Are Key To Avoid Persistent Deficits*.
[220] Kate Alexander, *Texas' Budget Challenges Could Persist Beyond 2011*, American-Statesman (February 1, 2011), available at http://www.statesman.com/news/texas-politics/texas-budget-challenges-could-persist-beyond-2011-1223479.html.
[221] Letter from Texas Comptroller Carole Keeton Strayhorn to Governor Rick Perry regarding the Perry Tax Plan (May 15, 2006), available at http://www.window.state.tx.us/news/60515letter.html.

structural deficit had resulted from the 2006 school finance reform package.[222] The new tax structure also increased pressure on the state's budget during periods of economic decline by replacing a relatively stable funding source, local property taxes, with state general purpose funds, a more volatile funding source that closely tracks the economic cycle.[223] Texas is one of just five states with no personal or corporate income tax. It is, thus, highly reliant upon sales taxes, which provided 55.1 percent of its general fund revenues in 2009 compared to the national average of 32.4 percent.[224]

Other policy choices helped insulate Texas from the full impact of the cyclical downturn, unlike California and Nevada. After the savings and loan crisis of the 1980s and 1990s hit the state especially hard, the Texas legislature tightened its mortgage regulations. This shielded Texas from the worst of the housing bust, and the state has not suffered from declines in home values and foreclosures to the extent many other states have.[225] The state has benefited from high oil prices, which soared in 2008 and remained high for much of the next two years.[226] Taxes collected on oil and natural gas also provide much of the state's rainy-day fund, which reached $9.5 billion in 2011. Lawmakers used $3.1 billion to cover a deficit in the 2010–2011 budget but ignited a controversy by refusing to tap the balance to help address the much larger deficit in the 2012–2013 budget, even as the state slashed funding for education and other vital services.

Texas's budget is among the leanest in the country. It ranked forty-seventh in per capita spending in 2009 at just $3,630, 28 percent below the national average.[227] Although the state's budget is among the smallest in the nation, the size and cost of its state workforce are near the national medians. State workers comprise 4.8 percent of all employees, ranking twenty-ninth,[228] and their labor costs consume 24.7 percent of total state expenditures, ranking twenty-seventh.[229] Texas's state pension plan was 84 percent funded in 2009, above the 80-percent level recommended by

[222] Alexander.
[223] Standard and Poor's, *Texas' Budget Challenge: Structural Changes Are Key To Avoid Persistent Deficits.*
[224] National Association of State Budget Officers, *2009 State Expenditure Report.*
[225] Merrill Goozner, *Perry's 'Texas Miracle' Isn't All It's Cracked Up To Be*, The Fiscal Times (July 8, 2011), available at http://www.businessinsider.com/for-rick-perrys-texans-there-will-be-cuts-to-employment-and-tax-revenue-2011-7.
[226] *Id.*
[227] Kaiser Family Foundation, *Total State Expenditures per Capita, SFY2009.*
[228] Schmitt, at 16.
[229] Calculated from data provided by the U.S. Census Bureau, *State Government Finances: 2009*, available at http://www.census.gov/govs/state/. Calculated by dividing "Salaries and Wages" by "Total Expenditure, adjusted to include benefits expense."

experts and the thirteenth highest level of any state.[230] The state ranks thirty-eighth in the share of state and local expenditures spent on public pensions, at 2.0 percent.[231]

In sum, there is no correlation between collective bargaining rights and state budget gaps, nor is there a correlation between bargaining rights and state pension underfunding. In addition, there is no correlation between bargaining rights and either the relative size or cost of state workforces. In the aggregate, expansive bargaining rights are correlated with better-funded pension plans and smaller budget deficits. Of course, there is variation among states. Some states with expansive protections for public sector employee bargaining have small budget deficits and well-funded public pension funds, and some have large budget deficits and underfunded pension plans. However, as we have shown with the in-depth analysis of California, Nevada, and Texas, state budget problems and underfunded pension plans are more likely to be caused by features of the state's economy, tax structure, and policy choices rather than by the public sector employee union demands.

III. COLLECTIVE BARGAINING AND SOLUTIONS TO STATE BUDGET PROBLEMS

The fact that public sector bargaining is not the cause of state budget crises does not necessarily lead to the conclusion that bargaining rights are irrelevant to the process of finding solutions. It is important, however, to remember that bargaining rights are not government employees' only legal protection against layoff or discharge. Without a union, and in the absence of individual employment agreements, state and local government employees would not necessarily be subject to immediate dismissal – for example, civil service and teacher tenure laws allow "bumping" rights – but government employers would have more latitude to fire or lay off workers or to substantially reduce their pay. Given the importance of labor costs to the overall budget of most governments, drastic cuts would close the budget gaps. Such measures likely would also decimate schools, law enforcement, fire safety, tax collections, and other government services. It may, thus, be that political opposition from the public would be as significant a constraint on the ability of governments to drastically reduce labor costs as are union

---

[230] Pew Center on the States, *The Widening Gap*, at 6.
[231] National Association of State Retirement Administrators, *State and Local Government Spending on Public Employee Retirement Systems*.

contracts. Nevertheless, the fact that government employees have individual or collective employment contracts constrains the government's ability to unilaterally impose somewhat less drastic measures, including outsourcing some work, laying off or furloughing some workers, or reducing pay, health care coverage, or pensions. It is important to note, however, that the extent to which collective bargaining agreements prevent governments from unilaterally adopting labor cost savings measures such as layoffs or furloughs depends on the law of the jurisdiction.[232] It is also important to note that state laws and, in many cases, state constitutions generally provide employees vested rights that prohibit reductions in accrued pension benefits. Although the particularities of vesting rules differ from state to state, reductions in vested rights can generally be obtained only by agreement. After first dispelling the notion that states could solve their budget crises by slashing public sector compensation through repudiating existing labor agreements or seeking to discharge them in bankruptcy, we suggest five ways in which public employees, through their unions, could partner with governments to close budget gaps.

Two especially controversial approaches to addressing the labor cost components of government fiscal crises have been proposed lately, as they have been in times of past government fiscal crisis: One is discharge in bankruptcy of collective bargaining agreements or pension and benefit promises for retirees, and the other is just an outright repudiation of collective bargaining agreements. Neither is a sensible solution because each is fraught with considerable legal doubt.

Bankruptcy

Under current law, only private people, entities, and municipalities may file for bankruptcy; as noted by other contributors to this volume, there is no legal authorization for states to declare bankruptcy. Even for municipalities, however, bankruptcy is of dubious utility as a means of modifying or repudiating wage, health benefit, and pension promises.

---

[232] In California, for example, both the governor and city councils unilaterally furloughed employees in 2009, and their power to do so was upheld against some legal challenges, although the power to do so was rejected as applied to other employees. *Professional Engineers in California Gov't v. Schwarzenegger*, 50 Cal.4th 989 (2010) (upholding power to furlough executive branch state employees); *City of Los Angeles v. Superior Court*, 193 Cal. App.4th 1159 (2011) (upholding unilateral furloughs of city employees); *California Attorneys v. Brown*, 195 Cal.App.4th 119 (2011) (rejecting power to unilaterally furlough employees of California Insurance Compensation Fund).

Bankruptcy as a strategy to modify or eliminate collective bargaining agreements emerged as a substantial issue in the late 1970s and early 1980s when unionized American industries in metal fabrication and manufacturing faced dramatic changes associated with globalization and recession. When a number of companies sought to discharge their collective bargaining agreements in bankruptcy, unions and the National Labor Relations Board urged that companies were obligated to bargain with their unions over modifications rather than seek bankruptcy court approval for a unilateral modification. The Supreme Court ultimately held in *NLRB v. Bildisco & Bildisco* that a bankruptcy court may authorize rejection of a burdensome collective bargaining agreement if the equities balance in favor of rejection. The Court also held that the employer may unilaterally modify the agreement after filing bankruptcy even before the court formally orders rejection of the contract.[233] Congress subsequently amended the Bankruptcy Act to legislatively overturn *Bildisco* by adding § 1113, imposing a duty to bargain with the union over modifications necessary to permit reorganization.[234] However, § 1113 applies only to reorganizations under Chapter 11 of the Bankruptcy Code, which is the provision used by private companies. Municipalities may file for reorganization under Chapter 9, which was not amended by § 1113. Thus, *Bildisco* continues to govern municipal bankruptcies.[235]

Scholars report relatively few efforts by municipalities to reorganize in bankruptcy and even fewer in which the debtor-government sought to modify or repudiate its collective bargaining agreement. In one relatively recent case, Orange County, California, filed for bankruptcy in 1994 following severe investment losses. The county sought to repudiate the seniority and grievance provisions of collective bargaining agreements so that it could lay off employees unilaterally without regard to the rights of senior employees to "bump" junior employees from jobs when the senior employee's job was targeted for layoff.[236] The bankruptcy court enjoined the repudiation, finding under the *Bildisco* standard that even the county's concededly dire financial situation did not necessitate making changes without negotiating with its unions.[237]

---

[233] 465 U.S. 513, 526, 534 (1984).
[234] 11 U.S.C. § 1113.
[235] See *Unilateral Alteration of Public Sector Collective Bargaining Agreements*, 59 Buff. L. Rev. at 20; Ryan Dahl, *Collective Bargaining Agreements and Chapter 9 Bankruptcy*, 81 Am. Bankr. L.J. 295, 297 (2007); *In re County of Orange*, 179 B.R. 177, 183 (Bkrtcy C.D. Cal 1995).
[236] *In re County of Orange*, 179 B.R., at 180.
[237] *Id.*, at 184.

Whether other municipalities would be able to persuade bankruptcy courts to allow repudiation of collective bargaining agreements would presumably depend, under the "balance of equities" standard of *Bildisco*, at least in part on the willingness of the unions to negotiate pay freezes, cuts, furloughs, or other cost-saving measures. It also depends on the municipality's other assets and obligations, not just its collective bargaining agreements. Although *Bildisco* gives the municipal leaders the power to threaten unilateral changes, ultimately the possibility that a bankruptcy court will enjoin the modifications as in the Orange County case makes bankruptcy a risky legal strategy if the principal goal is simply modification of the collective agreement rather than a wholesale reorganization of municipal liabilities and finances.

Repudiation and the Contract Clause

In the recent past, as in earlier periods of fiscal crisis, some governments have adopted legislation repudiating promises made in collective bargaining agreements for current employees or reducing pension benefits for retirees and for current employees who have not yet retired. Legislation repudiating a contract is subject to challenge under the Contract Clause of the U.S. Constitution and similar clauses in many state constitutions.[238] The Contract Clause was inserted into the Constitution to prevent states from enacting debtor-relief laws that might hamper commercial activity by allowing debtors to renege on their contracts without fear of litigation.[239] A state law that substantially impairs a state's contractual obligation is constitutional only if it is "reasonable and necessary to serve an important public purpose."[240] An impairment is "reasonable" only if changed circumstances were not foreseeable to the contracting parties at the time the

---

[238] U.S. Const. Art. I, § 10, cl. 1 ("No State shall ... pass any ... Law impairing the Obligation of Contracts"). See *Independence-National Education Ass'n v. Independence School Dist.*, 223 S.W.2d 131 (Mo. 2007) (school district's unilateral repudiation of collective bargaining agreement violates Missouri constitution).

[239] Erwin Chemerinsky, *Constitutional Law: Principles and Policies*, at 646 (4th ed. 2011).

[240] *United States Trust Co. v. New Jersey*, 431 U.S. 1 (1977). In *United States Trust Co.*, the Court invalidated New York and New Jersey laws changing the terms of bond agreements to allow Port Authority toll revenue to be used to subsidize rail transport. The Court reasoned that the states knew when they adopted the earlier provisions, which had been to assure Port Authority bondholders that revenues would be used to guarantee bonds, that changed circumstances might demand additional funding to support rail services. The Court also emphasized that the states had other means of raising money to fund rail service. *Id.*, at 29.

contract was formed and "necessary" only if there are no less drastic alternatives to serve the important public purpose.[241] The Supreme Court has explicitly cautioned, in its only contemporary case addressing the impairment of governmental contracts, that financial need is not a sufficient reason to abrogate a contract: "A governmental entity can always find a use for extra money, especially when taxes do not have to be raised. If a State could reduce its financial obligation whenever it wanted to spend the money for what it regarded as an important public purpose, the Contract Clause would provide no protection at all."[242]

Scholars who have analyzed the Contract Clause challenges to state legislation modifying government collective bargaining agreements and pension plans have concluded that the fact-intensive nature of the legal inquiry places great emphasis on the precise nature of and reasons for the impairment and on the terms of the collective bargaining agreement or pension plans in question.[243] In the past, courts have tended to allow impairments when the fiscal emergency was especially dire and unpredictable and alternatives were not readily available, when the impairment delayed (rather than reduced or eliminated) earned compensation or cut future compensation, or where the cuts spread the pain across the government rather than targeted a select group of employees.[244] Scholars have pointed out, however, that these factors are malleable, which makes it difficult to predict the likely outcome to a Contract Clause challenge to state legislation.[245] As applied to cuts to government employee pay and benefits in the current recession, the analysis might point in opposite directions. On the one hand, the recession was deep, and the budget problems of many jurisdictions are dire. On the other hand, the salience of contemporary political argument

---

[241] *Id.*, at 29.
[242] *Id.*, at 25.
[243] Befort, *Unilateral Alteration of Collective Bargaining Agreements*, 59 Buff. L. Rev. at 40; Paul M. Secunda, *Constitutional Contracts Clause Challenges in Public Pension Litigation*, 29 Hofstra Lab. & Emp. L.J. 263 (2011); *see also* Gavin Reinke, Note, *When a Promise Isn't a Promise: Public Employers' Ability to Alter Pension Plans of Retired Employees*, 64 Vanderbilt L. Rev. 1673 (2011) (discussing constitutional challenges to 2010 public pension plan changes in Colorado, Minnesota, and South Dakota and concluding that changes may impair contract obligations).
[244] Befort, at 40–44. *See Baltimore Teachers Union v. Mayor and City Council of Baltimore*, 6 F.3d 1012 (4th Cir. 1993) (upholding teacher furlough plan).
[245] Befort, at 40–44. For example, scholars criticized the Fourth Circuit's decision upholding the unilateral imposition of a teacher furlough plan in 1993. *See* Thomas H. Lee, Jr., *Balt. Teachers Union v. Mayor of Baltimore: Does the Contract Clause Have Any Vitality in the Fourth Circuit?* 72 N.C. L. Rev., at 1633, 1644–1648 (1994); Note, *Fourth Circuit Upholds City's Payroll Reduction Plan as a Reasonable and Necessary Impairment of Public Contract*, 107 Harv. L. Rev., at 949, 949 (1994).

over tax increases as compared to cuts in government benefits and services makes it particularly difficult to assess whether tax increases are feasible alternatives to pay cuts. Does the intransigence of some political leaders on the issue of tax increases mean that pay cuts are the only option, or does the intransigence suggest that government is unfairly targeting public sector employees and consumers of government services by asking them, rather than taxpayers, to bear a disproportionate share of the suffering?

Real Solutions

Unilateral repudiation of collective bargaining agreements and elimination of bargaining rights altogether are not the only ways that governments can confront budget crises. Unions can facilitate governments in finding solutions to budget problems in many ways. First, the evidence on the historical record of prior fiscal crises suggests that unionization of public workers facilitates the search for solutions to budget problems. Unions have recently, and in the past, negotiated solutions to severe fiscal crises. When New York City faced bankruptcy in the 1970s, a coalition of municipal unions representing more than a quarter million employees negotiated wage freezes, cuts, benefits reductions, productivity enhancements, and most important, investment of pension funds in New York City bonds and notes that, scholars argue, saved the city from bankruptcy.[246] More recently, in response to budget concerns during the Great Recession, unions representing state and local workers in California, New York, Massachusetts, Vermont, Connecticut, and many other states have negotiated pay freezes or cuts and reduced pension or health benefits or increased employee contributions to benefits plans.[247] In fact, a greater proportion of states with collective bargaining rights for most employees experienced layoffs during the most recent budget crisis than did states with no public

---

[246] David Lewin and M. McCormick, *Coalition Bargaining in Municipal Government: The New York City Experience*, 34 Industrial & Labor Relations Rev., at 175 (1981). See also Lewis, et al., at 16–19 (recounting the New York City experience and other examples of cost-saving negotiations between governments and public sector unions in times of fiscal crisis).

[247] State of California, Legislative Analyst's Office Report, Apr. 29, 2011 (California); Danny Hakim, *Cuomo Secures Big Givebacks in Union Deal*, N.Y. Times, June 23, 2011, at A1 (New York); Laura D. Francis, *House Panel Debates State Budget Problems*, Daily Labor Report, Apr. 14, 2011, at AA-1 (Vermont); Rick Valliere, *Boston City Unions Agree to Shoulder $70 Million in Health Costs Over Four Years*, Daily Labor Report, Apr. 15, 2011, at A-9 (Massachusetts); Peter Applebome, *Connecticut Workers Approve Contract They Had Rejected*, New York Times, August 18, 2011, at A1 (Connecticut).

employee bargaining rights.[248] It is easy to see why collective bargaining involving a wide cross-section of government employees facilitated agreement; it is a good deal easier both administratively and psychologically to get employees to agree to pay and benefits concessions if there is a mechanism to spread those cuts fairly across the workforce.

Moreover, in some cases it is not necessary for government officials to secure the agreement of unions to make changes. Scholars have noted that substantial numbers of collective bargaining laws and agreements allow governments significant latitude to implement unilateral changes in times of fiscal crisis.[249] Thus, it is possible for governments facing fiscal crises to reduce costs consistent with their bargaining agreements or to unilaterally reduce labor costs notwithstanding such agreements.

Second, cost reductions in government services are not only achieved through eliminating unions, reducing payrolls, outsourcing, or cutting employee pay and benefits. On the contrary, scholars have analyzed many examples of governments achieving substantial cost savings and efficiencies by working with unions to harness employee ingenuity.[250] A union that is empowered to assist employees to identify and implement cost-saving measures can provide the necessary personnel mechanism to coordinate information and to motivate employees to manage their work more efficiently. In Oregon and Michigan, for example, the government employees' unions bore the considerable expense of polling employees and hiring experts to study government operations to identify possible cost savings and improved efficiencies. Without a union, of course, the employer would have to create a personnel administration function trusted by employees to channel ideas and information between management and workers. For example, a government employees union in Oregon issued a report in March 2011 gathered from a survey of 1,600 state workers that included proposals for achieving $333 million in general fund savings and

[248] National Association of State Budget Officers, *The Fiscal Survey of States* (Spring 2011), available at http://nasbo.org/Publications/StateExpenditureReport/tabid/79/Default.aspx. Data are for fiscal year 2011.
[249] Befort, *Public Sector Bargaining*, 69 Minn. L. Rev., at 1256–1269.
[250] Martin H. Malin, *The Paradox of Public Sector Labor Law*, 84 Indiana L.J., at 1369, 1395–1396 (2009); Stephen Goldsmith and Mark E. Schneider, *Partnering for Public Value: New Approaches in Public Employee Labor-Management Relations*, 5 U. Pa. J. Lab. & Emp. L., at 415 (2003); Saul Rubenstein, *Unions as Value-Adding Networks: Possibilities for the Future of U.S. Unionism*, 22 J. Labor Research, at 581 (2001); *The Results of Union-Management Cooperative Efforts to Increase Productivity and Reduce Costs in the Federal Government Service are Provided in U.S. Office of Pers. Mgmt.*, Labor-Management Partnership: A Report to the President (2000), available at http://www.opm.gov/lmr/report/.

efficiencies. The report leveraged the observations of frontline workers to identify opportunities to trim expenses, for example, by reducing outsourcing where in-house workers could provide services at lower cost and by expanding the use of state programs with proven records of lowering expenses or growing revenues.[251] Similarly, a coalition of public employee unions in Michigan issued a report in 2011 finding that the state could achieve substantial cost savings by changing the ratio of non-supervisors to managers and by imposing cost reductions not only on government employees (as had been proposed) but also on contractors (who were paid more than 2.5 times what the government spent on its own workforce).[252] Teachers' unions in some jurisdictions have also been active in proposing cooperative programs to reduce expenses while maintaining educational quality.[253]

Third, state budgets are not necessarily benefited by cutting government services without regard to larger economic impacts. Unionization does not necessarily increase labor costs without producing corresponding increases in productivity or value; evidence from the private sector suggests that unionization is correlated with reduced turnover and higher levels of productivity and efficiency as compared to comparable nonunion work.[254] When cutting jobs involves outsourcing rather than eliminating work, the short-term cost savings often mask longer-term costs. State workers, especially the most highly skilled, are often cheaper than private sector workers who can perform the same work because, as noted, at the highest skill (and highest compensation) level, government employees earn substantially less than their private sector counterparts. Thus, to the extent that collective bargaining restricts wholesale outsourcing of government services, it is not clear that it increases government costs.[255] Moreover, state fiscal health is

---

[251] Service Employees International Union, Local 503, *Moving Oregon Forward: A Better Way* (March 22, 2011), *available at* http://ow.ly/4jCl9.

[252] Service Employees International Union, Local 517, *New Solutions for Michigan* (May 2011), *available at* http://www.seiu517m.org/files/2011/05/Fair-Economy-New-Solutions-for-Michigan-FINAL.pdf.

[253] Martin H. Malin, *Charter Schools and Collective Bargaining: Compatible Marriage or Illegitimate Relationship?* 30 Harv. J.L & Pub. Pol'y, at 885, 903–911 (2007).

[254] Richard B. Freeman and James L. Medoff, *What Do Unions Do?* ch. 11 (1984).

[255] *See* U.S. Government Accountability Office, Department of Labor: *Better Cost Assessments and Departmentwide Performance Tracking Are Needed to Effectively Manage Competitive Sourcing Program*, GAO 09-14 (November 2008) (finding that the methods by which agencies report and control costs in privatization programs affects the existence and degree of cost savings associated with outsourcing); *see generally* http://www.inthepublicinterest.org/node/457 (reporting studies showing that outsourcing does not reduce government costs as much as is sometimes asserted).

not necessarily improved by cutting government jobs. Obviously, firing all state tax collectors would cut government costs in the short term but at the expense of government revenue in the short, medium, and long term.[256] At a subtler level, government employment compensation levels and practices may have a beneficial effect on the economy. Governments distribute wages differently than do private sector employers, paying a comparatively greater share to the lowest paid workers. This helps the economy because higher payments have the greatest marginal value among lower paid workers, who are most likely to spend rather than save them. Public sector unions negotiate for better pay at the bottom end of the wage scale and lower pay at the top, which may have beneficial macro effects on consumption and social equality.

A fourth way in which unions could be part of the solution, even though they are not the cause of the problem, concerns public pensions. The evidence noted shows that the problems of public pension funds are not the result of collective bargaining but are, instead, the result of market downturn in every state. In some states, pension-funding deficits are caused in part by governments having failed to make the contributions to the fund that experts agreed were necessary to guarantee actuarial soundness.[257] There is no evidence that unions prevent solutions to these problems. On the contrary, a number of unions have advocated sensible reforms both in funding and in eligibility and benefit formulas. For example, the American Federation of Teachers (AFT) has recommended funding reforms, including that public employers should pay their annual required contribution every year, that future changes to benefits should be reviewed for their impact on the plan's long-term financial health, and that pensions should establish a reserve fund to assist in offsetting market volatility.[258] The AFT also endorses reforms in benefits formulas and eligibility, including imposing caps on maximum benefits, prohibiting the practice of significantly

---

[256] Minnesota effectively did this during the July 2011 government shutdown, and economists estimated that it would cost the state $52 million a month. http://www.bloomberg.com/news/2011–07–07/minnesota-shutdown-may-cost-state-economy-23-million-weekly-1-.html.

[257] Pew Center on the States, *The Trillion Dollar Gap* (finding that the failure of some states, including Illinois, New Jersey, and Kansas, to make annual contributions recommended by experts for actuarial soundness is the cause of pension underfunding, not the benefit levels).

[258] American Federation of Teachers, *Strengthening Retirement Security and Building a Better America: Final Report of the AFT Ad Hoc Committee on Revenues and Retirement Security* (April 2011), *available at* https://www.aft.org/pdfs/press/StrengthRetireSecurity0411.pdf.

increasing compensation at the end of a worker's career in order to inflate benefits when a pension is calculated based on the final years' salary (a practice known as "spiking"), and prohibiting employees from collecting a pension while employed in another job (a practice known as "double-dipping").[259] Some of the most high-profile abuses of public pension systems, including examples of six-figure annual benefits, spiking, and double-dipping, have involved high-level government employees (including school superintendents, police and fire chiefs, city managers, and others) who were not union members, not covered by union contracts, and whose pension benefits were negotiated individually, not by a union.[260] Moreover, because vesting rules in many jurisdictions prohibit unilateral reduction of vested benefits, agreement to reduce vested benefits is necessary. Unions may facilitate the negotiation of across-the-board reductions in benefits if they convince their members that the reductions are part of a program of shared sacrifice, whereas individual negotiations with individual pensioners may be more time-consuming and difficult.

The elimination of defined benefit pensions in favor of defined contribution plans for public sector employees should not be part of the solution for several reasons. First, it is not necessary: Sensible changes in funding rules, mandatory contributions in flush times, and recovery of the equities markets will address the long-term funding deficits. Second, it will not solve the problem of underfunded pensions because states will still need to pay for the vested benefits of their employees. Third, defined benefit plans offer economies of scale in the form of pooled asset management. This allows plan participants to have the benefit of expert investment management at a reasonable price and gives them bargaining power vis-à-vis investment managers. Fourth, defined benefit plans offer annuities on a fair basis over the life of the retiree, eliminating the possibility that a retiree will make rash decisions about how to manage his or her retirement funds. In the aggregate, the country benefits from a retirement income system in which every retiree is guaranteed some income for the entirety of his or her life. Fifth, only defined benefit plans spread the risk of longevity and investment

---

[259] Id.
[260] Marc Lacey, *School Official Finds Retirement Is Just a Higher Pay Grade*, N.Y. Times, Apr. 2, 2011, at A11 (noting examples of double-dipping by Arizona school superintendent and police chief); Duhigg, at A1 (noting that chief of police and deputy fire chief in Costa Mesa, California, and the heads of departments of lifeguards in Newport Beach and Laguna Beach received six-figure pensions, but not noting that, as department heads or supervisors, none of these officials is covered by a union contract and that their pay and pension benefits are individually negotiated).

loss over a long period of time and over a large number of people, which allows fund managers to adopt more efficient investment strategies that provide better long-term returns. Reliance on defined contribution plans, by contrast, puts the risk of investment losses and unexpectedly long life spans on each retiree, incentivizing more conservative investment strategies, which provide lower returns.

A fifth way in which unions can contribute to the solution of state budget problems is through their potential to broaden the public debate over the desirability of specific approaches to balancing state budgets. By advocating budget policies that reflect the interests of working people, unions broaden budget policy discussions that might otherwise be dominated by and reflect only the priorities of well-resourced commercial interests. For example, in Pennsylvania some public employee unions are reframing the public debate over what level of revenues and forms of taxes are desirable by campaigning for the adoption of an excise tax on natural gas extraction (unlike other states, Pennsylvania does not tax shale drilling).[261]

One policy unions could consider supporting, which could mitigate budget problems and thus efforts to cut labor costs in lean budget years, is to improve state rainy-day funds. Forty-five states presently have dedicated reserve funds in which they stockpile savings that may only be used when revenues decline or expenditures unexpectedly increase.[262] These funds can benefit state economies because they allow states to take countercyclical actions to increase spending (or to reduce cuts) during recessions, thereby limiting the need to cut spending and/or raise taxes, each of which reduces demand from the economy and thus exacerbates an economic downturn.[263] However, many states have rules that limit the effectiveness of these funds by capping contributions to the funds during periods of surplus or conversely requiring contributions during shortfalls; some states inappropriately limit the size of the fund or erect barriers to using the fund during years in which shortfalls occur. For example, Texas has one of the nation's largest rainy-day funds but requires a supermajority vote in

---

[261] Ian Urbina, *Regulation Lax as Gas Wells' Tainted Water Hits Rivers*, N.Y. Times, Feb. 26, 2011, at A1; Sharon Ward, *Close the Loopholes: Pennsylvania Needs Fair Taxes to Support the Services We Need*, Pittsburgh Post-Gazette, Apr. 15, 2011, at B7.

[262] Elizabeth McNichol and Kwame Boadi, *Why and How States Should Strengthen Their Rainy Day Funds*, Center on Budget and Policy Priorities, at 5 (February 3, 2011), available at http://www.cbpp.org/cms/index.cfm?fa=view&id=3387.

[263] Spending cuts and different forms of tax increases do not reduce economic demand in equal measure, however. Many economists believe taxes on upper-income individuals have a smaller impact on consumption relative to other methods of balancing state budgets. *Id.*, at 5.

the legislature to approve spending any of it, creating the counterintuitive situation in which it is more difficult to spend the rainy-day fund than to raise taxes, which requires only a simple majority.[264] As a result, proposals to use the fund to help close the state's most recent staggering deficit were not passed. During the Great Recession, unions in Texas and many other states advocated using rainy-day funds,[265] and by supporting reforms that strengthen these funds in coming years, unions may provide at least a partial alternative to wage and benefit cuts, furloughs, and layoffs in future downturns.[266] However, unions are unlikely to support reforms to divert revenues that might otherwise fund current contract improvements if they cannot trust that lawmakers will actually use these funds in future years to limit cuts. This trust may no longer exist in states like Wisconsin following the polarizing attacks on union rights by elected officials seeking to blame unions for problems they did not create.

CONCLUSION

Much of the literature blaming state budget problems on public employee compensation and collective bargaining appears animated by a normative belief, never stated, that government employees are paid more than they deserve, which in turn rests on unstated and controversial assumptions about how our society should determine the value of work. Although market dynamics set the outer boundaries for compensation – excessive levels

---

[264] Texas requires a three-fifths supermajority to use the fund in a current budget cycle and a two-thirds supermajority to use the funds to help write the next budget. Robert Garrett, *House Budget Chief Optimistic that Rainy-Day Funds Will Be Tapped*, Dallas News (March 3, 2011), *available at* http://www.dallasnews.com/news/politics/texas-legislature/headlines/20110303-house-budget-chief-optimistic-that-rainy-day-funds-will-be-tapped.ece. By contrast, only a simple majority is required to raise taxes. *Proposal Requiring a Two-Thirds Vote of Legislature to Raise Taxes Didn't Pass*, Austin American-Statesman (July 7, 2011), *available at* http://www.dallasnews.com/news/politics/texas-legislature/headlines/20110303-house-budget-chief-optimistic-that-rainy-day-funds-will-be-tapped.ece.

[265] *See e.g.* Elaine Marsillio, *Corpus Christi Teacher's Union Urges Public to Support Use of Rainy Day Fund*, caller.com (June 6, 2011), *available at* http://www.caller.com/news/2011/jun/06/corpus-christi-teachers-union-urges-public-to-of/; *Time to Tap Md.'s Rainy Day Fund*, The Baltimore Sun (October 19, 2009), *available at* http://articles.baltimoresun.com/2009-10-19/news/0910180055_1_rainy-day-fund-bond-rating-mental-hospital.

[266] For a policy discussion of potential reforms and which states may benefit from them, *see* McNichol and Boadi. The need for reforms is evident from the fact that rainy-day funds were sufficient to close just 5% of the cumulative state budget shortfalls during the most recent recession. *Id.*, at 8.

may overwhelm public budgets and crowd out other services, whereas insufficient levels will undermine the ability to recruit and retain a quality workforce – the data reviewed for this chapter have not shown states to be suffering from either problem.

The contemporary debate over the labor rights of government employees is really a debate about fundamental values. It is sometimes asserted that the problem with public sector bargaining is that it results in some public sector employees earning six-figure salaries or having the right to retire in their fifties, which are taken as examples of a broken system needing fixing. As we have shown, those assertions are often based on anecdotal examples of high-level nonunion officials, and on average, public employees are not paid more than their private sector counterparts. To the extent that the assertion is based in widespread practices, such as policies allowing or requiring public safety officers to retire in their fifties and giving public school teachers full health care coverage, there is room for policy debate. We can have a debate as a society about what public school teachers, park rangers, cops, firefighters, or lifeguards should get paid. In addition, we can have a debate about which government employees should remain on active duty into their sixties and what pension they should receive when they reach the age at which they can no longer safely perform their job. Reducing or eliminating collective bargaining rights for these workers will not solve the budget problems of their states, and it will not contribute to a sensible discussion or a fair policy about public employee compensation and retirement security.

APPENDIX

States Providing Collective Bargaining Rights to Substantially All Public Employees

State	Notes
Alaska	Alaska's Public Employment Relations Act covers state government employees and local government employees, unless the local legislature rejects application of the act by ordinance or resolution. Alaska Stat. § § 23.40.070–23.40.260.
California	California has a number of laws providing bargaining rights to various types of public employees. The Ralph C. Dills Act covers state employees. Other laws cover employees of local governments (including firefighters), public schools, and universities. Public transportation supervisors and public transportation labor disputes are covered by other provisions. *State Employees:* Cal. Gov't Code § § 3512–3539.5; *Local Government Employees:* Cal. Gov't Code § § 3500–3510, Lab. Code § § 1960–1964; *Public School Employees:* Cal. Gov't Code § § 3540–3549.3; *University Employees:* Cal. Gov't Code § § 3560–3599; *Public Transportation:* Cal. Pub. Util. § § 99560–99570.4 (supervisors), Cal. Lab. Code § § 1137–1137.6 (disputes).
Connecticut	Connecticut has three laws providing bargaining rights to various types of public employees. The main legislation covers state employees. Other legislation covers municipal employees and teachers. *State Employees:* Conn. Gen. Stat. § § 5–270 to 5–280; *Municipal Employees:* Conn. Gen. Stat. § § 7–467 to 7–479; *Teachers:* Conn. Gen. Stat. § § 10–153a to 10–153r.
Delaware	Delaware has three laws providing bargaining rights to various types of public employees. The main legislation covers state, county, and local government employees. Other legislation

(*continued*)

The law cited in this Appendix is current as of July 21, 2011.

Table (continued)

State	Notes
	covers teachers, police, and firefighters. *State, County, and Local Government Employees*: Del. Code Ann. tit.19, § § 1301–1319; *Police and Firefighters*: Del. Code Ann. tit.19, § § 1601–1618; *Teachers*: Del. Code Ann. tit.14, § § 4001–4018.
District of Columbia	The District of Columbia has one law that provides collective bargaining rights to all public employees of the D.C. government except judicial and nonjudicial personnel of courts and supervisors, management officials, or employees whose participation in a labor organization would result in a conflict of interest. D.C. Code Ann. § § 1–601.1 to 1–603.1, 1–605.1 to 1–605.4, 1–617.1 to 1–617.3, 1–618.1 to 1–618.17.
Florida	Florida has one law granting collective bargaining rights to public employees with a number of exceptions, including appointed or elected officials, agency heads, supervisors, managers, directors, administrators, and confidential employees. Fla. Const. art. I, § 6; Fla. Stat. ch. 447.201–447.609.
Hawaii	Hawaii's public sector labor relations law covers state, county, and local government employees. Haw. Rev. Stat. Ann. § § 89–1 to 89–23.
Illinois	The Illinois Public Labor Relations Act covers state and local government employees. Separate legislation, the Illinois Educational Labor Relations Act, covers educational employees. An executive order grants the right to bargain collectively to providers of home-based support services who receive state funds. *State and Local Employees:* 5 Ill. Comp. Stat. Ann. 315/1–315/27; *Educational Employees:* 115 Ill. Comp. Stat. Ann. 5/1–5/20; *Home-Based Support Services Providers:* Exec. Order No. 09–15.
Iowa	Iowa's Public Employment Relations Act grants collective bargaining rights to state and local government employees. Executive orders grant child care home providers the right to bargain collectively. Iowa Code § § 20.1–20.26; *Firefighters:* Iowa Code § § 679B.15–679B.27; *Child Care Home Providers:* 2006 Exec. Orders Nos. 45 and 46.
Maine	Maine has a number of laws providing bargaining rights to various types of public employees. The main legislation, the State Employees Labor Relations Act, covers state employees. Other legislation covers municipal employees, which includes school, district, and Maine Turnpike Authority employees; state university employees; judicial employees; and child care providers who receive state funds. Me. Rev. Stat. Ann. tit. 26, § 963; *State Employees:* Me. Rev. Stat. Ann. tit. 26, § § 979 to 979-Q; *Municipal Employees:* Me. Rev. Stat. Ann. tit. 26, § § 961–974; *State University Employees:*

State	Notes
	Me. Rev. Stat. Ann. tit. 26, §§ 1021–1035; *Judicial Employees:* Me. Rev. Stat. Ann. tit. 26, §§ 1281–1294; *Child Care Providers:* Me. Rev. Stat. Ann. tit. 22, § 8308.
Maryland	Maryland's main public sector bargaining law covers state employees of the principal departments within the executive branch, the state insurance administration, the state department of assessments and taxation, the state lottery agency, and nonfaculty positions in the state university system. Separate laws provide teachers and other certificated school employees, noncertificated public school employees, and police officers of the Maryland National Capital Park and Planning Commission (MNCPPC) with the right to bargain collectively. State law and an executive order grant family child care providers the right to bargain collectively, and an executive order grants independent home care providers that right. *State Employees:* Md. Code Ann., State Personnel and Pensions §§ 3–101 to 3–601; *Teachers:* Md. Code Ann., Educ. §§ 6–401 to 6–411; *Noncertificated School Employees:* Md. Code Ann., Educ. §§ 6–501 to 6–510; *MNCPPC Employees:* Md. Code Ann. art. 28, § 5–114.1; *Family Child Care Providers:* Md. Code Ann., Fam. Law §§ 5–595 to 5–595.6 and Exec. Order No. 01.01.2007.14; *Independent Home Care Providers:* Exec. Order No. 01.01.2007.15.
Massachusetts	Massachusetts' public sector labor relations law covers state, county, and local government employees except for employees of the Labor Relations Commission; employees of the departments of State Secretary, State Treasurer, State Auditor, and Attorney General; members of the militia or National Guard; and personal care attendants. Mass. Ann. Laws ch. 150E, §§ 1–15, ch. 180, § 17A; *Personal Care Attendants:* ch. 118G, §§ 28–33.
Michigan	Michigan's main legislation, the Public Employment Relations Act, covers state, county, and local government employees. Separate laws cover arbitration procedures for police troopers, police sergeants, police, and firefighters. Mich. Comp. Laws Ann. §§ 423.201–423.216; *Police Troopers and Sergeants:* Mich. Comp. Laws Ann. §§ 423.271–423.286; *Police and Firefighters:* Mich. Comp. Laws Ann. §§ 423.231–423.246.
Minnesota	The Minnesota Public Employment Labor Relations Act covers state, county, and local government employees. Certain requirements differ for essential employees – for example, firefighters, peace officers, confidential or supervisory employees, assistant county attorneys, and health care professionals. A comprehensive listing of essential employees appears at Minn. Stat. § 179A.03. Minn. Stat. §§ 179A.01–179A.25.

(continued)

Table (continued)

State	Notes
Montana	Montana's public sector labor law covers government employees at the state, county, and local levels. Separate legislation covers nurses at public health care facilities. Mont. Code Ann. §§ 39-31-101 to 39-31-409; *Nurses:* Mont. Code Ann. §§ 39-32-101 to 39-32-114; *Firefighters:* Mont. Code Ann. §§ 39-34-101 to 39-34-106.
Nebraska	Nebraska's main labor legislation, the State Employees Collective Bargaining Act, applies to state government employees. State, county, and local government employees, as well as employees at public utilities, also are granted certain organizing and bargaining rights under the Industrial Relations Act. A separate law covers teachers. Neb. Const. art. XV, §§ 13-15; Neb. Rev. Stat. §§ 48-217 to 48-219, 48-801 to 48-842, 81-1369 to 81-1390; *Teachers:* Neb. Rev. Stat. §§ 79-12,101 to 79-12,103.
New Hampshire	New Hampshire's public employees labor law applies to government employees at the state, county, and local levels. N.H. Rev. Stat. Ann. §§ 273-A.1 to 273-A.17.
New Jersey	New Jersey has several laws covering public employees. The main legislation covers state, county, and local government employees. A separate law covers impasse procedures for police and firefighters. In addition, family child care providers and community care residential providers for adults with developmental disabilities who receive state funds are given the right to organize and bargain collectively. N.J. Stat. Ann. §§ 34:13A-1 to 34:13A-13, 52:14-15.9e; *Police and Firefighters:* N.J. Stat. Ann. §§ 34:13A-14 to 34:13A-21; *Family Child Care Providers:* 2009 N.J. Laws 299; *Community Care Residential Providers:* 2009 N.J. Laws 270.
New Mexico	New Mexico's Public Employee Bargaining Act applies to state and municipal employees. In addition, family child care providers who receive state funds are given the right to organize and bargain collectively. N.M. Stat. Ann. §§ 10-7E-1 to 10-7E-26, 50-2-2; *Family Child Care Providers:* § 50-4-33.
New York	New York has a number of laws providing bargaining rights to public employees. The main legislation, the Public Employee's Fair Employment Act, commonly known as the Taylor Act, covers state, county, and local government employees. Local jurisdictions are authorized to adopt their own procedures as long as they are "substantially equivalent" to the Taylor Act. New York City has adopted a separate ordinance that covers employees of its mayoral agencies, except teachers and transit workers. N.Y. Civ. Serv. Law, §§ 200–214, N.Y. Gen. Mun. Law §§ 681–685; *Child care providers:* N.Y. Lab. Law §§ 695a-695g.

State	Notes
Ohio	Ohio's public employees labor law applies to state government employees and employees of municipalities with a population of at least 5,000. Ohio Rev. Code Ann. §§ 4117.01–4117.23.
Oregon	Oregon's public sector labor law applies to state, county, and local government workers. Solely for purposes of collective bargaining, the state is considered the public employer of record for home care and personal support workers. Executive orders grant adult foster home providers and family child care providers the right to bargain collectively. Or. Rev. Stat. §§ 243.650–243.782, 292.055, 443.705–443.785; *Adult Foster Home Providers:* Exec. Order Nos. 07–07 and 07–20; *Family Child Care Providers:* Exec. Order Nos. 05–10, 06–04, and 07–03.
Pennsylvania	The Pennsylvania Public Employee Relations Act applies to state, county, and local government workers. Separate legislation covers police and firefighters. An executive order grants family child care providers the right to bargain collectively. Pa. Stat. Ann. tit. 43, §§ 1101.101–1101.2301, 1102.1–1102.9; *Police and Firefighters:* Pa. Stat. Ann. tit. 43, §§ 217.1–217.10; *Family Child Care Providers:* Exec. Order No. 2007–06.
Rhode Island	Rhode Island has a number of laws providing bargaining rights to public employees. The main legislation covers state employees. Other legislation covers firefighters, police, teachers, municipal employees, state police, 911 employees, and corrections officers. *State Employees:* R.I. Gen. Laws §§ 36–11–1 to 36–11–13; *Firefighters:* R.I. Gen. Laws §§ 28–9.1–1 to 28–9.1–17; *Municipal Police:* R.I. Gen. Laws §§ 28–9.2–1 to 28–9.2–17; *Teachers:* R.I. Gen. Laws §§ 28–9.3–1 to 28–9.3–16; *Municipal Employees:* R.I. Gen. Laws §§ 28–9.4–1 to 28–9.4–19; *State Police:* R.I. Gen. Laws §§ 28–9.5–1 to 28–9.5–17; *911 Employees:* R.I. Gen. Laws §§ 28–9.6–1 to 28–9.6–16; *Corrections Officers:* R.I. Gen. Law §§ 28–9.7–1 to 28–9.7–17.
South Dakota	South Dakota's labor relation law applies to state, county, and local government employees. S.D. Codified Laws §§ 3–18–1 to 3–18–17, 60–8–3 to 60–8–8.
Vermont	Vermont has a number of laws providing bargaining rights to various types of public employees. The main legislation covers state employees and is known as the Vermont State Employees Labor Relations Act. Certain state employees – including managerial employees, those employed in the Department of Personnel, and certain employees in the Department of Finance and Management – are excluded from coverage. Other legislation

(*continued*)

Table (continued)

State	Notes
	covers municipal employees and teachers. Vt. Stat. Ann. tit. 3, §§ 901–1006; *Municipal Employees:* Vt. Stat. Ann. tit. 21, §§ 1721–1735; *Teachers:* Vt. Stat. Ann. tit. 16, §§ 1981–2010.
Washington	Washington has a number of laws providing bargaining rights to public employees. Separate legislation covers state employees, and other laws cover employees at institutions of higher education, civil service academic employees at community colleges, teaching and research assistants at the University of Washington, municipal employees, teachers, state ferry employees, and port district employees. *State Employees:* Wash. Rev. Code §§ 41.06, 41.56; *Higher Education Employees:* Wash. Rev. Code §§ 28B.16.015; *Community College Employees:* Wash. Rev. Code §§ 28B.52.010–28B.52.900; *Municipal Employees:* Wash. Rev. Code §§ 41.56.010–41.56.950; *Teachers:* Wash. Rev. Code §§ 41.59.010–41.59.950; *Ferry Employees:* Wash. Rev. Code §§ 47.64.005–47.64.910; *Port District Employees:* Wash. Rev. Code §§ 53.18.010–53.18.060.
Wisconsin	Wisconsin has several laws providing bargaining rights to various public employees. The main legislation covers state employees, including teaching assistants at the University of Wisconsin. It also covers home care providers who receive state funds. Other legislation covers municipal employees, including teachers, police, and firefighters. An executive order grants family child care providers the right to bargain collectively. Wis. Stat. Ann. §§ 111.80–111.97; *Municipal Employees:* Wis. Stat. Ann. §§ 111.70–111.77; *Family Child Care Providers:* Exec. Order No. 172.

States Providing Collective Bargaining Rights to Some Public Employees

State	Employees Covered
Georgia	Georgia has no generally applicable collective bargaining statute for public employees. Two separate laws cover firefighters in municipalities that elect coverage and Atlanta's subway employees. Ga. Code Ann. §§ 45–19–1 to 45–19–5; *Firefighters:* Ga. Code Ann. § 54–1301; *Subway Employees:* Metropolitan Atlanta Rapid Transit Act of 1965, § 20.
Idaho	Idaho has no collective bargaining statute for public employees. However, municipal employees can bargain collectively if no local ordinance prohibits it. Two separate laws cover teachers and firefighters. Idaho Code §§ 44–2001 to 44–2012; *Municipal Employees:* Idaho Code § 50–301; *Teachers:* Idaho Code §§ 33–1271 to 33–1276; *Firefighters:* Idaho Code §§ 44–1801 to 44–1811.
Indiana	Indiana has no generally applicable collective bargaining statute for public employees. In 2005, the governor rescinded executive orders that allowed public employees to establish bargaining units. However, state law provides certified public school employees with the right to bargain collectively. *State Employees:* Exec. Order dated 01/11/05; *Teachers:* Ind. Code Ann. §§ 20–29–4–1 to 20–29–4–3, 20–29–6–1 to 20–29–6–18, 20–29–7–1 to 20–29–7–4, 20–29–8–1 to 20–29–8–14, and 20–29–9–1 to 20–29–9–5.
Kansas	Kansas has two laws providing bargaining rights to public employees. The main legislation covers state employees. Local government employees are covered in those jurisdictions whose governing bodies elect coverage. Supervisory employees, with their employers' approval, can elect coverage. A second law covers teachers. An executive order grants family child care providers the right to bargain collectively. Kan. Const. art. 15, § 12; Kan. Stat. Ann. §§ 44–831, 75–4321 to 75–4337; *Teachers:* 72–5410 to 72–5437; *Family Child Care Providers:* Exec. Order No. 07–21.
Kentucky	Kentucky has no generally applicable public sector labor legislation. However, separate laws cover corrections personnel, firefighters, and police officers employed by certain county and local governments. *Firefighters:* Ky. Rev. Stat. Ann. §§ 345.010–345.130; *County Police:* Ky. Rev. Stat. Ann. §§ 78.470–78.480; *Local Police:* Ky. Rev. Stat. Ann. §§ 67C.400–67C.418; *Urban-County Corrections Personnel, Firefighters, Police Officers:* Ky. Rev. Stat. Ann. §§ 67A.6901–67A.6911.
Missouri	Missouri's public sector labor law covers state, county, and local government employees except police; deputy sheriffs; highway patrol employees; National Guard members; and teachers at schools, colleges, and universities. State law also grants personal care providers the right to bargain collectively. Mo. Rev. Stat.

(continued)

Table (continued)

State	Employees Covered
	§§ 105.500 to 105.530; *Personal Care Providers:* Mo. Rev. Stat. § 208.862.
Nevada	Nevada's Local Government Employee-Management Relations Act covers local and county government employees. Nev. Rev. Stat. Ann. §§ 288.010–288.280, 613.230–613.300.
North Dakota	North Dakota has no generally applicable labor relations act. However, it does have a law covering teachers and administrators in school districts. N.D. Cent. Code §§ 34-01-14, 34-09-01, 34-11-01 to 34-11-05, 34-11.1-01 to 34-11.1-8. *Teachers:* N.D. Cent. Code §§ 15-38.1-01 to 15-38.1-14.
Oklahoma	Oklahoma has no generally applicable public sector labor legislation, but it does have laws granting municipal employees, school employees, and firefighters and police officers the right to bargain collectively. The law requiring large municipalities to negotiate with public employees is repealed, effective Nov. 1, 2011. Okla. Const. Art. 23, § 1A; *School Employees:* Okla. Stat. Ann. tit. 70, §§ 509.1–509.10; *Firefighters and Police Officers:* Okla. Stat. Ann. tit. 11, §§ 51-101 to 51-112 and tit. 19, § 901.30; *Municipal Employees:* Okla. Stat. Ann. tit. 11, §§ 51-201 to 51-220 (repealed eff. Nov. 1, 2011).
Tennessee	Tennessee does not have a generally applicable collective bargaining statute for public employees after the Education Professional Negotiations Act of 1978, providing collective bargaining rights for teachers, was repealed by the passage of the Professional Educators Collaborative Conferencing Act on June 1, 2011.[a] Because the law changed so recently, and after the release of the data used for this report, we have coded Tennessee as a "bargaining rights for some public employees" state.
Texas	Texas has no generally applicable public sector labor relations statute. Police, firefighters, and emergency medical service personnel are granted collective bargaining rights. Op. Att'y Gen. M-77 (1967); Tex. Lab. Code Ann. §§ 101.051–101.053; *School Employees:* Tex. Educ. Code Ann. § 21.937; *County Employees:* Tex. Loc. Gov't Code Ann. § 155.001; *Police and Firefighters:* Tex. Loc. Gov't Code Ann. §§ 174.001–174.007, 174.023, 174.051–174.055, 174.101–174.109, 174.201–174.205, 174.251–174.253; *EMS Personnel:* Tex. Loc. Gov't Code Ann. §§ 142.151–142.157, 142.159–142.160, 142.162–142.163.
Wyoming	Wyoming's only public sector labor legislation is a provision granting firefighters the right to organize and bargain collectively. Wyo. Stat. Ann. §§ 27-7-108 to 27-7-115; *Firefighters:* Wyo. Stat. Ann. §§ 27-10-101 to 27-10-109.

[a] Richard Locker, *Tennessee Legislature OKs Ban of Teacher Bargaining*, The Commercial Appeal, May 21, 2011; Randall Higgins, *Teachers Adapting to Loss of Contract*, Timesfreepress.com, July 1, 2011.

States Providing Collective Bargaining Rights to Virtually No Public Employees

State	Notes
Alabama	Alabama's only public sector labor legislation is a provision granting firefighters the right to organize and present proposals on wages and other conditions of employment. However, the provision does not authorize bargaining. Ala. Code §§ 11-43-143, 25-7-1 to 25-7-54, 36-1-4.2 to 36.1-4.4.
Arizona	Arizona law allows public safety employees to organize and form employee organizations. The Department of Public Safety is obligated to recognize and bargain with an employee organization elected by the majority of department employees. However, wages are explicitly excluded from the scope of bargaining. Ariz. Const. art. XXV; Ariz. Rev. Stat. Ann. §§ 23-1301 to 23-1307, 23-1411 to 23-1412.
Arkansas	Arkansas has no collective bargaining statute for public employees. Ark. Const. Amend. 34; Ark. Code Ann. §§ 11-3-301 to 11-3-304, 19-4-1602.
Colorado	Colorado has no collective bargaining statute for public employees. State employees are authorized by executive order to designate an employee organization in a secret ballot election as their exclusive representative in negotiating a "partnership agreement." Colo. Rev. Stat. §§ 8-1-126, 24-50-104, 24-50-123; Exec. Order D 006 07.
Louisiana	Louisiana has no collective bargaining statute for public employees. However, where a private transit system has been acquired by a public entity, its employees are given the right to organize and bargain collectively. La. Rev. Stat. Ann. §§ 23:981–23:987, 42:457; *Public Transit Employees:* La. Rev. Stat. Ann. § 23:890; *Teachers:* La. Rev. Stat. Ann. §§ 17:100.4, 17:438; *Firefighters and Law Enforcement:* La. Rev. Stat. Ann. § 42:457.1.
Mississippi	Mississippi has no collective bargaining statute for public employees. Miss. Const. art. 7, § 198-A; Miss. Code Ann. § 71-1-47.
North Carolina	North Carolina prohibits public employees from joining unions. A court ruled this provision unconstitutional (*Atkins v. City of Charlotte*, 296 F.Supp 1068, 70 LRRM 2732 (W.D.N.C. 1969)) but upheld the section that forbids a government agency from making contracts or agreements with unions. N.C. Gen. Stat. §§ 95-78 to 95-84, 95-97 to 95-100, 143-3.3(g).

(*continued*)

Table (continued)

State	Notes
South Carolina	South Carolina does not have a collective bargaining statute for public employees. S.C. Code Ann. § § 8–11–83, 8–17–310 to 8–17–380, 41–7–10 to 41–7–90; *County and Local Employees*: 8–17–110 to 8–17–160.
Utah	Utah has no collective bargaining statute for public employees. Utah Code Ann. § § 34–32–1, 34–34–1 to 34–34–17.
Virginia	Collective bargaining for public employees is prohibited. Va. Code Ann. § § 2.1–116.05 to 2.1–116.012, 2.2–3003 to 2.2–3006, 40.1–55 to 40.1–69.
West Virginia	West Virginia has no collective bargaining statute for public employees. Op. Att'y Gen. (1962); W.Va. Code § § 12–3–13b, 29–6A-1 to 29–6A-11.

Source: **Unless otherwise noted, all data taken from** Bureau of Nat'l Aff., *Public Sector Bargaining – State Laws, available at* http://laborandemploymentlaw.bna.com/lerc/2445/split_display.adp?fedfid=1480271&vname=lecbnlaw&fcn=1&wsn=501128000&fn=1480271&split =0 (accessed 7/21/11).

Epilogue

DAVID A. SKEEL, JR.

What a difference a year makes. When this book was first conceived, superstar Wall Street analyst Meredith Whitney had recently predicted that fifty to a hundred municipalities and several states might default in the next few months, and a serious debate was underway as to whether Congress should enact a bankruptcy law for states. Although the past year has seen a handful of high-profile municipal defaults – including a bankruptcy filing by Jefferson County, Alabama, and an attempted bankruptcy filing by Harrisburg, Pennsylvania – the predicted wave of failures has not materialized. No state has defaulted. Instead, a number of states have taken steps, some drastic, to reduce their expenditures, particularly their obligations under their collective bargaining agreements with public employees.

A great deal of uncertainty remains, however. Many states are struggling mightily to meet their balanced-budget obligations. None of the states whose prospects were bleakest a year ago – California and Illinois preeminent among them – is ready to declare their mission accomplished quite yet.

I believe that this book, with its unparalleled collection of experts and extraordinarily insightful analysis, will have one of two possible futures. Perhaps the states have seen the worst of the recent crisis. If the next decade brings greater prosperity than the recent past, this book will provide an important resource for the future. When the next crisis hits, it will be essential reading for policy makers and scholars, much as the very best literature on the Great Depression and subsequent crises has been throughout the current crisis. If conditions darken further, on the other hand, the book will provide an urgently needed introduction to and assessment of the states' predicament, as well as a range of potential responses.

Which will it be? The brightening fiscal picture in many states suggests that perhaps we should see the glass as half full. A number of states – not just Wisconsin and Ohio, whose controversial retrenchments on their contracts with public employees have often been in the headlines, but New York, New Jersey, and other states as well – have indeed reined in some of their obligations. Illinois enacted a substantial tax increase. After a steep decline in tax revenues across the nation during the recent crisis, tax receipts have begun to pick up. In the first quarter of 2011, state tax revenues were up an average of 9.3 percent over the prior year, and more recent numbers are likely to show even more improvement. If these trends continue, even the most troubled states may well be on their way to recovery.

If we connect a different set of dots, however, the picture looks more ominous. In 2010 and 2011, the federal government directed a generous dose of stimulus funding to the states. That funding is expected to drop sharply in the coming year, from $59 billion in 2011 to $6 billion in 2012. Public pensions in California and especially Illinois are still egregiously underfunded, and there is little evidence that the gaps will soon be closed. If the American economy tumbles back into recession – either because the recent turmoil in Europe worsens or for some other reason – the most financially precarious states could quickly find themselves back in full crisis mode.

Although it is impossible to know where the states' fiscal health is headed right now, there is one thing we do know: As long as the states retain their status as sovereign entities within America's federalist structure, with the capacity to borrow money and primary responsibility for making good on their obligations, state fiscal crises will recur. This book surely will not be the final word on the issues they raise. But because the potential for state financial crises will always be with us, it should be an exceedingly valuable resource for many years to come.

Index

Adler, Barry, 200
Affordable Care Act, 90
AFL-CIO. *See* American Federation of Labor and Congress of Industrial Organizations
Age Discrimination in Employment Act, 261, 272
Ahmen, Neveen, 72
Aizenman, Joshua, 132, 145
Alabama, 109
Alaska, 59, 67, 70, 81, 218
Alesina, Alberto, 221, 222
Alexander, Lori, 124, 141, 284, 290, 291
Allegretto, Sylvia A., 268, 269, 270
Almeida, Beth, 277, 278
Alt, James E., 218
Amdursky, Robert S., 103, 109, 111, 117, 218, 227, 244
American Federation of Labor and Congress of Industrial Organizations, 3
American Federation of State, County & Municipal Employees, AFL-CIO v. Woodward, 257
American Federation of Teachers, 300
American Recovery and Reinvestment Act, 50, 53, 89, 135, 220, 278
Anderson, Gary, 58, 74
Angelo, Paul, 64, 67, 71
Applebome, Peter, 297
Argentina, 116, 129, 157, 160, 165, 166, 167, 168, 170, 173, 181, 182, 224
Arizona, 259
Arkansas, 12, 13, 43, 53, 54, 112, 113, 158
  fiscal crisis of, 46

ARRA. *See* American Recovery and Reinvestment Act
Ashton v. Cameron County Water Improvement District, 230, 231
Atkins v. City of Charlotte, 257
Aubry, Jean-Pierre, 74, 91, 273, 275

Bader, Lawrence N., 71
bailout, 109, 117–21, 123, 129, 130, 131, 132, 136, 140, 142, 147, 157, 159, 160, 161, 169, 177, 182, 184, 221, 238, 242
Bails, Dale, 219
Baird, Douglas G., 179, 222
Baker, Lynn A., 117
balanced budget requirements, 19–23, 28, 30, 32, 35, 37, 77, 118, 132, 134, 138, 141, 218, 221, 224, 278
Baltimore Teachers Union v. Mayor and City Council of Baltimore, 296
bankruptcy. *See* bankruptcy, municipal; United States Bankruptcy Code
bankruptcy, municipal, 3, 100–02, 104, 196, 197, 198, 203, 204, 229, 230, 231, 233, 237
  effects on collective bargaining, 107–08
  New York, 1970s, 44, 103, 114, 118, 247, 297
  Orange County, California, 105, 294
Barclays Capital Municipal Credit Research Special Report, 60, 61, 62, 65, 66, 69, 71
Barnet, Barry C., 180
Barro, Josh, 3, 82, 85, 90, 91, 95
Bayoumi, Tamim, 133, 145, 220
Befort, Stephen F., 246, 256, 260, 296, 298

317

Behn, Robert D., 217
Bender, Keith A., 263, 264, 266, 268, 276
Bergen, Kathy, 70, 71
Besley, Timothy, 285
Black, Fischer, 69, 71
Boadi, Kwame, 302, 303
Bohn, Henning, 60, 71
Boivie, Ilana, 278
Bolivia, 160
Bolton, Patrick, 181, 203, 208, 211
Bond v. United States, 1485
bonds, 26, 27, 34, 69, 104, 108, 109, 112, 113, 116, 119, 131, 136, 150, 156, 159, 161, 162, 163, 164, 168, 169, 173, 199, 247, 250, 252, 274, 297
Bowmar, Robert H., 117
Boyd, Donald, 79, 81
Brady Plan, The, 160–61, 164, 167
Brainard, Keith, 71
Braucher, Jean, 223
Brazil, 130, 159, 160, 165, 166
   Senate of, 130
Briffault, Richard, 27, 34, 39, 117, 218
Brown, Jeffrey R., 64, 65, 72
Brown, Kyle N., 74
Buchanan, James M., 128, 222
Buchheit, Lee C., 146, 147, 150, 152, 160, 161, 167, 169, 170, 175, 182, 183
Buffett, Warren, 5, 135, 137
Bunker, Nick, 262, 269, 281

Cain, Bruce, 10, 39
California, 2, 59, 66, 71, 80, 81, 82, 100, 102, 107, 119, 123, 133, 135, 136, 191, 194, 196, 205, 215, 218, 237, 255, 268, 269, 281
   collective bargaining in, 282–86, 297
   Proposition 13, 23, 84, 86, 285
   Proposition 20, 285
   state constitution of, 20, 22
California Attorneys v. Brown, 293
Cantor, Eric, 192
Canzoneri, Matthew, 220
capital gains income, 81, 284
capital gains tax, 80, 82
Case, Anne, 285
Cauchon, Dennis, 264
Center for Economic and Policy Research, 265, 269, 273
Center for State and Local Government Excellence, 268

Center on Budget and Policy Priorities, 53, 82, 83, 238, 254, 278, 302
Cernoch, Heather Hill, 287
Chemerinsky, Erwin, 295
Childrens' Health Insurance Program, 87, 217
Chile, 51, 160
CHIP. *See* Childrens' Health Insurance Program
Choi, Stephen J., 184
Christie, Chris, 78
Chrysler, 212, 240
Chun, John H., 180
City of Los Angeles v. Superior Court, 293
City of Santa Ana v. Santa Ana Police Benevolent Association, 283
Civic Federation, The, 59, 72
civil service, 58, 256, 257, 260, 283, 289, 292
Civil War, 10, 12, 13, 24, 40, 42, 43, 47, 110, 132, 141
Clark, Robert L., 58, 59, 72
Clinger, Andrew, 287, 288
Coffee, John C., 199
Cogan, John F., 221, 222
Cohen, Benjamin, 180
collective bargaining, 2, 59, 69, 95, 107, 118, 200–02, 209, 212, 216, 227, 236, 238, 244, 258, 259, 260, 263, 268, 270, 273, 275, 278–303
Colorado, 59, 65, 69
compensation
   public and private sector compared, 264–70
Conference of State Legislatures, 239
Congressional Budget Office, 18, 64, 90, 274
Connecticut, 59, 67, 71, 84, 101, 113, 204, 218, 297
Contracts Clause. *See* United States Constitution, Contracts Clause of
Cooper, Michael, 60, 72, 217
Corcoran, Sean P., 269, 270
Cornia, Gary C., 284
cost of living adjustments, 69, 70
Costa Rica, 160
counter-cyclical spending, 34, 40, 41, 43, 44, 45, 47, 49, 54–55, 219, 302
County Sanitation District v. SEIU Local 660, 283
Craig, Lee A., 59, 60, 72
credit default swaps, 69, 137, 138, 140

credit rating agencies, 57, 66, 126, 129, 140
  Fitch Ratings, 57, 65, 72
  Moody's Investor Services, 57, 61, 65, 74
  Standard & Poor's, 56, 57, 60, 65, 75, 284, 288, 290, 291

Dabney, Jr., H. Slayton, 101
Dadayan, Lucy, 81
Debevoise, Whitney, 179
Delaware, 262
Dodd-Frank Wall Street Reform and Consumer Protection Act, 204, 205
Dohm, Arlene, 272
Dominican Republic, 160
Doolittle, Fred C., 55
Drazilov, Mitra, 71
Dubrow, David L., 107
Duhigg, Charles, 255, 273, 276, 301

economic growth, 47, 49, 86, 91
Economic Policy Institute, 267, 268, 269, 270
Ecuador, 160, 164, 165, 167, 168, 172, 173, 177
Edwards, Chris, 264
Eichengreen, Barry, 128, 145, 180, 181
El Salvador, 160
Elliott Associates v. Banco de la Nacion, 1114
Epple, Dennis, 66, 72
Epstein, Richard, 224
Erler, H. Abbie, 218
European Excessive Deficit Procedure, 130, 142
European Monetary Union, 123, 129, 138, 142, 144, 145, 220
European Union, 4, 43, 45, 123, 129, 130, 137, 138, 142, 143, 144, 147, 169, 176, 183

Faitoute Iron & Steel v. City of Asbury Park, 1580, 1565
Federal Deposit Insurance Corporation, 157
federal grants, 133, 134, 136, 143
federal mandates, 103, 106, 134, 143, 153, 217, 220, 224, 235
Federal Medical Assistance Percentages, 50, 89
federal spending, 45, 46, 47, 55

federalism, 119, 123, 128, 129, 130, 132, 141, 143, 145, 216, 220, 229, 230, 232, 234, 235
Federation of Tax Administrators, 82
Feibelman, Adam, 4, 146, 150, 151, 154, 155, 158, 167, 168, 223
fiscal constitutions, 9
  apparent inconsistencies in, 33–36
  four main types of, 19–23
fiscal crisis, 11, 37
fiscal federalism, 4, 119, 123, 124, 126, 130, 214, 215, 216, 219, 220, 223, 228
Florida, 12, 67, 69, 84, 155, 259, 287
Flushing National Bank v. Municipal Assistance Corporation of New York, 44, 103, 115, 247, 251
FMAP. *See* Federal Medical Assistance Percentages
Ford, Gerald, 211
Fornia, William B., 277
Fox, William, 83
Francis, Laura D., 297
Frankfurter, Felix, 111, 197
Freeman, Richard B., 299

Galvis, Sergio, 180
Garcia, Monique, 70, 71
Garrett, Robert, 39, 226, 303
GDP. *See* United States, Gross Domestic Product of
Gelfand, M. David, 118
Gelinas, Nicole, 196
Gelpern, Anna, 148, 151, 152, 153, 154, 156, 158, 160, 162, 165, 166, 167, 168, 169, 170, 171, 173, 174, 181, 199, 214
General Motors Company, 125, 212, 240
Georgia, 84, 101, 114
Gerst, Jeremy, 219
Gianviti, Francois, 183
Gillette, Clayton P., 3, 102, 103, 109, 111, 117, 121, 216, 218, 227, 233, 244
Gingrich, Newt, 191, 214, 215, 216, 237, 238
Gold, Jeremy, 69, 71, 72
Goldsmith, Stephen, 298
Goldstein, Morris, 133, 145
Goodhart, Charles E. A., 220
Goozner, Merrill, 291
Gouraige, Jr., Chislain, 180

Government Accountability Office, 60, 67, 72, 72, 272, 273, 299
Government Accounting Standards Board, 61, 65, 73, 274
Great Depression, 13, 28, 40, 41, 43, 44, 45, 46, 47, 49, 52, 54, 100, 103, 111, 112, 158, 245, 249, 256
Greece
  fiscal crisis of, 41, 45, 46, 47, 130, 131, 137, 143, 144, 148, 168, 169, 176, 183
Greenhouse, Steven, 61, 69, 73
Grilli, Vittorio, 220
Grodin, Joseph R., 261, 282
Guatemala, 160
Gulati, G. Mitu, 146, 147, 150, 152, 160, 161, 167, 169, 170, 175, 181, 182, 183, 184, 199

Hakim, Danny, 297
Haldane, Andrew, 180, 181
Haley, John J., 74
Halonen, Doug, 215
Hamilton, Alexander, 124, 142
Harris, Alexandra, 69, 73
Haugen, Robert A., 242
Haughwout, Andrew, 106
Haverstick, Kelly, 74
Hawaii, 67, 78, 82, 259
health care, 2, 49, 56, 86, 87, 90, 92, 94, 95, 126, 217, 265, 283
health insurance, 49, 86, 90, 239, 284
hedge funds, 68, 162
Henes, Jonathan S., 191, 196
Hepp, Ralf, 220
Hessler, Stephen E., 191, 196
Heywood, John S., 263, 264, 266, 268, 276
Higgins, Randall, 303
Hodges, Ann, 256, 258, 259, 260
Hodler, Roland, 221
Home Building & Loan Association v. Blaisdell, 247, 249
Hou, Yilin, 218
housing bubble, 51, 52, 273, 284, 288
Hsin, Ping-Lung, 63, 65, 73, 74
Hubbell v. Leonard, 0222
Hurley, Timothy, 82
Hurwitz, Josh, 74, 273
Hustead, Edwin C., 58, 73, 74
Hustead, Toni, 58, 73

Iceland, 168
Idson, Todd, 266
Illinois, 2, 12, 59, 61, 66, 67, 68, 70, 84, 123, 136, 138, 194, 196, 215, 218, 237, 269, 273
income tax, 14, 50, 77, 78, 80, 81, 82, 84, 85, 86, 92, 93, 284, 287, 291
Indiana, 2, 12, 24, 66, 67
Indonesia, 159
inflation, 12, 49, 60, 62, 85, 87, 89, 90, 94, 95
infrastructure, 2, 10, 12, 18, 26, 27, 34, 36, 41, 45, 47, 49, 50, 56, 60, 124, 128, 132, 135, 141, 150
Inman, Robert P., 16, 39, 117
insolvency, 41, 55, 100, 105, 106, 121, 126, 130, 132, 141, 142, 168, 203, 204, 205, 233, 234, 243, 251
International Centre for Settlement of Investment Disputes, 179, 181
International Monetary Fund, 144, 148, 158, 159, 161, 164, 169, 170, 175, 176, 178, 179, 180, 183, 184, 203, 211
Internet sales tax, 51, 83
Iowa, 117
Iraq, 2, 157, 167, 168
Ireland, 45, 129, 131, 138, 168

Jackson, Thomas H., 39, 211, 213, 222
Jamaica, 160
Johnsen, Christopher, 222
Johnson, Lyndon B., 49
Johnson, Nicholas, 278
Jones v. City of Cortland Police Department, 272
Jones, Norman L., 73

Kaiser Family Foundation, 50, 90, 283, 287, 291
Kaplow, Louis, 244
Keating, Elizabeth K., 217
Keefe, Jeffrey, 264, 265, 267, 268
Kennedy, Frank R., 193, 217
Kentucky, 59, 113
Keyeshian v. Board of Regents, 257
Keynes, John Maynard, 217, 222
Keynesianism, 42, 48, 216, 217, 219, 220, 221
Kiewiet, D. Roderick, 39
Kimhi, Omer, 100
Klein, William A., 199

Kletzer, Kenneth, 220
Kochan, Thomas A., 260
Korea, 159
Kousser, Thad, 39
Krogstrup, Signe, 218
Krol, Robert, 218
Kroszner, Randall S., 245
Krueger, Anne, 176, 181, 183, 193
Kruger, Mark, 180, 181
Krugman, Paul R., 222

Lacey, Marc, 301
Lafayette v. Louisiana Power & Light Co., 232
Laffer, Arthur B., 204, 290
Langbein, John, 272
Latter, Gordon, 69, 72
Lav, I., 64, 73, 83, 238, 254, 273, 274, 276, 277
law enforcement, 50, 272, 283, 292
layoffs, 40, 48, 54, 219, 297
Lehman Brothers Holdings Inc., 144, 196
Lerrick, Adam, 181
Levitin, Adam, 4, 144, 145, 194
Lewin, David, 265, 297
Liberia, 160
Lipson, Jonathan C., 193
Little Hoover Commission, 64, 73
Locker, Richard, 299
London Club, The, 158, 161
Louisiana, 12, 59, 67, 101, 104, 110, 112, 113, 116, 218, 244
Lowenstein, Roger, 273, 276
Lowry, R.C., 218
Lucas, Deborah J., 69, 73

Madland, David, 262, 269, 281
Maguire, Steven, 66, 73
Mahmud, Tayyab, 157
Maine, 59, 84, 155, 262
Malek, Lauren, 158
Malin, Martin, 256, 260, 261, 298, 299
Manasse, Paolo, 160
Manhattan Institute for Policy Research, 238
Marsillio, Elaine, 303
Martinez, Robert, 84
Maryland, 12, 15, 82, 84, 114, 218
Massachusetts, 58, 59, 84, 85, 95, 118, 218, 297
Masson, Paul R., 220
Maurer, Raimond, 69, 73

McCaffrey, Edward J., 224
McCarthy, David, 74
McConnell, Michael W., 4, 104, 111, 112, 204, 223, 230, 232, 233
McCormick, M., 297
McCubbins, Mathew D., 39
McElhaney, Stephen T., 58, 73
McGill, Dan M., 58, 62, 74
McKinley, Jr., James C., 290
McNichol, Elizabeth, 53, 64, 73, 83, 219, 221, 238, 254, 273, 274, 277, 278, 279, 283, 287, 290, 302, 303
McRae, Duncan, 222
Medenica, Madeline, 74, 273
Medicaid, 40, 44, 48–50, 52, 53, 60, 87, 89, 90, 94, 133, 135, 140, 217, 219, 278, 290
Medoff, James L., 299
Mélitz, Jacques, 220
Meltzer, Allan, 181
Mexico, 51, 82, 159, 160, 180, 199, 224
Michigan, 12, 70, 101, 118, 218, 268, 269, 298
  fiscal crisis of, 110
military, 46, 51, 131, 154
Miller, Girard, 64, 74
Minnesota, 65, 69, 109, 110, 114, 268
Mishel, Lawrence, 269, 270
Missouri, 59, 259
Missouri v Jenkins, 226
Mitchell, Olivia S., 3, 58, 59, 63, 65, 71, 73, 74, 76
Monell v. Department of Social Services, 231
Monkkonen, Eric, 109
Moore, Stephen, 290
moral hazard problem, 4, 101, 117, 119, 120, 124, 127, 129, 177, 184, 195, 201, 221, 238, 239, 242
Morrill, Melinda S., 58, 72
Moule, Ellen, 39
municipal insolvency, 99, 104
Munnell, Alicia H., 61, 64, 66, 67, 74, 91, 273, 275
Muris, Timothy J., 222
Murphy, Brian B., 73

Nathan, Richard P., 55
National Association of State Budget Officers, 39, 278, 284, 287, 288, 291, 298

National Association of State Retirement Administrators, 69, 71, 74, 276, 286, 289, 292
National Council on Public Employee Retirement Systems, 74
National Education Association, 64, 74
National Governors Association, 239
National Labor Relations Act, 260, 283, 286
National Labor Relations Board, 294
National Labor Relations Board v. Bildisco & Bildisco, 107, 227, 294
National League of Cities v. Usery, 232
natural disaster, 43, 45, 243
NCPERS. *See* National Council on Public Employee Retirement Systems
Nelson, Ray D., 284
Nevada, 17, 21, 23, 28, 59, 67, 78, 105, 218, 281, 288
  collective bargaining in, 286–89
New Deal, 28, 39, 43, 45, 47, 48, 55, 133, 141, 232
New England, 24
New Hampshire, 81, 110, 218
New Jersey, 60, 66, 67, 68, 78, 82, 85, 95, 111, 209, 250, 251, 268
New York, 2, 19, 21, 63, 66, 67, 69, 82, 89, 94, 101, 105, 106, 110, 115, 182, 195, 196, 211, 215, 218, 250, 269
New York v. United States, 234
Noll, Roger, 10, 39
Nordhaus, William D., 222
North Carolina, 67, 89, 113, 259
Novy-Marx, Robert, 64, 66, 70, 74, 75, 274

Obama, Barack, 1
OECD. *See* Organisation for Economic Co-operation and Development
Oechsli, Christopher, 179
Office of Management and Budget, 46, 51, 52, 53, 79
Ohio, 24, 59, 60, 61, 71, 95, 209, 268
Oi, Walter, 266
Oklahoma, 67
Oliff, Phil, 278
Oregon, 69, 298
Organisation for Economic Co-operation and Development, 51, 85
Orszag, Peter R., 218, 219

Pakistan, 164
Panama, 160
Panizza, Ugo, 151, 153, 154, 158, 159, 171, 172, 177, 178, 184, 185
Paraguay, 160
Paris Club, The, 148, 158, 160, 163, 164, 178
Park, Youngkyun, 65, 75
Pasricha, Gurnain, 132, 145
PBGC. *See* Pension Benefit Guaranty Corporation
Pennsylvania, 12, 68, 74, 133, 140, 218, 269, 302
pension. *See* private pension plans; public pension plans
  average state and local benefit total, 276
  defined benefit plan, 58–71, 270–72, 277, 301–02
  defined contribution plan, 58, 70, 271, 277, 302
Pension Benefit Guaranty Corporation, 60, 75
Perotti, Roberto, 221
Perry, Rick, 290
Personnel Administrator v. Feeney, 261
Persson, Torsten, 222
Peru, 160
Peskin, Michael, 69, 75
Pew Center on the States, 54, 75, 107, 255, 273, 276, 285, 288, 292, 300
Picker, Randal C., 104, 111, 112, 179, 204, 223, 230, 232
Pisani-Ferry, Jean, 183
politically driven fiscal crisis, 45, 56, 92, 126, 136, 157
Porell, Frank, 278
Port of Mobile v. Watson, 109
Posner, Eric, 184
Poterba, James M., 132, 145, 218
private pension plans, 58, 62
Professional Engineers in California Government v. Schwarzenegger, 293
property tax, 14, 23, 27, 31, 50, 51, 59, 77, 78, 79, 80, 81, 84, 85, 86, 92, 93, 94, 226, 283, 290
public education, 2, 17, 26, 41, 50, 54, 56, 66, 86, 87, 88, 92, 94, 141, 150, 217, 255, 263, 267, 269, 284
public pension plans, 57–71, 90, 92, 134, 253, 255, 270–78
  accounting of, 61, 91, 140, 144

exhaustion date of, 66
funding of, 60
underfunding of, 63, 65, 69, 71, 91, 133, 238, 272, 273, 292
public safety services, 58, 66, 255, 267, 272, 283, 289, 292, 304

Quinby, Laura, 74, 91, 273, 275

Raffer, Kunibert, 180
rainy day funds, 16, 19, 22, 23, 29, 30, 31, 34, 35, 36, 38, 291, 302, 303
Rasmussen, Robert K., 242
Rauh, Joshua D., 63, 63, 66, 68, 70, 71, 72, 74, 75, 274
Reagan, Ronald, 54
    New Federalism and, 3, 54, 55
recession, 5, 9, 14, 48, 51, 52, 60, 66, 82, 100, 135, 222, 254, 278, 284, 287, 288, 290, 294
Reinhart, Carmen M., 224
reserve fund. *See* rainy day funds
retirement age, 59, 70, 255, 272
retirement plans, 58, 270, 275
revenue allocation, 17, 68, 284
Rhode Island, 84, 195
Rivlin, Alice, 41
Roberto v. Department of Navy, 261
Rodden, Jonathan, 4, 117, 120, 125, 132, 133, 145
Rodriguez-Tejedo, Isabel, 39
Rogalla, Ralph, 73
Rogers, Janet, 287
Rogoff, Kenneth, 159, 161, 177, 178, 179, 180, 181, 182, 222
Roubini, Nouriel, 135, 151, 152, 154, 156, 159, 160, 169, 172, 173, 175, 176, 179, 182, 184, 185
Rowl, Daryl, 61, 75
Rowley, Charles K., 222
Rubenstein, Saul, 298
Rueben, Kim S., 218
Russek, Frank, 64, 75
Russia, 161, 162, 163, 170
Rutan v. Republican Party of Illinois, 258

Sabelhaus, John, 72
Sachs, Jeffrey, 180, 220, 222
Sala-i-Martin, Xavier, 220
sales tax, 14, 50, 51, 77, 78, 79, 81, 82–84, 85, 92, 93, 94, 284, 287, 291

Salmon, Felix, 167
Sapir, Andre, 183
Schick, Allen, 222
Schieber, Sylvester J., 61, 74, 75
Schipper, K., 72
Schlesinger, Jr., Arthur M., 45
Schmitt, John, 264, 269, 279, 285, 288, 291
Schneider, Mark E., 298
Schwarcz, Steven L., 99, 147, 150, 151, 153, 155, 174, 175, 177, 181, 182, 183, 184, 185, 202, 214
Schwartz, Alan, 197
Scott, Robert E., 198
Scott, William A., 110
Segal Associates, 65, 75
Senbet, Lemma W., 242
Setser, Brad, 151, 152, 154, 156, 159, 160, 161, 162, 165, 166, 169, 170, 171, 172, 173, 174, 175, 176, 179, 182, 184, 185
Shepsle, Kenneth A., 222
Shiffrin, Steven M., 218
Sibert, Anne, 222
Silvers, Damon, 3, 141
Simko, Darryl B., 246
sinking fund, 18, 19, 23, 114
Skeel, Jr., David A., 4, 5, 60, 75, 147, 149, 181, 191, 192, 203, 208, 211, 214, 231, 234, 237, 238
Slater, Joseph E., 253, 255, 256, 257, 258, 260, 265
Slemrod, Joel, 224
Smith v. Arkansas State Highway Employees, Local 1315, 257
Smith, Daniel L., 218
Smith, R. Hal, 286
Smith, Stephen, 220
Snell, Ronald K., 65, 69, 70, 75, 275
SOA. *See* Society of Actuaries
social insurance, 47, 150, 223
Social Security, 48, 49, 57, 59, 70, 276, 289
Social Security Act, 48, 59
Society of Actuaries, 73, 75
South Dakota, 69, 82
Sovereign Debt Restructuring Mechanism, 176, 181, 182, 183, 193, 203, 208
special purpose governments, 26, 26
Spilberg, Phil, 284
Stabile, Susan, 272

Staman, Jennifer, 58, 64, 75
Steneri, Carlos, 166
Stern v. Marshall, 212
Strayhorn, Carole Keeton, 290
structural deficit, 238, 284, 287, 290
Sturges v. Crowninshield, 1286
Sturzenegger, Frederico, 151, 161, 162, 163, 164, 165, 166, 167, 170
subsidies, 44, 47, 48, 77, 135, 250
Super, David A., 217
Supplemental Nutrition Assistance Program/Employment and Training, 49, 55, 217
Svensson, Lares E. O., 222
Swaine, Robert T., 199
Szakaly, Kristin, 39

Tabellini, Guido, 222
TANF. *See* Temporary Assistance to Needy Families
Tangel, Andrew, 68, 75
Temporary Assistance to Needy Families, 217
Tennessee Professional Educators Collaborative Conference Act, 259
tenure, 59, 260, 292
Texas, 59, 191, 259, 281, 302
  collective bargaining in, 289–92
  Senate of, 290
  Supreme Court of, 290
Thailand, 159
Thompson, Robert, 167
Tieslau, Margie A., 219
Tobago, 160
Tollison, Robert D., 222
Torres, Zahira, 266
treasurer, 17, 112, 140
Triantis, George G., 209
Trinidad, 160
Troske, Kenneth, 266
Turkey, 159

U.S. Trust Company of New York v. State of New Jersey, 249, 250, 251
Ukraine, 163
unemployment insurance, 18, 40, 44, 47, 48, 49, 52, 60, 126, 217
unemployment rate, 45, 52, 54, 55, 217, 284, 287
unions. *See* collective bargaining; public safety services, public education

United Nations, 167
United States
  bankruptcy code of. *See* United States Bankruptcy Code
  Bureau of Labor Statistics of, 54, 87, 258, 262, 263, 264, 267, 268, 270, 271, 272, 284, 285, 287
  Census Bureau of, 42, 46, 47, 48, 49, 50, 54, 76, 77, 88, 262, 263, 267, 276, 281, 285, 286, 288, 291
  Congress, 1, 48, 49, 53, 107, 111, 135, 191, 205, 210, 229, 245, 294
  Department of Education of, 88
  Department of Health and Human Services of, 49
  1841 fiscal crisis of, 12, 13, 24–25, 37, 42, 131–32
  fiscal crisis of, 5, 9, 40, 48, 80, 123, 133, 191, 237
  General Accounting Office of, 42
  Gross Domestic Product of, 12, 13, 14, 45, 46, 47, 49, 51, 52, 53, 88, 90, 138
  national debt ceiling of, 1, 43, 136
  national debt of, 12
  Senate, 136
  Supreme Court of, 107, 108, 109, 110, 111, 112, 116, 155, 192, 193, 212, 213, 226, 229, 230, 232, 234, 235, 241, 245, 249, 250, 251, 294, 296
  Treasury Department of, 42, 160
United States Bankruptcy Code, 111, 224, 232, 236, 244, 251, 294
  Chapter 7, 198, 200, 223
  Chapter 9, 99–108, 149, 185, 193, 197, 203, 206, 208, 215, 223, 227, 229, 237
  Chapter 11, 179, 223, 225, 294
United States Constitution, 42, 142, 192, 236, 257
  Contracts Clause of, 111, 112, 155, 235, 245, 246, 249, 250, 251, 295
  Eleventh Amendment, 104, 110, 111, 112, 154, 231, 234
  Takings Clause, 197
  Tenth Amendment, 232
United States Trust Company v. New Jersey, 295
United States v. Bekins, 1456
Urbina, Ian, 302
Uruguay, 160, 166, 167
Useem, Michael, 71, 76

Index

Valliere, Rick, 297
van Wincoop, Eric, 220
Vekshin, Alison, 102
Venezuela, 160
Vermont, 60, 77, 218, 278, 297
Vest, Marshall J., 217
Virginia, 118, 258, 259
von Hagen, Jürgen, 220
Von Hagen, Jürgen, 128, 145, 219, 220
von Hayek, Friedrich, 128

Wagner, Richard E., 222
Wallis, John Joseph, 3, 9, 12, 24, 27, 28, 39
Walsh, Mary Williams, 65, 76
Wälti, Sébastian, 218
Ward, Sharon, 302
Warshawsky, Mark, 74
Washington, D.C., 39, 72, 73, 74, 75, 76, 109, 118
Wassmer, Robert W., 284
Weidemaier, W. Mark C., 146, 153, 154, 182
Weiner, Joseph, 199
Weingast, Barry R., 24, 39, 128, 222
Weisberger, June, 261
welfare services, 2, 12, 14, 28, 87, 141, 217, 218
West Virginia, 29, 273

White, Michelle J., 200
Wibbels, Eric, 120, 132, 145
Wilcox, David W., 64, 72, 76
Williams, Jonathan, 290
Wilshire Consulting, 62, 76
Wilson, Daniel, 219
Winklevoss, Howard E., 60, 62, 76
Wisconsin, 29, 69, 209, 218, 255, 268
  collective bargaining in, 2, 141, 144, 195, 253–56, 276, 281, 303
Wisniewski, Stanley C., 74
Woglom, Geoffrey, 133, 145
Wolk, Bruce, 272
Woo, Sarah, 226
World Bank, 10, 148, 158, 161
World War I, 46
WorldCom, 196
Wyoming, 218

Yang, Tongxuan, 71, 76
Yianni, Andrew, 158
York, Anthony, 285

Zahradnick, Robert, 83
Zeldes, Stephen P., 69, 73
Zettelmeyer, Jeromin, 151, 159, 161, 162, 163, 164, 165, 166, 167, 170, 177, 178, 179, 180, 181, 182
Zorn, Paul, 71, 73, 74
Zumer, Frédéric, 220